G000229784

The Supreme Court

The Supreme Court

RUADHÁN MAC CORMAIC

PENGUIN
IRELAND

PENGUIN IRELAND

UK | USA | Canada | Ireland | Australia
India | New Zealand |South Africa

Penguin Ireland is part of the Penguin Random House group of companies
whose addresses can be found at global.penguinrandomhouse.com.

First published 2016
001

Copyright © Ruadhán Mac Cormaic, 2016

The moral right of the author has been asserted

Set in 12/14.75 pt Bembo Book MT Std
Typeset by Jouve (UK), Milton Keynes
Printed in Great Britain by Clays Ltd, St Ives plc

A CIP catalogue record for this book is available from the British Library

ISBN: 978-1-844-88340-0

www.greenpenguin.co.uk

Penguin Random House is committed to a
sustainable future for our business, our readers
and our planet. This book is made from Forest
Stewardship Council® certified paper.

Do mo thuismitheoirí

Contents

Contents

Introduction

Fiat justitia ruat caelum ('Let justice be done, though
the heavens fall')

Inscription on the frieze of the Bridewell
Garda Station, behind the Four Courts

As soon as Adrian Hardiman had finished speaking and the five
judges had filed out of the courtroom, the State's lawyer made a dash
for the door. The court had just delivered a thunderbolt. Merrion
Street had to be alerted before the news got out.

On the other side of the Liffey, word spread fast. The Attorney
General's office contacted the Department of Justice, where officials
hurriedly briefed the minister, Michael McDowell. It turned out that
neither McDowell nor the Attorney General, Rory Brady, had even
known the decision was due. The Taoiseach, Bertie Ahern, was in
his office on the first floor of Government Buildings when he was
informed. 'This is a real problem', a senior government figure said at
a hastily convened meeting.

Within minutes, everyone's phone was ringing. Officials had been
caught off guard; the lawyers among them knew this was bad, but
nobody quite knew how bad. Some of them were aghast. 'What the
fuck have they done?' a high-ranking official thought when he heard
the news.

What the judges had done was strike down as inconsistent with the
Constitution the long-standing law that automatically made it a
crime for a man to have sex with a girl under fifteen. The rationale
was simple: as a general rule in serious criminal cases, a defendant can
claim that he or she made a genuine mistake and did not intentionally
commit a crime. But the 1935 law on sexual offences involving minors

did not explicitly allow this principle to apply. So, in a unanimous decision delivered to a half-empty courtroom on Tuesday, 23 May 2006, a five-judge Supreme Court declared it inconsistent with the Constitution. That meant the Oireachtas would have to scramble to enact a replacement law.

However, for the government the decision appeared to have a second and more alarming implication. A long-standing legal rule meant that when the Supreme Court found a law unconstitutional, it followed that it never had been constitutional: not only did it no longer exist, but it *never* existed. Did that mean that anyone who was serving a prison sentence for 'unlawful carnal knowledge' of a girl under fifteen would now walk free? 'My initial reaction was: how are we going to keep the floodgates closed', recalls one government figure.

Within minutes of the Supreme Court judgment, as the judges sat in their chambers largely oblivious to the storm raging outside, officials were rifling frantically through files to find out how many cases could be affected. A prison governor called the Department of Justice. 'Do you realize how many people you're going to have to release on foot of this? And who they are', he said.

The case that prompted the Supreme Court's decision had been brought by a man known as 'CC', who, as an eighteen-year-old, had consensual sex with a fourteen-year-old girl who told him she was sixteen. But for many years the law had been used to prosecute a much wider range of cases. An initial tally by officials in the Prison Service and the office of the Director of Public Prosecutions (DPP) was that there were seven men serving prison sentences solely on the basis of convictions under the now unconstitutional section of the relevant act, and that a further twenty were awaiting trial. Among the first group were believed to be some of the most serious sex offenders in custody, including John Adams, a 64-year-old from Ballymena, Co. Antrim, who had been convicted of unlawful carnal knowledge of girls aged six, eight and ten, and Michael O'Donnell from Dungloe, Co. Donegal, who had pleaded guilty in 2005 to nineteen sample counts of sexual assault and unlawful carnal knowledge of his first cousins over a nine-year period. 'It was nightmare stuff', recalls one Cabinet member.

The story went straight to the front pages. Distraught victims of child sex abuse began to call Joe Duffy's *Liveline* and the *Gerry Ryan Show*. The government's first instinct was to play it down in public and hold adamantly to the line that there was no need to panic. But behind closed doors the mood was dark, and it didn't improve when, two days after the original decision, the State had to go to court to withdraw sexual offences charges against two men, aged twenty-six and thirty-six. One had been awaiting trial for having sex with a girl while the other, who had pleaded guilty, had been due to be sentenced. This coincided with the revelation that, while the Department of Justice had been told by the Chief State Solicitor as far back as December 2002 that a constitutional challenge had been initiated against the section of the act, neither McDowell nor Brady had personally been told. That gave the opposition the ammunition it needed to attack the government. A legal headache was rapidly becoming a political crisis. One senior figure likens it to 'a landslide' that caught everyone unaware. 'We were completely blindsided by the whole thing. We didn't see it until it was far too late.'

It had been known for years that there could be problems with the 1935 act. In 1990 – sixteen years before the CC decision – the Law Reform Commission had recommended changing the law so as to explicitly allow the defence of honest mistake as to a girl's age. In the standard legal textbook on sexual offences, published in 1996, the academic Tom O'Malley suggested there could be a question mark over the constitutionality of the section.[1] The Supreme Court itself had flagged the problem in 2005, when it allowed CC to make that claim on the eve of his trial but said it would consider the broader constitutional issue later. Yet the State's lawyers were convinced the court would never go so far as to strike down the law. 'I had thought they would draw back at the consequences of the finding', says one insider. Now he and his colleagues found themselves appreciating the wisdom of the former Taoiseach Jack Lynch, when he had said, over two decades earlier, 'It would be a brave man who would predict, these days, what was or was not contrary to the Constitution.'

For the government, it was all the more galling to see that the court of five that decided the case was made up of people it knew

well. The author of the judgment, Adrian Hardiman, was a close
friend of both McDowell and Tánaiste Mary Harney. Chief Justice
John Murray, a former Attorney General in two Fianna Fáil-led governments, had worked closely with the Taoiseach when Ahern was
Charlie Haughey's chief whip in the early 1980s. The other three
judges on the case – Nial Fennelly, Hugh Geoghegan and Brian
McCracken – were all independent-minded jurists who, like Murray
and Hardiman, had been appointed to the Supreme Court by Fianna
Fáil–Progressive Democrat coalitions.

'When the court makes a decision, there's a certain amount of
respect around that', one official recalls. 'You don't ring them up and
say, *"What the fuck have you done here?"* But of course you said it to
yourself.' It didn't go unnoticed in government or in the law library
that there had been no women on the court. 'If you'd had any woman
on the court, they'd have had more sense than to make a judgment
like that', one judge told a colleague.

Even though the CC case was about sex between two teenagers,
the act had been used for years to prosecute adult sex offenders. That
was because, unlike with a rape charge, the State didn't have to prove
the absence of consent or put the victim through a cross-examination
in court. When taking their decision, the judges didn't know how
many cases might be affected. The issue hadn't come up once during
their meetings in the book-lined conference room adjacent to the
Chief Justice's chambers. In their view it was irrelevant. For the
judges, the key point was that people were being charged under provisions of an act that they had become convinced was contrary to the
Constitution. When the question went around the table one last time,
all five agreed and signed off on the judgment.

Justice had been done. Now the sky was about to fall. Or at least
that's how it felt in Government Buildings.

While officials worked flat out on drafting emergency legislation
to plug the hole in the law, ministers were grasping for a strategy.
Everyone was on the defensive, guarding their own patch and blam-
ing others for the debacle. Rory Brady sought advice from one of the
most respected senior counsel in the State on the implications of the
Supreme Court's decision. What came back was worse than anyone

in government had imagined – the memo advised that the government should immediately release everyone who had been convicted under the impugned act. It didn't take much political nous to see that the Fianna Fáil–PD coalition would struggle to survive the public uproar that would follow a government decision to release a clutch of serious sex offenders. McDowell rejected out of hand the idea of unilaterally signing release orders. He was backed up by the advice of a second senior counsel, who recommended fighting each case one by one. Finally, the strategy was agreed: the government would contest each case and 'make the High Court authorize each release in turn', as one senior figure puts it.

The first major test came a few days later, on Monday, 29 May, when the High Court heard an application for release by one of the seven men who were serving sentences. The 41-year-old, known only as Mr A, had been convicted of the statutory rape of a twelve-year-old girl four years previously. He had bought the girl four Bacardi Breezers and two vodkas in May 2002 before he had sex with her when she woke up to be sick. He pleaded guilty in 2004 and was jailed for three years in Arbour Hill Prison.

Arguing the State's case against releasing Mr A was Gerard Hogan, one of the leading constitutional lawyers in the country. In a presentation that stressed the national importance of the case, Hogan told the judge, Mary Laffoy, that it would be 'an appalling vista' if those who had pleaded guilty to very serious offences involving pre-teen children were to get a 'windfall bonus' from the Supreme Court judgment. Senior Counsel Conor Devally, on Mr A's legal team, told the judge there was no alternative: the warrant on which Mr A was jailed was based on a non-existent law. There was no legal authority for holding his client.

What happened next confirmed the coalition's worst fears. At 2pm the following day, Laffoy returned to a packed courtroom. Laffoy had unimpeachable credentials; she was fair-minded, smart and probably the High Court judge most admired by her colleagues. In a decision that took twenty minutes to read, Laffoy announced that the Supreme Court's decision left her with no alternative but to order the release of Mr A. The offence to which he pleaded guilty in June

2004 was not an offence at the time. His conviction was therefore 'a nullity', she said. 'The defect could not be more basic.'

Barrister Paul Anthony McDermott, another member of the State's legal team, immediately stood up and asked Laffoy to delay the release so the State could appeal her decision to the Supreme Court. Laffoy sighed and said she could not do that. Mr A, sitting in handcuffs a few feet away, was to be released. Listening to the news of Laffoy's decision on the radio that afternoon, some Supreme Court judges felt instinctively that it was wrong. Several others believed that, unpalatable as it seemed, Laffoy's decision was legally spot on.

The image of Mr A walking out of court with a coat over his head sent shockwaves through the political system. If he could get out, then so could at least six others. In the Dáil that afternoon, Ahern, McDowell and Harney sat ashen-faced as opposition leaders lined up to berate them. How had senior ministers not known that the constitutionality of the act was under threat, or even that the Supreme Court decision was coming? Why had emergency legislation not been prepared?

Fine Gael leader Enda Kenny said that, as a public representative and a father, he was appalled by the High Court's decision to release 'a pervert' back into society. 'Thanks to your breath-taking incompetence, Mr A has walked and so might Messrs B, C, D, E and F.'

Pat Rabbitte, the leader of the Labour Party, said the parents of Ireland were not interested in a dissertation on criminal law. 'They want to know if their children will be safe this weekend', he said.

That day, gardaí went to the house of Bridgeen Doherty in Co. Donegal to warn her that Michael O'Donnell, the man who had sexually abused her from the age of four, could soon be released. 'Lock up your little girls' read the banner headline on the front page of the *Irish Mirror*.[2]

Even had senior ministers known in advance that the Supreme Court decision was coming, there was nothing they could have done to change the outcome or mitigate its effects, at least as they applied to people who had already been convicted. But, in the heat of a fraught and tumultuous week, that didn't matter. To the public, two things were clear: child rapists were walking out of jail and the government was floundering. Coming less than a year before a general election and after two bad opinion polls for Fianna Fáil, backbenchers were aghast. 'There has been blind panic within Government Buildings and Leinster House', said Mark Hennessy, political correspondent of the *Irish Times*, on RTÉ's *Primetime* in the aftermath of Laffoy's judgment. 'Fianna Fáil TDs are going around in a state of shock. Guys are seeing their seats walk away from them.'

Privately, everyone blamed someone else, and tempers were fraying. The Department of Justice, the Attorney General's office and the office of the DPP each believed they were being unfairly blamed, and inside the administration there were sharp disagreements on how the State should argue the appeal against Laffoy's judgment in the Supreme Court later in the week. Tensions worsened when McDowell said publicly that the DPP's office had conducted the CC case on its own. That prompted a furious reaction from the DPP, James Hamilton, who made a call to the secretary general of the Department of Justice, Seán Aylward, to say he would go public unless it was acknowledged that the case had been jointly handled by the offices of the DPP and the Attorney General, as is standard in such cases. Harney defused the row by going into the Dáil and confirming that the Attorney General's office had been actively involved.

Attorneys General are only ever in the news when something has gone wrong. Brady, seeing his name on the front pages, felt under huge pressure. But, politically, it was McDowell who was in mortal danger. Arriving in New York for a United Nations conference on the Wednesday evening, Ahern apologized for the hurt caused to victims but said he had full confidence in his justice minister. Yet the key movers within government assumed that if the State lost its appeal against Laffoy's decision in the Supreme Court, McDowell would have no choice but to step down. Some worried that his departure would threaten the government.

Everything turned on what the Supreme Court would do next.

The Supreme Court is a small, intimate place. The judges' private meetings take place in a ground-floor conference room at the end of a narrow corridor lined with portraits of each of the Supreme Courts since the foundation of the State. The blue-green bookshelves are filled with statutes, law reports, textbooks and dictionaries, and in the middle of the room, on a red carpet, is the dark wooden table where the judges sit. The window, looking out onto the judges' car park, is opaque so passers-by cannot see in. The room has direct access to the Chief Justice's office and, via a few steps, to the Supreme Court chamber itself – a small, austere, high-ceilinged space that has changed little in the past eighty-five years.

The intimacy of the environment can make it an intimidating arena to argue a case. A barrister on his or her feet stands close enough to the judges to see each grimace, each raised eyebrow, each flash of momentary incomprehension on their faces. 'It also means that if things are not going well then you can practically hear the laboured breathing of your solicitor sitting a couple of feet in front of you and your clients sitting a few inches behind you', says one senior counsel.

The power imbalance is total. Barristers bow as they enter and stand when the judges stand. They meekly humour the crankier judges' bad moods and laugh ostentatiously at every joke from the bench. In return they can be flayed at any moment. 'It's the equivalent of the wall of death for barristers', says the senior counsel. The judges don't always interject one at a time; occasionally they speak over each other, spraying questions as they pop into their heads. For the barrister on his or her feet, the natural instinct is to take a couple of paces backwards, to regain composure. But there's no space; the physical confines of the room force him or her to stand still, immobile and exposed, watching the carefully crafted three-hour oration on the finer points of criminal law thrown out in three minutes flat.

The lawyers are not the only performers in the room: the judges too are alive to the drama. They sit on their elevated perch, surveying the room, occasionally interjecting and probing, all the while trying, however unsuccessfully, to maintain a veneer of inscrutability. 'I have nothing but sympathy for barristers, who have to crack up laughing at some banality from the bench', recalls one former judge. 'It's even worse for the judges who are sitting there. A lot of people think the entire bench are laughing along. What they're thinking is: will this person shut up and stop going on with this.'

A lawyer who loses in the High Court can take consolation in the knowledge that he or she can always appeal to a higher court. But the Supreme Court has the final word. When he was a barrister, the future Chief Justice Tom Finlay once stood up and told the court it didn't have jurisdiction to decide a certain point. One of the judges, Cecil Lavery, came back with an immediate retort. 'Mr Finlay,' he said, 'we are the Supreme Court, and under God we can do anything.'

Yet, though Supreme Court judges are powerful, influential people whose decisions can have far-reaching consequences for individuals and for the country at large, for the most part they go about their work quietly, largely unnoticed by the world outside the bubble of the Four Courts. Most of them never get recognized on the street. Only every few years does a case come along that pricks that bubble and thrusts the court under the glare of the media spotlight. The Mr A case was one of those. In private, discussions were taking place among the judges even before the hearing began. A number of them met for coffee in each other's chambers – a rare enough event both then and now. Newspaper reports were being sent between judges' chambers in sealed envelopes so they wouldn't be seen carrying them through the Four Courts. Their mood was growing tense.

The high-powered legal team selected by the Attorney General to mount the State's challenge comprised Gerard Hogan and George Birmingham as well as junior counsel Paul Anthony McDermott. Everyone in government seemed to have a view on how they should argue the case, so the night before the hearing the three lawyers agreed to meet for dinner at Hogan's house so they could have a final strategy discussion in peace. The pressure was intense; nobody on the team had eaten in days. At about 6pm, Birmingham received a call from Brady, who wanted a word with the barristers on the case. Birmingham explained that they were at Hogan's house. 'Listen, I'll come round for dinner', Brady announced. Later in the evening, McDowell called and said he'd come along as well.

The five men were sitting around Hogan's kitchen table when the nine o'clock news came on in the background and the newscaster began gravely to intone on the crisis. McDowell turned around and snapped, 'Turn that bloody thing off.' Later in the night, as the men were discussing possible concerns the court could raise, Hogan mentioned a famous and potentially problematic line by the former Supreme Court judge Séamus Henchy – a hero to everyone in the room. A finding of unconstitutionality amounted to 'a judicial death certificate' for a law, Henchy had written in a judgment in 1982. At that, McDowell picked up the CC judgment, held it in his hand and looked across the table at Hogan. 'Gerard, here's what I want you to say tomorrow. The only thing that died in this judgment is common sense. Tell them that tomorrow.'★

The following morning, just hours before the Supreme Court appeal was to be heard, more than 2,000 people marched along Molesworth Street and placed white flowers at the gates of Leinster House. Similar demonstrations took place in towns across Ireland. 'I felt like they should be told, it's the Four Courts you should be marching on, not the Dáil', recalls one government insider.

The composition of the Supreme Court to hear the State's appeal against Mr A's release was different from the CC case, with Susan Denham and Catherine McGuinness joining Murray, Hardiman and Geoghegan. Members of the court knew Denham was particularly annoyed by the CC decision. Just a year previously, when the case had first come before the Supreme Court, she had written a judgment in which she suggested a way of squaring the circle. Citing various authorities, she had argued that, while the defence of ignorance as to a girl's age was not explicitly contained in the act, it was such a well-established principle that the court should take it as given that it existed in the law. Others disagreed with Denham, saying that that was not what the Oireachtas had intended back in 1935. But now it

---

★ What Henchy had said immediately after his comment on a 'judicial death certificate' turned out to be of considerable assistance to the State's team. Even with that death certificate, he wrote, there were lots of situations where this may not be of any use to someone coming to court afterwards. Henchy wrote that a declaration that a pre-1937 law was unconstitutional 'does not necessarily carry with it the corollary that what has been done after 1937 in pursuance of that statutory provision will equally be condemned for lack of validity'. *Murphy v. The Attorney General* (1982).

was clear that, if the court had agreed with her back in 2005, the whole debacle would have been averted.

At the hearing the tension eased within ten minutes. It was clear that the State's legal team had the momentum. In the conference room afterwards, the judges spoke in reverse order of seniority – a long-standing tradition on the court. First came Geoghegan, followed by Hardiman, McGuinness, Denham and then Murray. Some of the judges felt that the media reaction was over the top and that the problems with the act had been flagged for years. The decision in *CC* may have been sound, but some believed a way should have been found to limit its effects. The choice before them now was stark: apply the logic of the court's own CC decision, and in effect approve the release of some of the State's most serious sex offenders, or find a way to bring about what everyone in the room instinctively believed was the most desirable outcome – the re-arrest of Mr A. For some the first answer had an elegant intellectual appeal, but they also knew the consequences – for victims and for faith in the justice system, not to mention for the court itself – could be dire. The alternative was also stark: keep a man in prison on foot of an offence that had never existed.

At either end of the spectrum of judicial decision-making are the theorists and the pragmatists. The theorists see themselves almost as automatons, embodying the French philosopher Montesquieu's claim that 'judges . . . are only the mouth that pronounces the words of the law, inanimate beings, who can moderate neither its force nor its rigor'.[3] The pragmatists are more result-oriented: they will the just outcome and then search for a legally permissible way to bring it about. No judge is entirely one or the other, and often an individual decision is a combination of the two approaches, but anyone who spends a few days sitting in the Four Courts will see that some judges are more Montesquian than others.

That day in the Supreme Court, the pragmatic argument won out. Very quickly, there was a clear consensus in favour of overturning Laffoy. Mr A had never claimed he had made an honest mistake as to his victim's age, and the group felt that in those circumstances it would be unjust and wrong for him to benefit from the CC decision.

Moreover, Mr A's case was over – to unpick it would undermine the certainty of the law, one judge said.

Counsel for the state Gerard Hogan had given the court enough case law to show there were limits to the retrospective application of a finding of unconstitutionality. For example, the Supreme Court's declaration in 1975 that the Juries Act was unconstitutional on the basis that it tended to exclude women from juries did not mean that every previous jury decision was therefore invalid.

Yet at the same time the Supreme Court was in effect about to order that people be kept in jail on the basis of an unconstitutional law. It was not the court's finest hour, and several of the judges knew it. 'A somersault', as one close observer puts it. 'A contortion', says another. Some were more comfortable doing so than others, but all eventually agreed.

Shortly before 4.40pm, the judges returned to the courtroom and issued a warrant directing that Mr A be re-arrested. By 7pm he was back in Arbour Hill Prison. Within hours a rapidly enacted replacement law was on its way to Áras an Uachtaráin for the President's signature.

A few days after the decision, some of the country's best-known lawyers attended a housewarming party at the home of the then High Court judge Frank Clarke in Blackrock, Co. Dublin. As Michael McDowell passed a group that included Catherine McGuinness, one of the judges who had decided the case, he raised his hands and motioned as if to make a theatrical bow.

The debate on the Mr A decision continues to this day. Several Supreme Court judges and their allies resolutely defended the decision in public, pointing out that it had been subsequently cited with approval by courts across the common law world. But the decision divided opinion closer to home. In the High Court, judges were so angry at the treatment of Laffoy, who they felt had been put in an invidious position by the Supreme Court, that one even muttered they should resign en masse. For some internal critics of the Supreme Court it exemplified a wider failure to see around corners and anticipate the real-life consequences of its decisions – a view captured in the common nickname for the Supreme Court among High Court judges, 'Ponder Park'. In a critical appraisal of the decision, the barrister Rossa Fanning wrote:

[Mr] A. was a spectacularly unsympathetic litigant. He asked the Supreme Court a very difficult question and caused significant public disquiet in so doing. A different outcome might have had ramifications, in a manner unprecedented in the history of the State, for the institutional respect that the Supreme Court is afforded by the public and the body politic. Put bluntly, it would be difficult to think of a much more unpopular decision than the premature release of a child molester on a legal technicality. The decision may have been expedient but doesn't mean that it was correct.[4]

A common view in the Four Courts was that the Supreme Court had performed a somersault to fix a mess of its own making. When the retired High Court judge Seán O'Leary died later that year, he left behind a scathing posthumous critique of the decision. 'The lengths to which the Supreme Court went to obfuscate the fact that the continued detention of a prisoner in an Irish jail . . . for an offence that did not exist in law at the date of his conviction smacks of an attempt to curry favour with a potentially hostile media.' One of his successors puts it more succinctly: 'They just invented stuff because they realized they'd made a balls-up.'

The episode left some judges rattled. '*CC* and *Mr A* is branded onto the consciousness of the present generation of judges more than any other case', says one. Within the Supreme Court, the unanimous decision in *Mr A* masked serious differences over how the court had found itself in the position of rushing to close the prison gates. Yet the court has its own way of dealing with internal disagreements: it avoids talking about them. Otherwise the conference room would become an even more claustrophobic place. And so, at their weekly lunch a few days after the decision, after some complaints about media coverage, the conversation quickly petered out. As a group, they never spoke about the episode again.

The Supreme Court is not accustomed to the sort of focus the Mr A case thrust upon it. Unlike ministers or TDs, whose every move is pored over, amplified and re-packaged as a form of national psychodrama, the work of judges – wrapped in a forbidding cloak of archaic, esoteric language and otherworldly courtroom conventions – can seem to exist at a distant remove, their power in inverse proportion to the level of public scrutiny its exercise attracts. The Four Courts is just a few kilometres from Government Buildings, but in other ways it can seem like another universe.

As guarantor and interpreter of the 1937 Constitution, and the Constitution of the Free State before it, the Supreme Court has been central to some of the key debates in Ireland since Independence. In the United States, the Supreme Court's awesome power derives in large part from how difficult it is to change the US Constitution. Senior Irish judges operate in a very different landscape. Bunreacht na hÉireann can be amended by a simple majority of those who turn out to vote, and referenda can be – and on many occasions have been – called to reverse the effects of a Supreme Court decision, or at least limit its effects.

Nonetheless, understanding the Supreme Court is vital to understanding how the State works, how society has evolved and why some of the biggest debates over much of the past century – on abortion, the Troubles, adoption, police power, the European Union, the role of women, contraception, the rights of the individual, referenda and the place of religion in society, to name but a few – have unfolded as they have. In some cases the court was an instigator of change, ushering in landmark changes or nudging the government to act. In others it was a mirror, reflecting the tensions and contradictions of the society it served. At times, by doing nothing at all, the court was making a point.

Yet the story of the Supreme Court is largely unwritten. Historians, stymied by a lack of source material emerging from a famously secretive institution, have generally steered clear of the subject. Conspicuous by their absence on the library shelves are comprehensive biographies of figures such as Hugh Kennedy, Cearbhall Ó Dálaigh, Brian Walsh or Séamus Henchy – just some of the most significant judges in the history of the court and, by extension, the history of Ireland in the twentieth century. The judges themselves have done little to help. Beyond their judgments, members of the court have remained largely silent. Supreme Court judges have written books on philosophy,[5] fishing[6] and the nature of evil.[7] One wrote a science fiction novel.[8] But none has published a memoir about life as a judge.[9] Barristers have been every bit as reticent. What exists, therefore, is largely oral history, a collection of stories and memories refracted and often distorted over time as they passed from one generation of lawyers to another. To his great credit, Kennedy was alone among senior judges in leaving the bulk of his private papers for future scholars to consult.

The result of all of these factors – the dearth of sources, judicial secrecy, arcane language and the shortage of historical writing – has been that the court has been left in the anomalous position of being at once powerful and largely impenetrable to most citizens. Discussion of its decisions tends to be dominated by practising lawyers, who work in a legal culture that requires them to bow when they approach a judge and to greet every judicial utterance with formulaic flattery. That deference inhibits serious critical analysis as much as the alternative account: one of heroes and villains, of an irredeemably tone-deaf bench lurching haplessly from case to case.

This book was written out of a sense that the story is more complex, and therefore more interesting, than either view would have it. But they're both right about one thing: the judges matter. And so this is above all a book about people: those who brought the cases, those who argued in court, those who dealt with the fallout and, above all, those who took the decisions.

A common judicial refrain is that, as trained technicians whose role is simply to apply the law, the judges' personalities are largely irrelevant. Only the least self-aware judges actually believe that. It may be true that most of the questions that come before the Supreme Court are relatively straightforward, but in key places the text of the Constitution is vague and ambiguous, and the regularity with which the court has divided on big cases over the past ninety-two years is proof of the room for manoeuvre the judges enjoy in interpreting it. As this book attempts to show, judges' backgrounds and relationships, as well as the internal tensions among them, are vital to understanding how the institution works. Shortly after Niall McCarthy was appointed to the Supreme Court in 1982, according to a story often retold in the law library, an old colleague passed him in a corridor and asked how he was getting on in his new surroundings. Very well, the flamboyant McCarthy replied. 'Last week they were my opinions. Now they're the law.'

If a focus on the judge as individual is one thread that runs through these pages, another is the relationship between government and the judiciary. So this book is as much about Irish society and politics as it is about the law. Tension is built into the system of government that allocates powers between three institutions – executive, parliament and judiciary – but how those tensions have played out between Government Buildings and the Four Courts is a largely untold story.

The book is neither a constitutional history nor an exhaustive compendium of cases, both of which have been produced by far more qualified authors. Nor is it a history of Ireland in the twentieth century. It takes its cases selectively, using them as a lens through which to view the judges themselves and the evolution of the court, or in an attempt to shed light on some broader shifts taking place in society. Its aim is to begin to write the Supreme Court into a story from which it has been largely absent.

In writing the book, I have drawn on new archival material on the courts and the judiciary, including recently released documents from the office of the Chief Justice and records from the Department of An Taoiseach, the Department of Justice and the office of the Attorney General – all of which are held by the National Archives of Ireland. The book also draws on hundreds of previously unseen letters between Brian Walsh of the Supreme Court of Ireland and William Brennan of the United States Supreme Court over a thirty-year period. This remarkable correspondence, which is due to be released to the public in 2017, is held at the Library of Congress in Washington DC. In addition, I have consulted the private papers of Hugh Kennedy, Cearbhall Ó Dálaigh and others at the UCD Archives, as well as hundreds of books, journals, essays and scholarly articles. Newspaper and magazine coverage of the courts over the past century has been another invaluable resource.

The key primary sources are interviews I carried out over two years with more than 140 individuals with particular insights into the Supreme Court, its history, its personalities and its internal workings. Nearly all were given on the understanding that anonymity would be guaranteed. In addition, I have drawn on a number of private papers, letters and emails that were provided to me on condition that their provenance would go unacknowledged.

1. Beginnings

'. . . the moment when the silence of the Gael in
Courts of Law is broken'

Hugh Kennedy

A thick dark plume rose from the Four Courts and drifted slowly out over the Liffey. Fragments of charred paper fluttered in the wind, like white birds against the black smoke. The great Gandon dome – a landmark of the Dublin skyline for more than a century – had collapsed, its Corinthian columns shattered and the interior blackened by fire.[1]

As night fell on 30 June 1922, the seat of Ireland's justice system lay in ruins – and with it had gone any hope that all-out civil war could be averted.

The ferocious three-day assault by the Free State Army on anti-Treaty forces occupying the Four Courts under the command of Rory O'Connor and Liam Mellows since Holy Thursday, 13 April, had culminated in two ear-splitting explosions – the second so powerful that it shook the building, smashed windows a mile away and ultimately brought about the occupying soldiers' surrender.[2]

When they had been removed and the fires had gone out, the destruction of the Four Courts was virtually complete.[3] The courtrooms, the law library, the judges' chambers and the Round Hall – the throbbing heart of the building, where just weeks earlier lawyers had met, mingled and cut last-minute deals on their way into court – were gutted. In the Public Records Office, which housed an irreplaceable archive of civil court cases, wills, deeds and other records – a social and legal history of Ireland over nearly eight centuries – everything was lost. Dispatched to assess the damage a few days later, the High

Court registrar, Con Curran, found the scene unrecognizable. In the ashes where the Round Hall once stood, he found the remnants of six statues of Irish judges; when he pressed his thumb into one of them, it had 'the consistency of cream cheese'.[4]

As court staff sifted through the smouldering ruins of the Four Courts, and judges and lawyers relocated to a makeshift home in the King's Inns, one of their number was hard at work elsewhere in the city, thrashing out what he hoped would be sweeping changes to the system whose symbolic citadel on the quays had been attacked. The Anglo-Irish Treaty had paved the way for the establishment of the Irish Free State, but for it to be activated the new state needed a Constitution. Hugh Kennedy, then law officer to the provisional government under Michael Collins (the post of Attorney General had not yet been created), was about to be thrust into the limelight.

A small, portly man whose high-pitched voice and rosy cheeks made him an easy target for press cartoonists, Hugh Kennedy had been educated at home by his father, the Dublin surgeon Hugh Boyle Kennedy, before going to University College in the 1890s. There he became the first editor of the student magazine, *St Stephen's*, where he published some of the earliest works of his contemporary James Joyce. Kennedy was Joyce's bête noire; the future judge once attacked a paper on Ibsen that Joyce gave to the Literary and Historical Society and subsequently beat him in an election for auditor of the society.[5] The enmity wasn't quickly forgotten. Joyce's biographer, Richard Ellmann, attributes to the writer's father, John Joyce, the remark that Kennedy 'had a face like a child's bottom, well-whipped'.[6] Ellmann thinks it likely that the 'prim and proper' Kennedy inspired the name of Hugh 'Blazes' Boylan, the caddish man-about-town in *Ulysses*.[7]

Kennedy was a Home Ruler, but had also made financial contributions to Sinn Féin[8] and was one of the few senior members of the Irish Bar to 'adjust with equanimity' to the new political order.[9] He had a strong interest in the Irish language, his Donegal-born father having been a fluent speaker, and through his membership of the Gaelic League the young lawyer met Pádraig Pearse, Éamonn Ceannt and Eoin MacNeill – all fellow members of the League's central committee. As a shrewd and well-regarded barrister, he quickly rose to prominence at the head of a clutch of lawyers who, in the immediate aftermath of the Treaty, found themselves in demand and on the ascent in the public life of the new State. 'The relative absence of lawyers in the pre-Treaty elite and their conspicuous presence in the early Free State elite is a crucial contrast; lawyers knew how to build law-bound states', writes historian Tom Garvin. 'The ideology of legalistic and unromantic electoral democracy became a cornerstone of their political position.'[10]

Yet in a conservative milieu, Kennedy himself was a romantic whose impatient insistence on the need for distinctly Irish institutions and ideas made him something of a radical. He saw English institutions as alien creations and believed that if the Irish people were to be won over to accepting the Free State, English forms would have to be replaced.[11] Nowhere was that more imperative, Kennedy believed, than in the legal system.

The new state faced formidable obstacles in creating a new system for the administration of justice amid the chaos of civil war. The judicial system inherited from the British had to be swiftly remodelled in a way that would command public support while maintaining some continuity and somehow incorporating the successful work of the so-called 'Dáil courts' – a parallel local justice system that emerged during the War of Independence and managed to gain a reputation for efficient and fair handling of disputes.[12]

The broad shape of the courts structure that would remain in place for much of the next century was outlined by the Free State Constitution, drafted in 1922 by a committee whose members included Collins and Kennedy. By then the career lawyer and the revolutionary figurehead had developed a close working relationship; after the Treaty negotiations Collins told Cosgrave he wished 'we'd had him in London for the Treaty'.[13]

At the heart of the plan was a High Court, which would handle the most serious criminal and civil cases, and below it a set of local courts where smaller disputes would be resolved and lower-level crimes prosecuted. At the apex of the system would be a court of final appeal: the Supreme Court.

But here the architects of the new system faced an in-built problem. The British had insisted that the Anglo-Irish Treaty include a requirement for a right to appeal the Irish courts' decisions to the judicial committee of the Privy Council in London. The prospect of judges in London – including, as it happened, the unionist leader Lord (Edward) Carson – having the final say over the decisions of the Free State courts threatened to undermine the Supreme Court before it was even up and running. Negotiations between Dublin and London ensued. The Irish side, led by Kennedy, was unable to fully exclude appeals to the Privy Council, but it succeeded in watering down the language in such a way that, the Irish delegation believed, appeals to London would only be allowed in rare and special cases. The language was sufficiently ambiguous to enable Kennedy to sell it as an important concession that shored up the new institutions. His efforts were largely vindicated when, in July 1923, the first post-Independence appeal went to the Privy Council and resulted in the Irish position – which Kennedy himself travelled to London to argue – being upheld. The judge, Lord Buckmaster, agreed the terms of the Constitution meant 'as far as possible finality and supremacy are to be given to the Irish Courts'. That put the Supreme Court on a stronger footing.

Its position was also strengthened by the fact that the new Constitution contained some innovative features that gave added weight to the courts' role. The independence of the judiciary was expressly guaranteed and protection was extended to civil rights such as personal liberty, free speech and religious freedom. Just as important, the document gave the judiciary the authority to review, and potentially strike down, laws enacted by the legislature – a tool that would turn out to be decidedly blunt in the Free State era but which, retained and strengthened by the drafters of the 1937 Constitution, would ultimately become the sharpest weapon in the Supreme Court's arsenal. It would be the source of its greatest power and the basis for recurrent, at times acute, tension between the judges and the politicians over the next century.

Kennedy saw the 1922 Constitution as a major achievement and was later to grow disillusioned with politicians' failure to harness its potential. In a powerful address to the American Bar Association in 1928, he described the document as 'a Constitution whose democratic character is manifest if Gettysburg still speaks'. He went on:

> This boast at least we may make without fear of challenge, that under the institutions as we have made them there is no room for ascendancy of class or religion, and the upgrowing youth of our state will compete, with equality of opportunity, in a free country to whose service they are now called to give of their best in conditions which realise what seemed the wild dreams of their fathers, conditions which end a feud of centuries and open up the economic and other possibilities which should flow from the reconcilement of historic enmity.[14]

The 1922 Constitution set out the principles that would underpin the new order, but the specifics — not least the vital question of who would preside over the new courts — had still to be worked out. The delicate task fell to a specially created judiciary committee appointed in early 1923 by W. T. Cosgrave, who was the first President of the Executive Council, or prime minister. The committee was chaired by Lord Glenavy (formerly Sir James Campbell), a former Lord Chief Justice and staunch unionist, but Kennedy, by then Attorney General, was an influential member and the most vocal champion of the reformist agenda. In addition to Kennedy and Glenavy, the all-male committee also included some who would become senior members of the Free State judiciary, including future Supreme Court judges Charles Andrew O'Connor, William Johnston,* John O'Byrne and the Protestant nationalist James Creed Meredith. Also on the committee was Timothy Sullivan, who was to be the first President of the High Court, and Cahir Davitt, son of the Land League founder, Michael Davitt. In a letter apparently drafted by Kennedy, Cosgrave wrote to each member of the committee, urging them to 'fashion an administration of justice upon which the people will lean with confidence and affection'. He went on:

---

*Johnston was the father of the writer Denis Johnston and grandfather of the novelist Jennifer Johnston.

In the long struggle for the right to rule in our own country, there has been no sphere of the administration lately ended which impressed itself on the minds of our people as a standing monument of alien government, more than the system, the machinery, and the administration of law and justice, which supplanted in comparatively modern times the laws and institutions till then a part of the living national organism. The body of laws and the system of judicature so imposed upon this Nation were English (not even British) in their seed, English in their growth, English in their vitality. Their ritual, their nomenclature, were only to be understood by the student of the history of the people of Southern Britain.[15]

Kennedy envisaged replacing the old order with an indigenous Irish courts system, completely independent of politics. At one point he wrote to Eoin MacNeill, now a minister in the new administration, that 'in so far as the existing system is based upon English history we hope to cut it out and start afresh'.[16] A long-standing practice under British rule was that, when the Lord Lieutenant – the head of the British administration in Ireland – was away, judges could be sworn in to act in his place. For Kennedy, that blurring of the lines between the judiciary and the executive was an example of how the judges had allowed themselves to become politicized. Appointment to the bench had become a tainted instrument of patronage, reserved as payment for political services, he believed, and these failings helped explain 'the bad repute of the Anglo-Irish Bench and its position as an enemy institution in the eyes of the people'.[17]

It was well recognised amongst those who sought promotion to the Bench, that the only safe avenue of promotion was the Whip's office of one or other of the political parties in England. Mere pre-eminence in the legal profession in Ireland . . . led nowhere, certainly not to the pre-eminent positions on the Bench. And this was a matter of common knowledge.[18]

The War of Independence had sealed the fate of the old judiciary. A string of habeas corpus decisions – cases in which the judges had upheld the British forces' right to detain people and even impose the death penalty – were seen by Kennedy and others as symptomatic of the Crown judiciary's worldview, one that was jarringly out of sync with the prevailing mood and left them heavily compromised. 'The war record of that judiciary is still branded upon the public memory', wrote George Gavan Duffy, the future President of the High Court and one of the signatories to the Anglo-Irish Treaty, in 1922.[19]

Yet while Kennedy felt the new courts needed to make a clean break with the past, and advised the committee that they should consider themselves 'untrammelled by any regard to any of the existing systems in this country', the proposals that emerged from their deliberations – perhaps not surprisingly, given that all but one of the members belonged to the legal profession – were hardly revolutionary. The most far-reaching changes occurred at the lower levels of the courts system, where the emphasis was on winning public support by making the machinery of justice more efficient and bringing it closer to the citizen. Drawing on the success of the so-called 'Dáil courts', also known as the 'Sinn Féin courts', set up as a parallel local justice system during the War of Independence, the committee proposed a network of District Courts to replace the part-time magistrates of the old regime.

The District Court would be the workhorse of the new system. The next level was the regional Circuit Court, which would deal with civil cases and all but the most serious crimes. These were to be handled further up the chain, in the High Court, which was to hear civil cases above a certain monetary threshold. At the top of the pyramid was the Supreme Court, which would consist of three judges, led by the Chief Justice. While the number of Supreme Court judges would increase, the overall structures would remain in place, with only minor changes, into the twenty-first century. 'A gentle evolution took place, rather than a radical revolution', writes Hugh Geoghegan, who sat on the Supreme Court in the 2000s.[20]

The modesty of the plans, particularly at the higher levels of the system, was partly a result of the new Constitution itself, which put an obstacle in the way of sweeping change by providing for the wholesale carrying forward into the new state of the laws and legal system inherited from the British. This appeared to exclude from the outset any attempt to replace the English common law with a continental-style civil code. But, as Chief Justice Ronan Keane would later point out, the committee also seemed happy to leave untouched many important aspects of Irish law that were clearly within their remit.[21] For example, they appear not to have considered the arguments for replacing the adversarial system with an inquisitorial one or bringing an end to the distinction between barristers and solicitors.

Even if Kennedy had tried to push through more radical changes, however, he would probably have met stern resistance. While he had allies on the committee, not least his old university friend Louis J. Walsh and two former Dáil Court judges, Cahir Davitt and James Creed Meredith, the group included a number of old regime judges whose appetite for sweeping changes may well have been limited. Then there was Lord Glenavy, with whom he had a strained relationship. In a letter to Cosgrave setting out his views on the old judiciary, in August 1923, Kennedy wrote scathingly that Glenavy's promotion to Lord Chief Justice of Ireland in 1916 owed less to his skill as an advocate than to 'his work in collaboration with Carson and his bitter diatribes on English Tory platforms against his own people, diatribes most wicked because he did not believe them but delivered them as the price paid for judicial promotion'.[22]

One of the issues that divided Kennedy and Glenavy was judicial attire. To Kennedy, replacing the traditional costume, adopted by barristers in 1685 when the Bar went into mourning at the death of King Charles II, would be an important sign of rupture with the past. He was convinced that if the new courts were to win public support and convince sceptics that the Free State government was more than a puppet regime, the new order would have to break with the trappings of the British legal system. Wigs and gowns were in his sights.

Kennedy's preference was for colourful new outfits modelled on the robes worn by the Brehons, or judges of the old Gaelic Ireland. In this he had the support of W. B. Yeats, then a member of the Free State senate, who put him in touch with the English artist Charles Shannon to discuss new designs. Kennedy saw this as an issue of 'national importance' and got closely involved in poring over sketches and illustrations.[23] He had a particular loathing for the horsehair wigs, which were not only a 'servile appendage'[24] but were also, he told Yeats, 'objectionable, stupid, ugly and cause headaches to people with sensitive heads'.[25]

But Kennedy didn't foresee the scale of the backlash from his own colleagues. In a letter to his friend Louis J. Walsh in October or November 1923, Kennedy wrote of the hostility that was greeting his plans among fellow barristers, who were 'obstinately hostile' to his changes and clung to the wig 'with the greatest intensity'.[26] The controversy rumbled on for more than two years, Kennedy gradually growing more despondent in the face of implacable opposition from the law library. He reserved particular ire for Glenavy, who, he told Walsh, appeared to be 'out for my blood' (in his response, Walsh agreed that Glenavy was 'a terrible old cod').[27]

By mid-1926 Kennedy had to concede defeat in his battle over the gowns. When the rules committee of the new judiciary finally delivered a firm rejection to his proposals, a resigned Kennedy lamented to Cosgrave that he was a 'lone voice without support'.[28] On 22 September he thanked Yeats for his help and hoped that they might succeed some time in the future. 'The legal profession is still [in] large majority of the old school, and very conservative', he wrote.[29] Kennedy's disappointment was compounded by the rejection of his proposed change to the form of address for judges in court. He wanted judges to be addressed as 'A Bhreithimh', the Irish for 'judge', but again his colleagues and the Executive Council overruled him. 'Now the position will be that we shall be addressed with the abominable "My Lord" and we wearing on our heads an emblem of subjugation, or subordination to external ideals', he told Cosgrave in July 1926.★[30]

★ It was not until 2006, under Chief Justice John Murray, that the mode of address was changed from 'My lord' to 'Judge' or 'the court'. When the proposed changes were under discussion within the judiciary, Adrian Hardiman objected to a colleague's suggestion that the Irish courts should adopt the American 'Your Honour'. To him, according to a friend, it was redolent of 'the old Irish peasantry tipping their cap'.

Kennedy's only sartorial success was in the District Court, where he won support for new gowns and headdresses modelled on those worn by Venetian doges, making the judges look like they had over-sized socks on their heads. But at the three higher levels – Circuit, High and Supreme Court – the pre-1921 costumes remained in place. (It would take almost ninety years for the Supreme Court to end the practice of wearing wigs in court.) Some of the district justices continued to wear the new hat, but in time it fell out of favour. All that remains of Kennedy's effort is the doge's hat which he had planned to wear in the Supreme Court and which is kept to this day in the Chief Justice's Chambers in the Four Courts.[31]

The relationship between Kennedy and Cosgrave, which had begun when Cosgrave approached Kennedy to write a legal opinion in the early days of his administration, developed into a close partnership. By March 1923, when he was appointed the first Attorney General of the Irish Free State, Kennedy had become a friend and adviser to Cosgrave. The collaboration extended beyond the law; when Collins and Arthur Griffith died, it was Kennedy who drafted Cosgrave's homages to both men.

Kennedy was ambitious and had keen political antennae, and it didn't take much effort to convince him to stand for the Dáil when the opportunity arose. In July 1923, having been urged to stand in Donegal, his father's home county, by his old university friend Louis J. Walsh, Kennedy ruled it out, stressing the importance of 'keeping the law removed from politics'.[32] Just a few weeks later, at Cosgrave's urging, he performed a swift U-turn by announcing his intention to stand for Cumann na nGaedheal in a Dublin South by-election. The demarcation lines between law and politics weren't so rigid after all. Kennedy threw himself wholeheartedly into politics, prompting his mother to write to his wife, Clare, with the hope that 'he may find a minute for his poor mother one day soon'.[33] Kennedy's increasing public profile brought its own disturbing hazards. His house at Waterloo Place in Dublin was attacked by opponents of the treaty in early 1923.

The lawyer-turned-politician was elected to the Dáil in October

1923, defeating the anti-Treaty candidate in a two-man race with 52 per cent of the vote. But he never saw his foray into politics as anything more than an interlude; Cosgrave had already broached the possibility of appointing him Chief Justice, and it was a job he coveted. In a personal letter to Cosgrave on 19 August 1923, Kennedy outlined what he saw as the failings of the old regime judiciary and suggested the qualities required of a Free State judge. Unlike the Anglo-Irish judges, the reconstituted bench would have to 'stand clear' of government and all other influences. Yet at the same time, he wrote, it would be a mistake to 'rush to the other extreme' and fill the bench with 'purely technical' lawyers.

> The legal pedant is as great a danger as (personally much less attract-ive than) the political job-hunter. The best type of judge is the man who not only is a sound lawyer and man of independent judgment but who also has had contact with affairs. The type of man who can tie and untie legal knots with uncanny skill but who has nothing of the practical everyday world in his composition does not often make a success in the practice of the legal profession and one may say never succeeds as a judge. On the other hand, the man who has a sound working grasp of legal principles combined with a practical business-like grasp of everyday mundane affairs, succeeds in the profession and succeeds on the Bench.

Kennedy's profile of the model judge sounded uncannily like a self-portrait. He suggested that, provided a candidate was not a 'mere political hack', some experience in 'the political affairs of this coun-try' was an added qualification. Cosgrave got the message. In June 1924, less than a year after he was elected, Kennedy resigned his Dáil seat. He would be the first Chief Justice.

Filling the senior positions on the new bench was a delicate task. On the one hand, Cosgrave and Kennedy wanted to inject new blood into the system, and Kennedy in particular hoped to appoint judges who shared his own enthusiasm for starting afresh. He made clear that Thomas Molony, a liberal and Catholic Dubliner who had suc-ceeded James Campbell as Lord Chief Justice in 1918, had been too closely associated with the British authorities and was therefore not politically acceptable. On the other hand, the pool of high-calibre candidates was dominated by unionist lawyers and judges of the old regime, and the government was conscious of the need to reassure the Protestant and unionist minorities that they would have a role to play in the new state.[34]

The result, in keeping with the pattern of appointments to the Seanad, where sixteen of Cosgrave's nominees were unionists, was a carefully weighted mix. The first of the two vacancies on the Supreme Court was filled by Sir Charles O'Connor, a well-regarded 69-year-old judge who had for the most part managed to avoid the political controversy associated with the habeas corpus cases in the War of Independence – cases in which people took challenges to the legality of their detention.[35] The third position on the court went to Gerald Fitzgibbon, who had represented Dublin University (Trinity College) as a unionist in the House of Commons and Dáil Éireann. As President of the High Court, a position that came with ex officio membership of the Supreme Court, the government chose Timothy Sullivan, a Catholic nationalist, which meant that the Supreme Court was equally balanced between the two traditions.* Appointments to the High Court followed the same pattern.

In all, just two of the senior Crown judges – Charles O'Connor and William Wylie, a Presbyterian from Coleraine who, like O'Connor, was not seen as hostile to the new order – were asked to stay on.

Overnight, the bench had been virtually cleared of judges who served under the British in Ireland. They had known for some time that the writing was on the wall. When the Treaty negotiations were taking place in October 1921, the old regime judges had lobbied London to protect them and tried to ensure they would be compensated when they lost office.[36] In May 1922, Lord Chief Justice Molony told a senior British official that the judges were 'simply waiting to see will the tide turn or engulf us'.[37] In September that year – three

---

* Today it is rare for the President of the High Court to sit in the Supreme Court, but in the early decades of the court it was more common.

months before his position as Lord Chancellor was abolished – John
Ross described the judges as being 'in a state of great anxiety' about
what lay ahead for them.[38] They got little sympathy from Kennedy,
whose disdain for the old judges made little allowance for the difficult situation in which they had found themselves during those
tumultuous years. During the upheaval that followed the Treaty
negotiations, the judges had worked under considerable pressure,
their lives at risk from attack or assassination. Their war record damaged them irrevocably in the eyes of an increasingly nationalist
population, while their perceived proximity to executive power
jarred with the principle of judicial independence that was to be an
article of faith under the new order. But the picture was not black-
and-white. As barrister Blathna Ruane points out, for example, the
Crown judiciary had privately successfully resisted attempts by the
British government to restore order by establishing a special tribunal
to try cases without a jury, thereby refusing to align themselves with
the wishes of an executive to whom they were supposedly joined at
the hip.[39]

In the end, the old judges were given the option of retiring with
compensation. All of them went to live in England initially, but 'in
varying degrees they each drifted back to Ireland later'.[40]

The choice of judges to sit on the Free State's first Supreme and
High Courts was the result of a careful balancing act, showing a
desire both to break with the past and to reassure southern unionists
and the British. Kennedy may have shown little sympathy for the
situation in which the old regime judges found themselves, but he
was adamant that the new system would send a signal of openness to
the Protestant minority. 'Although the population of the Free State is
largely Catholic, the majority of the Judges of the High Court are
Protestants. But the courts have the confidence of the people, and
nobody cares what the religion of the judges is',[41] Kennedy told the
New York World during a visit to the United States in 1928.*

---

* The *New York World* reporter described Kennedy as 'a blue-eyed, rosy-cheeked
man of medium height. When he laughs he unbuttons his coat. His hair is grey
and he talks with a British accent.'

On some issues, Kennedy was willing to go further than Cosgrave to accommodate Protestant concerns. Before Independence, for example, an Irish resident could get a divorce by seeking a private member's bill enacted in the Westminster parliament.[42] The 1922 Constitution was silent on the issue, but Kennedy was 'strongly of [the] opinion that we should make provision for those who approve of that sort of thing', and in February 1923 he approached Cosgrave to clarify the State's position. Kennedy did not see how they could 'prejudice the position of the minority in this country by depriving them of this little luxury',[43] but Cosgrave involved the Catholic hierarchy in the deliberations, and their intervention, which tallied with Cosgrave's own conservatism on moral questions, ensured the proposal went nowhere.

There were to be serious clashes of personality and judicial approach on the early, three-judge Supreme Court, particularly between Kennedy and Fitzgibbon, but in those days of 1924 the focus was chiefly on the mechanics of building an institution that could inspire public confidence in the justice system of the fledgling state.

A ceremony to inaugurate the new judiciary was held on 11 June 1924 in the upper yard at Dublin Castle, where Michael Collins had marked the surrender of the castle by the British administration two years before and where the courts had relocated from the King's Inns in 1923. The Supreme Court sat in St Patrick's Hall, one of the rooms in the State Apartments.* In the early summer drizzle, crowds gathered in the castle yards and watched from windows and balconies as the Chief Justice led the incoming judges, all dressed in morning clothes and silk hats, past a guard of honour from the south-east corner of the castle yard to the former Throne Room.[44] There, in the presence of Cosgrave and his ministers, Kennedy invited the new judges of the Free State to take their oath. The form of the event, largely devised by Kennedy himself, was 'an indication that he would be concerned, as head of the judiciary, to emphasize that a new legal order was now in being'.[45] Once the Attorney General, John O'Byrne,

* St Patrick's Hall is now the venue for presidential inaugurations.

had congratulated the Chief Justice and his brethren, Kennedy spoke in Irish and English and said the time had at last come when 'the voice of the Gael' would be heard in the courts of Ireland.

> This is surely a precious moment – the moment when the silence of the Gael in Courts of Law is broken, and that within what was once the Pale – the moment when, after a week of centuries, Irish Courts, fashioned in freedom by an Oireachtas again assembled, are thrown open to administer justice according to laws made in Ireland by free Irish citizens for the well-being of dearly beloved land and people.
>
> It is for us here in the seat of justice a moment of compelling emotions, and for me especially, to whom has fallen under Providence the unique and sacred favour of presiding at this very time and place, the joy and emotion are well-nigh overwhelming . . . [46]

The ceremony at Dublin Castle marked an important symbolic step for the new State and crowned a major achievement for Kennedy and Cosgrave. With striking speed, they had fashioned a new courts system to rank alongside the more celebrated successes of the early years after Independence, such as the establishment of An Garda Síochána.[47] Yet the rhetoric of rupture belied the relative modesty of the changes, at least at the apex of the courts system. While the system at District and Circuit Court level had been overhauled, for better or worse, the visitor to the Supreme Court in late 1924 would have found it a fairly familiar scene. Irish law remained rooted in the British tradition. Senior barristers, dressed in the same wigs and gowns, were known as King's Counsel and continued to address the judges as 'My Lord'. The harp may have replaced the royal coat of arms on the wall behind the bench, but ultimately the changes were the legal equivalent of splashing the red pre-Independence post-boxes with a coat of green paint.[48]

Some judges make a point of eschewing the limelight. Hugh Kennedy embraced it, cultivating a public persona while privately complaining about the strictures that his role as Chief Justice imposed on him. A magazine journalist who was invited to his home, Newstead in Clonskeagh, for a feature on 'Beautiful Irish Homes', described a house filled with books, his wife Clare's piano and a dining room where 'it is evident that the Chief Justice presides and gathers round him his colleagues of the Bar and his literary friends, and relaxes from judicial cares like a true Irish judge'. The journalist was told that Kennedy often sat up late, poring over his judgments till dawn. 'He does not smoke, but has contracted that old Georgian custom of carrying a snuff box, and with a pitcher of water by his side, spends the long night sometimes in his study.'

Like many judges, Kennedy liked the media attention (and kept all his press cuttings) while at the same time bemoaning journalists' perennial failure to do justice to his wise and learned judgments. Writing in his diary on 27 November 1929, Kennedy complained about the morning papers' coverage of the latest case at the court, sniping that the reports made it seem as though the judges had delivered 'incoherent balderdash' and expressing relief that they were printed on 'perishing paper' that wouldn't be available to future historians. 'I have appealed to both papers in vain to send a competent reporter into our court to relieve the deaf, aged and stupid crank who now tortures us; but they keep the competent young men for the police and criminal courts to provide what the reading public really wants', Kennedy wrote. Two days later, he bemoaned how at social occasions he had to try to keep avoiding people who wanted to talk business. It was, he conceded, 'part of the punishment one takes for the considerable stipend'.

Kennedy could be an acerbic, often petulant, critic. Remarque's *All Quiet on the Western Front*, which he read and reviewed in his diary in 1929, was a 'belly and bowels' story of the Great War. Harry Clarke's drawings showed 'exquisite line and colour' but were 'infused with a diseased mentality'. He complained of a fellow judge's persistent interruption of barristers, which was 'very trying to me and must be maddening to counsel'. The mundane concerns that filled his diary by the late 1920s – giving an insight into a personality that was by turns insightful and petty, lucid and vain – reflected the relative calm that had settled over the Supreme Court by that time. The bloody upheaval of the Civil War had given way to a measure of stability and the new courts were running smoothly.

Kennedy continued to be consulted by Cosgrave even after he became Chief Justice, and drafted a tribute for him on the assassination of his Justice Minister, Kevin O'Higgins, in 1927. Cosgrave also looked out for Kennedy, whom he affectionately addressed as 'the Brehon'. In a hastily written note in July 1925, Cosgrave reassured the Chief Justice he had managed to suppress publication of a reference to his attendance 'at a Masonic Garden Party . . . in Clonskeagh'. Kennedy's tone had grown lighter, but memories of the Civil War were still fresh. In a diary entry in February 1929, describing his attendance at a concert given by the Dublin Philharmonic Society, he wrote: 'The dead march in Beethoven's Symphony Eroica released floods of memory of murdered leaders and tramps to Glasnevin [cemetery] and that sense of despair for irreparable loss which has swept over one in these few years of sullied freedom.'[49]

This return to normality looked to be complete with the re-opening of the Four Courts in October 1931. The complex had been closed since its destruction in the Civil War, and the completion of the re-building work, which would allow the courts to return from their temporary home at Dublin Castle, was an occasion Kennedy thought should be marked with a grand ceremonial opening. He wrote to the Minister for Justice, James FitzGerald-Kenney, proposing an elaborate ceremony in the Round Hall that would culminate in the minister symbolically handing the keys of the courts to Kennedy before he led his colleagues into the Supreme Court and declared the courts open for business. At that point the tricolour would be hoisted over the building and the national anthem played.

The Executive Council thought this was all a bit much. They didn't want any ceremonial opening at all. For one, it was sure to go down badly with the public. In a letter to Kennedy, FitzGerald-Kenney said it would be impossible to justify the expenditure, given that Ireland and the world were still reeling from the economic crisis set off by the Wall Street crash. But the Council also advised that the security situation was less stable than it appeared. FitzGerald-Kenney said ministers were concerned that a high-profile re-opening would be akin to 'shaking a red rag in the face of an insane bull', providing a 'direct incentive' to anti-Treaty elements who might be intent on targeting the complex a second time. 'We are taking all possible precautions to see that the Four Courts are not blown up or otherwise destroyed some night', he told Kennedy.[50]

The re-opening of the Four Courts took place on 12 October without any formal ceremony, but Kennedy did manage to organize a religious service and some low-key speeches that ensured the occasion made it into the next day's papers.

The reconstruction of the Four Courts nine years after its destruction was a feat of engineering and workmanship, but it was also a symbolic milestone for the new State, heralding 'a return to political stability and normality following the devastation caused by the Civil War'.[51] At the heart of the restored building was the stuffy, walnut-panelled Supreme Court, where – after a brief statement to thank the architects and restoration team – the Kennedy court got to work.

Yet while the Civil War had ended, the threat of political violence hung over the country and the institutions of the new state remained relatively fragile. Just two days after the re-opening of the Four Courts came a reminder of the fraught political atmosphere: the government drafted a draconian law allowing for military tribunals with the power to impose the death penalty.

It was only a matter of time before the three judges of the Supreme Court would be drawn into the conflicts that raged outside.

2. Stand-off

'It may be necessary . . . for a responsible Executive to
save the people from irresponsible Judges.'

Stephen Roche

It was about 8.15pm when three strangers wearing dark coats knocked
on the door of Edward Kinane's remote farmhouse near Upper-
church, a small village tucked into the Slieve Felim hills in north Co.
Tipperary, and asked for a bucket of water for their car. It was an
unusual request, not least at this late hour, but Kinane said he was
happy to help. As the farmer made to walk across the kitchen, one of
the men followed him in and told him to put his hands in the air.
Kinane refused. The stranger repeated the order. Kinane stood still.
The man drew a revolver and pressed it into Kinane's chest, forcing
him to walk backwards towards the dining room.

Kinane's mother, Margaret, and his brother Martin, who were also
in the farmhouse that night, looked on in horror as Kinane lunged at
the gunman, grabbing the man's collar with his right hand and the
barrel of the revolver with his left. A shot rang out and a bullet flashed
past. A violent melee ensued. Kinane pulled the revolver from his
assailant's hand, but he quickly found himself outnumbered. A second man struck Kinane on the head and shoulder with a baton, and
the third shot him in the thigh. 'I've been shot!' he shouted as he fell
to the ground. The three men stood over him for two or three minutes, Kinane would later tell gardaí, but they said nothing. In the
skirmish Kinane's brother Martin had been hit by a baton on the
shoulder. Margaret Kinane turned to the attackers. 'What have ye
against us?' she pleaded. The men said nothing and left.[1]

A few days later, on Tuesday, 24 April 1934, an improvised sitting

of Thurles District Court took place at Edward Kinane's bedside in
the surgical ward of the local hospital. Four men accused of having
carried out the attack sat on chairs at the end of the bed, surrounded
by gardaí. With his head heavily bandaged, Kinane gave the local
District Justice (as they were called at the time) his account of the
events of the previous Saturday night. Responding to questions from
the local superintendent, Kinane said he had never seen his assailant
before that night.

'You know him now?' the garda asked.

'Oh, yes; I can put my finger on him.'

Kinane sat up in the bed and pointed at one of the men – a local
named Hubert Johnson. 'By Almighty God,' Kinane said, 'I can
swear that is the man.'

Johnson and his three co-accused – Jerry Ryan, John Harty and
James Cantwell – were indicted on a raft of charges, including
attempted murder, and sent for trial. The Minister for Justice issued
an order transferring the trial to the Military Tribunal at Collins
Barracks in Dublin.

In the course of a two-week military trial in the capital, prosecutors led by the future High Court judge George Gavan Duffy,
situated the attack on the Kinane farmhouse in the wider context of
the enmities that sprang from the Civil War and still simmered across
Ireland twelve years on. The court heard that Jerry Ryan, formerly a
colonel of the Free State Army, belonged to the central council of the
League of Youth, a group better known by its nickname: the Blueshirts. The right-wing organization had been established in the early
1930s ostensibly to provide protection for political groups such as
Cumann na nGaedheal from attacks and intimidation from the
anti-Treaty IRA, which had had a number of its prisoners released
after Éamon de Valera's Fianna Fáil came to power in February 1932.*
After the attack on the Kinane farmhouse, gardaí said they believed
all four accused were Blueshirts.

---

*Later, under the leadership of the former Garda Commissioner Eoin O'Duffy,
the Blueshirts drew increasingly on the policies, symbols and organizational style
of European Fascism, and some of its members went on to fight for the Fascists
during the Spanish Civil War.

The wounds of the Civil War were still raw in Thurles, and tensions had been running high in the weeks leading up to the attack on the farmhouse. A number of assaults and window-breakings had been reported to gardaí, but the catalyst for the attack, prosecutors argued, was the seizure earlier in April of three horses from local farmers for non-payment of rates. One of the horses belonged to John Harty's father. An auction for the seized animals took place in Thurles town centre on 12 April, but it soon descended into chaos after farmers from several miles around Thurles converged on the sale ground. 'By the time the sale started about 300 people were present, many of them wearing blue shirts', the *Irish Times* reported. James Kinane, the Thurles rates collector, was one of the chief targets of the farmers' fury. He took several blows to the head and at one point drew his revolver in self-defence. When the auction ended, the crowd marched in procession to the Main Street, where they were addressed by Col. Jerry Ryan.

According to prosecution lawyers, Edward Kinane was targeted simply because he was the local rates collector's stepbrother. The military tribunal sentenced Johnson to three years in prison and gave Ryan and Harty nine months each. Cantwell was found not guilty on all counts against him.

The attack on the farmhouse in rural Tipperary was but one incident among many in those turbulent years, and would have merited only fleeting mention in the national press were it not for the fact that the four suspects took a court challenge to the constitutionality of their detention. And that challenge would become the most serious and far-reaching case to come before the Supreme Court since it had been established. At stake was the very future of the Free State Constitution itself.

A strong, stable Constitution is one that is difficult to change. The drafters of the Free State Constitution knew that, and so one of the most radical parts of the new state's founding document was a requirement that any future amendment would have to be approved by referendum. Not only that, but the bar was set high: unless a majority of registered voters or two-thirds of those who actually turned out to vote said Yes, any referendum would fall. But in the final stages of the drafting process in the early 1920s a crucial caveat was inserted. For the first eight years after the coming into effect of the Constitution, the new clause stated, the text could be amended by a vote of the Oireachtas. The clause was intended simply to make it easier to clean up minor errors or technical flaws in the early years after Independence without having to go to the people for approval each time. Little did the drafters know that the Constitution would ultimately unravel because of that small, last-minute tweak. In 1929, after relatively little debate in the Dáil, the transitional period was extended by another eight years.

It was the government's crackdown on crime and a wave of unrest in the late 1920s that brought the issue to a head. From 1927, when the draconian Public Safety Act of 1923 was repealed, violence and intimidation, particularly of juries, began to rise and pose profound dilemmas for the Cumann na nGaedheal government.[2] Within two months of the repeal of the Public Safety Act, Cosgrave told Dáil Éireann in October 1931, one witness to a court case had been murdered and a juror was gravely wounded in Dublin. 'This signalled the breakdown of the jury system', he told the House. The final straw was an interview by Frank Ryan of the IRA in which he justified three recent killings and claimed the IRA was capable of more.[3] The government's response was to introduce an 'elaborate anti-terrorism law'[4] that granted the authorities extensive powers of arrest and allowed the government to ban public meetings. It also provided for the creation of immensely powerful military tribunals with the authority to impose severe penalties, including death, for any offence. Its verdicts would be final in all cases.

Jerry Ryan and his three co-accused went to court to challenge the legality of their detention. They challenged the constitutional validity of two laws: the one that extended by a further eight years the period in which the Constitution could be amended by ordinary legislation[5] and the one that allowed for the introduction of military tribunals.[6] They lost in the High Court but appealed that decision to the Supreme Court, where the case was heard at a special holiday sitting in a deserted Four Courts in August 1934.[7] Two high-powered legal teams lined up against each other in the Supreme Court that summer. Éamon de Valera's Fianna Fáil had swept to power in the general election two years previously, so, intriguingly, the barristers who found themselves challenging the draconian laws introduced by Cumann na nGaedheal were closely identified with Cosgrave's party. The team was led by John A. Costello, a former Attorney General and future Taoiseach, and with Charles Casey and Cecil Lavery alongside him it included two future Attorneys General and judges. Opposite them in the stuffy courtroom that summer were six formidable barristers representing the State, including the Attorney General and future Chief Justice Conor Maguire, a future President of the High Court (George Gavan Duffy) and three future Supreme Court judges (Martin Maguire, James Geoghegan and Kevin Haugh).

The case turned on the validity of the amendment to the Constitution pushed through by the Cosgrave government in 1929, purporting to extend from eight to sixteen years the period within which the Constitution could be amended by a simple vote of parliament. In other words, did the Oireachtas have an unlimited power of amendment of the Constitution during the transitory period? If not, then the military tribunals were unconstitutional and the Tipperary Blueshirts would be freed. If it was valid, then in effect it meant any government had an unlimited power to change the Constitution whenever it wished. That would mean the Constitution and the supposed 'inviolable' and 'guaranteed' rights it conferred on the people wouldn't be worth the paper they were written on. The stakes were high, and the three-man Supreme Court was badly divided. Hugh Kennedy sided with Jerry Ryan and his co-accused, but the Chief Justice found himself in a minority of one; Fitzgibbon and James Murnaghan were with the State.

Kennedy, Fitzgibbon and Murnaghan knew each other well. They had served together on the court since 1925 and would remain together until 1936, an eleven-year period that remains the longest stretch in which no personnel changes took place on the court. But it wasn't always an easy cohabitation for the three men.

Murnaghan, born to Irish emigrant parents in St Louis, Missouri,

before the family returned home to Omagh, Co. Tyrone, was a
wealthy northern nationalist who had been a contemporary of Kennedy's at UCD, where he had contributed to the student magazine,
St Stephen's, which Kennedy edited, and later went on to join him on
the committee that drafted the 1922 Constitution.* As an accomplished academic and one of relatively few suitably qualified Catholic
barristers after Independence – the law library was still dominated by
lawyers from Protestant and unionist backgrounds – Murnaghan had
risen rapidly from junior counsel to a position on the High Court
bench, an elevation explained partly by the government's desire for
balance between unionist and nationalist appointments to the judiciary.[8] When Charles O'Connor, the only former member of the
Crown judiciary to serve on the Supreme Court, retired in 1925, a
year after the new court was established, Murnaghan was appointed
his successor. He had a reputation as a solid, reliable judgment-writer,
but his position between Kennedy and Fitzgibbon made his the swing
vote in some key cases.

Fitzgibbon, a unionist with strong family ties to the law, had represented the University of Dublin in the House of Commons and
Dáil Éireann before he became a judge and had also served as a member of the constituent assembly that drafted the Constitution.
Although he, like Kennedy, was a close adviser to W. T. Cosgrave, it
appears unlikely Fitzgibbon shared Kennedy's desire for large-scale
changes to the legal system. In contrast to Kennedy's 'enthusiastic
nationalism',[9] Fitzgibbon's attitude towards the new state was one of
'pessimistic scepticism'.[10] In that he wasn't alone among judges of the
Free State era. For some of them, having been educated in a British
system where parliament was supreme and the Constitution was
unwritten, 'their background and traditions made the very existence
of an Irish state seem a perilous experience, and the works and pomps
of that State – whether declarations of fundamental rights or, at
the other extreme, the establishment of a standing military court –
the objects of deep suspicion'.[11] Their diverging views on the new

---

*Murnaghan, unlike Kennedy, had a good relationship with James Joyce and
remained friendly with the writer throughout his life.

state put Kennedy and Fitzgibbon at odds, and the tensions between the two men were a feature of the court's first decade.[12] In 1929, when Kennedy was hearing an application from the pre-Independence Attorney General Sir James O'Connor to be readmitted as a solicitor, Kennedy confided in his private diary that he suspected Fitzgibbon was advising O'Connor behind his back.[13]

The simmering tensions between Kennedy and Fitzgibbon would come to the surface in the Blueshirt case. Both men criticized the government for using the Constitution in a way that was not foreseen by the drafters, but whereas Kennedy ruled against the government Fitzgibbon reluctantly accepted that the authorities were acting within their powers.

Fitzgibbon's judgment was remarkable less for what he said than how he said it. He rejected the view that there were universal rights so sacred that no legislature could have the authority to deprive a citizen of them. He commented with withering sarcasm on how Fianna Fáil had denounced the draconian law-and-order powers while in opposition but then enthusiastically embraced them when in government. The sentiment reaches its apotheosis in his closing lines. In what Gerard Hogan, now a judge of the Court of Appeal, has described as 'the most remarkable language ever to be found in a judgment of the Irish Supreme Court', Fitzgibbon, laying bare his disillusionment with the new state, writes of the Constitution setting out 'the conditions under which liberty is enjoyed and justice may be administered in "this other Eden, demi-Paradise, this precious stone, set in the silver sea, this blessed plot, this earth, this realm, this Saorstát"'. The line is a reworking of a passage in Shakespeare's *Richard II*, with 'this Saorstát' replacing 'this England'. Fitzgibbon never seemed remotely comfortable with the new regime, but specifically he was concerned about the erosion of civil liberties under the Free State – a theme he would return to in other cases. Here he felt he had no choice but to wave through a law that would allow the state to hang people for relatively minor offences, but he wasn't happy about it. 'Have we really come to this?' he was in effect asking. Murnaghan, although 'staggered' by how the military courts departed from legal norms, reluctantly agreed with Fitzgibbon.

Kennedy, alone of the three judges, decided against the government. But his minority judgment, like Fitzgibbon's for the majority, was most significant not for his conclusions but for his means of getting there. His judgment took an hour and a half to read aloud in court. Noting that the constituent assembly had declared at the forefront of the Constitution Act that 'all lawful authority comes from God to the people', he said all legislation of the Oireachtas had to conform to what he called 'that acknowledged ultimate Source' or else it would be 'repugnant to the Natural Law' and therefore unconstitutional and invalid. That was a first. His citing of the natural law – the idea that certain rights or values are inherent, having been ordained by a higher source – foreshadowed its use in fraught debates on issues such as contraception and abortion later in the century.

Just as Fitzgibbon's judgment captured a strain of unionist disenchantment with the new order, Kennedy's provided a glimpse of the Chief Justice's frustration at his own increasing isolation. He was convinced that the government was using legal sleight of hand to manipulate the Constitution for its own ends, yet frustrated that his court – where, not for the first time, he found himself in a minority of one – chose not to stand in its way.

The Ryan case revealed deep flaws in the 1922 Constitution. Though the government won its case, the Supreme Court decision made it clear that the Constitution could be amended indefinitely by an act of parliament. In effect, the Constitution had the same status as ordinary legislation. Though it did not say so explicitly, with the court's decision, the document's death warrant had been signed. Yet by the time the judges issued the decision in the week before Christmas 1934, behind-the-scenes work was already under way across the Liffey on an attempt to identify what could be salvaged of the Constitution.

In May, de Valera – perhaps by now toying with the idea of a new Constitution[14] – had established a high-level committee to examine possible changes. One of the first issues the group discussed was how the relative powers of the government and the judiciary should be weighted. Establishing a pattern that would hold for the next century, the most vocal internal voice for keeping a lid on judicial power came from the Department of Justice. On 14 June, Stephen Roche, the secretary of the Department of Justice, circulated a memo to the three other members of the committee that made clear that he felt the judges needed to be reined in. What the country wanted, he wrote, was a 'strong Executive' not liable to be 'delayed, hampered and humiliated at every step by long arguments in the courts'. Further, he wrote:

> I believe that the doctrines of 'judicial independence' and 'the separa-
> tion of the functions' are being overdone and that the Courts have
> been given or have assumed a position in our civic life to which they
> are not entitled. There was a time in England when the Judges' job
> was to save the people from an irresponsible Executive: it may be
> necessary, in turn, for a responsible Executive to save the people from
> irresponsible Judges.[15]

It wasn't a unanimous view. In his copy of the memo, Michael McDunphy, who was Assistant Secretary in de Valera's department, placed a question mark beside the reference to 'irresponsible Judges' and added that a 'strong' executive could conceivably be a real danger instead of a blessing.[16]

While Roche was sceptical, verging on hostile, towards the idea of judicial review – an innovation of the 1922 Constitution – the committee's final report said this power was fundamental and should be retained. What the senior civil servants couldn't agree on was who exactly should have the power of deciding on the validity of laws: the Supreme Court alone, a special Constitutional Court or the High Court with a right of appeal to the Supreme Court? De Valera seems to have been open to the idea of a Constitutional Court. In the Dáil on 11 May he said other countries had set up special courts that could stand back and take a broader view than the ordinary courts, which interpreted laws from day to day. 'If I could get from anybody any suggestion of some court to deal with such matters other than the Supreme Court, I would be willing to consider it. I confess that I have not been able to get anything better than the Supreme Court to fulfil this function.'[17]

The idea of establishing a special court specifically to hear constitutional cases was radical and innovative, and would probably have provoked consternation in the legal profession if it had been leaked at the time. 'Hostility from the bar and bench had already killed off far more modest proposals for reform of court costume and dress in the 1920s and radical, avant garde proposals of this kind would doubtless have met a similar fate', writes Gerard Hogan.[18] In the end that idea was shelved, but other cornerstones of the 1922 Constitution survived. The committee's report to de Valera stressed the need to protect fundamental rights through a written Constitution and a system of judicial review (a procedure by which courts can review an administrative action by a government department or other public body). These principles duly made their way into the first draft of the Constitution, written by John Hearne, Legal Adviser at the Department of External Affairs – and remained intact throughout the process.

The committee's report laid the groundwork for the 1937 Constitution, which retained judicial review and expanded the fundamental rights provisions of the first document. In that it strengthened the role of the courts and came closer to achieving the ideals set out by Kennedy in the early 1920s. The adoption of the new Constitution was a watershed he didn't live to see, however. On Saturday, 12 December 1936, Kennedy died of a heart attack while at home in Clonskeagh. Announcing the news of the Chief Justice's death in the Dáil that evening, de Valera described Kennedy as a great lawyer and a great judge. 'He was also a patriotic Irishman, who gave fine service to his country. His death is a loss to the Bench and to the nation', the Taoiseach said. From the opposition benches, W. T. Cosgrave paid tribute to his old friend before deputies stood in silent tribute. His passing was 'a national loss', the *Irish Independent* reported.[19]

Today Kennedy is remembered as the chief architect of the Supreme Court. Its second courtroom was named after him in the 1990s, and his portrait is the first that visitors see when they leave the court. Kennedy's death, on the eve of the new Constitution coming into force, took from the Supreme Court not only its figurehead but also the man who, arguably more than any other, had steered the new courts system into being and staked out its place as an institution that projected stability and commanded bipartisan respect in the fraught years after the Civil War. As such, he is a major figure in the history of the State's formative years. As Chief Justice he was a staunch defender of judicial independence and his expansionist view of the court's role anticipated future developments.[20] One of the tragedies of his premature death was that he never got a chance to work with the 1937 Constitution, which gave the judges far more scope for innovation than the charter it replaced.

Yet for all his achievements, Kennedy cut a somewhat isolated figure by the time of his death, at the comparatively young age of fifty-seven. In a number of high-profile cases, he had found himself in a minority of one. For all his idealism and courage, he was weak at building alliances and lacked the diplomatic skills to succeed in bringing others around to his views. It still rankled, late in his life, that his hope of replacing the customs and trappings of the old legal system had been frustrated by opposition within the legal profession, while his relatively broad view of the court's role was stymied by a combination of his fellow judges' reservations and the in-built weaknesses of the Constitution they had to work with. The result was that, in the entire fifteen-year lifespan of the Free State Constitution, only twice did the court actually use its power to directly review the constitutionality of an act of parliament.

The frailties of the Constitution were a real obstacle, but most judges did little to push at its boundaries. That failure was largely a result of the hostility of the legal culture. The judges of this period had been trained in a system where parliament was king, inculcating in them a reluctance to overstep what they saw as the traditional limitations of the courts' role. As Keane points out, this conservatism cut across political lines; some judges who would have been considered as nationalists, Murnaghan among them, showed just as little inclination as their unionist brethren to ruffle feathers on the other side of the Liffey.[21]

What was true of the judiciary was also true of the law library. Judges can only decide the cases that come before them. They can only take up the arguments barristers present. But in the 1920s and

1930s, there were no queues of lawyers taking landmark legal challenges that would force the judges to grapple with their powers under the new system. Not until the early 1960s, arguably, did the law library – sensing that the winds were changing and that the judges were growing increasingly receptive to expansionist arguments – begin to take cases that relied on the Constitution to push back against political over-reach or seek to advance an agenda for social change.

Hugh Kennedy's death, which coincided with a government decision to increase the size of the Supreme Court from three judges to five, was followed by big changes in personnel. His replacement as Chief Justice was Timothy Sullivan, until then President of the High Court. Like Kennedy, Sullivan came from a nationalist background and had sat on the judiciary committee that designed the new courts system in the early 1920s, but he had little of Kennedy's reformist zeal or appetite for constitutional adventurism. He was joined on the Supreme Court, just before Christmas 1936, by two very different Fianna Fáil appointees: James Geoghegan[22] and James Creed Meredith.

Geoghegan, a Catholic farmer's son from outside Mullingar, Co. Westmeath, was a pro-Treaty Redmondite who practised as a solicitor and a barrister before joining Cumann na nGaedheal in the early 1920s. He remained a member until 1930, when, having come into contact with Fianna Fáil as one of six barristers who advised de Valera on the payment of land annuities, he switched allegiance and joined the then opposition party. He was elected TD for Longford-Westmeath in a by-election in June 1930.[23]

Geoghegan was unusual among Fianna Fáil TDs in having played no part in the War of Independence or the Civil War. That he had never held a gun worked to his advantage when the party came to power. De Valera, having to fill the sensitive position of Minister for Justice in March 1932, chose Geoghegan due to his legal expertise but also no doubt as a way of reassuring his opponents as to Fianna Fáil's intentions. After he and Frank Aiken received their seals of office, their first act was to go to Arbour Hill Prison to arrange the release of all political prisoners.[24] Geoghegan was Attorney General at the time of his appointment to the court.

Meredith, the third newcomer to the Supreme Court in December 1936, defied easy categorization. From a Protestant Dublin family, he had a stellar record as a scholar at Trinity College Dublin before becoming a barrister in 1901. During the Home Rule struggle he became interested in the nationalist cause and his advice was sought out by prominent republicans.[25] He joined the Irish Volunteers when the movement was founded in 1913 and was one of John Redmond's nominees to its national committee. When the volunteers imported arms from Germany in the summer of 1914 – the Howth and Kilcoole gun-running episode – a 39-year-old Meredith was a crew member of Sir Thomas Myles's yacht *Chotah*, which landed arms at Kilcoole that August.

His views appear to have become more radical because, after Kilcoole, he got involved in the establishment of the Dáil courts – the unofficial republican courts that sprang up during the War of Independence. It took 'a degree of moral and physical bravery' to do so, particularly for a barrister with an established practice.[26] These courts were frowned upon by the Bar Council, which in 1920 passed a resolution that it was professional misconduct for any member of the Bar to appear before such tribunals.[27] The British also had them in their sights: there are records of Dáil court judges being arrested and courts broken up by the authorities.[28] Meredith eventually became 'President of the Supreme Court of the Dáil Courts' – their most senior figure – and after the war he was asked by the provisional government for proposals on how to wind them up. In 1924, when the new courts system was set up, he was one of the first five government appointees to the High Court.

Meredith was a polymath with wide interests. Law was his day job, but he was also an athlete, a writer, a philosopher and a patron of art. His translations and annotations of key philosophical texts, including Immanuel Kant's *Critique of Aesthetic Judgment* (1911), include standard works that remain widely available today, and he contributed essays on philosophy to periodicals in London and Dublin. He was a member of the Proportional Representation Society of Ireland

and president of the Statistical and Social Inquiry Society, a forum for discussion between senior civil servants, academics, members of the professions and interest groups.[29] A lifelong art lover,[30] he had a key role in setting up the collection of Irish art at the Dublin Municipal Gallery of Modern Art (the Hugh Lane Gallery), to which he donated three paintings. Meredith published three plays and also has the distinction of being the only Supreme Court judge to have written a science fiction novel while on the bench. *The Rainbow in the Valley*, published in 1939, is a utopian text filled with philosophical digressions on evolution, dreams, religion, war, humour, nationalism, music and in-jokes about Irish politics. In it, an Irishman travels to remote western China and comes upon a settlement of scientists ('The Station') who have established communications with Martians.

The new Constitution came into force on 29 December 1937, but no sooner had it been adopted than the government's attention turned elsewhere, first to efforts to end the Anglo-Irish economic war, followed soon after by the countdown to the Second World War. The new Constitution brought little immediate change in the Four Courts. On 30 December – the morning after 'Constitution Day' – the Chief Justice, Timothy Sullivan, went to Government Buildings and swore the new oath in de Valera's presence, declaring that he would carry out the functions of Chief Justice 'without fear or favour, affection or ill will towards any man' and pledging to uphold the Constitution and the laws of the State. Sullivan then returned to the Supreme Court, where, in front of a smattering of onlookers, the other judges made their declarations in his presence. After the ten-minute ceremony normal business resumed. The structure and procedures of the courts remained the same, and there was no explosion in litigation by citizens seeking to vindicate the stronger rights they now enjoyed. Indeed, a whole two years were to pass before a case of any real significance came to court. But when it did come, that case would set off a constitutional crisis and thrust the Supreme Court into the unaccustomed glare of the public spotlight.

National security was again the backdrop. By early 1939, on the eve of the outbreak of war in Europe, renewed IRA activity after a few years of declining republican violence was causing increasing concern within the Fianna Fáil government. The surge in IRA activity came at a point of weakness for the organization itself. Its leadership was increasingly divided on strategy, its popularity was on the floor, and many of its members had made their peace with de Valera and joined Fianna Fáil. The rapid decline of the Blueshirts after 1933, when the group was banned and Fine Gael was formed, ironically delivered a double blow to the IRA, depriving it of an enemy while at the same time freeing up the security services to focus on the republicans.[31] De Valera's patience with the IRA had long been running out, and in the years leading up to 1939 he had been slowly turning the screw on his former comrades. In 1935 his government responded to IRA provocations with a series of raids and arrests, followed by the suppression of the republican newspaper, *An Phoblacht*.[32] In June 1936 the IRA was declared an illegal organization and its chief of staff, Maurice Twomey, was jailed for three years by the military tribunal.[33]

With the draconian Cosgrave-era Public Safety Act due to lapse with the coming into force of the new Constitution, discussions had been under way within the Fianna Fáil government from late 1937 onwards on new legislation that would give the authorities new powers to crack down on political violence. This was a sensitive point for Fianna Fáil, not least because it had bitterly criticized Cosgrave's coercive security laws when in opposition. But when, in January 1939, the IRA began a bombing campaign in Britain that would kill seven people and injure 200, the Department of Justice was finally given the all-clear to draft new security legislation, albeit with the express instruction to change Cosgrave-era phraseology as much as possible.[34]

The Offences Against the State Act was duly signed into law on 14 June 1939.[35] The legislation, which remains virtually unchanged on the statute books today, contained more safeguards around due process and the rule of law than the Cosgrave-era measures but was highly controversial nonetheless. It enabled the government to ban membership of proscribed organizations, possession of treasonable documents or the holding of certain meetings. The IRA's annual Bodenstown commemoration, which was due to take place later that month, was immediately banned. While the 1939 law granted extensive powers of arrest, search and detention, it was more restrained than the Cosgrave-era legislation. The power to detain was now confined to forty-eight hours, down from the previous seventy-two hours.[36] The most far-reaching and controversial provisions, however, were the establishment of a Special Criminal Court and the introduction of internment without trial. Within months they would provoke a crisis.

The first internees were arrested in September that year and brought to Arbour Hill Military Detention Barracks. Among them was James Burke of Ballinrobe, Co. Mayo, who was detained on foot of a warrant signed by Minister for Justice Gerald Boland which said he was satisfied Burke was 'engaged in activities calculated to prejudice the preservation of the security of the State'. Burke's lawyers went to the High Court, arguing that his detention was illegal. Before George Gavan Duffy, Burke's barrister, Seán MacBride, denounced the 1939 act, insisting it was unconstitutional because it gave the executive what amounted to judicial powers.

To the government's consternation, Gavan Duffy agreed. In a judgment delivered on 1 December the judge filleted de Valera's law, declaring that the internment provisions breached the constitutional guarantee of personal liberty and that even in times of emergency neither the Oireachtas nor the government could disregard the Constitution. The judge zoned in on one word in the law. In order for the minister to issue a warrant for someone's internment, he had to be 'satisfied' – rather than merely being 'of the opinion' – that he or she was a threat to state security. For Gavan Duffy, this meant the minister was in effect administering justice – and that was the role of the judges, not members of the Cabinet.

> The Constitution . . . is the Charter of the Irish People and I will not whittle it away. The right to personal liberty and the other principles which we are accustomed to summarise as the rule of law were most deliberately enshrined in a national Constitution, drawn up with the

utmost care for a free people, and the power to intern on suspicion or without trial is fundamentally inconsistent with the rule of law and with the rule of law as expressed in the terms of the Constitution.

The legal position would be different if Ireland were at war, the judge added, but this was not a war measure.

The upshot was dramatic: the internment provisions of the Offences Against the State Act were unconstitutional, so James Burke walked free. The High Court's thunderbolt caught de Valera's government off guard. It immediately sought to appeal to the Supreme Court, but in that court MacBride successfully argued that the court had no right to hear an appeal in a case such as this. Citing pre-1922 practice, he claimed that a habeas corpus decision, much like an acquittal on a criminal prosecution, belonged to a different category from a normal court decision, and was in effect beyond the State's right to appeal. Chief Justice Sullivan accepted MacBride's argument. Gavan Duffy's decision was final.

For the government, the fallout from this legal reverse was swift and embarrassing. With the Supreme Court's refusal to hear the State's appeal, the government decided – in circumstances that have echoes today of the aftermath of the CC/Mr A episode in 2006 – that it had no option but to release fifty-three other prisoners who had been detained under the same act.[37] Then, on 23 December – twelve days after the Supreme Court decision – the Magazine Fort, the Defence Forces' main ammunition depot at the Phoenix Park, was raided by the IRA in a military-style operation. Around fifty raiders made off with thirteen lorries carrying more than a million rounds of ammunition.[38] The audacious theft was a propaganda coup for the IRA and a humiliation for the government, which found itself in the awkward position of having to explain how, overnight and in a time of war, subversives had managed to steal most of the army's stock of ammunition. The government's first reaction, in the days after Christmas, was to place an army cordon around Dublin. That resulted in some of the stolen arsenal being recovered in the days after Christmas. But ministers were also determined to have their way on the legislation, and for that they needed a new strategy.

The plan, decided on at a special Cabinet meeting on New Year's Day 1940, was to draft a new section of the legislation that was substantially the same as the old one except for one crucial difference: the authorities would be empowered to detain a person if the Minister for Justice was 'of the opinion' that he or she was engaged in activities that threatened the public peace or the security of the State. By abandoning the requirement that the minister be 'satisfied', the government believed, it could overcome the High Court's concern about ministers assuming the functions of judges.

Of course, the government would still be running the risk of a second embarrassing rebuff from Gavan Duffy or another judge in the High Court as soon as the Offences Against the State Act was passed. So the government's strategy had a second prong, which became clear in a report in the *Irish Press* on the same day as the special Cabinet meeting. Presumably drawing on sources within Fianna Fáil, the paper said the President 'may shortly refer a Bill to the Supreme Court, in accordance with Article 26 of the Constitution, for a decision as to whether any law is "repugnant to the Constitution"'.

Article 26, which had never been used up until that point, gave the President of Ireland – then Douglas Hyde – the power to refer a bill to the Supreme Court to decide on its constitutionality. It was his decision alone, but before taking it he was required to convene a meeting of the Council of State, an advisory body comprising some of the most senior current and former public office-holders in the State, including the Taoiseach, Tánaiste, Attorney General and Chief Justice. If the council could persuade Hyde to refer the bill, the government could take its chance in the Supreme Court. According to Gerard Hogan, it appears the government had come up with a pre-arranged plan whereby the Article 26 procedure would operate as 'a substitute form of appeal' from Gavan Duffy's decision.[39]

But first the government had to get the law through the Oireachtas. In the Dáil, senior government figures aimed both barrels at the Four Courts. Minister for Justice Gerald Boland said he was satisfied that, had it not been for the judges' decisions, the raid in the Phoenix Park would not have occurred. Taoiseach de Valera made little effort to contain his annoyance at the courts for finding the original law unconstitutional and made clear that this was far from how he had envisaged the Constitution working. He told the House:

> The Government, and all those interested in the passing of the Constitution were taken by surprise when they found that an Act which was passed by the Oireachtas last year was held to be unconstitutional. We were still more surprised when we found that the Supreme Court held that there was not a right of appeal even in a case in which the validity of an Act . . . was in question.

An instrument designed to preserve the safety of the public had been 'broken in our hands' by the court's decision, he added, and that had to be remedied. 'I say if the Constitution which was brought in here, which used common-sense language and which had to be submitted to the people for enactment, is not to have the meaning which the legislature and which the people think it has and if we cannot get some common ground on which there is an understanding of words, then we certainly cannot get on', he said pointedly. 'If the legislature and the judiciary are going to be at loggerheads in that way we shall have to change the situation.' It's difficult not to see in de Valera's language a veiled threat to the Supreme Court.

President Hyde duly convened the Council of State and, no doubt encouraged by de Valera and the other political representatives around the table, referred the bill to the Supreme Court on 8 January.

Now a delicate situation arose. On the day Hyde sent the bill to the Supreme Court, the five judges on the court were Sullivan, Murnaghan, Meredith, Geoghegan and William Johnston, a Dublin Presbyterian with northern roots who had been appointed the previous year. Conor Maguire, the President of the High Court and a former Fianna Fáil TD, was an ex officio member. But, as it happened, Johnston was due to retire on 18 January, and there was no way the court could hear the arguments and deliver its judgment before then. That meant that the government had the chance to appoint a new judge to the Supreme Court on the eve of one of the most sensitive cases that had ever gone to the court.

On 18 January, de Valera's government nominated John O'Byrne, an experienced judge who had served on the High Court for fourteen years. In some ways it was a surprising choice. As Gerard Hogan points out, O'Byrne had been Attorney General in the Cosgrave government in 1924–6 and had been 'a thorn in the side' of the Fianna Fáil administration during the turbulent years 1933–4. As a High Court judge, he had ordered the release of General O'Duffy following his arrest in December 1933 at the height of the Blueshirt controversy, a decision that had been greeted 'with jubilation by Fine Gael leaders, who interpreted it as a major setback and embarrassment for the government'.[40] However, O'Byrne was seen as a safe pair of hands. After all, he had been 'a pro-Treaty supporter whose views on security matters and the threat posed by IRA violence had been hardened by bitter experience of the Civil War and its aftermath'.[41] In general, de Valera took a relatively bipartisan approach to judicial appointments; a number of his government's nominees for the Supreme Court either had no Fianna Fáil lineage or were closely associated with Fine Gael. Sullivan, de Valera's choice as Chief Justice after Hugh Kennedy's death, was seen as a Fine Gael supporter.

When the court came to decide on the constitutionality of the bill, the five judges hearing the case were Sullivan, Murnaghan, Geoghegan, O'Byrne and Maguire. Meredith had been expected to sit on the court, but on the morning of the hearing it was reported that he 'may be unable to attend owing to an indisposition', and he was replaced by Maguire.[42] On 14 February the court upheld the constitutionality of the bill. De Valera could breathe a sigh of relief.

In a judgment that would be unpicked almost in its entirety by later Supreme Courts, Sullivan rejected the claim that the government was in breach of the Constitution by giving itself the power to indefinitely detain individuals without trial or judicial supervision. He dismissed the argument that this breached the personal rights provisions of Article 40.3.1, saying the task of harmonizing personal rights was a matter exclusively for the Oireachtas.

One of the most intriguing remarks from Sullivan that day came not in the judgment itself but in the brief remark he made before he began reading the text. 'The decision now announced is the decision of the majority of the Judges and is, within the meaning of Article 26.2.2 of the said Article, the decision of the court', he said. Did that mean the decision was not unanimous? The law library rumour mill went into overdrive.

A few days later, on 21 February, when the Ceann Comhairle informed the Dáil that President Hyde had signed the bill into law, the opposition TD James Dillon stood up in the chamber and made an intriguing claim. Was it not the case, 'as a matter of fact', that judges Geoghegan and Murnaghan believed the bill was unconstitutional, Dillon asked. And did this not mean that of six superior court judges who had considered the legislation, including Gavan Duffy, three believed it was unconstitutional? Dillon's claim cannot be corroborated, but as a barrister – albeit one who had never practised – he was well connected in legal circles. If Dillon was right that the outcome was 3-2, it meant O'Byrne – appointed to the court on the eve of the case – was the swing vote and that the bill had only narrowly survived. 'I do not know where the Deputy got the information', de Valera replied tersely.

The intrigue didn't end there. In 1967, almost three decades after the judgment, the American academic Loren Beth made a sensational claim about Meredith's unexplained absence from the court that week in January 1940. It was 'of considerable political interest to note', Beth wrote, that Meredith 'absented himself from this case and was replaced by a substitute, the President of the High Court, Conor Maguire, who was known to support the Bill'. Since the majority was 3-2, Beth suggested, this 'manoeuver' may have created the majority by which the bill was upheld. 'At the least, it leaves the unpleasant suspicion that the Government, in effect, tampered with the Court.'[43] It was some claim: that Meredith withdrew or was withdrawn, either because of a conscientious objection to the bill or because the Chief Justice wanted to ensure a certain outcome. But Beth offered no proof and subsequently withdrew the claim, acknowledging it was 'quite unfounded'.[44] Nonetheless, the speculation about divisions in the court in that case prompted the government, the following year, to arrange for the Oireachtas to add a new clause to the Constitution: from then on, when the Supreme Court was considering the constitutionality of a bill, the court had to issue its decision as one, single judgment.[45]

Even though the Supreme Court eventually upheld the constitutionality of the re-worked Offences Against the State Bill, thereby taking the heat out of the controversy and sparing the government another embarrassing reverse, the episode showed the potential for acute tension that lay beneath the outwardly cordial relationship between the government and the judiciary. At that point, the Supreme Court had never held any bill to be unconstitutional. That it even came close on this occasion was significant. 'The fact that the judiciary had been so evenly divided over the constitutionality of sensitive security legislation, at a time when a question mark hung over even the very survival of the State, ought to have sent its own signal that the Constitution had indeed endowed the judiciary with potent powers which might well be used to rebuff the other organs of government in more settled times', writes Hogan.[46] Tentatively, the Supreme Court was finding its feet, taking the measure of its new powers, marking out its place in the new constitutional landscape. And laying down markers for the future.

3. Separating powers

'Gentlemen, we have a Constitution. Yet no one seems
to know what it means.'

Cearbhall Ó Dálaigh

In the late twentieth century, the assumption took hold that Irish
constitutional law began in the 1960s. It was true that in that decade
the courts, reflecting broader shifts in society and a new willingness
to push the boundaries of judicial power, adopted a more expansionist view of their role and effected wholesale changes to the
constitutional order. But judicial innovation works by accretion, like
a building that takes shape with the addition of each new block. And
the groundwork for the flowering of the 1960s was being laid much
earlier. Dotted through the reports of the 1930s and 1940s are cases
that show constitutional points were being argued – not always successfully, but argued nonetheless. They show how, in the first decades
after the enactment of the new Constitution, judges were grappling with the possibilities and responsibilities of judicial review, and
that the three branches of government – executive, legislative and
judicial – were negotiating and testing the contours of their respect-
ive powers.

Many of these cases, on one side or the other, involved barristers
such as Tommy Conolly, Seán MacBride, John A. Costello and Cecil
Lavery. In every generation at the law library there is a small group
of practitioners who, usually owing to their experience and reputation, have the ear of the Supreme Court: they get the full attention of
the judges and are allowed to finish their sentences, run through their
arguments in the order they choose and generally dictate the agenda.
In the early decades of its existence, these four were among the

leading advocates in the state, and, on constitutional law, Conolly in particular broke new ground.

Today Tommy Conolly is largely forgotten – unlike judges, whose reputations live on through their judgments, barristers tend to fade from memory within a generation – but to his contemporaries Conolly was in the vanguard of constitutional innovation in Ireland. When the rare constitutional cases appear in the law reports of the 1930s and 1940s, the name T. J. Conolly almost invariably appears for one side or the other. 'It is no exaggeration to describe Tommy Conolly as the "onlie begetter" of modern Irish constitutional law', write Rex Mackey and Ronan Keane.[1]

In the early 1980s young barristers would marvel at the quiet reverence afforded by the Supreme Court to this small, bird-like veteran with a shock of white hair and a tendency to mumble. But by then Conolly had attained an aura as one of the great constitutional lawyers at the Bar. He made his name in some of the great cases of the 1960s and 1970s, but his authority was rooted in his status as a pioneer in an earlier era.

Conolly's trademark courtroom manoeuvre was to avoid making a point directly, believing it was far more useful to plant an idea in a judge's mind and let them believe they had come up with it themselves. He did this by speaking around his point at length until eventually an impatient judge would intervene to state the obvious. 'Mr Conolly, surely you mean . . .', the judge would say. 'Your Lordship,' Conolly would reply, 'I couldn't have put it better.'

'He was like a fisherman throwing a fly, waiting for the fish to rise', says a former colleague. 'An extraordinary style of advocacy, but very effective. Eventually they got to know what he was at, but they still loved him for it.'

Conolly had a razor-sharp intelligence, but his demeanour – rumpled, vaguely eccentric, with a line of ash perpetually drooping from his mouth – only added to his aura. When colleagues from the law library would come to his house for case meetings, they would have to negotiate not only Tommy but also the fierce macaw he kept in the house. The bird – who, Anthony Cronin recalled, said 'Howya' with a Dublin accent – 'was liable to take the finger off anybody who attempted to stroke or touch it.'[2]

On one occasion, Cearbhall Ó Dálaigh, when Chief Justice, adjourned the court until Conolly had recovered from an indisposition, observing that 'the case before us is so important that we felt that such a constitutional matter should not be decided in the absence of his submissions'.[3]

Conolly's indisposition may well have had something to do with his famously prodigious drinking. He had 'a touch of the drawback', as one contemporary gently puts it. On a Saturday morning Conolly and his wife, Angela, often drank with their friend Brian O'Nolan, aka Flann O'Brien, in the Dawson Lounge on Dawson Street or, later, in Tobin's on Duke Street. During the week their locales of choice were Sinnott's or Neary's.[4]

In the early hours of one morning in the early 1950s, according to Anthony Cronin, Conolly was O'Nolan's passenger when they were stopped and taken to Donnybrook Garda Station. O'Nolan insisted he was not drunk but, as the law allowed at the time, the gardaí on duty sent for a doctor to carry out the usual tests: walking in a straight line, picking objects off the floor and pronouncing difficult words. While waiting for the doctor, O'Nolan suggested to the desk sergeant that Conolly should be allowed to go out and get him a drink. The sergeant raised no objection, so Conolly crossed the street to Long's and returned with a naggin of whiskey. 'He handed it, unopened, to O'Nolan, who, looking the sergeant straight in the eye, unscrewed the cap, raised the whiskey to his lips and drank it virtually in one gulp', Cronin writes. '"Now", he said, "you can get all the doctors you want."' The case was later thrown out of the District Court.[5]

In the court's early decades, major decisions could spring from unlikely circumstances. *Buckley v. Attorney General*, commonly known as the Sinn Féin funds case, was ostensibly a financial dispute between estranged friends. But it put the judiciary and the executive at loggerheads and culminated in seminal judgments that put down an important marker on the separation of powers.

Having established itself as a broad church of nationalist opinion in the years leading up to 1921, the ratification of the Anglo-Irish Treaty by the Dáil in January 1922 caused a catastrophic split in Sinn Féin, splintering the party into the rival political groupings that would ultimately become Fianna Fáil and Fine Gael. De Valera took most Sinn Féin TDs with him when he finally broke with the party in 1926 and formed Fianna Fáil after a dispute over Sinn Féin's policy of abstentionism. The rump abstentionist Sinn Féin he left behind was hammered in the election of June 1927, its seat total collapsing from forty-seven to five, and when the next election came round in September of the same year, the party did not contest a single seat due to lack of funds.

In the aftermath of the Sinn Féin split, one of the most contentious issues was ownership of the original party's funds, which on legal advice in 1924 the party had lodged in the High Court to the credit of the trustees of the organization. As Hogan points out, the money was of both symbolic and practical value.[6] If it could prove itself the rightful owner of the pre-1921 party coffers, post-Civil War Sinn Féin would strengthen its claim to be the true successor to the original party. Just as importantly, getting its hands on such a considerable sum of money – by 1924 the funds amounted to £8,610, equivalent to around €557,000 in 2016 – would have given the anti-Treaty side a major financial boost at a time when it was struggling to stay afloat.

The dispute simmered for almost two decades before finally ending up in the High Court in January 1942, when Sinn Féin – in the name of its then president, Margaret Buckley, and eight other officers and members of the party – initiated legal action seeking a declaration that the funds, which by then stood at £24,000 – or roughly €1,232,000 at today's values – were the property of their organization.

The prospect alarmed de Valera, the then Taoiseach, who argued at a private meeting in February 1942 that the money had been donated by 'all classes of the people' for the 'national objectives' pursued by the party he led in the period 1917–21. He believed it should be put to some 'national purpose' that reflected the general aims of that period.[7]

By this point Sinn Féin was a spent political force, and the dispute over a relatively small sum of money paled into insignificance compared with the problems the State was facing in the immediate post-war years. What transformed it into a political storm – and, eventually, a defining stand-off between the government and the judiciary – was what de Valera did next. In March 1947, just as Buckley's case was about to be heard in the High Court, the government published the Sinn Féin Funds Bill 1947, a piece of legislation stating explicitly that all legal actions concerning the funds were to be dismissed by the courts. Under the bill, the money was to be transferred to a new board chaired by the Chief Justice, which would disperse it to people who had been members of a number of named bodies, including the IRA, during the 'critical period' (1916–21) or their dependants.[8]

It was a blatant incursion into judicial territory. In effect, the government, through the Oireachtas, was telling the judges how to decide a case that was already in progress. When he was asked for his advice, the Attorney General, Cearbhall Ó Dálaigh, saw no problem with the bill and confidently predicted that its constitutionality would be upheld. In his view, the Constitution did not expressly prohibit legislation that had retroactive effect. Surprisingly, he did not even refer to what was the central feature of the legislation: that it was overtly designed to intervene and stop a live case before the courts. In March/April 1947, on the eve of the bill's publication, Ó Dálaigh visited the Chief Justice, Conor Maguire, to inform him of the parts of the bill that affected him directly.[9] Maguire saw nothing unusual about the meeting; to him it was 'in conformity with the usual practice in regard to Bills affecting the Judges or the Courts'.[10] Maguire complained to Ó Dálaigh that having responsibility for the funds would eat into his busy schedule and take him away from his day-to-day duties, but he appears not to have expressed a view on potential constitutional problems with the draft – either he didn't see a problem or he felt expressing a view either way would be inappropriate.[11]

As soon as the bill was published, it began to backfire on the government. In an editorial headed 'A Dangerous Innovation', the *Irish Independent* lambasted de Valera's attempt to 'supersede' the courts by attempting to halt proceedings.[12] Later, the same paper ran a full-page

editorial denouncing the government's attempt to 'usurp' the functions of the judiciary.

> The public must bear in mind that this arrogant claim to 'take any
> case from the Courts', if once conceded to any Government, may be
> invoked tomorrow or the next day to prevent individual citizens or
> organisations of civil servants or teachers or trade unions asserting
> their rights against the Executive. If this precedent were once estab-
> lished, the Judiciary could no longer protect the rights of the
> citizen.[13]

Media misgivings were as nothing compared to the hostility de
Valera met in the Dáil, where the opposition scented blood. And not
only was the government in its sights but so was the Chief Justice as
well. During a debate on the bill, Independent TD James Dillon
homed in on the government's decision to involve the Chief Justice in
its scheme, which he decried as a 'loathsome outrage on the law'. If
the President of Ireland referred the act to the Supreme Court to
decide on its constitutionality, Dillon demanded to know, what
would the Chief Justice do? Would he have to step down? What
exactly had been said by the Attorney General to the Chief Justice?
Was the House to take it that the Chief Justice approved of the
arrangement?

'The office of the Chief Justice is the keystone of the arch of freedom in our society', Dillon said in the Dáil. 'Fracture that and all will
ultimately come down. If this section passes, the office of Chief
Justice is disreputable in the land.'[14]

As the opposition was well aware, Conor Maguire was closely
connected to Fianna Fáil. From impeccable republican stock – his
father had been a leading figure in the Gaelic League in Connacht
and a close associate of Pádraig Pearse and Douglas Hyde – Maguire
had been imprisoned in Sligo for six months in 1919 for publicizing
the Dáil loans (bonds issued in 1919–21 by the Dáil of the
self-proclaimed Irish Republic) and was involved in drafting the
rules for the Dáil courts in 1920. His anti-Treaty stance led to his dismissal from the land courts (later the Land Settlement Commission)

in July 1922, but after qualifying as a barrister in the same year he turned to politics and finally won election to the Dáil at the third attempt in the 1932 general election. From then on, he rose rapidly through some of the State's most senior legal and judicial positions: first Attorney General, then High Court judge, High Court President and, from April 1946, after the death of Timothy Sullivan, Chief Justice.

Maguire's political ties to de Valera's party were not lost on the opposition. In a scathing broadside against the Chief Justice, Fine Gael's Richard Mulcahy told the Dáil that Maguire had shown himself incapable of resisting being made a tool of the party that put him into office, and doing so 'in full and secure knowledge of the blow he is striking at our courts as independent institutions which ought to act independently'. His voice rising, Mulcahy went further: by 'degrading his own personality . . . and the office', Maguire had shown he was not fit to occupy the position of Chief Justice.[15]

DE VALERA: Is this an attack on the Chief Justice?

MULCAHY: Certainly, and a deserved attack on the Chief Justice. The Taoiseach has given us ample evidence that the Chief Justice deserves to be attacked.

DE VALERA: The Taoiseach is here to answer for himself.

DILLON: Who brought the Chief Justice into the House but yourself?

DE VALERA: I am prepared to deal with the matter on a proper basis, but I thought there was a rule here that individuals in the courts would be protected.

MULCAHY: They are degrading themselves and at the dictation of the Party.

DE VALERA: Loud shouting will not do.[16]

Despite the protestations of the opposition, the Sinn Féin Funds Act was signed into law on 27 May 1947. Two weeks later, with the passage of the act into law having apparently taken the heat out of the controversy, barrister Andreas O'Keeffe went to the High Court on behalf of the State and applied to have the pending proceedings over the Sinn Féin funds struck out. He applied initially to Judge Kevin Dixon, but as Dixon, in his previous post as Attorney General, had advised de Valera's government on the funds saga, he asked O'Keeffe to bring the application to the President of the High Court, George Gavan Duffy.

If O'Keeffe thought his application was a mere formality, he was in for a shock. In the President's court, he was immediately on the back foot. Gavan Duffy zoned in on the constitutional question. He wanted to know if there was any precedent for 'interfering with a pending action' in this way. Unless O'Keeffe could say anything in favour of the constitutionality of the act, he would turn down the application, the judge said. O'Keeffe suggested a precedent from earlier in the decade but Gavan Duffy was not impressed. The barrister was on the ropes.

> O'KEEFFE: The only thing I find difficult is to determine in what way the Act could be unconstitutional. I am at a loss to appreciate that.
> GAVAN DUFFY: Because judicial power is vested in the Courts. This is a judicial matter brought before the Courts for judicial determination. No other organ of the State, in my view, has the right to interfere pending that judicial determination.[17]

Gavan Duffy then put his hand in his pocket, took out a prepared decision and proceeded to read it out. The act was unconstitutional, he concluded, on the ground that it interfered with the principle of the separation of powers.[18] Gavan Duffy 'had driven a coach and four through the Sinn Fein Funds Act,' his biographer writes, 'rendering it a dead letter'.[19]

The State's appeal against Gavan Duffy's decision opened in the Supreme Court on 23 June. Reflecting the importance of the case, three senior counsel lined up on each side, among them some of the most prominent lawyers at the Bar. Richard McGonigal, Richard McLoughlin and Tommy Conolly were briefed by the Attorney General, while John A. Costello, Charles Casey and Seán MacBride appeared for the trustees of the Sinn Féin funds.*

---

*According to one former judge who knew a number of those involved, de Valera, in the aftermath of Gavan Duffy's decision, insisted on a personal consultation with the new counsel who were brought in to argue the state's appeal. When the Taoiseach was advised by his own lawyers that his side faced an uphill struggle to win in the Supreme Court, according to the source, de Valera mused,

Conor Maguire excused himself from the appeal, owing no doubt
to the fact that the legislation made him chairman of the board that
oversaw the funds and also perhaps because of his having been consulted by Ó Dálaigh before the bill had been published. He was
replaced for the appeal by Martin Maguire, the second most senior
High Court judge after Gavan Duffy, giving Maguire the fifth seat
on the court alongside Murnaghan, Geoghegan, O'Byrne and William Black. Black, the son of a Methodist clergyman from Holywood,
Co. Down, had been active in Sinn Féin (and later Fianna Fáil) and
had campaigned in the general elections of 1918 and August 1923
alongside his future colleague in the judiciary Conor Maguire. Black
had joined the Supreme Court in 1942 to replace the retiring James
Creed Meredith, his appointment ensuring that the court retained a
Protestant judge.[20]

As the Sinn Féin funds law had been enacted after the coming into
force of the new Constitution, the 'one-judgment rule' applied. Under
the Constitution, the court had to make a single judgment, without
revealing the opinions of individual judges, in two types of cases –
when a bill has been referred to it by the President, and when an
appeal concerned an act passed by the Oireachtas since 1937.* So in
this case the court had to speak with one voice and not reveal any
dissenting views. As Hogan points out, the newspaper reports of the
four-day oral argument suggest that Black, who repeatedly and
aggressively pressed Costello with his questions, was decidedly hostile towards Gavan Duffy's decision and may well have argued that it

---

perhaps playfully, as to whether it would be possible simply to pass legislation so
as to allow for additional judges to be appointed to the Supreme Court before the
Sinn Féin funds appeal was heard. 'This was greeted with silence,' according to
the former judge. 'Dev said, "Well, of course, the people mightn't like it." "I don't
know about the people, Taoiseach," said Tommy Conolly, "but there would be
great rejoicing in the law library."' The appointment of two or three new judges
would have allowed for their barristers' work to trickle down to their colleagues
in the Bar.

* The one-judgment rule in cases relating to post-1937 acts was removed by referendum in 2013, although it remains in place when the Supreme Court considers
bills referred to it by the President.

should be overturned when the judges went into conclave.[21] If he did, he was outnumbered. Whereas Gavan Duffy in the High Court had focused on the separation of powers, the Supreme Court also homed in on the private property rights guarantee in the Constitution. At the hearing, the Attorney General's team had argued that the State was entitled to take away a citizen's property rights – in this case, the Sinn Féin money – and that that was for the Oireachtas to decide based on 'the exigencies of the common good'.[22] It was quite a stretch, and the Supreme Court rejected it out of hand.

The court's judgment, delivered by O'Byrne, was a spectacular reverse for de Valera's government. For only the fourth time, a piece of legislation enacted by the Oireachtas was found unconstitutional. This was probably the most significant. By upholding Gavan Duffy's defence of the separation of powers, the Supreme Court 'gave a clear signal to future governments that they would trespass on the judicial domain at their peril'.[23] The press reaction shows more than a hint of disbelief that a court in which four of the five judges had been selected by Fianna Fáil (Murnaghan was the one exception) would use de Valera's own Constitution to deliver such a damaging blow to the government. Not only was there no subsequent attempt by the Oireachtas to intervene in cases that were in progress, but future governments were exceedingly careful in using their power, left untouched by the Sinn Féin funds case, to use legislation to reverse the consequences of a decision of the courts.[24]

For Margaret Buckley, the Sinn Féin president who initiated the case, the decision turned out to be far less significant. After a hearing in the High Court the following spring, Judge Kingsmill Moore concluded that the existing Sinn Féin was not in any legal sense 'a continuation of the organization which had held its two Ard-Fheiseanna in 1922 and which had melted away in the course of that year as the result of the political strife culminating in the Civil War'. That meant Buckley's group had no claim on the money. A case that re-kindled Civil War antipathies, drove a wedge between the judges and the politicians and lit a path to the emergence of modern constitutional law, itself ended with a whimper.

★

The Supreme Court's constitutional workload, and its prominence in public debate, was by now greater than at any point since the new Constitution had come into force. In July 1947, just weeks before its decision in the Sinn Féin funds case, the court had struck down part of the Trade Union Act on the ground that, by decreeing that specified unions alone should have the right to organize workers of a particular class, the Oireachtas was in breach of the constitutional guarantee of freedom of association.[25]

It could have been an even more spectacular year for the court had President Seán T. O'Kelly acceded to opposition calls to refer the Health Act to the court to decide on its constitutionality. The bill's provisions, including compulsory medical inspection and immunization, alarmed the Catholic hierarchy and some doctors, and would have forced the court to flesh out what were then little-invoked constitutional provisions on personal rights, the family and the inviolability of the dwelling. O'Kelly convened the Council of State but, having been assured by Ó Dálaigh that the bill was 'clearly constitutional' and should be left open to future challenges, the President signed it into law.[26]

But 1947 would turn out to be more of an anomaly than a sign of things to come. Gavan Duffy's death in 1951, and O'Byrne's three years later, robbed the senior judiciary of two of its most original thinkers on the Constitution, and in the years that followed the High Court, powered by judges such as Dixon and Kingsmill Moore, was arguably the stronger of the two courts.[27] Between 1947 and 1958 there was little novel constitutional law to enliven the Supreme Court, and no major decision striking down legislation. Instead, through the 1950s it plodded for the most part through a fairly dull diet of local government, company liquidation, revenue and low-level criminal procedural law.

The Chief Justice sets the tone of the court, and in Maguire the judiciary had a good leader but one who showed little inclination to stretch the boundaries of his role. It is striking that even Ó Dálaigh, who would later be seen as a leading light of the constitutional revolution of the 1960s, made scant impression in the early years after his appointment to the court in 1953.

As always, the court was at the mercy of the cases that came to its door. And the decline of political violence in the late 1940s and '50s, at least until Operation Harvest – the codename for the IRA border campaign in the period 1956–62 – staunched the flow of controversial cases. Up to that point Supreme Court controversy was generally linked to its role in adjudicating the legality of State responses to republican activity; once that activity declined, the court was able, for a time at least, to step back from political controversy.

Not that the court was entirely uncontroversial. In the 1950s it particularly antagonized two groups: Protestants and trade unionists. In 1951 the court upheld a decision by Gavan Duffy in a dispute between a husband and wife about the religious upbringing of their children.[28] The husband had agreed before the marriage that the children would be brought up as Catholics but later attempted to repudiate that agreement. Gavan Duffy concluded, correctly, that the old common-law rule of paternal supremacy had not survived the enactment of the 1937 Constitution and that the husband had entered into a binding agreement.[29] But he did so in a way that implied Catholicism had a privileged status in Irish law. Although the Supreme Court distanced itself from Gavan Duffy's language, it upheld the decision – an outcome that was considered deeply objectionable to the Church of Ireland and was still recalled by many within the church as recently as the 1990s.* Later, the Supreme Court

---

* Religion was at the heart of another case decided by Gavan Duffy, *Schlegel v. Corcoran and Gross* (1942), which has a strong claim to be the worst decision ever made by an Irish court. Teresa Schlegel, a devout Catholic, had refused to allow Nathaniel Gross to take over the lease on a sub-let room in her family home on Harrington Street in Dublin, on the ground that he was Jewish. In court she argued that she objected because she 'could not have an anti-Christian living in the house where I live'. The law empowered Gavan Duffy to over-rule Schlegel's objection if he felt she had 'unreasonably' refused Gross. He declined to do so, concluding that Schlegel's actions were reasonable. In his own words: 'Anti-Semitism . . . far from being a peculiar crotchet, is notoriously shared by a number of other citizens . . . the antagonism between Christian and Jew has its roots in nearly two thousand years of history and is too prevalent as a habit of mind to be dismissed off-hand, in a country where religion matters, as the eccentric extravagance of a bigot, without regard to the actual conditions under which

held that 'closed shop' trade union arrangements breached the constitutional guarantee of freedom of association.[30]

Changes in judicial personnel, Maguire's leadership style and relative
calm in the country may have contributed to the well of constitutional cases running dry, but the absence of any serious attempt to
explore the potentially rich personal rights provisions in the 1937
document, for example, was also due to the fact that the lawyers
who alone could take the cases showed little inclination to take on
the task.

Most judges were not enthusiastic either. The fear of crossing into
the political domain – and therefore outside of what they understood
to be the courts' bailiwick – was spelled out by High Court judge
Henry Hanna in a constitutional case in 1939. He recoiled from an
attempt to make him find an act unconstitutional. The case put to
him was that the legislation in question was contrary to 'peace, order
and good government' and violated the 'principles of social justice' as
set out in Article 43 of the Constitution. Hanna said it would be difficult, if not impossible, for any court to define such terms and that,
in any case, interpreting them was for politicians, not judges. 'The
phrases seem to me to be in the nature of political, economic or socio-
logical tags, used in common language with different meanings by
different people and devoid of any legal connotation whatsoever', he
wrote.[31]

When the future Supreme Court judge Donal Barrington joined
the law library in 1951, he later recalled, there was 'a general feeling
that the Constitution was a broken reed'.[32] The Constitution was
regarded as the last resort of a barrister who knew his case was going
nowhere. The personal rights provisions in Article 40.3 were seen as
general guarantees that applied to everyone, and the job of deciding

---

consent was withheld.' Deplorable as the language is, however, the law as it stands
in 2016 allows for the same outcome. The Equal Status Act 2000 exempts the leas-
ing of a dwelling which is part of one's own family home from the scope of
anti-discrimination legislation. See Gerard Hogan, 'Duffy, George Gavan', in
McGuire and Quinn (eds.), *Dictionary of Irish Biography*, and G.M. Golding, *George
Gavan Duffy*, pp. 129–33.

how the rights of the individual were to be reconciled with the rights of the community at large was seen as a matter for the Oireachtas rather than the courts.

There had been stirrings of change in UCD, where students from 1934 onwards were taught constitutional law by Professor Patrick McGilligan, a strong believer in the concept of judicial review. But even in the late 1940s, when Barrington and his generation were in UCD, the standard textbook on constitutional law was a book written by the British legal theorist A. V. Dicey in 1885.[33] Preceding generations of lawyers, such as the judges in the Four Courts in the 1950s, had been educated in that British tradition, where parliament was supreme and the judges' job was to ascertain the will of the politicians through their laws.

However, by the end of the 1950s the days when the judges considered themselves subservient to parliament were coming to an end. Donal Barrington recalls sitting in the Supreme Court some time in the 1950s, watching a case, when Ó Dálaigh was an ordinary member of the court. 'Suddenly Cearbhall looked up from his papers and, so far as I can recall his words, said, "Gentlemen, we have a Constitution. Yet no one seems to know what it means."'[34] Ó Dálaigh, it appeared, was growing impatient with the failure of the legal profession to grapple seriously with the new Constitution. Mining the rich potential that lay largely unexplored within it would turn out to be the mission of the court in the decade that followed.

4. Changing of the guard

'It was just that each of us had this particular outlook . . .'

Brian Walsh

At the stroke of midnight on Thursday, 28 September 1961, Ireland's court system lost all its powers and ceased to exist. The hiatus, which lasted for just a few hours, was little more than a historical curiosity. The courts had been set up under the 1922 Constitution but were never re-established under the document that replaced it in 1937. For years lawyers had speculated as to whether this meant the courts did not actually exist in law. Although the Supreme Court had rejected the claim when an enterprising lawyer put it before them in the 1950s, Seán Lemass's Fianna Fáil government opted to clear up any confusion. It enacted a law that temporarily abolished the old system in its entirety and almost immediately re-created each of the courts, from the Supreme to the District.

The public barely noticed this relatively inconsequential event, but the legal world marked the change with great pomp and ceremony. At noon on Friday, 29 September 1961, the Chief Justice, Conor Maguire, emerged from the Four Courts in morning dress to be greeted by an army trumpeter sounding a salute. With a motorcycle escort, the entire judiciary was driven to Áras an Uachtaráin, where President de Valera, accompanied by Lemass and other government figures, gave each judge his new warrant of appointment. When the new legal term began the following week, Maguire received a military guard of honour before entering the Supreme Court and witnessing each judge make the declaration required of them on taking office. The business of the Four Courts then resumed as normal.

A far more momentous change was about to take place with little fanfare. Less than three months later, when Conor Maguire stepped down on reaching retirement age, the Government Information Bureau issued a terse statement. It began:

> Acting on the advice of the Government, the President has appointed Cearbhall Ó Dálaigh, a Judge of the Supreme Court, to be the Chief Justice to fill the vacancy created by the retirement of Mr Justice Conor A. Maguire.
>
> To fill the vacancy created by the appointment of Mr Justice Ó Dálaigh, the President, acting on the advice of the Government, has appointed Brian C. Walsh, a Judge of the High Court, to be a Judge of the Supreme Court.
>
> Both appointments take effect from today.[1]

The Fianna Fáil government had ample reason to know and trust Ó Dálaigh, who was a long-time supporter of the party and had twice run unsuccessfully for a seat in Dáil Éireann before serving as Attorney General in two Fianna Fáil governments. His appointment was nonetheless greeted with surprise. In the law library, the favourites to succeed Conor Maguire were Cecil Lavery, by then the most senior judge on the court after Maguire, and Cahir Davitt, President of the High Court.

Lavery had been a star barrister before he joined the bench, and stories of his skill as an advocate had already entered law library folklore. A very tall man with a northern accent – he was born in Armagh and moved to Dublin as a teenager – Lavery was known for his distinctive style of cross-examination. 'He would ask a witness a question and then turn on his heel', recalled his contemporary Ralph Sutton. 'He would do a complete pivot and then look at the witness again. This was very disconcerting for the witness. In the end, when he had the witness nearly beaten, he'd take off his glasses and he had queer lizard-like eyes which he would fix on the unfortunate victim. He was most dramatic.'[2] It was said that on one occasion, exasperated at not managing to get his point across to a judge in the Supreme Court, Lavery returned to the library, placed his papers on the table and announced of one of the judges: 'To put a law report in the hands of [that judge] is like putting a loaded pistol in the hands of a child.'[3]

As a former Fine Gael TD, and Attorney General to the inter-party government led by John A. Costello from 1948 to 1951, Lavery's politics would have counted against him when Lemass came to fill the vacancy. It was also felt that he had made more of a mark as a barrister than as a judge. But missing out on the top job must have been especially galling for Lavery, as he had previously come within a whisker of the second most senior judicial post in the State. Lavery had been appointed to the Supreme Court to fill the vacancy created by the retirement of James Geoghegan in 1950, and when George Gavan Duffy died a year later, he was seen as the front-runner to replace him as President of the High Court. Costello, who was Taoiseach at the time, certainly wanted to appoint him.[4] But Thomas Coyne, the secretary of the Department of Justice, raised doubts as to whether it was technically permissible to appoint a Supreme Court judge to be President of the High Court. Lavery felt there was no validity to Coyne's point, but, apparently in order to spare Costello any embarrassment, he reluctantly withdrew his name and Cahir Davitt was appointed instead.

When the vacancy arose in the Chief Justice's office a decade later, in 1961, Costello made a point of writing to Lemass to encourage him to appoint Lavery. In a letter marked 'strictly personal', Costello said he felt obliged to write 'in the interests of what I conceive to be justice to a former colleague of mine'.[5] He explained to Lemass about the mess-up that deprived Lavery of the High Court post, and said he was concerned that that could jeopardize Lavery's chances of becoming Chief Justice, as the President of the High Court was a more senior position in the judicial pecking order than an ordinary member of the Supreme Court. Costello offered gushing praise for Lavery, describing him as 'the outstanding legal personality of the last half century in this country' and 'the greatest legal genius in this country'. Lemass wrote a non-committal response the following day. 'I think I should let you know that I have received it and assure you that it will have my most careful attention', he wrote. Later that month, Lemass was again lobbied to select Lavery – this time by Cardinal d'Alton of

Armagh, who said he had been asked by a bishop to 'put in a word with you' in support of his fellow northerner.[6]

Temperamentally, Lavery and Ó Dálaigh were opposites. Lavery was pugnacious, intellectually assertive and occasionally gave barristers appearing before him the impression that he wished he was on his feet arguing the case himself. Ó Dálaigh, seventeen years his junior, was gentle, almost diffident, with a quieter, more consensual style. While Ó Dálaigh was a consummate lawyer, he had nothing like the practice Lavery had. He did have wide interests: his passion was for languages – he spoke fluent Irish, French and Italian – and was a champion of the arts.

Although both men would have had reason to consider themselves outsiders in the law library – Lavery was a nationalist from Armagh who had sat on the unofficial Dáil courts in the early 1920s, while Ó Dálaigh was the son of a fish shop manager from Bray, Co. Wicklow – Lavery, the son of a solicitor and an alumnus of Castleknock College, came closer to fitting the classic mould set by previous (and future) judicial appointees. That could have endeared Ó Dálaigh even more to Lemass, a fellow Christian Brothers boy.

When Ó Dálaigh was appointed, Lavery made no secret of his resentment at having been overlooked in favour of his more junior colleague, and one whose practice at the Bar had been dwarfed by his own. In the years after Ó Dálaigh's elevation, his relationship with Lavery grew severely strained, the tension sometimes apparent even in their body language in court. T. C. Kingsmill Moore, an influential judge who remained on the court with the two men until he and Lavery retired in 1966, felt Lavery was desperately unfair to Ó Dálaigh, and later he would tell friends how his admiration for Ó Dálaigh greatly increased when he saw how the chief stood up to Lavery. In time, Kingsmill said, Lavery realized he had underestimated Ó Dálaigh and the tensions eased.

If Ó Dálaigh was a comparatively youthful Chief Justice, Brian Walsh, the 43-year old High Court judge who was promoted to the Supreme Court on the same day, was so young that, as the *Irish Times* noted, 'some of his colleagues could have rocked his cradle'.[7] Walsh had been on the High Court for just two years, but, like Ó Dálaigh, his relative inexperience as a judge was outweighed by his reputation as a lawyer and his personal connections to leading figures in Fianna Fáil.

Born in Dublin in 1918, Walsh was the eldest in a family of three sons of Patrick Walsh, an Irish speaker who worked in the Department of Education, and his wife, Elsie, who died when Brian was a boy. He was sent to Coláiste na Rinne in Co. Waterford, Scoil Mhuire and Scoil Cholmcille in Dublin before completing his schooling at Belvedere. At UCD he studied legal and political science and did a Masters in economics while simultaneously taking classes in the King's Inns, where barristers are trained.[8] Like Ó Dálaigh, he spoke fluent French and loved to travel; their curiosity about the world and their openness to outside influences were to have a profound effect on the court's development.

In his early years in the law library, Walsh also served part-time in the local defence force, the forerunner to the FCA,[9] during the war years, and it was through this that he established a friendship with Charles Haughey, who was Minister for Justice by the time he was appointed to the Supreme Court.[10] Although Walsh was regularly briefed by Fianna Fáil as a barrister, his relationship with the party was never as formal as that of Ó Dálaigh. According to Charles Lysaght, who worked closely with him on the Law Reform Commission in the late 1970s and early 1980s, Walsh felt alienated from the Fianna Fáil government over its treatment of the national schoolteachers, which led to a strike in 1946 (all four of his grandparents had been teachers). Through his friend Noel Harnett, a barrister and Clann na Poblachta supporter, he met Noël Browne, Minister for Health in the inter-party government led by John A. Costello, and advised Browne on the controversial Mother and Child scheme, which provided for state-funded healthcare for all mothers and children aged under sixteen. The government's decision to abandon the scheme under pressure from the Catholic bishops prompted Browne to resign, and after the 1951 election it was Walsh who organized the meeting between Lemass and Browne that resulted in Browne and his followers supporting Fianna Fáil, thus ensuring its return to government after three years in opposition. Walsh subsequently took part in discussions with Browne about forming a new party, but Browne eventually joined Fianna Fáil and the idea came to nothing.

With Cearbhall Ó Dálaigh's appointment leadership of the Supreme Court passed to a new generation. At fifty, there was every prospect that he could remain at the helm for twenty-two years. A tenure of that length would give any chief justice the time and space to exert a huge influence on the court and on the law. His and Walsh's appointments were widely welcomed by the press, which saw in them a refreshing emphasis on youth and a departure from a tendency of previous governments to prefer seniority over other considerations when filling vacancies on the bench.[11] Ó Dálaigh was praised for being meticulous and conscientious, and for his support of the arts, Walsh for his energy and track record as a lawyer. But there was little in either man's record, outwardly as least, to suggest that their appointments represented a turning-point.

As de Valera's Attorney General in the 1940s, it was Ó Dálaigh who advised the government there was no constitutional problem with passing a law that ordered the courts to decide a pending case in a certain way – a proposition swiftly and roundly rejected by both the High and Supreme Courts.[12] Ó Dálaigh was on the court when, in 1958, it sent an important signal on the separation of powers by deciding unanimously that the power to strike a solicitor off the rolls was too serious to entrust to a professional body and should be a task exclusively for the judiciary. But for the most part the 1950s were arid years for constitutional development, and in his eight years as an ordinary judge on the court there was little to hint that he harboured expansionist inclinations.

The same was true of Walsh, who was known to have an interest in constitutional law but had been on the High Court for such a short time that he had left little footprint. He delivered only two reported judgments, from November 1959 and December 1961.[13]

Over the following twelve years, however, the Supreme Court, with the Ó Dálaigh–Walsh axis at its heart, would breathe new life into the Constitution, with consequences that were to have a profound effect on Irish society over the next half-century. They were far from the first judges to wrestle with the Constitution. In the decades since 1937, as J. P. Casey has pointed out, the Supreme Court had delivered important decisions on issues such as freedom of association,[14] property rights,[15] judicial power[16] and the personal liberty of the citizen.[17] But those cases were isolated. Under the Ó Dálaigh court, the pace accelerated. From his appointment as Chief Justice in December 1961 until his resignation in December 1972 to become a judge of the European Court of Justice in Luxembourg, the Supreme Court dealt with as many constitutional cases as had arisen in the entire period 1937–61. At the height of the expansionist era, in the mid-1960s, one ground-breaking judgment followed another as the court embarked on a drive to expand citizens' individual rights, enhance the protections for defendants in criminal law and rethink fundamental legal principles such as judicial review and the separation of powers. In the process the court became a more powerful institution, and exerted greater influence over the lives of citizens, than ever before.

The genesis of the shift, and the extent to which it was a grand design, have been debated ever since. A quarter of a century later, at the European Court of Human Rights in Strasbourg, where he was then a judge, Walsh gave an interview to the Australian lawyer Garry Sturgess, who was preparing a radio documentary and a book on courts around the world. Walsh told Sturgess that on the day Lemass offered him the position on the Supreme Court, the Taoiseach said he would like to mention one thing and would never again refer to it. '[H]e said he would like the Supreme Court to become more like the United States Supreme Court', Walsh said. 'Obviously it was [Lemass's] wish that the court should be more active in its interpretative role. It was put very briefly but quite clearly.'[18] Walsh said he subsequently learned that Lemass had said something similar to Ó Dálaigh around the same time.

The implication was that Ó Dálaigh and Walsh had direct political encouragement for their judicial activism. But quite what Lemass might have meant is far from clear. In 1961 the US Supreme Court under Chief Justice Earl Warren had yet to deliver most of the landmark liberal judgments that made it an inspiration to expansionist-minded judges and lawyers around the world. It was not until later in the decade that the Warren court created a general right to privacy (*Griswold v. Connecticut*, 1965), limited public figures' right to take defamation actions (*New York Times v. O'Sullivan*, 1964), gave poor defendants the right to state-funded counsel (*Gideon v. Wainwright*, 1963) and required that criminal suspects be read their rights by police (*Miranda v. Arizona*, 1966). Lemass cannot have been suggesting that the Supreme Court follow an example that had not been set. Nor is it likely that he was telling Walsh and Ó Dálaigh that he wanted the court to take over the business of social change. 'I'm not certain that Lemass's appointment of Walsh might have indicated a wish on his part for more "liberal" reforms . . . Lemass's instincts were in my view always more dirigiste than liberal', says Lemass's biographer, John Horgan.[19]

Yet coming after the 1950s, when the court had made scant impression beyond the Four Courts, Lemass may well have seen it as perfectly compatible with his own reform agenda that the Supreme Court should take a more prominent role in national life and open itself more enthusiastically to influences beyond the country's shores. 'From my own understanding of Lemass, I have no difficulty in accepting that he was – not least because he was conscious of his own failing health, even in this period – a man in a hurry, increasingly frustrated by the slow pace of political, institutional and constitutional reform', says Horgan.[20]

Ireland had joined the United Nations six years earlier in December 1955, and the government's thoughts were increasingly turned towards future participation in the European project. A livelier, more internationally minded Supreme Court would have sat quite comfortably with Lemass's view of the world and Ireland's place within it.

'I am not saying that [Lemass's words] necessarily influenced me in any particular way, because I think the horse was chosen for the course', Walsh told Sturgess. 'He probably felt he was talking to somebody who had much the same views. I certainly was very much influenced by the American experience. I had studied it to a very considerable extent and kept myself familiar with it all through my career.'[21]

Walsh played down any suggestion that he and Ó Dálaigh set out with a plan to refashion the constitutional landscape. The internal workings of the court did not lend themselves to close collaboration among judges, as at the time case conferences – a regular feature of the court's work in later decades – were relatively rare.

'Nothing that was designed happened', Walsh said of their partnership. 'It was just that each of us had this particular outlook and, as we constituted two-fifths of the court and the others were not unsympathetic to our point of view, it was a question of making the running. And in most cases the other judges, or most of them, would agree.'[22]

In his view, the judicial activism of the 1960s was above all a reflection of broader trends in society and the coming of age of a new generation of judges, barristers and solicitors. Lawyers of his generation, who had gone through university from the mid-1930s, had seen the first stirrings of 'a different outlook on law, and it's when their impact began to be felt as practitioners later on that these points arose'.[23] Just months before Walsh was appointed to the Supreme Court, a young academic named John Kelly published the first edition of what was to become a hugely influential book, *Fundamental Rights in the Irish Law and Constitution*.[24]

'I think it was a fairly natural evolution. New generation of lawyers. New generation of judges. And perhaps a greater emphasis in public generally on individual rights and the necessity for not allowing the State to have absolute power.'[25] Most importantly, Walsh believed, that meant the court started getting the cases.

> From 1961 onwards the Constitution became very much part of life and its impact could be felt among the ordinary people, who suddenly became conscious of the fact that they had a constitution, that it could be implemented and that, in fact, many parts of it were self-executing and did not require any supporting legislation. The consciousness of this suddenly burst upon the public and it just happened to be that, in the years commencing around about 1960–61, the court, for a variety of reasons, became very active. The most important reason was that it got the cases. The court is not self-starting and

depends on cases. So it was a happy coincidence of the right cases coming along at a time when the court was most receptive to new ideas.[26]

A few weeks after their interview in Strasbourg, Walsh met Sturgess in his chambers in the Four Courts. In previously unpublished material preserved on tape, Walsh elaborated on that happy coincidence.

> We had sufficient knowledge of the subject, in particular the American jurisprudence, to see the significance of it all, and to provide the remedies which we thought the particular occasion, and even the decade, required . . . It would have been far more difficult without [Ó Dálaigh's] leadership. Being Chief Justice, especially one who was as highly thought-of as he was, added considerable weight to what in many cases would be regarded as strange new ideas and doctrines, and made them all the more acceptable to everybody.[27]

Ó Dálaigh and Walsh certainly took up their new positions at a time of optimism and change. By the early 1960s the stultifying climate of the previous decade was giving way to a new confidence underpinned by a growing economy and rising living standards. The shift in policy direction represented by the First Programme for Economic Expansion, set out by the Department of Finance's dynamic young Secretary, T. K. Whitaker, resulted in a rise in the value of the country's exports of 35 per cent from mid-1959 to mid-1960 alone, powering the domestic economy and in turn staunching the devastating flow of people leaving the State in search of work. In just two years the level of emigration had declined dramatically – from 44,427 in 1961, to just 12,226 in 1963.[28]

The rise of a new generation of judges and barristers was mirrored by trends in politics, the media, sport, the arts, religion and business.[29] In July 1960 a Garret FitzGerald column in the *Irish Times* was given the simple headline 'Good Times Coming'. The year Ó Dálaigh became Chief Justice, RTÉ launched its television service. A month after his appointment, the IRA formally abandoned the border campaign that had begun in December 1956. 'It was a time of rude energy, a contempt for tradition, in which the material fruits of postwar sac-rifices and reconstruction could be enjoyed', writes Fergal Tobin in his book *The Best of Decades*. 'Like all such times, it threw up a generation that believed itself to have discovered the world anew and to have cracked codes that had eluded its elders.'[30] As Diarmaid Ferriter points out, the impression of the decade as a golden era – a perception he sug-gests was no doubt heightened by the reappearance of depression and emigration in the 1980s – 'does not do justice to the complexities and subtleties of the decade'.[31] Yet by the time the Supreme Court sat at the beginning of the new term in January 1962, it was clear that the gen-eral air of change extended far beyond the Four Courts.

The sense that the State was beginning to reconcile itself with its past while casting forward optimistically to a more prosperous and outward-looking future, however reductive it might have been, reached something of an apotheosis with the visit of John F. Kennedy in June 1963. The US president's return to the country of his ancestors was an occasion of euphoric celebration, his charisma and movie-star glamour bringing excitable crowds out onto the streets of Dublin, Wexford, Limerick, Cork and Galway. Kennedy acknowledged the achievement of Irish Independence and was the first foreign head of state to attend a ceremony at Arbour Hill, resting place of fourteen executed leaders of the 1916 Rising. But he also, in a speech to the joint houses of the Oireachtas, referred to 'a new and peaceful revolution, an economic and industrial revolution . . . you have modernised your economy, harnessed your rivers, diversified your industry, liberalised your trade, electrified your farms, accelerated your rate of growth, and improved the living standard of your people'.[32]

For Kennedy the Irish visit, just five months before his assassina-tion in Dallas, was a nostalgic and emotional coda to a historic European trip that would be remembered for his resonant 'Ich bin ein Berliner' speech in Berlin the previous week. For Ireland it was a chance to showcase modernity, project self-confidence and bask in the reflected glory of a returning son.

It went publicly unnoticed at the time, but a month after Ken-nedy's visit, the second most powerful Catholic Irish-American in Washington also visited Ireland. William Brennan had been a justice

of the United States Supreme Court since 1956. His parents, William
and Agnes, were both from Co. Roscommon but met as emigrants in
the United States and never returned to Ireland. Brennan was keen to
see Roscommon for himself, so during his private visit in July 1963 he
travelled west and met his relatives, in whose homes his own picture
took pride of place on the wall after those of Kennedy and Jesus. He
was disappointed to see that his father's home had been razed long
ago, so his relatives made sure to point to a house where his mother
might have been born. 'He was happy and accuracy wasn't the order
of the day', his relative Paula Smith told Brennan's biographers.[33]

At a dinner before he returned to the US, Brennan met Brian
Walsh, who by then was eighteen months into his tenure on the
Supreme Court in Dublin. The two men hit it off straight away. They
talked about the big issues of the day and exchanged views on some
of the legal questions the courts in both countries were grappling
with at the time, including the 'exclusionary rule' – the law that pro-
hibits the use of illegally obtained evidence in a criminal trial. Before
they parted, Walsh gave Brennan a copy of *The Old Munster Circuit*,
Maurice Healy's affectionate portrait of life at the Irish Bar in the
early twentieth century.

Back in Washington, Brennan wrote to Walsh to tell him he had
devoured Healy's book on the voyage home. Picking up on their
'intensely interesting' discussion about the exclusionary rule, Brennan sent Walsh copies of three judgments the American court had
given on the issue in the recent past. He also told Walsh that he would
arrange with his office to have a 'slip opinion', or an unformatted
early draft, of every US Supreme Court judgment posted to Walsh as
soon as it was available.[34] This arrangement would remain in place for
almost thirty years, until both men retired in 1990.

In his thirty-four-year tenure Brennan would become one of the
most influential members of the US Supreme Court in the twentieth
century. His major decisions through the activist era of the 1960s and
'70s, and in particular his opposition to the death penalty and support
for abortion rights, cemented his place in the pantheon for many
liberal Americans. And for the duration of his time on the Supreme
Court, Walsh had copies of the American court's judgments long

before they appeared in the official reports. That flow of information, and the lifelong friendship the two men were to form, were to have a profound impact on the Irish court.

She smiles confidently at the camera, the columns of the Four Courts just about visible behind her fur hat. For fifteen months in the early 1960s, the photograph was ubiquitous. Gladys Ryan, a housewife from Drumcondra, became a household name, an object of public fascination, the finer details of her challenge to the State pored over almost daily in the national press. Her case eventually ended in defeat, and Ryan withdrew from the public eye as abruptly as she had been thrust into it. But in time her name would become synonymous with a seminal shift in how judges – and the country at large – saw the Constitution and its potential as a vehicle for social change.

Gladys McConaghie was born in 1921 and grew up on Leeson Street in the tumultuous early years of the Free State. A serious illness in her teens interrupted her education, but a job in Switzer's department store on Grafton Street enabled her to pursue her ambition and study to be a singer. In 1948 she married Corkman John Ryan, with whom she had five children. The couple threw their energy into Dublin's emerging ecology movement.[35]

In 1960 the Fianna Fáil minister for health, Seán MacEntee, introduced the Fluoridation of Water Supplies Act, which provided for the health authorities to add fluoride to the water supply across the country. The policy, designed to reduce the level of tooth decay in children, was becoming a tenet of preventative dental care in the United States and elsewhere, but a vocal environmental lobby argued that it was actually damaging to health. Before local authorities could act on the new law, Gladys Ryan – through her solicitor, the Fine Gael TD Richie Ryan★ – initiated legal action to have the fluoridation stopped and the law declared unconstitutional.

Ryan's case, argued on her behalf by a formidable team of senior

★ Ryan, who later became Fine Gael's spokesman on health, remained a lifelong opponent of water fluoridation. See *Hot Press*, 8 May 2013, and *Sunday Business Post*, 1 September 2013.

counsel in Seán MacBride, Tommy Conolly and Séamus Egan,[36] was rooted in a claim that the act was a violation of her personal rights and those of her children. She objected to the putting of fluoride into the public water supplies because she considered it an infringement of her parental rights, arguing that it was her role to see to the children's upbringing and to decide what they should eat and drink. Preventing caries in her children's teeth was solely her and her husband's responsibility, Ryan said, and they took it very seriously.

'Every case which involves the validity of a law is obviously of very considerable importance', MacBride told the judge, John Kenny, in his opening speech on 14 March 1963. 'This case is even of greater importance than most.'[37]

For MacBride, that was partly because it raised so many questions about major, and still relatively unexplored, parts of the Constitution, in particular the personal rights guarantees. The key section was in Article 40.3, which provided that 'The State guarantees in its laws to respect, and as far as practicable, by its laws to defend and vindicate the personal rights of the citizen'. It then goes on to identify some of those rights. 'The State shall, *in particular*, by its laws protect as best it may from unjust attack and, in the case of injustice done, vindicate the life, person, good name and property rights of every citizen' (author's italics). The 'in particular' was important because, as Kenny was later to suggest, it implied that there were other personal rights that did not actually appear in the text.

MacBride also flagged at the outset that his case set a lot of store by the concept of natural law. The idea that humans have certain superior rights by virtue of being human had largely lain dormant since it was invoked in a dissenting judgment by the then Chief Justice, Hugh Kennedy, in 1935.[38] The 1937 Constitution contained far more natural law language than the 1922 document it replaced. In Article 41, the State recognizes the family as 'a moral institution possessing inalienable and imprescriptible rights, antecedent and superior to all positive [i.e. statute] law'. But what were these rights that were superior to the legislation passed by the Oireachtas? On that the Constitution was silent.

Gladys Ryan's was the longest civil case in the history of the State.

Over sixty-five days from March to July 1963 the High Court heard
a mass of scientific and medical evidence from an array of experts
called by the plaintiff and the defendant. Kenny and the legal teams
pored over international scientific literature on fluoridation going
back over the previous thirty years.

As the case was drawing to a close, however, it became clear that
the issue Kenny was grappling with above all else was MacBride's
claim that the personal rights guarantee in the Constitution included
an implicit but unwritten right to what MacBride called personal
integrity. The Attorney General's senior counsel, William Finlay,
could see that Kenny had latched onto this, and knew that, if he
accepted the concept, it could be a small step to siding with Ryan. He
pushed back strongly in his closing speech in late July. But Kenny
wouldn't let it go.

JUDGE: Is it conceded that one of the personal rights is the right of
personal integrity?

FINLAY: I don't know what personal integrity means. It is an ample
phrase. It could correspond with the personal right that a citizen be
saved harmless from real danger being done to him. But in a wider
sense, no. Integrity would often mean the right to freely choose
how one should feed and nourish oneself. I don't think the rights in
this Article are anything of that order. I think it is a right to protect
the body of the Citizen from attack to his detriment.

JUDGE: In 'Pacem In Terris' one of the personal rights is the right of
personal integrity. What does it mean?

FINLAY: That the body should not be subjected to attack or damage.

JUDGE: Or interference?

FINLAY: Interference causing damage, but it is a question of har-
monising. I don't conceive that personal integrity has any vague
meaning.

'Pacem in Terris', or 'Peace on Earth', was a papal encyclical on
nuclear non-proliferation issued by Pope John XXIII on 11 April
that year – a month into the Ryan hearings. It was seen as a
ground-breaking charter, setting out the Catholic Church's position
on human rights and natural law, and its publication was a major

event. The *New York Times* published the text in its entirety (a first for the paper), and it was the subject, two years later, of a major UN conference. The passage Kenny was referring to read as follows: 'Man has the right to live. He has the right to bodily integrity and to the means necessary for the proper development of life, particularly food, clothing, shelter, medical care, rest, and, finally, the necessary social services.'

Finlay refused to concede that the Constitution contained an implied right to personal or bodily integrity that would amount to a right to have one's body free from interference. But even if it did exist, the barrister insisted, that integrity would only be interfered with if the fluoride was harmful. And at the fluoride levels the State proposed to add to the water supply, it would cause no harm.

MacBride could see that, on this point at least, he was pushing at an open door. Adopting the language in the encyclical in his own closing speech the following day, he was adamant that the Constitution contained certain rights that were so self-evident they did not have to be spelled out. 'We say [the personal rights] include physical integrity and the right to obtain the elements that are necessary for one's survival. There are many obvious rights not mentioned in the Constitution e.g. a right to marry, a right to have children, a right to fresh air, a guarantee of freedom of movement, a choice of residence, and so on.'[39]

Just a few days later, on 31 July, the protagonists reconvened to hear Kenny's decision. In a summary of his judgment that took two hours and ten minutes to read out, the judge rejected nearly all of Gladys Ryan's arguments. He wasn't convinced that she had shown that fluoride was damaging to human health. And in any case, he found, any citizen who objected to fluoridated water could, 'by the expenditure of a few pounds', remove almost all the fluoride ions from the water coming through the piped water supply.

But the real significance of Kenny's judgment lay elsewhere. The latter part of the High Court hearing had been taken up with discussion on whether the general guarantee of personal rights in Article 40 extended to rights that were not actually written into the Constitution. Kenny concluded that they did. One of these unspecified rights, he said, was the right to 'bodily integrity', a term the judge took directly from the encyclical. The fluoridation of the water supply was not a violation of Ryan's right to bodily integrity, Kenny said, but the right did indeed exist.

'I think that the personal rights which may be involved to invalidate legislation are not confined to those specified in Article 40 but include all those rights which result from the Christian and democratic nature of the State', Kenny said. With that, natural law was firmly back in play. And the doctrine of unenumerated, or unspecified, rights was born.

Gladys Ryan was dejected. Her punishing and drawn-out legal saga had ended in defeat, and now she was lumped with costs estimated by the press to be approaching £250,000, an astronomical sum at a time when £2,500 could buy a good house. She immediately lodged an appeal to the Supreme Court, where the case was heard by a five-judge court comprising Chief Justice Ó Dálaigh, Cecil Lavery, T. C. Kingsmill Moore, Kevin Haugh and Brian Walsh over eight days the following February. The transcript of the High Court case was 3,500 pages long, and the stenographer had died before the transcript had been fully written up, so the barristers and judges agreed that the court should dispense with the usual practice of reading the evidence into the record at the outset. If they were to do so, Séamus Egan estimated, it would take a month to read.

When the Supreme Court appeal was under way, barristers for the Attorney General made a surprising concession. Having strenuously resisted the idea in the High Court, they now accepted that the personal rights guarantee in Article 40 was not confined to those that were spelled out in the document. Among the unspecified rights, Finlay conceded, was 'a right to integrity of the person'.

The Supreme Court worked on its decision for four months, sifting through reams of scientific evidence and legal precedent from Ireland and abroad, including the United States. It was a difficult judgment to write, because in addition to the volume of material, the case came under the one-judgment rule, so the court had to cast it in a way that would be acceptable to all five members. On 5 June 1964, a month before the court gave its judgment, Walsh wrote to William Brennan and informed him about the case.

> In our own Court we have not done any particularly exciting case for the last year or so, save one Constitutional case challenging the validity of a statute which gave powers to the Minister for Health and to the Local Authorities to fluoridate the public water supply as an aid to preventing dental caries in children. From the cases we had cited to us I saw that this matter had engaged a number of the Supreme and Appeals Courts in your various States. We have had the rather heavy task of having to read and study the great mass of documentary material available in this matter together with the transcript of the evidence taken in the High Court at a trial which so far as evidence was concerned lasted over sixty days.

Walsh was conscious of the need for the court to get the science right. 'I am sure we feel we could always survive the criticism of lawyers but we are not in quite the same strong position to command the charity or tolerance of the scientists of the world', he wrote. Walsh did not spell out the court's thinking for Brennan and, in laying out the grounds of Ryan's case, did not refer to the concept of unspecified rights.

To many observers at the time, it would have seemed unthinkable that the Supreme Court could be persuaded to embrace such a radical and potentially far-reaching idea. But the court did just that. While it upheld Kenny's decision against Ryan, it gave its stamp of approval to his conclusion that the personal rights in the Constitution were 'not limited to life, person, good name and property right', as Ó Dálaigh said on behalf of the court. He didn't list those implied rights, but he made clear that there were others to be found. 'To attempt to make a list of all the rights which may properly fall within the category of "personal rights" would be difficult and, fortunately, is unnecessary in the present case', the judgment concluded.[40]

With the Supreme Court hurdle passed, Dublin Corporation activated the fluoridation plan that had been on hold for three years. The State never sought its costs from Gladys Ryan, but any sense of relief at that was tempered by the disillusionment she felt after her long, ultimately fruitless, legal battle. 'The whole thing was so unpleasant that I just want to put it out of my mind', she told the *Irish Press* in a rare public comment twenty years later.[41]

Looking back on his time on the Supreme Court more than a quarter of a century after the Ryan case, Brian Walsh said the Ó Dálaigh court, in its early years, was conscious that it could 'put down markers' for future events. 'By laying down markers one might inspire practitioners to pick them up and use them in the next case', he said.[42] In taking Kenny's lead in Gladys Ryan's case and in effect announcing the era of implied, or unenumerated, rights, the first big marker was laid.

It was a watershed moment. The Constitution contained rights that didn't actually appear in the text. And that meant the only people with the authority to identify them – the judges of the Supreme Court – had just made themselves immeasurably more powerful.

5. *Vive la révolution!*

'Perhaps not surprisingly, our views do not find full favour with the police authorities or indeed with the Department of Justice.'

Brian Walsh

On 6 July 1963, Philip Anthony Quinn walked out the door of Mountjoy Prison having completed a six-month sentence for attempted robbery. As he left the prison complex in Dublin's north inner city, the 31-year-old, from Clonakilty in Co. Cork, was approached by a garda who told him there was a warrant for his committal to Limerick Prison for two weeks for failure to pay a fine. He said nothing about arresting him. Accompanied by two other men, the garda walked with Quinn to the North Circular Road, where he was ordered to get into a car and, once inside, was told there was a British warrant for his arrest. It was read out to him on the short drive to the Bridewell.

The warrant charged Quinn with stealing £3,000 worth of transistor radios and other electrical equipment in August 1962 from a London-based company where he had been working at the time. But there was a problem with the warrant – Quinn's first name was listed as Patrick rather than Philip – so the following day his barrister, P. A. Ó Síocháin, went to the High Court to have the case thrown out. While those court proceedings were pending, the British authorities, in consultation with the gardaí, issued a second warrant, this time with Quinn's first name corrected.

At 11am on 15 July the gardaí went into the High Court and told the court president, Cahir Davitt, that they accepted the warrant was invalid and as a result had no objection to Quinn being released. They didn't mention that they had received a replacement warrant just an hour before coming to court. Released by the judge, Quinn left the court accompanied by his junior counsel. The barrister had to appear briefly in another court, so while he was waiting, Quinn stepped outside the Four Courts building.

And then he disappeared.

When the barrister emerged from court and could not find his client, he and the rest of the legal team began working the phones. In vain they contacted Dublin Airport, Limerick Prison and Garda Headquarters, but nobody knew of Quinn's whereabouts. At 9pm, senior gardaí informed Quinn's lawyers that he was not in custody anywhere in the Dublin Metropolitan Division.

Eventually it emerged that Quinn had been re-arrested the minute he stepped out of the Four Courts before being put into a car with a garda and two British police officers and driven immediately to the border. From there he was brought by ferry to Britain and driven to London. Even though Quinn was by now in a jail cell in London, his lawyers went back to the High Court to seek his release. But after a hearing of several days, the court found that the second warrant was valid, that Quinn was in lawful custody and that the gardaí had acted properly.

The Supreme Court saw it very differently. Its judges, led by the normally mild-mannered Cearbhall Ó Dálaigh, were furious. Having surveyed the evidence, Ó Dálaigh said, it was 'clear that a plan was laid by the police, Irish and British, to remove [Quinn] after his arrest on the new warrant from the area of jurisdiction of our courts with such dispatch that he would have no opportunity whatever of questioning the validity of the warrant'. The Chief Justice believed the police had chosen to 'whisk' Quinn across the border rather than taking him directly to Britain by plane or by sea as any delay would have given Quinn's lawyers the time to challenge the new warrant in the courts. 'In plain language the purpose of the police plan was to eliminate the Courts and to defeat the rule of law as a factor in Government', he said.

At the time, the only procedure for enforcing a British warrant in the Republic was a century-old law called the Petty Sessions (Ireland) Act 1851. Ó Dálaigh's court wanted rid of it. In a unanimous judgment, the judges concluded that the act indeed permitted the removal of an Irish citizen from the State without having the opportunity to challenge the arrest. As a result, the court found, the act was inconsistent with the Constitution.

It was in some ways a curious saga – later, acting much like a criminal trial court, the Supreme Court held that the British police officers were in contempt of court, even though the court had previously acknowledged that their actions had been in accordance with the law as it stood at the time. But the judgment on the constitutional issue, written by Brian Walsh, was to become one of the cornerstones of Irish constitutional law, insisting as it did on the rule of law, the value of personal liberty and the right of access to the courts. That insistence, combined with the stress on defendants' rights and the firm stance towards the gardaí, presaged some of the themes of the coming decade. Walsh also took the opportunity to lay down an important marker by suggesting in his judgment that the Supreme Court should not be strictly bound by its previous decisions.[1]

The judgment's force is encapsulated in one of the most famous assertions by the court of its view on citizens' fundamental rights. The intention of the Constitution, Ó Dálaigh wrote, was that

> rights of substance were being assured to the individual and that the Courts were the custodians of these rights. As a necessary corollary it follows that no one can with impunity set these rights at nought or circumvent them, and that the Courts' powers in this regard are as ample as the defence of the Constitution requires. Anyone who sets himself such a course is guilty of contempt of the Courts and is punishable accordingly.

In 1965 Minister for Justice Charles Haughey responded to the judgment by introducing the Extradition Act, which explicitly stated that no suspect could be handed over to the British until he had had a chance to challenge the warrant in the High Court.

Beyond its practical consequences, the judgment in Quinn's case was a clear signal of intent from the Supreme Court. The rule up to then, applied by the Supreme Court itself, was that once it made a decision on a legal point, then this would always be followed by a later Supreme Court. Now the court was repudiating that rule while giving barristers a nudge to the effect that it would be as well to look west, towards the United States, for inspiration, rather than relying on English law and precedent. In the judgment, Walsh dismissed the idea that just because the post-Independence Irish courts had adopted the old English common law system, that meant they should use English methods that were, after all, not designed for interpreting a written Constitution.

> In this State, one would have expected that if the approach of any court of final appeal of another State was to have been held up as an example for this court to follow it would more appropriately have been the Supreme Court of the United States rather than the House of Lords.[2]

This had been a bugbear of Walsh's for some time. 'What used to drive him mad was any suggestion that [the court] was bound by the House of Lords', says one former colleague. 'That was enough to send him berserk.'

In the early years of the Free State, the influence of US law had been fairly limited. It was true that in some respects the 1922 Constitution borrowed from its American counterpart, and one of its greatest innovations – judicial review – was essentially an American invention. But the transatlantic links were above all personal, the influence primarily indirect.[3] In 1928 Hugh Kennedy, the first Chief Justice, made a lengthy visit to the US, where he addressed the American Bar Association. He remained in touch with members of the legal profession there, and in 1933, when he was engaged in discussions with the government on judicial salaries, he contacted the chairman of the association to seek information on how the US dealt with the issue.

While the relative paucity of major constitutional cases in the first decades after the enactment of the 1937 Constitution limited the opportunities for judges to borrow from American case law, there were nonetheless signs of tentative change by the late 1940s. In the landmark 1947 case of *National Union of Railwaymen v. Sullivan*, in which the court used the constitutional guarantee of freedom of association to strike down part of the Trade Union Act, two US cases were among those cited to the court. In the same year, in the Sinn Féin funds case, barristers on both sides used American cases to argue for different approaches to the Constitution. The American influence was seeping into the Irish system in these years despite the fact that the law departments in the main universities were virtually silent on legal developments on the other side of the Atlantic. 'While Constitutional issues were being discussed in UCD, and that became a fertile seed bed for ideas that subsequently came to prominence, there is no indication that the teachers or the students looked for inspiration to the US', Donal O'Donnell writes.[4]

In the space of just a few years in the early 1960s, that changed dramatically. In case after case, barristers would invoke American precedent, knowing they now had a receptive ear on the bench. 'When I came to the Bar first, you had the Irish Reports and the English Reports and that was it', says one retired barrister who joined the law library in the 1950s.

> Once you got involved in constitutional law, you found that the American Supreme Court had usually said something on the subject – usually on both sides. I don't know which happened first, but I started quoting American cases to the court, and Cearbhall Ó Dálaigh, ultimately, at the end of a case, would say, 'Has the American Federal Supreme Court anything to say about this problem?' So you had to acquaint yourself with American law.

In the 1960s Ó Dálaigh and Walsh's ties to the States deepened as a result of their developing relationships with their US counterparts, occasional visits and their conscious effort to break with the traditional reliance on English courts' decisions and methods. Walsh sought out anything he could find about US law in his weekly copies of *Newsweek* and *Time*, and was a voracious reader of popular books about the US Supreme Court. As the 'slip opinions' continued to make their way from Washington to the Four Courts and Walsh's friendship with William Brennan deepened, he was able to glean new insights into the workings and thinking of the US court.

Walsh sought to import American ideas not only about the law itself but also on how the court in Dublin could improve its ways of doing business. In the mid-1960s, when he was a member of a committee appointed by government to review the courts' practices and procedures, Walsh wanted to introduce a new system whereby barristers would submit papers outlining their case in advance of the Supreme Court hearing. Until then every submission was made orally, a process that was time-consuming and disliked by Walsh and the rest of the court. The US court insisted on written submissions, so in December 1966, at Walsh's request, Brennan sent him some 'briefs' that had been submitted to the court for cases that year.* The relationship between Walsh and Brennan was developing, their correspondence increasingly familiar. Walsh wrote to Brennan in December 1964 to offer condolences on the death of his mother, just as he had the previous January after John F. Kennedy's assassination. 'It has been a very great shock to all of us here in Washington and I can't say that we are as yet fully reconciled', Brennan wrote to Walsh a month after Kennedy's death.

Through the early 1960s, the Supreme Court – comprising Ó Dálaigh, Cecil Lavery, T. C. Kingsmill Moore, Kevin Haugh and Walsh – was delivering one landmark judgment after another. One of the areas in which the new departure was most striking was criminal law, where the court placed defendants' rights front and centre and put the police on a tighter rein. Within a period of just a few years, the court was to overhaul a largely informal system in which illegally obtained evidence was regularly used to convict people, suspects were detained 'for questioning' for a number of days by the gardaí and bail was practically unavailable for serious crimes.[5]

A key figure in these years, and one whose relatively low profile belied his impact, was Kingsmill Moore, known as 'KM' to his colleagues on the bench. His track record and experience – he was the

* Around the same time, Walsh travelled to Paris and sat in on the deliberations of the Cour de Cassation – the closest equivalent in France to the Irish Supreme Court – and asked for copies of its own submissions. He visited the House of Lords in London for the same purpose. The requirement for parties to a case to provide the court with written submissions was duly introduced in the late 1960s.

oldest member of the court by the early 1960s – gave a steadying authority to a relatively young group of judges, while his civil libertarian views made him a particularly influential voice at a time when the court was eager to mine the personal rights guarantees in the Constitution in a more systematic way than it had ever done.

The son of a Church of Ireland clergyman, Kingsmill Moore was educated at an English public school before returning to Ireland to study classics at Trinity College in the years leading up to the Easter Rising. Following a period in the Royal Flying Corps in 1917–18, he worked as a correspondent for the *Irish Times* during the Civil War before returning to practice in the law library. A stint as an independent member of the Seanad for Dublin University from 1943 revealed some of those features of his personality and outlook – thoughtfulness, liberalism, a flair for writing – that would later come through in his judgments on the High and Supreme Courts. Walsh, in particular, looked up to Kingsmill Moore, who sat beside him on the bench for five years and became something of a mentor. Walsh admired his older colleague's 'natural inclination to be humane and liberal', his tendency to look out for the weak and the 'infinite pains' he would take to write with style and clarity. He also respected Kingsmill's cosmopolitanism, noting that he too always kept abreast of legal developments from the US and elsewhere. 'His approach to the law was not a narrow doctrinal one', Walsh wrote after Kingsmill's death in 1979. 'He was fully aware that the law was to be appraised as a means of service to justice.'[6]

Not that Walsh and Kingsmill always agreed. In March 1961 the court – including Walsh, who was drafted in from the High Court for the case – had to decide whether evidence that was obtained in breach of a constitutional right could be used to convict someone of an offence. Gerald O'Brien and his brother Patrick had been found guilty of stealing after a trial in which the State's case was built largely on items found by gardaí during a search of 118 Captain's Road, the house where the two brothers lived in the Dublin suburb of Crumlin. But it emerged that the wrong address had inadvertently been written on the search warrant: instead of 118 Captain's Road, the warrant authorized a search of 118 Cashel Road, which was also in Crumlin.

In the Supreme Court, the O'Brien brothers' lawyers argued that the gardaí had broken the law by not having a valid warrant. Not only that, they said, but the authorities had violated the constitutional guarantee of the 'inviolability' of every citizen's dwelling. At the time, common law courts across the world were grappling with this very question, and indeed Walsh and Brennan discussed it when they met in Dublin in the summer of 1963, in the long gap between the hearing of the O'Brien case and the delivery of the judgment. Nearly all common law countries, including England, took a relaxed attitude to illegally obtained evidence. The general approach was: if it's relevant, it can be used in court. But in the period between the hearing of the O'Brien case in the Supreme Court and the delivery of the decision, the US Supreme Court issued a decision of its own in a case, *Mapp v. Ohio*, that covered similar terrain.[7] In the decision, which would have been posted to Walsh by Brennan as soon as it was delivered, the Washington court took a more hard-line approach by saying that no evidence that was obtained in violation of the Constitution could be used by any US state in a criminal prosecution.

There is no way of knowing how the Supreme Court would have decided had it not seen the *Mapp v. Ohio* decision after its own case had been argued, but the court clearly took it into account – despite US material apparently not having been mentioned by counsel at the original hearing, *Mapp v. Ohio* and other American cases are cited in the judgments. What the court attempted was to strike a middle way between what had been the prevailing common law view and the radical departure just effected by Brennan and his colleagues in the US.

The Ó Dálaigh court was unanimous on what should happen in the O'Brien case: the authorities were entitled to use the evidence, the court agreed, and the men's appeal was rejected. But on the constitutional principle itself the judges differed. The majority judgment, written by Kingsmill Moore and supported by Lavery and Frederick Budd (a judge of the High Court who had been drafted in to sit in for Kevin Haugh on this case), found that evidence obtained in a deliberate and conscious breach of a constitutional right should 'in general' and 'normally' be excluded. Walsh's judgment, with which Ó Dálaigh agreed, was slightly more radical, arguing that evidence obtained in intentional or conscious breach of a constitutional right should always be excluded except in extraordinary circumstances.

The difference between Kingsmill Moore and Walsh was one of degree, but overall both were cautious. They were ready to break with the mainstream view of English and most other common law judges, but they were not yet prepared to go as far as the US Supreme Court. The case was nonetheless a milestone, a hint of things to come, and the exclusionary rule was a topic the court would wrestle with for decades. In 1990, in Walsh's final case on the court, his colleagues gave him a big going-away present by finally accepting the more absolute position he had taken in the O'Brien case, although that decision was itself overturned in 2015.

If the early 1960s heralded a change in the court's thinking about defendants' rights, it also brought a striking shift in tone within the courtroom itself. In a setting where judges had often been aloof, intimidating and cranky, Ó Dálaigh went out of his way to be polite and accommodating to those who appeared before him. He and Walsh were concerned that judges in the lower courts refused to hear applications from prisoners who had already been sentenced. So Walsh drafted a form that was to be sent to the prisons and made available to anyone who wanted to bring a case to the courts.[8] Until then prisoners had always been referred to in court simply by their surname; now they were to be called 'Mr', Ó Dálaigh insisted.

'For a period, there was a vogue among members of the prison population – perhaps encouraged by the well-known concern of the Chief Justice for the protection of human rights – to apply in person to the High Court and Supreme Court to quash their convictions on various technical grounds', writes Rory O'Hanlon.[9] During one particular hearing, recounted by O'Hanlon, Ó Dálaigh wanted to consult a textbook on criminal law but found himself in the odd position of having to borrow it from the prisoner who was presenting his case. It turned out that the man had written from jail to ask for some books so he could read up on the law in advance of his case, and the Chief Justice had instructed staff to pass on his own copy of the text.[10]

All of this was viewed with bemusement if not scepticism by many older barristers. Senior counsel would mutter about having to wait their turn while Ó Dálaigh and his colleagues listened patiently to another convicted criminal. Of more consequence was the attitude of the government. By the mid-1960s, the Department of Justice, in particular, was watching developments at the Four Courts with increasing alarm. Officials at the department's headquarters on St Stephen's Green grew convinced that the court had become a soft touch, and resented what they saw as its enthusiasm for curbing garda powers at every turn. Previous governments had lost cases in the Supreme Court over the decades, but to some in the civil service in the 1960s it seemed the court was now becoming openly hostile to the interests of the political establishment.

The relationship grew considerably more strained in December 1966, when Roger O'Callaghan, a Cork man with no fixed address, went to the Supreme Court to challenge the High Court's refusal to release him on bail. O'Callaghan had been charged with a dauntingly long list of offences: larceny, breaking and entering, malicious damage, receiving stolen property, resisting arrest and assault – all of which he was alleged to have committed in Cork City the previous September – and was due to go on trial in the Central Criminal Court. When the District Court refused him bail, he appealed to the High Court but got the same answer.

It had become almost par for the course for the State to oppose bail on the ground that the accused person might use his freedom to commit further crimes. That was the argument used by the gardaí in O'Callaghan's case, and the High Court judge, George Murnaghan, had accepted it. For Murnaghan, this was the type of routine case he had heard – and rejected – many times before. He was so exasperated by how many prisoners were coming to court with what he saw as futile attempts to get out on bail that he decided to use the O'Callaghan case to set out the eleven principles he used to refuse them. He asked that the list be made available in the prisons so that the courts would not have to waste their time on such cases in future.

By doing that, Murnaghan opened the door for the Supreme Court to review the entire bail system. It grabbed the opportunity enthusiastically.

In a judgment that would reverberate in government for decades, the court zoned in on the notion that someone could be refused bail simply because he might commit another offence. It was anathema to Ó Dálaigh and Walsh's view of the Constitution. In a lacerating judgment with which the other members of the court all agreed, Ó Dálaigh said the idea amounted to 'a denial of the whole basis of our system of law'. Bail was not meant to be a punishment, he said.

> It transcends respect for the requirement that a man shall be considered innocent until he is found guilty and seeks to punish him in respect of crimes neither completed nor attempted . . . The courts owe more than verbal respect to the principle that punishment begins after conviction, and that every man is deemed to be innocent until tried and duly found guilty.

Walsh was every bit as critical:

> In this country it would be quite contrary to the concept of personal liberty enshrined in the Constitution that any person should be punished in respect of any matter upon which he has not been convicted or that in any circumstances he should be deprived of his liberty upon only the belief that he will commit offences if left at liberty, save in the most extraordinary circumstances . . . to secure the preservation of public peace and order or the public safety and the preservation of the State in a time of national emergency or in some situation akin to that.

Ó Dálaigh was keen to go even further and rule out the practice at bail hearings of giving a judge details of an accused person's previous convictions, but on that point he failed to win the support of his colleagues.

The government was incensed by the Supreme Court's decision. For some in the administration, it confirmed their suspicion, based on previous decisions such as those on extradition and the use of unconstitutionally obtained evidence, that the court was now actively working against the interests of the gardaí and the Department of Justice. Jack Lynch believed the bail decision showed a lack of common sense. Others put it more bluntly. One official who was involved in government discussions about the potential fallout at the time describes it as 'a phenomenal mistake', a 'thieves' charter' and 'the most notorious decision in the history of the Supreme Court'.

'They had over-interpreted their mandate. They were beginning to legislate', the former official says, still angry fifty years on. 'Judges should be careful not to overstretch their position. It's one thing to put a check on government. It's another thing to be creating whole new branches of rights. It was a colossal failure of insight. A huge mistake.'

Officials were also irritated by the court's open door for prisoners, which – because of the busy flow of prisoners who had to be brought to the Four Courts – was seen in the department as a costly and point-less imposition. 'The prison officers reported that the court had become something of a joke among the prison population: the judges would listen to anything they said and it was a great day out.'[11]

Tension between the Department of Justice and the Supreme Court had been a theme since the foundation of the State. As the depart-ment with the closest relationship with the security services and primary responsibility for law reform, it was an assiduous guardian of its own authority, as well as that of the gardaí, and saw court judg-ments that constrained the security forces' room for manoeuvre as a threat.

That suspicion went as far back as the 1937 Constitution. Stephen Roche, secretary of the department when the Constitution was being prepared, had urged de Valera against including the fundamental rights guarantees or allowing judicial review of legislation and expressed serious concern about the potential for judicial activism. In a memo he sent to Michael McDunphy, assistant secretary to the Executive Council, in April 1937, Roche expressed his disdain for 'the whole idea of tying up the Dáil and the Government with all sorts of restrictions and putting the Supreme Court like a watch-dog over them for fear that they may run wild and do all sorts of indefens-ible things'.[12]

It's not clear whether de Valera fully understood the power that judicial review would bestow on the courts. However, as Gerard

Hogan points out, given the critical views of Roche and others within government, 'It cannot be said that he had not received adequate advance warning about the direction which the draft Constitution might have been taking.'[13]

Many of Roche's successors harboured similar reservations about the judges' powers. Among them was Peter Berry, a wily official with a security background who, as department secretary in the 1960s and early '70s, was arguably the most powerful civil servant in the country. As the activism of the Ó Dálaigh era gathered pace, the relationship between the court and Berry's department deteriorated further.

The government appears not to have conveyed its concerns to the Supreme Court directly, adhering to the convention that discussion about cases is a no-go area between politicians and the judges. There was no need: Walsh and his colleagues were well aware of the department's unhappiness. Behind the scenes government figures were not slow to approach senior judges when they wanted to raise concerns.

In the years leading up to and immediately after Ó Dálaigh's appointment as Chief Justice, for example, the government had been exercised by what it saw as inconsistent penalties being handed down by the District Court. In November 1959, the then Taoiseach Seán Lemass wrote to Chief Justice Conor Maguire to remind him that the high rate of burglary, theft, house-breaking and assault was attracting a lot of public comment and was causing the government 'great anxiety'.[14] One reason for the spike, Lemass had been told, was the leniency of judges in the District Court when handing down penalties, and he wanted Maguire to give the matter his 'earnest consideration'.

Lemass must have known it was unusual to write to a Chief Justice in effect asking him to make sure judges gave more stringent penalties.

It is after considerable hesitation that I have decided to communicate with you on this matter, and I wish to emphasise that there is no question of any attempt by the Government to bring improper influence to bear on any branch of the Judiciary. I have felt compelled to take this step, however, by the belief that a grave and urgent question affecting the public interest is at stake.

Despite his disclaimers, the Taoiseach's letter put Maguire in an awkward position. At first he was at a loss to see what he could do, but after a meeting with Lemass the following month he agreed to go into the Court of Criminal Appeal and make a statement that would indirectly, through the coverage in the next day's newspapers, bring the issue to the judges' attention. But he was 'very reluctant' to 'lecture' the District Court judges on how they carried out their duties, as Lemass appears to have suggested at their meeting.

'I fear that they would possibly refuse to listen to any criticism I might make or to accept any guidance from me as to the punishment of offenders. They might claim that their independence guaranteed by the Constitution renders them immune from any criticism even by me as head of the Judiciary', Maguire wrote. Instead, he suggested that one way of dealing with the supposed problem was to change the law so as to allow the State to appeal against a sentence on the ground that it was not sufficiently severe. If public policy required that, the people would probably accept it.[15]

The issue did not go away, however. Four years later, in December 1963, the Minister for Justice, Charles Haughey, wrote privately to Cearbhall Ó Dálaigh. Again the topic was inconsistent imposition of fines and other penalties in the District Court. 'As you are aware, no doubt, the wide disparity of penalties imposed by different Justices for offences of a similar character and gravity has attracted unfavourable public attention from time to time.' He suggested that Ó Dálaigh address his colleagues on the District Court about the issue.[16]

Like Maguire before him, Ó Dálaigh struggled to see what he could do and had 'many misgivings' about Haughey's suggestion that he approach the judges directly.[17] Instead, a meeting was organized among the District Court judges themselves, and that appears to have mollified Haughey. In a follow-up letter, he told Ó Dálaigh he would take no further action, 'hoping that the Justices, of their own volition, will put their house in order'.[18]

The O'Callaghan case intensified the misgivings some ministers and officials had harboured for years towards the Ó Dálaigh–Walsh axis. Some within the administration could see and even admire what the court was doing in breathing life into the Constitution, de-Anglicizing the legal system, making the courts less formal and insisting on the rights of the citizen. But to their minds it was all happening too quickly.[19]

The sense that the court was intent on systematically curbing State power was especially galling to Fianna Fáil in that Ó Dálaigh and Walsh had both been seen as close to the party before they became judges. Successive governments made no secret of the fact that they would like the courts to have more scope on bail than the Supreme Court allowed them in its 1966 judgment.[20] Special legislation was discussed on several occasions but never drafted, because of a belief that the court would almost certainly find it unconstitutional. Ultimately the government got its way, but it took a full thirty years. In 1996, the people undid the O'Callaghan judgment by approving a constitutional amendment that explicitly authorized the courts to deny bail on the ground that an individual might commit another crime.

Inside the court, the judges stuck proudly to their decision, convinced that they had upheld the constitutional right to liberty and the individual rights of the citizen. They knew of the anger in the Department of Justice but were not particularly surprised by it. Ó Dálaigh and Walsh knew how the political system worked. In February 1969, when Walsh learned that a debate was taking place in the US about the bail issue, he sent Brennan a copy of the O'Callaghan judgments and filled him in on the case and the fallout.

> The decision is an interesting one because it represents the culmination of what was a fairly long standing difference of opinion between the Supreme Court and other courts on the practice and law applicable to the granting of bail. This particular case provided a very good opportunity for us to lay down the matter once and for all because the High Court judge in question (who always had strong views on this matter) on this occasion enumerated quite elaborately the principles which he thought should apply and we took the opportunity of dealing with the matter in some detail.

Since then, I am glad to say, bail applications in all courts are disposed of strictly in accordance with the principles laid down in our judgments. I should add that, perhaps not surprisingly, our views do not find full favour with the police authorities or indeed with the Department of Justice but nevertheless when our judgment appeared a Bill which was then in the course of its passage through parliament and which would have, among other things, in some ways restricted the granting of bail, was immediately amended to delete the provisions relating to bail so that the law, as it stands at the moment, is as set out in our judgment . . . We firmly rejected all concepts of using bail as a form of preventive justice. That particular argument always reminded me of the reasons assigned by Shakespeare to Brutus in his justification of the assassination of Caesar, namely, that he should be killed not for the evil he had done but for the evil he might do if he should be allowed to live.[21]

By the time of the O'Callaghan decision, the Department of Justice saw Ó Dálaigh and Walsh as the prime movers behind the court's activist turn. Ó Dálaigh they knew well – he had twice been Attorney General and as Chief Justice he had a public profile – but Walsh was relatively little known to the public beyond the Four Courts. As the officials watched developments on the court, they began to see his fingerprints all over the new expansionism that had taken hold. Or, as writer Colm Tóibín put it in his ground-breaking profile of the court in the mid-1980s, while Ó Dálaigh might have been firing the bullets, Walsh was loading the pistol.*

Ministers and their officials also got to know Walsh through his role as one of several judges who informally represented the judiciary in discussions on judges' pay with government throughout the 1960s. This had always been a sensitive topic. In order to shore up the principle of judicial independence, the 1937 Constitution contained an explicit ban on reducing the pay of a serving judge. But while that

---

* Colm Tóibín, 'Inside the Supreme Court'. Tóibín's remarkable second novel, *The Heather Blazing* (1992), is the story of a High Court judge. He has said that it was inspired partly by his encounters with the Supreme Court judges for the *Magill* feature.

clause blocked governments from cutting pay, the power to increase judges' salaries remained in the gift of the politicians. And if the government decided not to pass on wider public sector pay increases to the judiciary over an extended period, it could in effect reduce their income. That was a fear judges held since the courts system was set up in 1924, and it was to be a recurring source of tension between Government Buildings and the judiciary through the twentieth century.

That tension grew particularly acute in the 1960s, when salaries were rising in both the public and private sectors and the judges were adamant that they were entitled to a pay rise of their own. The issue turned into an acrimonious dispute that, while never revealed in public, floated beneath the surface throughout the decade.

In February 1963, having been lobbied by a number of judges, Charles Haughey signed off on a memo to government arguing that it should consider increasing judicial salaries to reflect pay increases elsewhere in society. He pointed out that there had only been three increases in judges' pay since 1924 and proposed an increase of 25 per cent for all judges. Haughey was alive to the sensitivities, and told fellow ministers that they should be careful not to annoy the judges too much. 'It is scarcely necessary for the Minister to mention the importance of a contented Judiciary: irritation and dissatisfaction with remuneration could have a harmful effect on Judges in the performance of their duties', the memo stated.[22] In July, Ó Dálaigh, accompanied by Lavery, Walsh and Richard McLoughlin of the High Court, met the Minister for Finance, James Ryan, to press the judges' claim for a salary increase. Ryan was non-committal, telling the judges' delegation merely that he 'reserved judgment'.[23]

The judges were getting nowhere with their claim, and Ó Dálaigh was coming under increasing pressure from within his own ranks to take a more assertive stance on the issue. Most of the judges on the Supreme and High Courts had taken a pay cut by leaving private practice to join the bench and watched enviously as their former colleagues and friends in the law library made more money than they did. They knew better than to make a pay claim during the economically stagnant 1950s, but by the following decade, as they watched secretaries and assistant secretaries of government departments get pay hikes, the judges grew insistent that they should have the same. The Department of Justice was initially receptive to the argument, but the Department of Finance was staunchly resistant. Nor was the judges' case helped by a dip in the public finances in the middle of the decade. Through 1965 and 1966 the judges kept lobbying the government to no avail.

In a joint memo on behalf of all judges to the government in December 1967, they pointed out that the real pay of judges had been greatly reduced since 1924, when the new courts system came into operation after Independence. They said the real remuneration of a Supreme Court judge in 1967 was less than that of a Circuit Court judge in 1924, and in real value was equal to only 53 per cent of the 1924 salary of a Supreme Court judge. An example they cited was Cahir Davitt, who, when he retired as President of the High Court after thirty-nine years on the bench, had a salary that was 'appreciably' lower in real value than the salary he had had as a Circuit Court judge when first appointed to the bench. They also noted that a County judge in Northern Ireland earned £350 more each year than a Supreme Court judge south of the border. They were not seeking a pay increase but rather the restoration of their 1924 levels, they said.[24]

The judges had a strong case. Salaries in the public and private sectors had risen to compensate for the fall in purchasing power. Part of the problem the judges faced in making their argument, however, was that the same pattern of long-term reduction had applied to two other offices: the President of Ireland and government ministers. That meant there was little sympathy for their case around the Cabinet table. If, for instance, the judges were to have their pay adjusted to reflect their 1924 income, they would have to receive a big increase. Having received small increases in 1962 and 1964, a Supreme Court judge in 1967 earned £4,950, compared to £3,000 in 1924. The increase they sought amounted to £9,330 a year.

As it happened, one of the unofficial shop stewards for the judiciary was Brian Walsh. While formal correspondence between the two sides went through Ó Dálaigh and the relevant ministers, Walsh had attended meetings between delegations from the judiciary and the Department through the 1960s. In January 1967 he took a different tack and wrote privately to the then Minister for Finance, Brian Lenihan. In a strongly worded letter following the latest rebuff from government, Walsh told Lenihan, whom he addressed by his first name, that the judges had been making their case for years without success and had pulled back from pressing their case during the period of deteriorating public finances for fear of 'embarrassing' the government. Yet while senior public service officials had received increases, Walsh wrote, the judiciary was getting nowhere. 'The result can scarcely be regarded as an incentive for forbearance in the future', he wrote. 'The decision is difficult to understand in the light of the indisputable fall over the years in the real value of the salaries concerned even without taking any account of the increased incidence of taxation.'

But Walsh then went further. 'As it stands, I am afraid that it is open to the interpretation that it is becoming a matter of actual policy to achieve the down-grading of the financial position of the members of the judiciary', he told Lenihan. 'The present position is so completely at variance with the spirit of the Constitutional guarantee in this matter as to make nonsense out of the latter.'[25] It was a big claim: was the government actively trying to keep judges' pay down? Walsh did not suggest why the government might want to do that.

Lenihan forwarded the letter to the Taoiseach, Jack Lynch, but nothing was to happen until a year later, when the government announced that it would increase the pay of all judges. The pay hike was about half of what the judiciary had been seeking, and on the day the news broke the *Irish Times* quoted mutterings 'in legal circles' that the figures still failed to bring the purchasing power of judicial salaries up to pre-war figures.[26] The tensions continued to simmer. In late 1969, realizing that they lacked any structure through which to make their case on pay and conditions to government, members of the judiciary set up a Judges' Association, which was designed to act as a quasi-trade union. Meanwhile, Ó Dálaigh continued to lobby Lynch, pointing out regularly that the judges were getting none of the gradual increases afforded to senior figures in the public service.

Finally, in July 1971, judges of the Supreme and High Courts were given the increase they had sought five years before. But Lynch's administration was concerned that giving judges more money would go down badly with the public. An *Irish Times* report on the planned increase quoted a government spokesman who was at pains to point out that judges would not receive the last two rounds of public pay increases 'and that their salaries generally are subject to heavy income tax and surtax'.[27]

That took the sting out of the decade-long pay dispute – one that foreshadowed an even more bitter row in the early twenty-first century. But its resolution did little to dampen the growing mutual suspicion between the judges of the Supreme Court and the government that had appointed them.

6. The limits of activism

'Brian Walsh is writing the constitutional law of this country.'

Tommy Conolly

The Minister for Justice was sitting at his desk at the department headquarters on St Stephen's Green when Peter Berry came rushing in with a piece of paper. The night before, he explained, an officer from the Garda Special Branch had attended a meeting of the Irish Soviet Friendship Association and drawn up a list of everyone who was there. Among the names reported to Berry was that of the Chief Justice, Cearbhall Ó Dálaigh.[1]

The idea that the Supreme Court might be a hotbed of ardent communism would have been amusing to anyone who was familiar with the court, but Berry's agitation reflected a broader sense of alarm within the department at the judges' activist turn. By the mid-1960s it was increasingly clear that the Ó Dálaigh court was tearing up the rulebook, invigorating the institution and making it a more assertive and central player than ever before.

These were heady times in the Four Courts. The Supreme Court, with Ó Dálaigh at the helm and Brian Walsh in the engine room, was plotting a new course and moving ahead with dizzying speed. In the mid-1960s the court was turning out a landmark judgment every few months, throwing out rules, laws and conventions that had stood unquestioned, like immovable monuments, for as long as anyone in the law library could remember. The court was methodically unlocking the Constitution's potential, which had lain largely dormant for decades, to be pressed into service as a guarantor of personal liberties and as a brake on overweening executive power. That all of this was happening in a building that was widely seen as a conservative bastion, with its otherworldly customs, its veneration of tradition and its social homogeneity – the Four Courts was an overwhelmingly male, urban and middle-class environment: the epitome, or so it seemed, of the Dublin establishment – made it all the more surprising.*

This was essentially a project of legal nationalism executed by judges who were determined to breathe life into the Constitution, forge a distinctly Irish constitutional law and break with the traditional reliance on English law and legal methods. And while strengthening the personal rights of the individual was a central plank of that agenda, their ambition was much broader. It encompassed nearly all branches of the law and was designed to 'impress on the public mind the Constitution's potential for the redress of grievances which had somehow contrived to escape the attention of the legislature'.[2] That desire to elevate the Constitution, to drive home the message that it was the benchmark against which every other law could be tested, was central to the project. And it led to one surprise after another. 'Things that nobody thought could happen did happen', as Walsh himself later put it.[3]

At the outset, however, one obstacle stood in the judges' way. Under a long-standing legal principle, reaffirmed by the Supreme Court as recently as 1953, the court was bound by its own previous decisions. That meant that every judicial utterance since 1924 was apparently sacrosanct. But in 1965, in a judgment written by Kingsmill Moore, the court simply swept the principle away, declaring itself free to depart from any previous decision that was 'clearly wrong'. That gave the court a clean slate to work from.[4]

Seminal judgments could spring from relatively mundane circumstances. When a Dubliner, Reginald Deaton, was about to be fined £327 by the Revenue Commissioners for smuggling large quantities of butter into the country with the intention of selling it on, Ó Dálaigh used the case to deliver a wide-ranging judgment on the

---

* Frances Elizabeth Moran became the first woman senior counsel in 1941, but it was not until 1980 that the High Court had its first female judge, in Mella Carroll. The Supreme Court had to wait until 1992, with the appointment of Susan Denham, to reach that milestone.

right of the citizen to be tried in the courts, and not by the Revenue or any other body. '[It] is inconceivable to my mind that a Constitution which is broadly based on the doctrine of the separation of powers . . . could have intended to place in the hands of the Executive the power to select the punishment to be undergone by citizens. It would not be too strong to characterise such a system of government as one of arbitrary power', he wrote.*

In the same month that the court heard the Deaton case – December 1962 – David McDonald went to court to challenge the decision of the greyhound racing authority, Bord na gCon, to ban him from attending any greyhound race track in the country. The court, this time through Walsh, ruled that any decision by Bord na gCon must adhere to 'natural justice' or 'constitutional justice' and that any decision it took could be reviewed by the courts.[5]

This was developed further in 1970, when the East Donegal Co-Op challenged a law that gave the Minister for Agriculture the power to refuse, grant or withdraw licences for livestock marts. The act, peppered with phrases such as 'if he so thinks fit' and 'as he shall think proper', gave the minister huge scope for discretion. In what remains a touchstone judgment today, Walsh upheld the constitutionality of the act but used the judgment to emphasize the scope of judicial review, stressing that the minister had to act within the confines of 'constitutional justice' and did not have an absolute or unqualified power. In other words, the doors of the courts were open to anyone who felt aggrieved by the minister's actions.[6]

The three cases, which are still cited almost every week in the Four Courts, were typical of the era. An alleged butter-smuggler, a dispute over greyhounds and a row about livestock mart licences may have looked like inauspicious raw material for seminal decisions, but

---

* *Deaton v. Attorney General and the Revenue Commissioners* [1963] IR 170. Through the second half of the twentieth century, the price differentials between various household goods gave rise to extensive cross-border smuggling. Butter was considerably cheaper in Northern Ireland than in the Republic. In May 1975, Minister for Finance Richie Ryan assured the Dáil that butter-smugglers were being prosecuted and that mobile customs patrols were 'operating continuously' near the border in order to contain the illegal butter trade. Dáil Éireann, 6 May 1975.

for the Supreme Court they provided an opportunity to sharpen and hone its thinking on the courts' power to review decisions taken by other arms of the state and to push back against any government attempt to use its own power arbitrarily. The three cases also pointed to a theme that has run through the court's thinking to the present day: its jealous guarding of its own power. When, in the early twenty-first century, the court had to rule on the powers of tribunals or Oireachtas committees to make findings against individuals, it continued to push back against any attempt by those bodies to assume judicial-style roles.

Setting down principles that would be of future use to the court was one thing. But in a number of cases the judges took decisions that the government realized immediately would change the way it would have to deal with the courts and potentially expose the State to significant expense. Up until the early 1970s, it was established practice that when a minister was involved in a court action, he could claim privilege and refuse to release records requested by the other side in preparing their case. That meant the person suing the minister over a decision he took often had no idea why the decision had been taken. The practice was unjust and ripe for abuse because it allowed ministers to withhold potentially embarrassing information. The Ó Dálaigh court took the first opportunity to throw it out. In a judgment on behalf of the court, Walsh concluded that since the Constitution entrusted the administration of justice solely to the courts, it was judges, not ministers, who had the final say on the production of evidence in court.[7] 'We said: "No, not any more. The court will look at the documents and we'll decide whether they're privileged or not"', Walsh said later.[8] Politicians and civil servants duly noted that they could no longer take the judges' attitudes for granted.

The legal profession quickly picked up on the signal from the court that its door was open to barristers who wished to think creatively about the Constitution. Among the first movers – inspired by the example pioneer barristers such as Conolly had set in ploughing a lonely furrow since the 1940s, and emboldened by the sweeping changes of the Ó Dálaigh court – was Donal Barrington.

Barrington's father had been a senior civil servant, but his death from pneumonia, when Barrington was two years old, left his mother to look after the five children on her own. There being no pensions for widows at the time, all his mother received was a letter from the government thanking her for the services her husband had rendered to the State and enclosing the balance of his salary for that month. 'We really were as poor as church mice from then on', Barrington later recalled.[9] He was brought up mainly in Dublin but spent a lot of time in Co. Clare, where his uncle had a farm, and went to St Patrick's School in Drumcondra and then Belvedere. 'I suspect – I don't know, because my mother would never tell you a thing like that for fear it would undermine your confidence – that the [Jesuits] never charged any fees for me, and I am grateful to them for my education.' At Belvedere he threw himself into debating in Irish and English and had the first inkling that he would like to be a barrister. When he came home and told his mother about the idea she professed to be delighted, but in retrospect he thought her heart probably sank. The family had no connections at the Bar, after all.

Barrington immersed himself in student life in UCD in the late 1940s. As the law lectures all ended by 11am, he would wander into lectures on all sorts of subjects – the French Revolution, the Abbey theatre, the history of political thought. He was hugely impressed and influenced by some of his lecturers: Michael Tierney on Greek civilization, Canon O'Keeffe on political theory and George O'Brien on economics.

> I remember, in the first week in second year, walking through Iveagh Gardens and hearing this voice behind me. 'Mr Barrington, Mr Barrington.' I turned around and there's my professor [George O'Brien]. Firstly, amazingly, he knew my name. Secondly, he said, 'Mr Barrington, I'm having a few friends in for a glass of sherry on Sunday and I'd be delighted if you could join us.' I was doubly stunned by this. I said, 'Of course, yes.' I was reading a book, Somerset Maugham's *Cakes and Ale*, which I thought was quite a risky book, having been brought up in Catholic Ireland. I was kind of holding it behind me, and George said, 'What book have you there?' I gave it to him shyly.

He looked at it and he said, 'Oh Mr Barrington, I wish I were young again and reading *Cakes and Ale*.' That was part of my education. It made such an impact.

If Barrington's mother was worried that the family's lack of connections would hold her son back in the law, his early days in the Four Courts would have done little to allay her concerns. Barrington was one of nine people called to the Bar on the same day in 1951. After they went into the library, each of the other eight was called almost immediately and given a complementary brief by his father or his uncle or a relative who was a solicitor. Barrington got nothing. 'I realized then for the first time that I was up against it. I sat in the law library for fifteen months before I got a brief', he recalled.[10] His first piece of work came from a close friend and colleague, John Cassidy, who had two cases on the same day, so passed one of them – an alcohol licensing case – on to Barrington. The judge was George Shannon, a stiff man with a fearsome reputation. When the other barristers stood up and announced their presence at the start of the hearing, Barrington lost his nerve and said nothing. So after a few minutes he scribbled a little note for the judge, saying who he was and who he was appearing for. The judge took the note, tore it up and threw it in the waste-paper bin. Ultimately, however, the case worked out well for Barrington. His opposite number was Billy FitzGerald, who was one of the most senior and successful barristers in the law library at the time. In the closing stages of the case, Barrington found a point that FitzGerald had missed. It swung the case in his favour and eventually the judge ruled against FitzGerald's side. The incident caused a stir in the Four Courts.

As he was trying to stake out a place for himself in the law library, Barrington was slowly rising to prominence beyond the Four Courts through his role as a founding member of the study group Tuairim. Established in 1954 by a group of recent university graduates, Tuairim was a reaction against the intellectually calcified atmosphere of the mid-1950s, where the economy was stagnant, politics was still haunted by the Civil War and society was being hollowed out by the ceaseless outward flow of people of their own generation. The year before

Tuairim was set up, the American Jesuit John A. O'Brien published a collection of essays under the title *The Vanishing Irish: The Enigma of the Modern World*. It argued that Ireland's depopulation was unprecedented, inexplicable and could well result in the country ceasing to exist as a political entity.

'Our idea was to look at Irish society, which was doing so badly in the 1950s, and to make suggestions', recalled Barrington.[11] The founders set a maximum age limit of forty for membership and attracted a wide range of young people who would go on to be leading figures in politics (Garret FitzGerald, Brian Lenihan, Michael D. Higgins), the law (Barrington, Ronan Keane, John Kelly), business (Miriam Hederman, Con Smith), trade unionism (Charlie McCarthy), science (Frank Winder) and other fields.

Attempting to carve out a place in what Tomás Finn calls 'the market of ideas', Tuairim wrote papers and pamphlets challenging orthodoxies on subjects as diverse as education, partition, childcare, censorship, economic policy, Ireland's role in the United Nations and the controversial relocation of UCD from Earlsfort Terrace to Belfield.[12] It may have sacrificed some of its radicalism by what John Horgan has called its 'unrealistic yearnings for political consensus', but in many areas Tuairim was far ahead of its time. It opposed censorship and suggested the creation of an Ombudsman's office long before either idea was acted on.

Tuairim's far-sighted proposals on Northern Ireland stand out. In its first pamphlet, 'Uniting Ireland', Barrington, who had connections to Fianna Fáil, set out the prescient argument that the consent of the northern parliament would be essential if unification of the island was ultimately to be achieved. The pamphlet was a strong critique of the capacity of Irish nationalism to transcend religious sectarianism and of Irish politicians and diplomats' failure to foster what de Valera once called a unity of wills in support of unity.[13] Barrington argued that if better relations were to develop in Ireland there would have to be 'self-restraint and sacrifice from the three parties primarily concerned – the Northern Protestants, the Northern Catholics and the South'. The pamphlet made a big impact. It sold 10,000 copies and was reprinted in full in the academic journal

Studies, and in 1969 Fianna Fáil minister Erskine Childers said it had 'changed thinking on the subject and had been an important factor leading to the meetings between [Seán] Lemass and [Terence] O'Neill. Garret FitzGerald later wrote that the pamphlet was "the first major challenge to traditional irredentist anti-partitionism", thus tracing a rethinking of the Southern approach to Northern Ireland to Donal Barrington.'[14]

Tuairim's rising prominence, and Barrington's emergence as a public intellectual, attracted widespread attention. The Department of Justice asked the Special Branch to investigate the group, but a branchman who went along to one of the meetings reported back that they were utterly harmless and nothing to worry about. John Charles McQuaid, the powerful Archbishop of Dublin, was not so sure. Concerned that Tuairim was exerting an influence in government, he had someone on the group's committee who would report back to him on its activities, and at one point wrote to the Papal Nuncio saying these young people would need careful watching. Barrington believed that the controversy surrounding Tuairim's pamphlet opposing UCD's move to Belfield, which outraged UCD President Michael Tierney and also took the opposite stance to Archbishop McQuaid, ultimately cost him the position of Chair of Constitutional Law at UCD.[15]

Barrington's first decade at the Bar was a fairly barren period for constitutional innovation, but he watched the ground-breaking changes of the Ó Dálaigh court, which coincided with his having firmly established himself as a barrister, with a keen interest. He had great respect for both Ó Dálaigh and Walsh, and their court's new-found willingness to liberalize aspects of Irish law, assert the importance of human rights and question long-held assumptions about the law and the State tallied with many of the views Barrington had held since the early days of Tuairim. One day Tommy Conolly, whom Barrington regarded as a hero, turned to him and said: 'Brian Walsh is writing the constitutional law of this country.' Barrington could not but approve.

★

While Ó Dálaigh and Walsh's Supreme Court was indeed a liberal driving force on issues such as criminal law and many individual rights questions, that was just part of the story. On key social issues, there were clear limits to how far it was willing to go. That was to become apparent in Donal Barrington's first major constitutional case.

In the late 1950s Kathleen Donnelly, a young woman from Galway, was working as a waitress in a café in Haringey, a borough of north London where a thriving garment industry had drawn thousands of Irish emigrants in the post-war years. Donnelly was in a relationship with the owner of the café, Leon Nicolaou, himself an immigrant who belonged to the burgeoning Greek Cypriot population in the area. They lived together for a few months until, in July 1959, Kathleen's brother came to London and took her back to Ireland.

A short time after returning home, Kathleen found out that she was pregnant. She told Leon, who immediately asked her to marry him. He was about twenty years older than her, but she was willing to marry him, and her parents approved, but only on condition that Nicolaou, who was a member of the Greek Orthodox Church, became a Catholic. He agreed, and Kathleen travelled back to London to be with him. The marriage was delayed while they waited for paperwork, and in the meantime, in February 1960, Kathleen gave birth to a baby girl at a hospital in north London. The parents were registered as Kathleen Sheila Donnelly and Leontis Nicolaou. They named the baby Mary Carmel.

In the weeks after giving birth, Kathleen grew unsettled and depressed. The paperwork that confirmed they were eligible to marry finally came through, but by then she was hesitant about the whole thing. In court many years later, Leon would say he had been willing to look after the child if Kathleen wanted to return to Ireland. He said he was also willing to accept it, albeit reluctantly, if she wanted to return home to Ireland with the baby, hoping that she would come back to London when she felt better. Meanwhile, back in Galway, her mother was urging Kathleen either to marry Leon or else leave him and have their child put up for adoption. Leon was firmly against adoption, he said.

When she filed an affidavit in the High Court in Dublin four years later, Kathleen said that at the time she was worried about the child being illegitimate. She was not prepared to marry Leon unless and until he became a Catholic, and she was not willing to leave the child with him for fear that she would not be brought up as a Catholic. She decided that she should go to a 'Catholic home', where she could work to keep herself and the child, so she made contact with the Crusade of Rescue, a London-based adoption organization, which put her in touch with the Catholic Protection and Rescue Society, on South Anne Street in Dublin. The society specialized in bringing young Irish women back to Ireland so as to ensure their babies did not fall into non-Catholic hands. It was officially designated by Archbishop McQuaid, on his accession to the Catholic See of Dublin in 1941, to operate a repatriation programme for Irish mothers of 'illegitimate' children.[16]

Having told Leon of her plan, Kathleen packed her bags and left for Dublin with Mary Carmel. Leon did not try to stand in her way. Later he would say that he understood she was going to live in an institution in Ireland and that he thought it was essential that the child be with its mother. In any event, he said, he thought the child could not be adopted without his consent.

Back in Ireland, Kathleen was admitted with Mary Carmel to St Patrick's Mother and Baby Home, a municipally funded institution run by the Sisters of Charity of St Vincent de Paul on the Navan Road in Dublin, where she spent a few months working for her own and the child's maintenance.

In the middle decades of the twentieth century thousands of women passed through St Patrick's, or St Pat's as it was known, a home that provided food and shelter to unmarried women before and after their babies were born. Among similar religious-run institutions, as journalist Mike Milotte points out, St Pat's was known in particular for two things. First, it was the only home of its kind that would take in a woman who became pregnant out of marriage a second time – 'second offenders' as Fr Cecil Barrett, who was head of the Catholic Protection and Rescue Society, put it in 1952.[17] Elsewhere, they were simply turned away. Second, St Pat's had a reputation for exceptional harshness. It was also centrally involved, as were many Mother and Baby Homes across the country, in the practice of sending the children of unmarried mothers to the United States for adoption. The nuns at St Pat's sent more than 250 children to the US from the 1940s to the 1970s.

Kathleen Donnelly had asked the society to try and find a home for Mary Carmel, and within a few months they had identified a couple who wanted to adopt. In September 1960 Kathleen brought seven-month-old Mary Carmel to the office on South Anne Street and left the baby with staff there.

In July, having heard nothing from Kathleen for a while, Leon wrote to her mother in Galway to ask for news. The following month Kathleen replied, saying that she thought she had made it clear that it was all over between them. He should forget about her and the child and start a new life for himself. In the letter she told Leon that, while he was Mary Carmel's father, she could not leave the child with him for fear that she might not be reared a Catholic. If he had any 'plans with regard to the child's future' – as the Supreme Court later paraphrased Kathleen's words – he should let her know before she got the child adopted as that would mean the baby would not be his any more. Leon did not reply to the letter, but towards the end of September he turned up at the house in Galway and asked Kathleen where the baby was. She had given her away, Kathleen said.

Nicolaou returned to Dublin, where he immediately contacted a solicitor, John Redmond. On his client's instructions, Redmond wrote to Kathleen to say that unless she replied within seven days and was willing to return the child to the father he would take legal action in the High Court to compel her to do so. Kathleen wrote back to say she had written to Nicolaou about the adoption during the summer but that he had not replied. She said the Catholic Protection and Rescue Society had found a good home for the child and that the adoption would be legally finalized within six months. Redmond then wrote to An Bord Uchtála – the adoption board – to say that he had been instructed to initiate legal proceedings to block any adoption and that it should take no further steps pending the outcome in the High Court. The board wrote back merely to say the matter had been noted.

Leon did not act on the threat of legal action. But as all of this was going on Kathleen was still seriously upset about the whole situation. Some time towards the end of 1960 or early 1961, she suffered a nervous breakdown and spent ten or eleven weeks under treatment in Ballinasloe Mental Hospital. She had no contact with Leon until later that year, when they began to write to one another again. But by then the adoption board had formally made the order for the adoption of Mary Carmel by a married couple in Dublin.

In the following months Leon and Kathleen began writing love letters to one another. The correspondence went on for more than two years. From time to time she would ask him for money and he would put some notes in an envelope for her. In the spring of 1963, and again in the summer, Kathleen had spells of treatment in the Ballinasloe hospital. And in August she returned to London and took up her old job as a waitress in the café in Haringey. Arrangements were made for the couple to marry. But not long after that, Kathleen grew upset again and told Leon she could not go through with it. It was around this time that Leon learned definitively that Mary Carmel had been adopted.

He made various unsuccessful attempts to find out where the child was and eventually instructed his solicitor, Redmond, to take a legal challenge against the adoption board in Dublin. And so began a chain of events that led all the way to the Supreme Court.

Redmond briefed the barristers John Cassidy and Donal Barrington, young rising stars at the time, to argue the case in the High Court. When they read the material and learned that the adoption board had not informed Nicolaou that the child had been adopted, let alone sought his consent, they thought it was outrageous. All the more so since the board did not dispute any of the facts as set out by Nicolaou. Its case was simply this: it doesn't matter that we didn't tell Nicolaou because he had no right to know. Yet almost as soon as the case opened before a three-judge High Court, it started to go against Nicolaou. The three judges – George Murnaghan, Séamus Henchy and Tommy Teevan – seemed to have doubts about his version of events. Murnaghan appeared quite quickly to form the view that there was something fishy about the case, some truth that had not emerged.

At this point Nicolaou's legal team only knew about a small number of letters that had passed between him and Donnelly. When Murnaghan asked to see one particular letter, Barrington initially agreed – only to be told by Cassidy, his own partner in the case, that they could not do that. The problem, unbeknown to the court, was that Donnelly had agreed to swear an affidavit saying Nicolaou was the father of the child, but only on condition that she would not have to come to court – a prospect that terrified her. So Cassidy and Barrington found themselves in the awkward position of having to refuse to show the court any letters that had passed between Nicolaou and Donnelly. To do so, as they knew, would have meant that Donnelly would be called to give evidence and they had no intention of putting her through that. The letter would perhaps not have changed all that much, as the facts were not in dispute between the two sides, but it only seemed to add to the judges' suspicions that there was something amiss. The refusal to hand over the letter torpedoed the case. The judges were furious with the two barristers. Cassidy and Barrington were beaten around the court for a few days before Nicolaou's case was rejected.

Not only did Nicolaou lose, however. He case was torn apart by the judges. At one point in the judgment Murnaghan writes that Nicolaou 'deposed that he is the natural father of the infant' – apparently implying that paternity was in doubt, even though the birth certificate showed he was the father and nobody in the case disputed this. Murnaghan called one of Nicolaou's statements 'evasive, tendentious and misleading' and zoned in on the legal team's 'flat refusal' to reveal the letter despite the court asking for it. He wrote:

> One can only conclude that the contents of the letter are damaging to [Nicolaou's] case. One is tempted to speculate as to what attitude was adopted or what matters were disclosed by Miss Donnelly in that letter which [Nicolaou] considers to be so harmful to his case that he is prepared to flout the wish of the Court to see a copy of the letter.

Nicolaou's lawyers were convinced they had been wronged and immediately lodged an appeal to the Supreme Court. But before the hearing was due to take place, they did some investigating of their

own. Badly stung by the treatment they had received in the High
Court, the three lawyers – Redmond, Cassidy and Barrington –
decided to travel to London to check Nicolaou's version of events for
themselves. In London they consulted all the records and found that
everything Nicolaou had told them stood up. Around lunchtime
they turned up at Nicolaou's little café in Haringey. Nicolaou, who
was hard at work, was amazed to see them. Over lunch they asked
him whether he had anything else that might cast any light on his
case. 'I have some letters', he said. He went upstairs and returned with
a huge stack of paper. The lawyers were amazed by what the letters
contained. Above all it was the tone that struck them: these were
clearly love letters, and a huge volume of them, that had passed
between the pair for more than two years after their daughter's adoption. They learned all about the money being sent to Donnelly in
Galway. There were also friendly, confidential letters from Kathleen's
mother to Nicolaou in which she told him she could not understand
why her daughter would not marry him.

It was freezing in Dublin in mid-November 1965, and the heating
in the Supreme Court was broken, so Nicolaou's appeal began with
the judges – Cearbhall Ó Dálaigh, Cahir Davitt, Cecil Lavery, Kevin
Haugh and Brian Walsh – wrapped in blankets. Cassidy and Barrington were still so angry about the High Court judgment that they
departed from the usual practice by refusing to read it out at the outset, Barrington even telling the court that he would prefer to talk
about the essence of the case rather than 'detain the court with matters
which should not have happened'. Haugh in particular seemed shocked
by that. Nicolaou's lawyers were so preoccupied with the treatment
they had received in the lower court that, at one point, Lavery told
them to take a deep breath: they would get a fair hearing.

Both sides did get a fair hearing, but it was clear in court that the
judges were uneasy that three High Court judges had for some reason
decided that this was a fishy case. 'There was this lingering doubt
in [their] mind', as one participant puts it. 'Could three High Court
judges possibly be so wrong?' The judges were perfectly polite and
civil, but it wasn't looking good for Nicolaou.

At the very end of the case, after almost ten days of argument,

Barrington rolled the dice for a final time. He stood up and asked Ó Dálaigh whether his side could produce further evidence – the correspondence between Kathleen and Leon. They had no right to have new evidence considered, as they had refused point-blank to produce it in the High Court, but Ó Dálaigh allowed them to submit the material. So Nicolaou's lawyers approached the bench and handed the judges an enormous affidavit containing the love letters they had discovered in London. The court adjourned so the judges could retire to read the material.

When they returned, the mood had changed completely. Clearly what the judges had read had made a big impression. Their new insight into the relationship between Kathleen and Leon seemed to have softened their stance. For a while Nicolaou's team started to think that they might even win.

But they were wrong.

The nub of the case, as argued by Nicolaou's legal team, was that the Adoption Act 1952, which had made adoption legal and regulated it for the first time, was unconstitutional because it allowed the authorities to make an adoption order without hearing the view of the child's natural father. The act made clear that several other people's opinions could be heard – including those of the mother, the guardian, the person who had charge of the child, a relative or a priest – but if the adoption board chose to hear the natural, unmarried father, that was at its own discretion.

Central to Leon Nicolaou's case was Article 40.1 – the so-called equality clause of the Constitution – which states: 'All citizens shall, as human persons, be held equal before the law.' His lawyers had argued that the Adoption Act infringed that clause because it discriminated against natural fathers by not giving them any entitlement to be heard in the adoption process. In 1965 this was a novel argument: the Supreme Court had barely, if ever, been invited to explore the equality clause and interpret what it meant.

On this occasion the Supreme Court followed the High Court's thinking and side-stepped the constitutional issue entirely. Upholding the constitutionality of the law, the court found that there was no question of Nicolaou's personal rights being infringed. The law was clear: a natural father was not necessarily entitled to be heard prior to the making of an adoption order. That was fine, because the equality clause did not 'envisage or guarantee equal measure in all things', it found. Delivering the judgment on behalf of the court, Walsh wrote:

> When it is considered that an illegitimate child may be begotten by an act of rape, by a callous seduction or by an act of casual commerce by a man with a woman, as well as by the association of a man with a woman in making a common home without marriage in circumstances approximating to those of married life, and that, except in the latter instance, it is rare for a natural father to take any interest in his offspring, it is not difficult to appreciate the difference in moral capacity and social function between the natural father and the several persons described [in the act] as having a right to be heard by the adoption board.[18]

The Nicolaou decision is one of the worst the Supreme Court has ever made. It was partly a product of its time, yet it was also true that there were voices, as far back as the mid-1950s, when the Adoption Act became law, that had queried the constitutionality of denying a natural father a right to be heard. In other areas, the court showed imagination and flair. Not here. The constitutional scholar John Kelly, in a book published just a year after the decision, restricted himself to calling it 'disappointing' but gave a searing critique of the reasoning in both the High and Supreme Court.[19]

Today, the circumstances that gave rise to the case are forgotten. It is primarily remembered as the case in which the Supreme Court spelled out that the family under the Constitution was grounded in marriage – a ruling that remains the law. In 1998, after the European Court of Human Rights ruled against Ireland over its failure to protect natural fathers' rights, the adoption law was overhauled.

Yet the Nicolaou case did reveal an important aspect of the court's personality in the 1960s. While the Ó Dálaigh court was groundbreaking in its approach to civil liberties, and took a broadly liberal stance on criminal law and other issues, it was much slower to move on moral or social questions, where its position was conservative. Perhaps if Nicolaou had taken his case a decade later, he would have won. But in 1965, as a participant in the case now remarks, 'it was just too soon'.

Redmond, Cassidy and Barrington were left badly bruised by the experience, and felt their reputations had been traduced. In the long run it did them no real harm; they would go on to have stellar careers. Shortly after the Supreme Court decision, a young barrister named Paul Carney – the same Paul Carney who would become Ireland's best-known criminal law judge later in the century – was called in to see Ó Dálaigh in his chambers. The Chief Justice and the nervous young barrister were chatting away until Ó Dálaigh got around to asking who Carney was 'devilling' with – a barristers' term for a type of apprenticeship. Carney told him he was devilling for Donal Barrington. 'Well,' Ó Dálaigh told him, 'if you're talking to Mr Barrington, you might tell him that we here would like to see him in again shortly, wearing a silk gown.' Ó Dálaigh was telling Barrington he should become a senior counsel and indicating that he had a bright future. Obviously he and his colleagues on the Nicolaou case should consider their reputations fully vindicated.*

Not that any of that was of much help to Leon Nicolaou, whose long legal battle had come to an unsuccessful end. By the time the Supreme Court decided the case, his daughter was five years old. He hoped, somehow, that he would meet her some day.

Sitting in a café in Dublin half a century on, the spring sunshine streaking through the windows, Mary Carmel cups her mug with two hands as she recounts the fragments of a story she has spent so

---

* Thirty years later, in 1996, Barrington was a Supreme Court judge when an adoption case known as *W. O'R v. EH* presented the court with a perfect opportunity to overturn the Nicolaou decision. Acknowledging in his judgment that he had acted for Leon Nicolaou in the original case, Barrington said that the reasoning in *Nicolaou* was 'fundamentally flawed' and that it was not possible 'to develop a coherent code of rights in relation to non-marital children and their parents while that reasoning stands'. Yet none of Barrington's colleagues on the court – Liam Hamilton, Hugh O'Flaherty, Susan Denham or Frank Murphy – was willing to overturn the original decision, so Barrington dissented alone. *W. O'R v. EH* [1996] 2 IR 248.

many years trying to assemble. A warm and friendly 56-year-old, with blonde hair, sallow skin and an infectious appetite for life, Mary Carmel beams as she shares the photographs of her two beautiful daughters on her iPad. She flicks through some of her own childhood photographs, reflecting on a saga that still feels every bit as sad and mystifying as it did when she first learned about it as a child. As she takes up the story, she speaks wistfully, pausing occasionally to pick up the thread.

When Kathleen gave her up for adoption, Mary Carmel was taken in by a warm and loving couple in Dublin. Her childhood was 'fantastic', she says, and her home was filled with love and affection. At first they lived in a one-room tenement, but as the family grew – the couple had a son whom they had also adopted – they gained a second room and then a third. She grew up in a close-knit community and she had good friends and neighbours who looked out for her like she was one of their own.

Their parents told Mary Carmel and her brother at a young age that they were adopted, but in her early years she knew virtually nothing about her birth parents and the landmark legal battle her adoption had set off. All of that changed when she was around twelve years old, when her brother went rifling through a wardrobe and found a stack of old letters. There were lots of them, all addressed directly to Mary Carmel, each one dating from the late 1960s and early '70s and signed not with a name but with a distinctive star-shaped symbol. Slowly she draws the symbol: four slanted, crisscrossing lines bisected by a single, thicker line with a semi-loop at the tail.

They were the affectionate letters of a father to a daughter. In them, Leon would tell Mary Carmel about his life, his background, and his fervent hopes of seeing her one day. The last one, dated 1973, told the girl her cousins in Cyprus were dying to see her.

Mary Carmel had never received the letters – she thinks it likely that her adoptive parents, who are now dead, thought it would be too difficult for her – and reading them came as a shock. Slowly, vague memories began to make sense. As a young child there had been a mysterious man who would stand near the schoolyard or near the house now and then. It worried her adoptive parents so much at the time that they called the gardaí, and for a time she would be accompanied to school every day by two officers. The man approached her once, when she was at a school sports day in the park. 'He called me over and whispered in my ear. My aunt, who was with me, ran over and took me by the hand and had words with him. She asked me what he said. I didn't understand at the time. I told her he said: "You are my Madonna. You are my Madonna."'

After a while he stopped appearing. Later she learned that the authorities had intervened somehow to keep him away. 'I think he had become obsessed', she says softly. She would also find out that her adoptive father ('a softie') gave Leon some photographs, including one of her on the day of her First Communion.

The more she knew, the more the pieces began to fit together. She recalled how one Christmas a parcel arrived with her name on it. She was just about old enough to recognize her name, so she grabbed it the minute it landed in the house. Inside was a beautiful silver-and-blue book that told the story of the Nativity. The accompanying letter had this strange squiggle at the end of it. She had no idea who had sent it, and she didn't give it much thought at the time.

She also recalled in a new light an incident that occurred when she was around seven or eight, when her Dad went downstairs and came back up with a visitor, a young woman – she thought of her as a girl at the time – who had brought her a box of sweets. Her adoptive mother introduced the woman, saying, 'This is your friend, she's from England.' The visitor sat down and asked Mary Carmel about school and how she was getting on. Mary Carmel didn't pay that much attention; she was focused on the gift. She remembers the brand – Weekend chocolates. 'It was her. I had no idea who she was at the time.'

In the early 1990s, when she had reached her thirties, Mary Carmel decided to try and find her birth mother. At the records office a staff member took out her file. On top of all the papers was a Christmas card addressed to Mary Carmel. Her mother had left it there in 1960 in case her daughter ever tried to find her.

When mother and daughter finally came face to face later that year, 'It was like we knew each other. She was beautiful, so lovely . . .

It was like a dream. We just sat down and started talking. She told me she loved Doris Day, and so did I. So she started singing a Doris Day song, and I joined in, there in the office.' She pauses for a moment, savouring the memory.

Kathleen and Mary Carmel got to know each other well. They would meet in a café outside Dublin – Kathleen never liked coming to Dublin, she told Mary Carmel, because it reminded her of coming to the city to give her daughter away – and they would talk and talk. They write to each other regularly. The ring Mary Carmel wears on her right hand – a gift from her birth mother – originally belonged to Kathleen's grandmother and has been passed through the generations of women in the family. She takes out a photo of the two of them together, Kathleen clasping her long-lost daughter tightly to her side. Only a week ago, she says, Kathleen phoned and sang her Happy Birthday down the line. 'She said she always thought I'd blame her for it all', she says. 'She was terrified that I wouldn't forgive her.'

Mary Carmel did not blame anyone. And the more she got to know Kathleen, the more she wondered about Leon. Kathleen did not like talking about those difficult times and tended to steer the conversation to other topics. But she filled Mary Carmel in on some things: that she never had another child, that she married later in life but that her husband died after a few years, that it was Leon who gave her the adoptive family's address in Dublin that time she came with the chocolates. She also told Mary Carmel that, when they were in St Patrick's Mother and Baby Home, the authorities there told her that they had found a couple in the United States who would like to adopt her baby. Kathleen refused; she wanted her daughter to remain in Ireland.

Of Leon, Kathleen said very little. One day, a few years ago, mother and daughter were sitting in the summer sunshine together, relaxed and momentarily silent in each other's company. Out of the blue, Kathleen said: 'His birthday is January 14th 1918.' 'I said, "Who?" She said, "Leon." . . . I think she loved him.'

Mary Carmel has spent years trying to find her birth father. She has contacted the Cypriot embassy in London, Cypriot emigrant associations and the owners of the premises where Nicolaou once ran his café. All to no avail. 'I have no anger towards him. It was a sad and difficult time for both of them.' He would be well over ninety now, and she thinks it unlikely that he is still alive. 'For years it was about meeting him. Now I just want to know where he is, where he lies.'

For years the Supreme Court judgment contained the sum total of Mary Carmel's knowledge about her origins. Those pages of dense legalese make for tough reading. 'I thought it was shocking, I really did.' Still, every so often she dips into it and reads a few paragraphs. And as she reads and re-reads she thinks to herself, 'My God, what did they go through?'

7. In the government's sights

'It would be a brave man who would predict, these days,
what was or was not contrary to the Constitution'

Jack Lynch

Of all the claims that could be made for the Irish judiciary in the decades after the enactment of the Constitution, diversity was not one of them. The typical judge appointed between 1937 and 1969 was male, Catholic, came from Dublin, had been to UCD, had one or more lawyers in his family and described himself as a liberal with a middle- or upper-middle-class background. His first self-supporting job was as a barrister or solicitor, and he was almost certainly a politically active member of Fianna Fáil at the time of his appointment. While he still sympathized with the party while on the bench, if not quite as enthusiastically as before, he was convinced he had been appointed solely because of his professional standing.

The trend held in the Supreme Court, where, of the nine judges appointed in that thirty-two-year period, seven were Catholic, five had been affiliated with de Valera's party, eight had lawyers in the family, seven had gone to UCD, six described themselves as upper-middle-class and only two claimed to be ideologically right of centre.

The information, collated by the American academic Paul C. Bartholomew when he visited Dublin in 1969 and carried out anonymous interviews with nearly every serving or retired judge from that period, painted a picture of striking uniformity.[1] Bartholomew noted that while certain criteria had to be met in order to qualify for appointment – for example, appointees to the Supreme, High and Circuit Courts had to be barristers of at least ten years' standing – that did not necessarily mean that the best person available was always selected. Though, he wrote, 'usually those named are of judicial calibre'.[2] Nonetheless, with few exceptions, 'a person named as judge will be one who is favourably regarded by the Government, perhaps out of gratitude for past services either to the party or to the state'. Even in the rare event that someone linked to the opposition party was appointed, 'this may well be for indirect advantage to the Government party in that such a "nonpartisan" appointment projects an image of objectivity to the public'.[3]

Observing a phenomenon that would endure into the twenty-first century, Bartholomew remarked that partisan political considerations were 'almost the only influence' behind District Court appointments, but that usually the role of political allegiance as a factor in appointments reduced the higher up the courts pyramid an appointee went.[4]

At the time that Bartholomew was carrying out his study, Fianna Fáil had been in power for all but five of the previous thirty-eight years. That largely explained the dominance of judges with prior allegiance to the party. The irony, of course, was that the law library was considered a Fine Gael bastion. It was an axiom in the early 1970s that Fianna Fáil were dominant politically but that Fine Gael were always in the ascendancy at the Bar.

While control of judicial appointments was the most obvious effect of Fianna Fáil's long-term possession of the keys to Government Buildings, another – which had a more immediate impact at the law library – was that State briefs tended to be handed out to counsel with party links. Both parties were guilty of it and the practice accentuated the already deep party divisions inside the Four Courts in these years. 'In the 60s and 70s, it was assumed and almost certainly true that State work at the Bar was given out according to political affiliation', says one former barrister who was a Fine Gael member at the time. 'I never got a State brief until the change of government in 1973. Then I got lots.'

There is no way of knowing whether the era of judicial expansionism that began in the 1960s would have taken place, or taken place when it did, had the court been run by Fine Gael appointees. One close observer from the time suggests Ó Dálaigh and Walsh's political and social heritage was critical to what was an essentially nationalist project to de-Anglicize Irish law and create a thriving, indigenous legal system that had the Constitution at its heart. It was no accident, on this analysis, that the little man – the defendant, the convict, the worker wronged by the State – was front and centre of the activist project. 'Both Walsh and Ó Dálaigh had been part of this populist party, Fianna Fáil, which represented the small man, the small farmer, the small shopkeeper, the working class of Dublin', one observer remarks. That was certainly the party's self-image.

There were differences between Fianna Fáil and Fine Gael appointees, but, much like the parties themselves in the latter half of the century, those differences were less ideological than cultural. Fine Gael's legal culture had a greater attachment to the common law, and was more heavily influenced by English case law. Fianna Fáil's was more open to rupture, more sceptical of the reliance on English law and more heavily influenced by the United States and its written constitution. There were judges who confounded those stereotypes, of course. Tom O'Higgins, a former Fine Gael minister and a party man to his core, was Chief Justice in the 1970s, when the court consolidated many of the developments of the previous decade while making landmark advances of its own. But he was a rare example.

While social background and party affiliation were important ingredients in a judge's make-up, neither was necessarily the most useful predictor of an individual's thinking once he joined the court – as Jack Lynch, who would grow increasingly frustrated with the court at a time when it was led by Fianna Fáil appointees, was to discover. In other words, appointments may have been party political but decisions were not.

Although Fianna Fáil appointed every Supreme Court judge in Ó Dálaigh's twelve-year term as Chief Justice, there were serious divisions between them. This was particularly clear from the end of the 1960s, when the retirements of T. C. Kingsmill Moore and Cecil Lavery resulted in an important reconfiguration. From 1969 the court's five members were Ó Dálaigh, Walsh, Frederick Budd,

William ('Billy') FitzGerald and Richard McLoughlin, while the President of the High Court, Andreas O'Keeffe, would occasionally step in as a substitute. As the second-longest-serving judge on the court, Walsh followed court tradition by moving to the chair just to Ó Dálaigh's right.

On some of the major cases in the late 1960s and early '70s, the court broke down 3-2, with Ó Dálaigh and Walsh joined by Budd to form the majority and FitzGerald and McLoughlin, who sat beside each other on the bench, united in a two-man opposition that consistently resisted some of the more sweeping changes. Budd's swing vote therefore put him in a pivotal position between two pairs of colleagues with fundamentally different views of the court's role. Just like his predecessor (and, as it happened, fellow liberal Protestant) Kingsmill Moore, without Budd some of the most important judgments from this era might never have been delivered. He was also strong on technical areas of the law, which made him an even more important ally of Ó Dálaigh and Walsh.

The key figure in the minority was FitzGerald, who had had a hugely successful and lucrative practice at the Bar before going to the bench. He was a 'leg and arm' man – a personal injuries specialist who, it was said, knew the monetary value of every limb in the human body. FitzGerald had a been a member of Fine Gael for many years, and there was widespread surprise when a Fianna Fáil government under Seán Lemass plucked him from the law library to fill one of the two vacancies on the Supreme Court in 1966.[5] FitzGerald seems to have had little interest in constitutional law and his conservative instincts put him in conflict with the more liberal-minded triumvirate of Ó Dálaigh, Walsh and Budd. Given that they formed a majority on the five-member court, FitzGerald's near-default position was to write the dissent.

This division was crystallized by one of the most important cases of the era, known today as *Byrne v. Ireland*. Once again, the circumstances behind the case could scarcely have been more run-of-the-mill.

In September 1965 Kathleen Byrne, a nurse from Kilmacanogue in Co. Wicklow, broke her leg when she fell into a trench dug outside her house by staff from the Department of Posts and Telegraphs, who were laying cables in the area at the time. Byrne's solicitor wrote to the department threatening to sue, but received a dismissive reply pointing out that, in law, the State as an entity could do no wrong and could not be sued. It then offered her £13 10s. towards her medical expenses. The paltry offer infuriated Byrne's solicitor, so he went to the law library and got the barristers Niall McCarthy, Donal Barrington and John Cassidy to agree to come on board and take the case.

A carry-over of the British regime – rooted in the idea that the Crown was sovereign and could do no wrong – was that the State was immune from being sued by one of its citizens. So the idea of suing 'Ireland', put forward by her legal team on Byrne's behalf, was unheard of. In the High Court, Byrne's lawyers argued that the State had no immunity from being sued, and that, like any other legal entity, it could be pursued in the courts for the actions of its employees. 'She Wants to Sue Ireland', was the almost incredulous *Irish Press* headline on its initial report of the High Court proceedings.[6]

But the judge, George Murnaghan, was not only unconvinced. He was hostile. 'He just couldn't grasp this concept of rights that could be enforced in the courts', Barrington later recalled.[7] Barrington spent several days boring Murnaghan about human rights, the rule of law and the State being subject to the courts – ideas the judge clearly had little time for. In the end, not surprisingly, he ruled against Byrne, remarking that he found it difficult to take Barrington's submissions seriously, and then promptly ordered Byrne's side to pay all the costs of the case. Finally, he delivered a wounding *coup de grâce*. 'Mr Barrington', the judge said. Barrington stood up. 'I'd like to inform you that your submissions in this case, by their fortuity, have reduced the High Court to the lowest level it has reached in my time on the bench or at the Bar.' Barrington sat down without saying a word. 'I was almost in tears walking out of court', he later recalled. As he made his way out the door, Barrington was approached by an official from the Chief State Solicitor's office. 'Don't worry, Mr Barrington', he said, 'you'll win in the Supreme Court.'

As it turned out, the official was right. This was an ideal case for the Ó Dálaigh court at that moment. It ticked all the boxes, offering the Supreme Court the opportunity to stand up for the rights of the individual while at the same time taking another big step in its programme to de-Anglicize the Irish legal system.

When Kathleen Byrne appealed Murnaghan's decision to the Supreme Court, she was pushing at an open door. The court duly grabbed the opportunity her case presented.

In a letter he sent to William Brennan in Washington a day after the Supreme Court hearing of the case concluded, Walsh asked his American counterpart for guidance on the situation in the US. 'All this is probably very well trodden ground in your jurisdiction but it is relatively new territory in ours', he wrote.[8] Walsh indicated that, given the references in the US Constitution to the power coming from the people, and other references to the people in the text, 'perhaps the people is the sovereign authority and that the state, being but the creation of the people under the Constitution, cannot claim itself to be the sovereign authority'.[9] This would be a major departure from the legal situation in the US. Since 1899, the US Supreme Court had held to the position that the state was fully entitled to invoke sovereign immunity. Walsh wanted to know about any cases where the issue had arisen. Brennan obliged less than a fortnight later with recommendations for some academic articles on the subject.[10]

When the judgment in the Byrne case was finally delivered, Walsh was emphatic, ruling that blanket immunity for the state was inconsistent with the personal rights guarantees in the Constitution. While the sovereign authority in Britain might be the Crown, he said, in Ireland it was the people.

Walsh was joined by Ó Dálaigh, Budd and O'Keeffe, giving him a clear majority. FitzGerald was appalled by the decision and stood alone against it. In a typically short dissenting judgment, he said the majority's decision to make the state liable to be sued in the courts involved 'such a radical change in the accepted view both of the Courts and of the Legislature that this Court should decline to undertake such a step'.

Walsh himself was immensely proud of his Byrne judgment. Whenever he was asked, later in his life, to pick out one case that he remembered with particular fondness, it was this one. 'That made a big difference', he said twenty years later. 'That was a big breakthrough in the sense that, when it was done, the reaction of most people was, "It's a wonder it wasn't done years ago, it seems so obvious." It has always been resisted by the executive. They'd never admit it.'[11]

'The Byrne case was the legal equivalent of taking the Union Jack down from the mast of the Castle', Colm Tóibín wrote.[12] 'It changed the whole attitude', Barrington later concurred. 'Once the State became a corporation subject to the law, it changed the whole nature of society.'[13]

Throughout the late 1960s and early '70s, Brian Walsh remained in close contact with William Brennan. By now Brennan had emerged as one of the key figures in the Earl Warren court, and he was the chief liberal voice behind a series of landmark majority judgments on criminal procedure, free speech and civil rights. His influence was so pervasive that colleagues nicknamed him 'the deputy chief'. In these years the tone of the correspondence between Walsh and Brennan grew increasingly familiar, and by August 1968, after they had met again at a conference in New York, they dropped the formal 'Mr Justice' and 'Justice' in their correspondence and began to address one another as 'Brian' and 'Bill'.[14]

The flow of information went in both directions. When the Irish court, in a decision written by Walsh, dealt with the question of whether the constitutional guarantees accorded to an adult accused of a crime should be extended to a young accused person,[15] Brennan noticed parallels with a case his court was working on. The American case, taken in the name of a fifteen-year-old named Gerald Gault, resulted in a landmark decision that found that juveniles accused of crimes must be afforded the same due process rights as adults. While the Warren court was working on its decision in early 1967, Brennan wrote to Walsh to ask for a copy of the Irish decision, known as *State (Sheerin) v. Kennedy*. Brennan read it with 'fascinated interest' and felt it had significance for the case he and his colleagues were considering, so he passed it on to his colleague, Justice Abe Fortas, who was writing the decision for the majority. Fortas duly included a reference to the Irish case in his judgment, with which Brennan concurred.[16]

Walsh also turned to Brennan in March 1969, when the Irish court faced a difficult decision on religious discrimination. Feargal Quinn, then managing director of Quinn's supermarkets, took a challenge to a ministerial order that imposed restrictions on butcher shops' trading hours but expressly exempted shops selling kosher meat. The exemption had been inserted in the order to ensure that Jews could buy fresh meat after the end of Sabbath, after sunset on Saturdays. But Quinn, whose meat counters had to close at 6pm because of the order, argued that the differential treatment was unconstitutional in that it amounted to religious discrimination and contravened the equality guarantee in the Constitution.

On 5 June 1969, as he was working on the court's judgment, Walsh wrote to Brennan and confided in him about the dilemma he faced. He asked Brennan if he could recommend any American cases or academic work on the topic. He also asked whether, in Brennan's opinion, the Irish exception for kosher shops would, under the First Amendment of the US Constitution, be regarded as fostering the establishment of the Jewish religion. 'Needless to say, if you choose to express an opinion on this I shall be more than delighted to receive it', he wrote. Brennan could think of no case that directly answered Walsh's question, but he pointed him towards a number of other decisions of his own that addressed the general issues. He signed off by conveying his sympathy to Walsh. 'It's really an agonizing kind of decision to make', he wrote.[17]

Ultimately, in a judgment that quoted extensively and approvingly from a number of Brennan decisions, Walsh found that the exemption went further than was necessary for the protection of religious observance. But he also set down an important principle: discrimination in favour of a specific religion was allowed under the Constitution if it was necessary so as to allow people to practise that religion freely.

By the time Brian Walsh became the second most senior member of the court, in 1969, the speed of reform had eased somewhat after the frenetic pace of the previous eight years. But neither the appetite of the court's majority for radical change nor the unease of the government over what it saw unfolding in the Four Courts abated. 'It would be a brave man who would predict, these days, what was or was not contrary to the Constitution', said a caustic Jack Lynch in the early 1970s. His first term as Taoiseach, from 1966 to 1973, coincided with some of the court's most significant judgments under Ó Dálaigh.

Des O'Malley, who was Minister for Justice under Lynch, says the Taoiseach had real misgivings about the court's increasing prominence:

> The Supreme Court [had been] deferential, kept its distance and kept its mouth shut. It was very conscious of the limitation on its own powers, and in particular was very conscious of the convention that the Supreme Court never wanted to become involved in anything that might even vaguely be described as a policy matter. Policy was not their field.
>
> With the transition that began to take place at that time, led by Ó Dálaigh and Walsh, the Supreme Court began to see itself as a legislative branch and not just a judicial one. And naturally that caused a reaction . . . If the people don't like a policy being put forward by a party, they can vote for other parties. But when the superior courts are making the law, the public can't change it. They can't express their disapproval of it.
>
> The resentment that a very mild and modest man like Lynch felt, which I don't think he ever expressed publicly, was legitimate. It wasn't because they were treading on his personal corner, it was because they were essentially in breach of the separation of powers.

The reservations felt by senior figures in government towards the Supreme Court's expansionism was underlaid by wider misgivings. Some were nonplussed by what they saw as the relaxed work practices in the Four Courts, such as the long summer holiday and relatively short court hours. It was true that being a judge was not the most stressful job, particularly compared to a busy practice in the law library. While the explosion in litigation towards the end of the century stretched court lists and put the judges of the Supreme and High Courts under pressure, a typical member of the bench in the early 1970s could have a relatively relaxed professional life. One barrister who was appointed to the High Court in that decade applied for the job because, by his own admission, he wanted more time to read and write books.

The problem of the lazy judge – the one person in the group who does not carry his share of the workload – has always been a feature of life on the Supreme Court and High Court, with the result that on nearly every court the heavy lifting has fallen disproportionately to certain individuals. On one occasion in the middle of the century the President of the High Court had such trouble getting judgments out of one colleague that he gave him time off to catch up with his writing – only to find out that the judge had gone off to Lord's to watch the cricket instead. On the Ó Dálaigh court, there was one judge who acquired the habit, before going into court in the morning, of cutting out the crossword from the *Times* of London and pasting it into his judges' journal. He would then proceed to do the crossword in court while the innocent barristers assumed he was studiously taking notes on their incisive arguments.

In the early 1970s, the Minister for Justice, Des O'Malley, himself a solicitor who knew the Four Courts well, decided to encourage the King's Inns, where future barristers must study before they can practice, to modernize and improve their legal education. Ireland was about to join the European Economic Community, and O'Malley believed the Inns should put more emphasis on European law, perhaps at the expense of Roman law, which was one of the obligatory courses. He was told that was a matter for the Benchers, an august group that includes judges of the Supreme and High Courts and a number of elected barristers. It took O'Malley ten months to secure a meeting with the Benchers. When he sat down with two of their members, he made his argument that Roman law was becoming less relevant, whereas European law was rapidly growing in importance, and perhaps the Inns should reflect this in their curriculum.

The elder of the two benchers, he said to me, 'I'm not sure, Mr O'Malley, whether or not you're a Latin scholar, but I must point out to you that our motto is *Nolumus Mutari*. If you're not a Latin scholar, I will explain to you that the word *Mutari* can be either a transitive or an intransitive verb. And as far as we are concerned, Mr O'Malley' – he wouldn't call me Minister – 'you can take it either way, because we will neither change nor be changed.'

To some extent, the government's suspicion about the judiciary was reciprocated. Some senior judges felt the politicians had been slow to appreciate the fundamental changes brought about by the 1937 Constitution, in particular that the concept of judicial review and the fundamental rights clauses gave the courts significant powers that the judiciary was duty-bound to use as required. In their eyes, the separation of powers was just as the name suggested – a carefully weighted apportioning of responsibility to the three branches of government – and occasionally that would put each of them in conflict. In addition, they were annoyed that when they made a finding of unconstitutionality the government and the Oireachtas were often slow to enact a replacement law.

Senior figures also had little respect for how politicians had dealt with the death penalty over the years. A number of judges, Walsh included, were fundamentally opposed to capital punishment. Walsh had been junior counsel for the prosecution in the trial for murder of Michael Manning, who was, in April 1954, the last man to be executed in the Republic. He was profoundly affected by the experience and made a point of receiving communion on the morning of the execution.[18] The government had had the power to recommend to the President that a death penalty be commuted, but it did not always use that power. Some judges felt the reasons for not doing so had too often been grounded in politics rather than morality.

Practical concerns were a factor too in the judges' wariness of politicians. Members of the judiciary resented the way they had had to fight for almost a decade to secure the same pay increases as senior civil servants.

When judges met politicians or officials at receptions, meetings or social occasions, they were perfectly friendly and civil to one another. At a personal level many of them got along well. But through the late 1960s and '70s these tensions were simmering beneath the surface. And that left both sides in a somewhat awkward position in

November 1970, when Peter Berry, the secretary of the Department of Justice, initiated a legal action of his own in the High Court.

Berry was a vastly influential figure in government. He had joined the Department of Justice in 1927, at the age of seventeen, and had served under fourteen Ministers for Justice. From 1936 he had been heavily involved in security work and even wrote a number of booklets on the IRA and left-wing organizations that were circulated on a 'top secret' basis to staff and ministers in the department. In the war years the then minister, Gerry Boland, appointed Berry to a special security position, where he coordinated all security information and activity. His appointment as secretary in 1961 made him 'a central cog in the State's security nexus',[19] and the shifts in the government's focus towards security matters after the outbreak of the Troubles put him in an even more influential position. The Garda Commissioner regularly reported directly to Berry, as did the head of the Special Branch.[20]

Given that Berry had been in situ throughout the years of the Ó Dálaigh court – he became department secretary in the same year that Ó Dálaigh was appointed Chief Justice and Brian Walsh joined the court – he had had a close-up view of the fallout from the major criminal law decisions on bail, the use of evidence and other issues – all of which were seen in the department as having curtailed garda powers. As it happened, funding for the operation of the courts was controlled by the Department of Justice.

On 25 September 1970 the *Irish Times* published a photograph showing two demonstrators and a placard. The placard read: 'Peter Berry – 20th Century Felon-Setter – Helped Jail Republicans in England'. The image accompanied a news story about the occupation, the previous day, of the offices of an English company on Grafton Street by fifteen Sinn Féin members. The poster was apparently a reference to two Irishmen who had been sentenced to seven years' imprisonment in Britain after being convicted of taking part in a raid to steal arms.

Berry believed the publication defamed him and decided to sue the *Irish Times*. When the case came to the High Court in April 1971, by which time Berry had taken early retirement, his lawyers argued that he had been the victim of a 'grave libel'. The only witness called was Berry himself. Answering questions from his barrister, Frank Griffin, Berry said he was 'appalled and distressed' when he saw the photograph. 'I cannot think of anything more ugly, more horrible in this life than being called an informer because it is a peculiarly nauseating thing in Irish life', he said. The newspaper argued that the image was a fair and accurate photographic report which was in the public interest and which they had a duty to communicate to the public.

It took the jury just half an hour to reject Berry's claim. The jurors agreed with his view that the photograph suggested he had helped in the jailing of Irish republicans in England, but they did not agree that that was defamatory.

A disappointed Berry duly appealed to the Supreme Court, where, in July 1972, he came face to face with Ó Dálaigh and Walsh, along with Budd, FitzGerald and McLoughlin. Over two days, Berry's side argued that the jury's decision was perverse and contrary to the evidence in the case. They also took issue with the High Court judge's handling of part of the case. The *Irish Times* pushed back, insisting the case had been correctly decided.

The court split 3-2, with Ó Dálaigh, Walsh and Budd dismissing Berry's appeal and FitzGerald and McLoughlin siding with the civil servant. In his judgment for the majority, Ó Dálaigh wrote:

> It is perhaps surprising that the Supreme Court should be asked to hold, as a matter of law, that it is necessarily defamatory to say of one of the citizens of this country that he assisted in the bringing to justice in another country of a fellow countryman who broke the laws of that country and who was tried and convicted for that offence in the ordinary course of the administration of criminal justice. This Court is bound to uphold the rule of law and its decisions must be conditioned by this duty.

Not only was Ó Dálaigh rejecting Berry's appeal, but he was also attacking him for taking it in the first place. In effect Ó Dálaigh was asking this: what was so bad about saying that Berry helped the British authorities arrest people who had committed a crime? After all, his job was to uphold the law. When Ó Dálaigh had finished reading his judgment, Walsh said, 'I agree'. Then Budd said the same.

FitzGerald and McLoughlin were disgusted. They were convinced Berry had a cast-iron case. FitzGerald wrote:

> It appears to me, and I think it would appear to any Irishman of normal experience and intelligence, that the words complained of were clearly a libel. 'Felon-setter' and 'Helped jail republicans in England' were not words in respect of which one has to have recourse to a dictionary to know what they meant to an Irishman; they were equivalent to calling him a traitor. The words are now admittedly untrue. They were a concoction by the author of the placard.

FitzGerald believed a 'gross injustice' had been done to Berry and said the case should be retried. For McLoughlin, the libel was 'beyond all argument'. The words in the photographs suggested that 'this Irishman, the plaintiff, has acted as a spy and informer for the British police concerning republicans in England, thus putting the plaintiff into the same category as the spies and informers of earlier centuries who were regarded with loathing and abomination by all decent people', McLoughlin wrote.

The Berry case was probably the nadir in relations between the court and the Department of Justice in the Ó Dálaigh era. Berry was not the only one to take it badly. 'The department viewed the Supreme Court judgment as being motivated by spite and dislike of Berry, although there was no evidence for this', writes Colm Tóibín. 'After a decade of initiatives by the court, this was the last straw.'[21] Now, the Ó Dálaigh court was in its sights.

Yet while the court's bitter divisions over the Berry case were plain to see from the judgments, there was one important aspect that neither the government nor the public ever knew about. In court on the day the decision was announced, it was Ó Dálaigh who delivered the majority judgment. It has been ascribed to him in the official law reports and in every legal textbook to this day.

But in fact Walsh wrote every word of the judgment. Before they went into court to announce the outcome of the case, Ó Dálaigh approached Walsh and asked him if he could deliver the judgment Walsh had written. Walsh agreed without asking for an explanation. It was only later that he figured out what must have been behind Ó Dálaigh's unusual request.

What Ó Dálaigh knew in July 1972 – but Walsh and the rest of his colleagues on the court did not – was that he was unlikely to be Chief Justice for much longer. By the time the Berry judgment had been delivered, Ó Dálaigh had privately indicated to the government his interest in becoming Ireland's first judge of the European Court in Luxembourg. He knew the Berry judgment would be controversial, and probably felt he had less to lose than Walsh, who would be on the court for many years more and would also be the favourite to replace Ó Dálaigh as Chief Justice when he left.

This was certainly Walsh's interpretation of Ó Dálaigh's actions. In an unpublished letter written in 1989 – a year before he retired from the Supreme Court – Walsh confirmed that he wrote the Berry judgment but that Ó Dálaigh asked to deliver it.

> I did not question his reasons at the time but I feel that perhaps he knew the storm it would cause and that as he was about to leave the Court very shortly to go to Luxembourg perhaps he thought he was saving me from the storm. I surmise this simply in retrospect because at the time I did not know he was going to Luxembourg and I did not question him as to why he wished to read it, but looking back on it now I feel that he did it because he thought in some way he would perhaps protect my future interests.[22]

In his letter, Walsh was at pains to insist that there was nothing personal in the judgment against Berry. The 'whole key to the case' was that no innuendo was pleaded. For example, if Berry's lawyers had pleaded that in some way there was an innuendo to the effect that Berry had acted out of 'base motives', then 'the case might have gone very differently before the jury'. But as it turned out, Walsh wrote,

> because of the way the case was fought the jury rejected the claim that it was libellous to say of a person that he assisted in bringing

law-breakers to justice. It would be expecting a bit much of any
Court much less the Supreme Court to hold that as a matter of law to
say of a person who assists in bringing [law-breakers] to justice that
he has done something which must hold him up to public odium,
ridicule or scorn.

Walsh was also keen to stress that his own relations with Berry
were actually 'quite good, so there was no question of any animus
against him in the mind of the writer of the judgment'. He went on:
'The fact that the plaintiff occupied a very high position in the
administration and in a very sensitive area was not a reason for holding that the words were defamatory, as the test must be what normal
right-minded people would think, not what might be thought in the
law-breaking fraternity.'[23]

On 16 August 1972, just over two weeks after the Berry judgment,
Ó Dálaigh wrote a letter to Walsh from Paris, where he was taking a
French course at the Alliance Française during the legal holiday. That
morning, Ó Dálaigh had found a day-old copy of the *Irish Times*. In
it, to his considerable annoyance, was the news of his imminent
appointment to the Luxembourg court.

'I am sorry that, through no fault of mine, you should not have
heard from me personally of my decision to go to Luxembourg before
the matter was made public', he told Walsh. 'I had stipulated with the
Minister that I should have an opportunity to do this. But however it
happened, it has turned out otherwise. Here in Paris today, I see the
news in a copy of yesterday's *Irish Times* – it was leaked reliably after
a government meeting yesterday.'[24]

Explaining his decision to leave the court after almost twenty
years, eleven of them as Chief Justice, Ó Dálaigh said it was taken
'with reluctance' but that it seemed the right one. 'I have been a member of the Court for too long', he told Walsh. He wrote of the

leadership . . . [which is] called for if the Court is to be held to the
lines which, in recent years, have earned it the respect and trust of
ordinary people.

That is a task which I could not hope to fulfil – at my age and with
my temperament. For the task great patience is needed, backed by

erudition, and it is therefore better, I think, that I should go and that you should remain.[25]

Walsh got the letter in his summer house on Achill island. The following day he wrote back to Ó Dálaigh. The news did not come as a surprise, Walsh wrote, as to him it was 'always clear that you were the only person the Government could ask if they wanted to indicate clearly what importance our country attaches to our entry into the [European] Communities'. But Walsh also struck a wistful tone, knowing that the close alliance between the two men, which was instrumental in effecting a revolution in the law and the place of the courts in society, was about to come to an end.

> I had always looked forward to sitting beside you in the Supreme Court for at least the next ten or eleven years secure in the knowledge that the Court would be led with the integrity, regard for principle, and courtesy which made the first decade of your tenure as C. J. so outstanding and which earned for the Court the high respect which I believe it now enjoys.
>
> I felt another decade of the Ó Dálaigh court could only be for the everlasting benefit of the country. I cannot at all agree with your reference to your age and temperament and patience. I am only too conscious that on many occasions I have put the last virtue to the test and still did not (apparently) exhaust it. Your departure will be a great personal loss to all of us and to the Bar.[26]

The exchange shows the affection the two men held for one another, and the sense Walsh in particular had that they had arrived at the end of an era. 'There is also something I find it easier to write than to speak', Walsh wrote in conclusion:

> That is to thank you for the great pleasure and happiness I have derived for thirty years from your friendship and support both at the Bar and on the Bench and away from the law. In particular I am conscious of the fact that I joined the Supreme Court on the same day as you became Chief Justice and I shall always regard the eleven years as the most satisfying and valuable years of my professional life. With a Chief Justice of a different and less sympathetic temperament things

would have been very different. It is a matter of deep regret to me that our professional paths must now part. As I said earlier I had looked forward to another decade of companionship on the Court. But whatever the next decade holds I shall always be proud to recall, and to be remembered for, being a member of your court for the entire of its period and to have been the only judge who can ever claim that distinction.[27]

The two judges' thoughts naturally turned to the succession, which they knew would have a huge bearing on the future direction of the court they had done so much to re-mould. Ó Dálaigh hoped that Walsh would be made Chief Justice. 'In the interest of the Court, in everyone's interests, I have no doubt how things should be ordered', he wrote, adding that 'in a few years the position will be sufficiently consolidated to leave you free to follow into Europe'.

Walsh was certainly the favourite for the job: he was the senior ordinary member of the court and the pre-eminent constitutional lawyer on the bench. Walsh's feel for politics was sharper than Ó Dálaigh's, however, and he was much less certain that the government would choose him. 'I also have the suspicion,' he told Ó Dálaigh in his letter from Achill, 'that the administration may also avail of the opportunity so to adjust the leadership and the personnel of the Court to reduce the risk of a continuation of the Court's "initiatives" of the past decade.'

Brian Walsh's instincts were correct. The government had no intention of appointing him Chief Justice. And one of the factors working against him was his friendship with Charlie Haughey. Since he had been acquitted of smuggling arms two years earlier, Haughey had been in the political wilderness. That the charges against him were intimately bound up with the events that had then been convulsing Ireland, north and south, made him a controversial figure and toxic for many.

By the autumn of 1972 there was no sign of the turbulence in Northern Ireland abating. What had started in 1968 as a civil rights campaign in reaction to gerrymandering and discrimination against the Catholic/Nationalist minority in areas such as housing and jobs had quickly escalated. Within the year Derry was in turmoil and violence was spreading in Belfast. In the summer of 1969 British soldiers were deployed on the streets of the north after civil rights marches were attacked by the RUC and loyalist crowds. It was estimated that in Belfast, where Catholics came under attack and dozens of homes were burned out, 30 per cent of the Catholic population were displaced.[28]

The aftershocks of the upheaval in the north reverberated south of the border, forcing the government to come up with a coherent response. In August 1969, Jack Lynch gave a televised address to the nation in which he declared that the government could 'no longer stand by and see innocent people injured and perhaps worse'. Lynch said the Stormont government was no longer in control of the situation and that 'the reunification of the national territory can provide the only permanent solution for the problem'. He called for negotiations with London about the future of the Northern state and for the intervention of the United Nations to keep the peace.[29]

The northern crisis set off convulsions in Fianna Fáil. As Diarmaid Ferriter points out, Lynch was 'caught between the opposing poles of the Fianna Fáil party: hardline and emotional or caustic and realistic'.[30] The tensions within the party hit the national consciousness in sensational fashion when, in early May 1970, Neil Blaney, Minister for Agriculture, and Haughey, Minister for Finance, were sacked over an alleged plot to arm Northern nationalists. Three weeks later Haughey was arrested and charged with conspiracy to import arms and being party to a plot to use State money to arm the IRA.

Haughey was arrested at his mansion, Abbeville, in Kinsealy, north Dublin. Not long after the arrest, senior figures in government were told that Brian Walsh had been at the house when gardaí arrived. An explanation that Walsh was simply returning a book did the rounds (and is still mentioned in legal circles). But for a number of people in government, including Lynch, the story confirmed their sense that Walsh was too close to Haughey, who had long been one of his chief rivals in the party.

Blaney, Haughey, an army captain, James Kelly, and a Belgian businessman, Albert Luykx, went on trial in September before the President of the High Court, Andreas O'Keeffe, but the case collapsed after a week when the judge took exception to comments made about him by the barrister Ernest Wood, discharged himself and aborted the trial.

Fellow High Court judge Séamus Henchy and his wife, Averil, had just arrived home after a holiday in Tenerife when the phone rang. It was O'Keeffe wanting to know if Henchy would be willing to preside at a new trial. Henchy agreed and within a few days gardaí had arrived at his home in Foxrock to build a garden hut that was to serve as a base for a twenty-four-hour security detail.

The retrial took place in October amid saturation media coverage. In his summing up to the jury, Henchy said there was an irreconcilable conflict in testimony between Haughey and another government minister, Jim Gibbons, and made it clear that one of the two men must have been lying. Haughey was acquitted, but Henchy's observation was damaging to Haughey and continually rehearsed by political opponents in the years after.[31]

In 1980 suggestions that there was unease among officials about Walsh's relationship with Haughey in the early 1970s came from a sensational source. In December that year the current affairs magazine *Magill* published the memoirs of Peter Berry, who had died two years previously. Berry had written these after his retirement but had drawn, he said, on diaries and notes he kept during his long career in the Department of Justice. They contained explosive revelations about the build-up to the Arms Trial and the relationships between Haughey, Lynch, O'Malley and the Department of Justice. An entry dated 7 September 1970 – two weeks before Haughey and his co-accused went on trial – contained the following:

> On September 7, 1970, the Minister [O'Malley] arrived off holiday in the afternoon and asked me to brief him up-to-date on what had gone on. Amongst other things I told him that Mr. Haughey had visited Mr. Justice Brian Walsh at Achill on Saturday and that earlier in the week he had been at Tralee races where he had been observed in the company of a Minister which had given rise to police comment. I named Mr. [Brian] Lenihan at his request.

When *Magill* hit the news stands, its editor, Vincent Browne, received a phone call from Walsh, who was still a member of the Supreme Court. Walsh told Browne he had libelled him very seriously. What did Walsh want him to do? Browne asked. Walsh wanted two things: a correction and a commitment that he would not publish it again. Browne agreed.★

The perceived relationship with Haughey put paid to Walsh's chances, slim as they were, of becoming Chief Justice. But there were other reasons for overlooking him. There was ministers' ongoing exasperation about some of the court's decisions on criminal law in the previous decade, which they felt elevated the rights of defendants above the necessity for the State and the security services to find, prosecute and convict criminals. Though it had been delivered years earlier, Jack Lynch was still particularly incensed by the court's judgment in the O'Callaghan case: to him it was ridiculous that an individual could not be denied bail on the ground that he might commit a crime while awaiting trial. At a dinner in the early 1970s, he confided to one person his view that the bail decision showed a lack of common sense. 'That doesn't mean that's why he did it,' the person says, referring to Lynch's decision not to promote Walsh, 'but that's the reason he gave for it.'

That sense of irritation over judgments that seemed to impose constraints on the gardaí was heightened by the onset of the Troubles, which the government regarded as a major threat to the security of the State. Des O'Malley says the period from the mid-1960s onwards was 'a watershed time in judicial-legislative relations':

★ Several years later, however, by which time Browne was editor of the *Sunday Tribune*, the paper published an extract from the Berry papers that included the very same sentence about Haughey visiting Walsh in Achill just weeks before the Arms Trial. Browne had completely forgotten about his conversation with the judge years earlier. After publication, Walsh again phoned Browne. 'You've done it again!' he said. At first Browne did not understand what Walsh was saying, so he picked up a copy and scanned the articles. 'Oh Jaysus', Browne thought. What should he do? Browne asked the judge. Walsh's demand was the same as the last time: correct it and don't do it again.

That was a time when one would hope that senior judicial people would become more cognisant of the need to protect the citizens of the State and its institutions, and less cognisant of individual personal rights. But it became evident from judgments that were being given by the courts [that it] was almost certain that the steps one took in protection of the common good and the public welfare would be found to be unconstitutional. So that caused a lot of anxiety.

Ó Dálaigh's departure, which coincided with Richard McLoughlin's death, finally gave Merrion Street the opportunity it had been waiting for to re-orient the court. Yet while Walsh's scepticism about his own chances of succeeding Ó Dálaigh turned out to be justified, neither he nor anyone else could have predicted that the government would opt to appoint Billy FitzGerald as Chief Justice.

FitzGerald had had a stellar career as a barrister. He was, Ronan Keane writes, 'a particularly devastating cross-examiner notable for a much envied ability to catch witnesses off guard with a series of staccato questions delivered in a rasping voice'.[32] But FitzGerald made much less of a mark as a judge. He had made little impression since his surprise elevation directly from the law library in 1966, giving no significant judgments and showing scant interest in the Constitution. He was appalled by the more radical departures of the majority formed by Ó Dálaigh, Walsh and Budd, and was most notable for writing judgments that registered his disgust at the direction of the court.

Lynch's decision to promote FitzGerald in 1972 was greeted with mystification. But to those close to Lynch it made a lot of sense. FitzGerald may have been a Fine Gaeler, but he was also a fellow Corkman. When Lynch was a young barrister he had known him; they had played golf together, and Lynch held him in high esteem personally. 'He was seen as someone who was a very businesslike individual', says one political source from the time. But the purpose was clearly to dampen the court's expansionist ardour. 'They appointed FitzGerald as Chief Justice because he was seen as a safe pair of hands', says another high-ranking government figure. 'Judges should be careful not to overstretch their position. It's one thing to put a check on government. It's another thing to be creating whole new branches of rights.'

While promoting FitzGerald, Lynch used the vacancies left by Ó Dálaigh's departure to Europe and McLoughlin's death to appoint Séamus Henchy and Frank Griffin, two High Court judges who had Fianna Fáil links but were regarded as solid and not much given to constitutional adventurism.

As a result of all the changes, the government was convinced its concerns had been addressed. As ministers saw it, Walsh and Budd would be in a minority and FitzGerald would preside over a quieter, more responsible court. They could scarcely have been more wrong.

Cearbhall Ó Dálaigh's tenure in Luxembourg would turn out to be short-lived. After the sudden death of the President of Ireland, Erskine Childers, in November 1974, the political parties – their finances depleted after a general election and a presidential election in the previous year – agreed that if Ó Dálaigh was willing to accept the office, he should be put forward as an unopposed candidate. He was duly inaugurated as President that December.

Just two years later Ó Dálaigh's presidency came to an abrupt end. In 1976 he used one of the few powers the President has by referring to the Supreme Court for review a new Emergency Powers Bill that gave the authorities the ability to detain suspects for up to seven days without charge. The court upheld its constitutionality. Subsequently, at an army function in Mullingar, Minister for Defence Patrick Donegan criticized Ó Dálaigh for the referral and described him as 'a thundering disgrace'.

Ó Dálaigh was incensed by the criticism and wrote a strongly worded letter of protest. He duly received an apology from Donegan, but he was still unhappy about what he saw as the half-hearted response by the Taoiseach, Liam Cosgrave, and the minister. Ó Dálaigh resigned the day after Donegan's apology, saying this was 'the only way open to me to assert publicly my personal integrity and independence as president of Ireland and to protect the dignity and independence of the presidency as an institution'.[33]

That brought Ó Dálaigh's public life to a close. He retired to

Sneem, Co. Kerry, and in March 1978 he died suddenly following a heart attack. When news of his death reached Dublin, the Supreme Court interrupted its normal business and, before a packed court-room, its judges paid generous tribute to their former figurehead. Even at that stage Ó Dálaigh's years at the helm were regarded as path-breaking, and this was reflected in the remarks of the Chief Justice, Tom O'Higgins:

> As a Judge of the Supreme Court and as Chief Justice he will be remembered for his fearless integrity, his zeal in the pursuit of justice, his innate humanity, and his clarity of expression. He presided in this Court at a time when the implications of what the Constitution meant in the lives of ordinary citizens was first recognised. In many cases in the 60s he demonstrated his concern that constitutional rights and guarantees should both be understood and respected . . . Here to-day we remember him as a lawyer, as a Judge, and as one who was amongst us and left his mark.

8. *McGee v. Attorney General*

> 'I'd prefer to see her use contraceptives than be placing
> flowers on her grave.'
>
> Séamus McGee

If a single day could have encapsulated the spirit of an era in which, both at home and abroad, the horrors of entrenched conflict co-existed with the hopeful stirrings of social change, it was 8 June 1972. That Thursday, a South Vietnamese plane dropped a napalm bomb on Trang Bang, a village that had been attacked and occupied by North Vietnamese forces. A press photograph of nine-year-old Kim Phúc, naked and severely burned, fleeing the hellish inferno of her village that day, became one of the most haunting images of war in the twentieth century. Just hours earlier, in Europe, where the Iron Curtain cast its long and menacing shadow, an airline pilot was shot dead when ten Czechs attempted to hijack a plane in the hope of escaping to West Germany. And in Ireland, where memories of Bloody Sunday were still fresh in the mind, the death toll of the Troubles continued to mount when a man and a woman were shot dead in Belfast and a garda inspector died of injuries he suffered after a remote-controlled bomb exploded on the Cavan–Fermanagh border.

Yet in the midst of war and bloodshed, this was also a time of optimism and vitality, at least south of the border. That day, 8 June, President Éamon de Valera signed into law the outcome of the previous month's referendum on membership of the European Economic Community, which had been approved by 83 per cent of voters. Across an increasingly urban society, emigration was slowing down, the women's movement was gaining in strength, incomes were rising and a very young population – close to 50 per cent were under twenty-six – was making its presence felt through a burgeoning youth culture and a questioning of old orthodoxies.

That was the background to another significant event that occurred on 8 June 1972: May McGee went to court.

A 27-year-old from Skerries, north Dublin, May lived with her husband, Séamus, in a mobile home in the nearby seaside village of Loughshinny, where she looked after the couple's four young children. There was no sanitation or sewage in the mobile home, which was located in the garden of Séamus's mother's house, and its confined living quarters of two bedrooms and a small kitchen left them with hardly enough room for the family. Money was extremely tight. May had gone to school at the local convent on a scholarship but left to care for her ailing mother just before sitting her Leaving Certificate. She had worked at the Plessey electronics factory in Swords, but had had to give up her job when she got married in 1968. Séamus, whom May had known since they were children, was a fisherman who spent a lot of time at sea. He took a percentage of each catch, which came to about £20 a week, but when the weather was poor he could go several weeks without any income. 'I wanted to keep working, because the fishing life was very unstable', May recalls, sitting with Séamus in their Skerries home more than forty years later. 'But you had to stop working because it wasn't allowed at the time.' She used to walk to her mother's house in Skerries, an hour away on foot, to save the bus fare. One Christmas Eve, Séamus recalls, he arrived home and 'we didn't have the price of the dinner'.

May and Séamus had four children, including twins, over a period of three years. The children brought them immense joy, but it was also a difficult time for the couple. As far back as the birth of their first child, Martin, May had developed toxaemia – a form of blood poisoning from a local bacterial infection – and as a result went into labour prematurely after thirty-two weeks. It was a complicated delivery, and May had difficulty walking afterwards.

After that experience, May and Séamus decided not to have another baby. Their local GP, Dr James Loughran, spoke to May about the Pill, she would later tell the High Court, but she was wary.

'I was very religious then', she said in the witness box. 'I was afraid God would punish me.' The doctor offered her advice about the rhythm method and gave her a thermometer and a temperature chart to help her follow her fertility cycle and compute her 'safe period'. But she struggled to understand the system and in the summer of 1969 became pregnant for the second time.

In November that year, Dr Loughran was called to see May urgently at the mobile home in Loughshinny. She was complaining of violent headaches and was 'afraid that something would happen to her', he would recall in the High Court. At first Dr Loughran could not find an explanation, but the problem became clear the following month, on New Year's Eve 1969. Just as May's due date was approaching, she was working in the kitchen and suddenly 'felt something give in her head'. A cup slipped out of her hand and she found herself unable to speak. Having rushed to the mobile home, Dr Loughran found that she had signs of stroke and was obviously extremely ill. What she described, he said, were symptoms of cerebral thrombosis on the right side of her brain. She was rushed by ambulance to the Coombe Hospital in Dublin, where she gave birth to her second child, Gerard, and was later transferred to the Richmond Hospital for further specialist brain investigation.

A few months later, Dr Loughran and Mrs McGee sat down to discuss family planning. He advised her not to use the Pill because of the episode of thrombosis, which, if it recurred, could endanger her health and mean she might not be able to care for her family. Dr Loughran would tell the High Court he strongly advised May that she should not become pregnant again, and discussed alternative methods of contraception with her. After talking it through with Séamus, May decided she would like to be fitted with a diaphragm. Dr Loughran was satisfied with that, but told her the device would only be reliable if it was used with a spermicidal jelly or cream. They agreed to go ahead with it.

Yet before May could have the diaphragm fitted, there came another surprise: she was pregnant again. It was upsetting news; she was not yet over the difficulties of her previous pregnancies, and both she and Séamus worried whether they had the money or the space to look after more children. The twin girls, Sylvia and Sharon, were born on 15 November 1970. They were beautiful and healthy, but again the birth took its toll on May, bringing serious complications that required a blood transfusion. A post-natal examination in December showed her blood pressure had risen to an unusually high level for a young woman. Her situation was so grave, she would tell the court, that doctors advised her it would be inadvisable for her to have further pregnancies and her life might be in danger if she did.

In early January, Dr Loughran fitted May with a diaphragm and gave her a prescription for Staycept, a brand of spermicidal jelly. He told her she could obtain it from the International Planned Parenthood Federation in London.

Under the law at the time, it was not illegal to use or make contraceptives in Ireland, but it was illegal to sell, offer, advertise or import them. So when the Staycept jelly was posted to May, the package was seized by customs officials and she was served with a notice informing her that it had been intercepted. In March 1971, May wrote to the Revenue Commissioners explaining her situation and appealing to them to reconsider. Dr Loughran followed up with a letter of his own in which he told the commissioners that the jelly was essential for his patient's mental and physical health. He also submitted a certificate stating that she had cerebral thrombosis and that she was urgently in need of contraceptive jelly for use with a diaphragm. Having received no reply, McGee again wrote to the commissioners asking if they could please do something for her. In a reply the next day, a Revenue official wrote: 'I am to inform you that the contraceptive preparation called Staycept jelly is prohibited to be imported under the Criminal Law (Amendment) Act 1935, and consequently the Revenue Commissioners are not empowered to allow its release for delivery in the State. A copy of your letter has been forwarded to the Department of Justice.'

May McGee took that to mean that she could end up in jail. Under the 1935 act, the penalty for importing contraceptives was a fine of £50 or six months' imprisonment. 'We looked at the letter, then went to the doctor', Séamus recalls. 'He explained it to us. She got annoyed over it. We mind our own business. We don't bother anyone. This is

supposed to be discreet. Then they come along and send you a letter –
not a very nice letter – to say that we could be put in jail for what
we're doing?' After a short pause, he adds: 'Then it just snowballed
from there.'

Dr Loughran had been a founding member of the Irish Family
Planning Association, which had openly operated a family planning
clinic in Dublin since 1968. He was also involved in the Irish Family
Planning Rights Association, which advised those who, in 1972, set
up a company called Family Planning Services Ltd – a mail order
service that took orders for contraceptives from across the country. When May asked Dr Loughran what she could do, he said he
could put her in touch with a solicitor he knew called Dudley
Potter. 'He [Loughran] realized this was a classic case, and that if we
couldn't win this we couldn't win anything', one member of the legal
team says. It was her decision, Dr Loughran told May. She gave the
green light. 'We sat down and he [Potter] told me he'd be interested
in trying to do something about it', May recalls. The solicitor duly
wrote to the Attorney General to say that he had been instructed
to begin legal proceedings seeking a declaration that the act was
unconstitutional.

When he came to assemble his team, Dudley Potter first approached
Donal Barrington. His growing reputation as a constitutional specialist meant he was by now a busy practitioner, with one impossible
case after another landing on his desk. On one occasion, Barrington
was briefed as a senior counsel to appear in a tax appeal case – an area
of law he knew little about. When he pointed out his ignorance, he
was told he was only expected to sit there, and by his presence give
the Revenue Commissioners the impression that their constitutional
status might be in some doubt.[1] Potter also contacted Seán MacBride,
convinced that his stature as a founding member of Amnesty International and as secretary general of the International Commission of
Jurists would enhance McGee's chances of winning. The two senior
counsel agreed to argue the case, along with the junior Anthony
Kennedy.

On the opposing side, the Attorney General had briefed a formidable team led by Tommy Conolly and Niall McCarthy, with Richard Cooke leading for the Revenue Commissioners.

The selection of MacBride, who by then was a republican elder statesman and a figurehead of the international left, was a calculated risk. His standing, not least on the global stage, was very high, but it was also known that the President of the High Court, Andreas O'Keeffe, had an intense dislike of him. The antipathy was partly personal, but there was also a political dimension to it. O'Keeffe was a son-in-law of Éamon de Valera, a long-time political opponent of MacBride's. De Valera and MacBride had both opposed the Anglo-Irish Treaty, and MacBride even served as private secretary to de Valera for a period in the mid-1920s, but they parted ways acrimoniously after the establishment of Fianna Fáil. MacBride became the IRA's chief of staff in the 1930s and later founded Clann na Poblachta in the hope that it would one day replace de Valera's party. Even all these decades later, there was no love lost between many in Fianna Fáil and MacBride.

Early in their preparations, McGee's legal team agreed that if O'Keeffe, who as High Court president had responsibility for allocating cases to individual judges, decided to hear the McGee case himself, they would probably lose. At first they had good news on this front: rumour had it that O'Keeffe had asked a different judge, Denis Pringle, to preside in the case. But Pringle, according to the story, then asked if he could pass on the case. 'He didn't want the wrath of the country upon his head', says one contemporary. In the end O'Keeffe took the case himself. And that meant that McGee's legal team opened their case in the High Court on 8 June 1972 on the assumption that they would probably end up in the Supreme Court.

There were two main planks to McGee's case. First, she claimed the law that prevented her bringing contraceptives into the State was inconsistent with the Constitution because it infringed what it was submitted was the implied right to privacy that was guaranteed to all citizens under Article 40, which concerns personal rights. Second, citing Article 41 (the family), she argued that the importation ban

violated what the Constitution called the 'inalienable and imprescriptible' rights of the family in a matter that was 'peculiarly the
province of the family itself' in that it attempted to frustrate a decision made by Mrs McGee and her husband for the benefit of the
family as a whole.

MacBride and Barrington also argued that it violated her freedom
of conscience. All of the claims were denied by the Attorney General
and the Revenue Commissioners.

As May and Séamus, now in their early seventies, reminisce about
the case, they laugh together at the thought of how unlikely it all
seemed. When the case began, neither of them had any idea of its
wider significance. 'It was a test case, I suppose. But at that stage we
didn't think it was a big thing. We were looking for our right to live
and do what we want, which is the way it should be', Séamus says.
'We had enough to do at home here without worrying about what
the world was thinking about.'

The case garnered huge publicity. During the High Court hearings, May's brother came home from college one day and said to her,
'Who's this Mary McGee that's in the papers?' The couple in court
were Mary and James; at home they were always May and Séamus.

'I said, "I haven't a clue"', May says. 'Mum looked at me, because
I'd had to tell her quietly . . . When he did find out afterwards, he
said, "I would never have expected you to do anything like that . . .
I don't believe it." I said, "I might be quiet, but when I make a sound
I make a sound."' At the kitchen table, May and Séamus burst into
laughter.

May's abiding recollection of the opening day in the High Court,
when she and Séamus both took to the witness box, was just how
intimidating it was. 'It's not a nice place, the Four Courts. It's cold
and scary. It was my first time ever in a court, and it's an awful place
to be. But I just said to myself, "I'm here now, let's just hope I'll get
this sorted and it'll be grand. I won't have to come here again".'

In the run-up to the hearing, MacBride had warned the couple
that they would have to face intimate and difficult questions from
both sides. Yet nothing quite prepared them for the minute scrutiny
to which they would be subjected. Questioning May on the opening

day, Barrington asked whether she felt she and her husband 'should live as brother and sister for the rest of your lives and look after the young children'.

> MAY MCGEE: We are only human. Religion is important, but I still think we have a right to live as human beings. We are husband and wife, and we cannot live as brother and sister.
>
> BARRINGTON: Have you views about what you are doing?
>
> MCGEE: What I am doing is not wrong. I have my children to consider. They have not had a proper home except for the eldest boy.
>
> BARRINGTON: Do you see any alternative to what you are doing?
>
> MCGEE: No, apart from living as brother and sister.
>
> BARRINGTON: Do you think it would be right for you to live as brother and sister with your husband?
>
> MCGEE: No.[2]

May's cross-examination by the lawyers for the Attorney General and the Revenue Commissioners did not take long, but she recalls the day as a humiliating experience. 'I remember thinking to myself, "For Heaven's sake". They try to make you feel so small. But you have to try and keep your head all the time, just answer the questions as much as you can.' She would look at the judge – she had been instructed to address her answers to him – and she could see he was uncomfortable with the intimate questions.

When it was his turn, Séamus told the court that after the twins had been born, he and May had talked about the future. May's health was poor, money was scarce and they had so little room in the mobile home that one of the boys was staying with his mother in her house. Quite apart from the risk to May's health, he said, they did not think they could look after any more children.

Later that day, there came a moment that would lodge itself in the minds of several of the people who were in court. During his cross-examination, Séamus was asked if he liked to see his wife using contraceptives. He replied: 'I'd prefer to see her use contraceptives than be placing flowers on her grave.'

The room went silent for a few seconds. 'It was a stunning answer', says one of those who was in court.

When Dr Loughran was pressed as to whether there was any doubt in his mind as to the wisdom of the advice he gave his patient, he replied: 'None whatever.'

MacBride's problem was that O'Keeffe could not see any right to privacy in the Constitution. MacBride insisted it was there. He argued that laws and constitutions could never stand still. They were 'a dynamic process' of 'adjusting to the times'. O'Keeffe pushed back against this idea of constant evolution. Even the Supreme Court could not rewrite the Constitution, he told MacBride. He was not asking for it to be rewritten, MacBride replied, only for it to be applied.

Tommy Conolly gave as good as he got. Surely, he said, the idea of contraception was repellent to society's ideas of common sense and propriety. It had not been shown that the right to use contraceptives appeared anywhere in the Constitution or that it was 'a natural right of mankind'.

'It is wrong to suggest', he said on the second and final day of the High Court hearing, 'that the interpretation of the Constitution should vary in accordance with the norms of religious thinking. If this was an objectionable piece of legislation, the way to get rid of it was not by approach to the Courts but by having the Act repealed. The result of this Act being condemned as unconstitutional would be that contraceptives could be freely sold all over Ireland, and hawked from door to door.'[3]

The Constitution may not have contained an explicit right to privacy, but since Gladys Ryan's fluoridation case in 1964, the judiciary had begun to identify what they found to be unwritten, or un-enumerated, rights. Conolly now had to argue the opposite of what he had argued in that case, when he represented Gladys Ryan. 'When did this position, according to my learned friend, arise that the sale of contraceptives, by virtue of some hidden magic in the Constitution, be validated in the country, and that their importation must be free? I respectfully submit that such a right cannot be derived', Conolly said.

MacBride and Barrington felt their best chance of winning was by focusing on Article 41, which is the article of the Constitution that lays down the rights of the family. There was no 'social object' to be gained by depriving May McGee of the right to be a 'full companion' to her husband, Barrington told the judge. If they had the right to marry, they had a personal right to regulate their marriage. The case was clearly one of freedom of conscience, he argued. Mrs McGee had made her decision and believed it to be the right thing for her to do. The real importance of freedom of conscience was whether a person was allowed to act in accordance with his or her conscience, subject to the restraints of public order and morality. 'To construe the guarantee of freedom of conscience in the sense that you are entitled to your conscience but you are not entitled to act in accordance with it, would be to deprive freedom of conscience of all life and reality', Barrington told the judge. He did not skirt around the terrible human dilemma at the heart of the case. What the people had tried to do to Mrs McGee in this legislation, he told the court, was 'a cruel thing'.

O'Keeffe dismissed May McGee's constitutional challenge less than two months later, on 31 July 1972. The right to freedom of conscience was a freedom to choose a religion and to act in accordance with its precepts, he found. It was not a freedom for the individual to act 'in furtherance of his private welfare within the limits set by his own conscience'. The act was not inconsistent with the authority of the family, and, crucially, the personal rights in the Constitution did not include a right to privacy of the kind claimed by Mrs McGee. O'Keeffe added, however, that there was nothing in his judgment to preclude the Oireachtas from repealing the disputed section of the act if it so wished. From this point on, May recalls, she grew more determined than she had ever been. 'I was disgusted', she says of the High Court decision. 'I didn't believe it. "OK", I said, "what can I do now?"'

The McGee case did not take place in a political or social vacuum. For the previous two years, the women's movement had been gaining in strength and controversy over the contraception laws had been growing increasingly intense. When, in February 1971, Taoiseach Jack Lynch had told the Fianna Fáil Ard-Fheis of his party's willingness to 'grasp nettles' which might stand in the way of the reunification of the country, it was generally assumed that the law on contraceptives was one of the nettles he had in mind. 'Where it can be shown that attitudes embodied in our laws and Constitution give offence to liberty of conscience, then we are prepared to see what can be done to harmonize our views so that, without detracting from genuine values, a new kind of Irish society can be created, equally agreeable to North and South', Lynch had said.[4]

The Catholic Church was implacably opposed to any liberalization of the legal regime, however. In March 1971, a month after Lynch's Ard-Fheis speech, the bishops issued a joint statement saying that they fully shared 'the disquiet, which is widespread among the people at the present time, regarding pressures being exerted on public opinion on questions concerning the civil law on divorce, contraception and abortion'. They said civil law on these matters 'should respect the wishes of the people who elected the legislators and the bishops confidently hope that the legislators themselves will respect this important principle'. The stance was expressed even more firmly by the Archbishop of Dublin, John Charles McQuaid, who published a pastoral letter in March 1971 in which he said that to change the law to allow access to contraceptives 'would, without question, prove to be gravely damaging to morality, private and public; it would be, and would remain, a curse upon our country'. The church was in a very strong position. The 1971 census showed that the proportion of the population describing themselves as Catholics had fallen only fractionally in the previous decade, from 94.9 per cent to 93.9 per cent. And among these Catholics, levels of church-going remained very high.[5]

But society was nonetheless changing, and Catholic moral teaching did not have the hold it had once done. Shortly before the McGee case was heard, the International Planned Parenthood Federation released figures showing that at least 1,210 Irish women had had legal abortions in Britain the previous year. That was considered a conservative estimate, given the likelihood that many Irish women seeking abortions simply gave addresses in Britain.[6] On the issue of contraception, dissenting voices were making themselves heard. Members of the Irish Women's Liberation Movement, which had been established in 1970, responded to McQuaid's pastoral letter by picketing the archbishop's residence. McQuaid was defiant, 'but the fact that the women were prepared to confront him publicly was yet another sign that his domination and unquestioned obedience to his church's teaching was coming to an end and the contraception debate was not one he could contain'.[7]

Two months later, the same organization attracted huge publicity when its activists visited Belfast and bought contraceptives* before returning to Dublin and declaring them defiantly at the customs barrier at Connolly Station.

The aims of the women's movement were primarily economic and political – including the achievement of equal pay, better representation of women in public life and better treatment for single mothers.[8] But the campaign to relax the contraception laws gained significant traction and it put politicians under pressure. In June 1971, the National Health Council recommended to the Minister for Health that contraceptives be made available to women who required them on health grounds. In the same month, a survey carried out for *This Week* magazine reported that 39 per cent of men and 29 per cent of women in Ireland favoured the sale of contraceptives without any stated safeguards.

The first parliamentary attempt to change the law came the following month, in July, when a bill was introduced in the Seanad in the names of Senators Mary Robinson, John Horgan and Trevor West. It was refused a first reading after a vote of 25 to 14, however, and it was not until February 1972 that Labour Party TDs introduced an identical bill to that which had been defeated in the Seanad. The Fianna Fáil government rejected it, a stance that so delighted the Fine Gael TD Oliver J. Flanagan, who voted with the government, that he crossed the floor to shake the hand of Brian Lenihan, the minister who set out the government's position in the House that day.

Notwithstanding the advances of their campaign, by the end of

---

* In fact, the 'birth-control pills' they brandished were unwrapped packets of Aspirin. They had not realized they could not buy the contraceptive pill without a prescription. Nell McCafferty, *Nell*, p. 225.

1972 many in the women's movement were despondent at what they saw as the slow pace of progress. Writing in the *Irish Times* on 30 December, under the headline 'Women in 1972: Not Much To Be Triumphant About', Mary Maher argued that the momentum of 1971 had stalled and that May McGee's defeat in the High Court was illustrative of a wider trend.

In 1972, after all, women had to leave the public service on marriage, they were paid less than men for the same work and were in effect excluded from sitting on juries. To qualify for State support, a deserted wife had to prove she had done her best to reconcile with the deserter, while unmarried mothers had no statutory claim at all to State help.[9] In marriage, the husband was the legal guardian of the children, and a wife's legal domicile was where her husband said it was. As Maher pointed out, the courts had just that year restated that a wife could be regarded as chattel; in June 1972, the month May McGee took her case, the High Court had confirmed that a man was entitled to damages if his wife 'was seduced and enticed away from him'.

Maher was not entirely disheartened, however. 'And yet,' she wrote, for all of that, 1972 wasn't without its hopeful moments, and Women's Liberation, 'like all good civil rights movements, appears to be making its impact in a kind of underground influence. There has been a change of atmosphere: more women are speaking up, more are prepared to take the decisive step toward action.'[10]

May McGee took her appeal to the Supreme Court in November 1973. 'It was a bit awesome, looking at these lads', she recalls of the five judges who heard the case: Chief Justice Billy FitzGerald, Brian Walsh, Frederick Budd, Séamus Henchy and Frank Griffin. May sat through the four-day appeal but says she could only follow parts of the legal argument. She whiled away a few of the long hours by doing some knitting.

Henchy and Griffin had been promoted to the Supreme Court by Jack Lynch's government in the previous twelve months to fill the vacancies left by Cearbhall Ó Dálaigh's departure for Luxembourg and the death of Richard McLoughlin. Both men had loose

Fianna Fáil connections, and they tended to vote together in the major cases, but if Lynch had hoped that their appointments would result in the court taking a back seat in national affairs, he was to be disappointed.

Henchy, in particular, was to emerge as one of the major figures in the history of the court. From Corofin in Co. Clare, he was a Celtic scholar and had been active in the early 1940s in Craobh na hAiséirghe, a radical Irish-language group within Conradh na Gaeilge.[11] As professor of law at UCD, he taught many future lawyers and politicians – among them Des O'Malley, the Minister for Justice in the government that appointed him to the Supreme Court in 1972. His performance on the High Court was regarded as 'unexceptional: steady and solid', only rarely showing the touches of inspiration that would distinguish him as a judge of the Supreme Court.[12]

Although Walsh and Henchy were of the same generation – there was only a year between them – and shared Fianna Fáil connections, the two men had a poor relationship in their years on the court. Their personalities were very different. Whereas Walsh was media-friendly and gregarious, Henchy had a reputation for being gruff and stand-offish and was, as he happily admitted, utterly incapable of making small-talk. Walsh relished the camaraderie of the Bar and was adept at cultivating relationships, while Henchy was extremely private, preferring to pass his time gardening or playing a game of billiards in the Royal Irish Yacht Club to mixing with colleagues. There were also substantial differences in outlook between them, including on extradition and the concept of natural law, and these were to surface repeatedly in their time on the court. What the two men shared was their brilliance as lawyers and judges; in time they would be regarded as giants in the Four Courts.

On 19 December 1973, just over a month after the McGee appeal was heard, barristers, journalists and onlookers got to their feet and the five judges filed into the Supreme Court in their wigs and their black gowns.

Initially it looked bad for McGee. FitzGerald, the Chief Justice, ruled against her. The act was not unconstitutional, he said, echoing O'Keeffe in the High Court, not least because it did not actually ban

the use of contraceptives. While one must naturally be sympathetic with Mrs McGee in her difficult circumstances, FitzGerald
said, 'these appear to me to be natural hazards which must be faced by
married couples with such fortitude as they can summon to their
assistance'.

But as the rest of the judges read their judgments into the record, it
became clear that McGee had won decisively, by a 4-1 margin. One
by one, Walsh, Budd, Henchy and Griffin ruled in her favour –
all finding that the act breached her constitutional right to marital
privacy. In what was to become one of his most celebrated judgments, Walsh issued a strong statement of the importance of the
Constitution's long-neglected fundamental rights provisions:

> Articles 41, 42 and 43 of the Constitution emphatically reject the
> theory that there are no rights without laws, no rights contrary to
> that law and no rights anterior to that law. They indicate that justice
> is placed above the law and acknowledge that natural rights, or
> human rights, are not created by law, but that the Constitution con-
> firms their existence and gives them protection. The individual has
> natural and human rights over which the State has no authority; and
> the family, as the natural primary and fundamental unit group of
> society, has rights as such which the State cannot control.[13]

In Walsh's view, it was a matter exclusively for the husband and
wife to decide how many children they wished to have, and it was
outside the competence of the State to dictate to them on the issue.
The sexual life of a married couple was of necessity and by its nature
an area of particular privacy.

> If the husband and wife decide to limit their family or to avoid hav-
> ing children by use of contraceptives, it is a matter peculiarly within
> the joint decision of the husband and wife and one into which the
> State cannot intrude unless its intrusion can be justified by the exi-
> gencies of the common good . . . It is outside the authority of the
> State to endeavour to intrude into the privacy of the husband and
> wife relationship for the sake of imposing a code of private morality
> upon that husband and wife which they do not desire.

According to Walsh, Article 41 of the Constitution, which deals with the rights of the family, guaranteed the husband and wife against any such invasion of their privacy by the State. 'It follows that the use of contraceptives by them within that marital privacy is equally guaranteed against such invasion and, as such, assumes the status of a right so guaranteed by the Constitution.'

Henchy's judgment was a tour de force. The effect of the act, he said, was:

> to condemn the plaintiff and her husband to a way of life which, at best, will be fraught with worry, tension and uncertainty that cannot but adversely affect their lives and, at worst, will result in an unwanted pregnancy causing death or serious illness with the obvious tragic consequences to the lives of her husband and young children. And this in the context of a Constitution which in its preamble proclaims as one of its aims the dignity and freedom of the individual; which in . . . Article 40 casts on the State a duty to protect as best it may from unjust attack and, in the case of injustice done, to vindicate the life and person of every citizen; which in Article 41, after recognising the family as the natural primary and fundamental unit group of society, and as a moral institution possessing inalienable and imprescriptible rights antecedent and superior to all positive law, guarantees to protect it in its Constitution and authority as the necessary basis of social order and as indispensable to the welfare of the nation and the State; and which, also in Article 41, pledges the State to guard with special care the institution of marriage, on which the family is founded, and to protect it against attack.[14]

In other words, Henchy performed a sweeping *tour d'horizon* of the Constitution and concluded that, if you take as a whole everything that the document protects, it implies or permits a protected zone of individual freedom where the State cannot interfere. If May McGee was to observe the ban, which she was bound under the law to do, she would

> endanger the security and happiness of her marriage, she will imperil her health to the point of hazarding her life, and she will subject her family to the risk of distress and disruption. These are intrusions

which she is entitled to say are incompatible with the safety of her life, the preservation of her health, her responsibility to her conscience, and the security and well-being of her marriage and family. If she fails to obey the prohibition, the law, by prosecuting her, will reach into the privacy of her marital life in seeking to prove her guilt.

Budd went even further than his colleagues, expressly recognizing not only a right to marital privacy but also a general right of privacy.

Everyone listened intently as the judgments were read out. 'The man sitting beside me whispered: "He said 'Yeah'," May recalls. 'The last two went quickly. Then he said, "You've won!" I just thought, "Thank God, I can get home now." I don't think I realized the enormity of what it was.'

As journalists scribbled in their notebooks, McGee's supporters and lawyers hugged and shook hands. Séamus was not there; his uncle was sick at the time, so he was skippering the fishing boat off Dunmore East in Waterford. When the judgment was delivered, someone called the local pub in Dunmore and left a message for him. 'That's how I found out. I had my uncle's car down. The weather was bad. It was near the weekend. I said, "Right." I hopped into the car in the middle of the night, around four o'clock in the morning. I was home the next morning with her.'

The dramatic conclusion to May McGee's long legal battle was front-page news. The Family Planning Clinic in Dublin hailed it as a 'big breakthrough'. The anti-contraception campaigner Desmond Broadberry, who was the father of eighteen children, described the judgment as 'a sad day for Ireland' and said that most of his fellow campaigners never considered for a moment that Mrs McGee would win her case.[15]

For their part, the Catholic bishops reiterated their view that the use of contraceptives was 'morally wrong'. Emerging from the Four Courts to be greeted by a phalanx of reporters, May said it was a great weight off her mind but she had not yet taken it in. 'What I want is the right to decide with my husband on family planning. It's up to every couple what form of contraceptive they use.'[16]

★

The lawyer William Binchy, citing a contemporary opinion poll from the early 1970s, said the court was ahead of public opinion on contraception.[17] It was certainly ahead of the politicians, who had prevaricated on the issue for years, and the decision showed that even on controversial and sensitive issues the court was willing to take a lead and nudge the executive and the legislature into action. Yet subsequent events were to reveal a paradox at the heart of *McGee*. A decision that many of those campaigning to liberalize Irish society considered a major breakthrough came with an ironic coda in the form, a decade later, of a successful campaign to add an anti-abortion amendment to the Constitution.

The four judges in the majority in the McGee case found that the idea that the law did not specifically ban the use of contraceptives was a red herring. The clear purpose of the act was to apply criminal sanctions in order to prevent the use of contraceptives. Finding in McGee's favour, they based their decision on the right to marital privacy, which they said was implied in the Constitution.

But while the headline was the 4-1 decision, even within the majority there were crucial nuances. The main judgment, written by Henchy, specifically located the right to marital privacy in Article 40, which is the article devoted to personal rights. Budd and Griffin also opted for Article 40.

Walsh arrived at the same outcome by a different route. For him, marital privacy was located in Article 41, which is the article about the family. In other words, this was the plaintiff's right because she was Mrs McGee, not because she was May McGee.

It was also notable that Henchy (as well as Griffin) cited recent US Supreme Court cases, in particular *Griswold v. Connecticut*, a momentous 1965 decision that found that the US Constitution protected a right to privacy. *Griswold v. Connecticut* was on the lips of every constitutional lawyer in 1973, because it was that right to privacy that led directly, in January that year, to *Roe v. Wade*, the controversial decision of the US Supreme Court to extend that right to privacy to a woman's decision to have an abortion. Henchy also cited *Eisenstadt v. Baird*, a 1972 US Supreme Court decision that established the right of unmarried people to possess contraception on the same basis as married couples.

Walsh, whose good friend William Brennan had been in the majority in both *Griswold v. Connecticut* and *Eisenstadt v. Baird*, conspicuously avoided citing either of the American cases. In his judgment he referred to this absence, saying his reason for not relying on the American decisions was not because he did not find them helpful or relevant but because he 'found it unnecessary to rely upon any of the dicta in those cases to support the views which I have expressed in this judgment'.

One possibility is that Walsh, who was strongly anti-abortion, did not cite *Griswold v. Connecticut* because he was well aware that there was a direct line between it and *Roe v. Wade*. The authority that *Roe v. Wade* relied on was *Griswold*, after all. And if that direct line had been established in the US, then there was no obvious reason why a personal right to privacy in *McGee v. Attorney General* could not, in the hands of this or a future Supreme Court, be relied on to bring about an Irish *Roe v. Wade* and thereby introduce legal abortion.

The American decisions were certainly pored over by the Supreme Court. On 8 November 1973, in the middle of the Supreme Court hearing of McGee's appeal, Walsh mentioned the case in a letter to Brennan:

> At the moment your name and opinions are very much in my mind because we are currently engaged on a constitutional case to decide whether or not the laws prohibiting the importation of contraceptives are unconstitutional. Your views in Griswold's case and in Eisenstadt are being closely studied as are those of your colleagues. You may find it strange that the case should turn upon the question of importation but the reality of the situation is that they are not manufactured at all in this country and are only available by importation.[18]

If Walsh was alive to the possibility that *McGee*, by identifying a right to marital privacy, could lead to the courts introducing abortion, he certainly was not alone. Herein lay the seeds of the abortion debate that would convulse Ireland within the decade. It was precisely the fear that the Supreme Court would follow the example of its American counterpart and apply the right to privacy to abortion that drove anti-abortion campaigners in their push for a referendum to insert a 'pro-life' amendment into the Constitution in 1983.

'It certainly was a catalyst for the pro-life amendment campaign, as they were called, which brought about the 1983 amendment and subsequently the X case', says the lawyer, senator and women's rights activist Ivana Bacik. 'So *McGee* has had a huge influence – not just in furthering women's rights but, ironically, I think, in setting them back.'[19]

The McGee decision was arguably the most significant the Supreme Court has ever taken. It marked a high point of the doctrine of un-enumerated rights and showed that natural law still exerted a strong hold on judicial thinking. It drove home the potential of judicial review and demonstrated to the public in a way that few other cases had the possibilities that lay within the Constitution as a tool for social change. The judgment had consequences far beyond May McGee or even the Four Courts. 'The decision in *McGee* started a social revolution, the consequences of which are still being played out', said Gerard Hogan in 2014. In its implications, he suggested, the decision bore comparison with *Brown v. Board of Education*, the US Supreme Court decision on racial de-segregation. 'Both decisions changed their countries irrevocably and both decisions required real judicial courage and a high degree of judicial imagination.'[20]

The decision transformed the political debate on contraception. 'The question was no longer whether the law should be relaxed. The law *was* relaxed.'[21] But the two largest parties in the Dáil, Fianna Fáil and Fine Gael, were still hopelessly divided on the issue. The problem first fell to the Minister for Justice, Patrick Cooney of Fine Gael. He introduced a bill that would permit the import and sale of contra-ceptives under strict conditions, but opposition from Fianna Fáil combined with a free vote of Fine Gael TDs – granted by the party leadership to accommodate its bitter internal divisions – resulted in its defeat in the Dáil. Even the Taoiseach, Liam Cosgrave, voted against his government's own bill.

When Fianna Fáil took power in 1977, it consulted widely and again resolved to settle the issue. In February 1979, Minister for Health Charles Haughey rose in the Dáil and proclaimed that he had found 'an Irish solution to an Irish problem'. His Family Planning Bill, like Cooney's, was highly restrictive, allowing people to buy contraceptives on prescription 'for the purpose, *bona fide*, of family planning or for adequate medical reasons'. While the Labour Party opposed the draft law on the ground that it did not go far enough and Fine Gael again allowed a free vote, Fianna Fáil this time applied the whip and secured its comfortable passage through the Oireachtas. It had taken almost six years, but finally the legislature had acted on the Supreme Court decision.[22]

May McGee looks back fondly at the case that made her a household name in the early 1970s. It was only later, she believes, that she realized the significance of what she had done. Today, she and Séamus beam with pride at the memories. 'Afterwards, I sat down and thought about it, and I just said: "I'm glad. I hope that helps a lot of women now to stand up for themselves."

'I like to think [the children] feel proud of what we did. I've always told them, "Stand up for yourselves. If you believe in something, go for it." I really do believe that . . . I won't say I'm brave – no way – but I'd like to think I helped women to stand up for themselves a little bit more.'

May was worried about her mother's reaction, but there was no need to be; she was 'chuffed' at her daughter's achievement, if a little worried that there might be a backlash. 'She was very surprised – never once did anyone say anything nasty to her. They might have said, "I never expected May to stand up for herself like that." Mam came home one day afterwards and said, "Do you know, a lot of people agree." I said, "Maybe it's time for change."'

Shortly after the Supreme Court judgment, May and Séamus were at Mass when the priest made a pejorative remark from the altar about some 'people in this town'. They felt it was clearly aimed at them. 'So we stood up and we walked out.'

There were one or two similar incidents, but on the whole the couple were relieved to receive such a positive response. Letters of congratulation arrived from all over the world. A newspaper offered them £1,000 for an interview; they used the money to put a deposit on the house where they now live. People would approach them on the street and greet them warmly. 'Without saying anything, they were letting me know, "It's OK"', May says. They also had discreet visits from some younger priests, one of whom May remembers telling her, 'You do what you have to do, don't be worrying about anyone else.'

A few years after the judgment, when life had returned to normal, the twins, Sharon and Sylvia, came home from school one day with a question for May. In class that day, their teacher had been telling them about women's rights and suggested to the girls that their mother would be a good person to talk to about this.

'At that stage I hadn't said anything. So they came home and told me, "Mam, the teacher said if we want to know about this bit of history, we've to ask you." So I said, "OK, we'll sit down now and have a chat."

'"Well", I said, "I had a little disagreement with the government . . ."'

9. Holding the line

'It's immortality of a kind – it's probably the only kind of
immortality which I can hope to achieve.'

Máirín de Búrca

His lone dissent in the McGee case was to be one of Billy FitzGerald's
last major acts as Chief Justice. Within a year he was dead, having
succumbed to a short illness that brought a premature end to his
leadership of the judiciary after less than two years in the role. If
Jack Lynch had chosen FitzGerald over Brian Walsh in 1972 on the
assumption that the conservative Fine Gael man would be a steady
hand at the tiller, he was proved correct. In two of the major constitutional cases that came before the court in his time, FitzGerald had
indeed resisted the temptation to push judicial boundaries. FitzGerald's problem was that his colleagues were united in ruling against
the State in the Byrne and McGee cases, leaving him in a minority of
one on both occasions. FitzGerald did not rock the boat, but the rest
of the court enthusiastically upended it, leaving the government
thrashing in the rippling waves.

By the time of FitzGerald's passing in 1974, Jack Lynch's Fianna
Fáil government had been replaced by a coalition led by Fine Gael's
Liam Cosgrave as Taoiseach. Again the political stars did not align
for Walsh. The government chose as FitzGerald's replacement the
Fine Gael blue-blood Tom O'Higgins, who at that point was the
most junior judge in the High Court. O'Higgins had unassailable
pedigree: the state's first Minister for Justice, Kevin O'Higgins, was
his uncle and godfather; his father – also Thomas – was a Fine Gael
minister; and his brother Michael was a Fine Gael TD and leader of
the Seanad. After becoming a barrister in the late 1930s and practising

on the Midland and Northern circuits, O'Higgins had moved into politics with an unsuccessful run for Fine Gael in Dublin South in the 1943 general election. He was a founder of the Central Branch of Fine Gael, a group of younger middle-class activists, and of the policy review magazine *The Forum*. In 1948 he became Fine Gael TD for Laois-Offaly, his father's former constituency, a seat he held until 1969.[1]

O'Higgins was appointed Minister for Health in the 1954–7 inter-party government, and when Fine Gael was ousted from power in the 1957 general election he combined his opposition front bench position with a resumed career at the Bar. Within the party, O'Higgins belonged to an urban, broadly centre-left group that saw modernization and a more socially oriented platform as the way forward. With Declan Costello and Alexis FitzGerald, he founded a study group, the National Research and Information Centre, which published a monthly journal called the *National Observer*. From this milieu came 'Towards a Just Society', the 1965 policy document that urged Fine Gael to embrace social democratic policies over small-government conservatism. 'O'Higgins was seen as a key moderniser, with a good grasp of economics and an ability to build common ground with the Labour Party and more conservative members of Fine Gael', write Patrick Maume and Kevin Costello.[2]

With a presidential election around the corner in 1966, O'Higgins suggested Seán MacBride and John A. Costello as potential Fine Gael candidates to run against the 83-year-old incumbent, Éamon de Valera. Neither name gained traction, and eventually he was persuaded to run himself. As a candidate, O'Higgins sought to position himself as a refreshing antidote to Civil War politics – and, by implication, to the ageing incumbent, who refused to campaign on the basis that as president he was above politics.[3] To drive home that message of rupture, O'Higgins ran what was in effect the first modern presidential campaign – a high-energy cross-country blitz, heavily influenced by US politics, that put his wife, Therese 'Terry' Keane, and their five children front and centre.[4] 'Tom and Terry' were presented as an Irish equivalent to John and Jacqueline Kennedy. And it very nearly worked. De Valera defeated O'Higgins by just 10,717 votes – a margin of less than 1 per cent of the votes cast.[5]

O'Higgins's performance was all the more remarkable since RTÉ had responded to de Valera's shunning of the campaign trail by refusing, in the interests of balance, to cover his campaign at all. O'Higgins's stock soared within Fine Gael. At the 1969 general election he moved from Laois-Offaly to Dublin South, where he topped the poll. He then became deputy leader to Liam Cosgrave. Later, Garret Fitz-Gerald remarked that, had O'Higgins remained in the Dáil, he, not FitzGerald, would have succeeded Cosgrave as Fine Gael leader in 1977.[6]

By now O'Higgins had spent more of his adult life as a politician than as a practising lawyer, but it was an electoral defeat that precipitated his move back to the Four Courts. O'Higgins did not contest the February 1973 general election. Instead, three months later, when de Valera's second term at Áras an Uachtaráin came to an end, he stood in a presidential election that he seemed certain to win. A shock defeat to the Fianna Fáil candidate, Erskine Childers, however, left O'Higgins bruised and out of work. He returned to the law library, and had only been back in practice for a few months when, that December, his former colleagues in government made him a High Court judge. His remarkable ascent was complete less than a year later, in October 1974, when he leap-frogged every other senior judge to be installed as Chief Justice.

In common with many of those whose careers straddle the Four Courts and Leinster House, O'Higgins occupied an ambiguous position; he was seen as a lawyer among politicians and a politician among lawyers.[7] While his experience as a barrister and his genial personality helped contain open hostility towards his appointment, the exceptionally close links between O'Higgins and the government that appointed him did not escape comment. In the Dáil, Jim Gibbons of Fianna Fáil saw O'Higgins's elevation as evidence of nepotism on the government's part.[8] The *Irish Press*, in its report on the announcement, observed:

> To the victors go the spoils in politics, love and war. Since the foundation of the State, the legal professions, regrettably, have been bound hand and foot to party politics. The annual list of sums paid to State

counsel shows this strong connection. But nowhere is it seen more nakedly than in the appointments of the judiciary. Down the years, judicial appointments were given to those who had loyally served the party or parties then in office. Whilst in the latter years of Fianna Fáil Government, the tendency was against this practice, the Coalition have reverted totally to it.[9]

The paper (founded and controlled by the de Valera family and Fianna Fáil in its sympathies) saw further evidence of that trend in the appointment to the High Court on the same day of Liam Hamilton, a long-time Labour Party supporter.

In the law library itself, there were plenty of sceptics who watched closely for signs that in office O'Higgins would favour the government in his judgments or attempt to row back on the judicial expansionism of the previous decade. Early verdicts on his term were lukewarm. It was noted that in a relatively high number of cases he did not write judgments, and it was true that as a doctrinal lawyer he was outshone by colleagues such as Séamus Henchy and John Kenny. He also adopted 'a more deferential attitude towards the political process' than some of his colleagues and predecessors.[10] Writing in 1979, the legal academic Nial Osborough found evidence in two cases decided by the O'Higgins court that 'the work of constitutional expansionism intimately associated with Mr Justice Walsh and the late Cearbhall Ó Dálaigh is now at an end'.[11]

The Ó Dálaigh court had rewritten so many basic concepts and principles, and at such breakneck speed, that it was perhaps natural that a period of consolidation would follow. It had been so immersed in major constitutional questions that it had left many more technical questions to one side. Who could take a case? What legal issues fell under the court's authority? 'Perhaps such matters only begin to give trouble when a system has reached a certain degree of sophistication', writes J. P. Casey. 'At any rate the O'Higgins court often had to confront them.'[12]

Yet, looking at O'Higgins's record, the most striking aspect of his ten-year tenure is the continuity of the work the Ó Dálaigh court had commenced. While, under O'Higgins, there was a shift in tone, and the rhetorical high notes of the sweeping Ó Dálaigh-era judgments on defendants' rights or the powers of the courts gave way to a more coolly analytical style, on many issues the O'Higgins court continued to build on the achievements of the previous decade. It still took any opportunity to apply the fundamental rights clauses in a way that was not necessarily in the interests of the government of the day.

O'Higgins joined forces with Brian Walsh to resist and eventually prevail against moves – no doubt supported by the gardaí – to dilute the rule under which any evidence obtained in breach of a suspect's constitutional right could not be used in court.[13] The court also imposed further restrictions on garda conduct towards political detainees by recognizing that suspects were entitled to a series of novel constitutional rights, including the right to legal advice and medical treatment.[14]

The constitutional guarantee of freedom of expression had rarely been invoked before the 1970s. The O'Higgins court began to grapple with it, putting in place the broad shape of a law of contempt that attempted to strike a reasonable balance between freedom of expression and the due administration of justice.[15] The same court saw a big surge in cases over the property rights guarantees – another issue that had lain dormant for many years.[16]

One of the most significant cases in the early years of the O'Higgins court was brought, once again, by women who came to court to have their rights confirmed over the heads of an unwilling government.

On the night of 4 August 1971, about 500 people joined a demonstration in central Dublin organized by left-wing and civil liberties organizations. The object of their anger was a draft law, due to pass through the Oireachtas that night, that would make squatting, or the encouragement of squatting, a criminal offence. The Prohibition of Forcible Entry and Occupation Bill was largely designed to curtail the activities of the Dublin Housing Action Committee, which, to the government's consternation, had coordinated direct action, including squatting, in protest at housing shortages in the capital. In its protest against the bill, the action committee was joined by the

Labour Party, both wings of Sinn Féin (the Marxist Officials and militaristic Provisionals), trade unions and the Union of Students in Ireland.

Watched by around 150 gardaí, the crowd that summer's night marched around St Stephen's Green, down Grafton Street and on to Leinster House. The protesters made their point but, by 10.30pm, when the government forced the parliamentary debate to a close, the crowd started to thin out and had all but disappeared by the time the deputies began to file out of the building. An *Irish Times* reporter at the scene described an atmosphere of 'resignedness and ineffectiveness', adding rather dismissively: 'It was a dignified but useless and singularly futile gesture.'[17] In its final paragraph the report noted that shortly after midnight two women and a man were arrested following incidents – later described by one of those arrested as 'a bit of a schemozzle' – at the Merrion Square entrance to Leinster House.[18]

The two women were Máirín de Búrca and Mary Anderson, both activists with the Irish Women's Liberation Movement. They were charged with obstructing a police officer in the execution of his duties. Having pleaded not guilty, both women chose to have the charges tried before a jury. They were then released on bail and sent forward for trial at the Circuit Criminal Court.

At the time, the law on juries was as set down in the Juries Act 1927, which, following a nineteenth-century British model, stated that jury service was decided on the basis of occupation of land set at a specified rateable value. The 1927 law provided that Irish citizens aged twenty-one or upwards and under sixty-five who were on the electoral register, and who possessed the relevant land qualification, were eligible for jury service. It also expressly provided that women should not be liable for jury service, even if they met the property-owning requirement (which was unlikely), unless they themselves made an application to serve. This meant it was extremely rare to see a woman on a jury.

From the late nineteenth century, the women's movement had often drawn a link between the right to vote and the extension of jury service for women. Parliaments that resisted the idea that women should sit on juries generally put forward two arguments. First, that women (especially married women) should not be required to serve on juries where this would conflict with their duties in the home. Second, that the features of certain criminal trials, notably those involving sexual offences, would be too onerous for women of a certain (delicate) temperament.[19]

In Ireland there had been stirrings of change in the 1960s, when calls for sexual equality grew louder with the first wave of the feminist movement. In a report on jury service in 1965 the Committee on Court Practice and Procedure, chaired by Brian Walsh, had recommended fundamental reform of the selection system. On the property qualification, it noted that there had been a 'great social revolution' since the enactment of the nineteenth-century British law on which Ireland's regime was based, notably 'universal adult suffrage and universal education'. The committee agreed that the property qualification had the effect that juries were not representative of the country as a whole but tended to be 'predominantly male, middle-aged, middle-minded and middle class'. The committee, by a 9-3 majority, recommended that women should no longer be exempt from jury service. The majority, including Walsh, accepted the view 'that women should have equal rights and duties with men in this matter [and that women's] presence on juries will result in a more balanced view being taken of cases in general'.

Among the three minority voices was John Kenny, the High Court judge who, while deciding on Gladys Ryan's challenge against water fluoridation the previous summer, had introduced the concept of unspecified, or unenumerated, rights (in that case, a right to bodily integrity). Kenny was somewhat less avant-garde on women's rights. As jury service might require a married woman to serve on a jury until late in the evening, the minority noted: 'If a married woman returns to her home at seven o'clock in the evening and finds an irate husband and three hungry children waiting for her, we think it unlikely that they will accept the importance of jury service as a convincing excuse.'[20]

That report was gathering dust on a shelf in Government Buildings seven years later, when de Búrca and Anderson, awaiting trial over the incident on Merrion Street, met their lawyers to decide on how to bring a challenge against the jury system. 'We were politically aware people but it was only at that point that we realized that we were eventually going to come before a jury of twelve property-owning men on an issue which dealt with the poor and housing', de Búrca recalled fifteen years later. 'We consulted with our legal advisers and they said that the only way of challenging this was to challenge it on a constitutional issue – that it was unconstitutional to have a jury comprised of [only] property-owning men.'[21]

The case opened before Denis Pringle in the High Court on 29 March 1973. On the two women's side were the senior counsel Donal Barrington and Séamus Sorahan along with Patrick MacEntee and the up-and-coming barrister and campaigner Mary Robinson. The women's solicitor, Dudley Potter, was the same lawyer who had taken on Mary McGee's case. Opposite them, representing the State, were Tony Hederman[22] and the senior counsel D. P. Sheridan along with the junior counsel Paul Carney.[23]

The challengers' case was that the Juries Act of 1927 was invalid because, by in effect excluding women, it breached a number of fundamental rights clauses in the Constitution. Barrington and Robinson claimed that it raised two key points that went to the heart of the Constitution and the legal system. First, jury service was a right and a duty placed on all Irish citizens. Second, an accused person had the right to a balanced jury, by which was meant a jury that consisted of a random selection of citizens.

Under the 1927 law, they told Pringle, women were eligible as jurors but they were not compellable. This meant that jury panels had been 'grossly unrepresentative' of the citizens. It also meant that women seldom if ever appeared in criminal jury cases, although, as press reports on the day added, 'one woman appeared in Green Street [court] in recent years'.

Pringle pushed back. Was it not up to the women themselves to serve? Barrington replied that if men were not compellable there would probably be no men either, as the mass of citizens, in his opinion, regarded jury service as a burden they had to carry.

The legal team acting for de Búrca and Anderson zoned in on the property requirement. Not only was it wrong to have it in the law in the first place, but it varied dramatically from county to county. In some parts of Ireland one could be eligible for jury service if one owned a holding valued at more than £10, whereas in Dublin the value was £25. Because of that variation, a person could be brought from an area where his or her case would be tried by people of a particular property qualification to an area where it would be tried by people with a different qualification. After listing the different qualification rates by county, Barrington told the court: 'It seems to me that a citizen on trial in Wexford is being tried by a jury of richer men than if he went for trial in Tipperary North.'

Despite the obvious disparities and the clear evidence that very few women actually appeared on juries, it was a difficult argument to make because, as Pringle kept pointing out, women had the right to serve on juries. Barrington and Robinson knew they were getting nowhere. After one long day on his feet, Barrington slumped into his seat with his head in his hands. As he sat there, de Búrca came up beside him. 'Tell me, Mr Barrington,' she said, 'why have you a cushion under your fat arse and I have to sit on a hard bench?' (In the mid-1990s, when Hugh O'Flaherty was given responsibility for supervising the redecoration of the Supreme Court, he recalled this anecdote and insisted that all the benches should have padded seats.)

Under the law, Barrington told the High Court, half the population was exempted from service by virtue of their sex. Had the act said 'mothers' or 'mothers with young children' instead of just 'women', the exemption would have some reference to an individual's function in society.

> PRINGLE: I could understand that if they were absolutely exempted, but they are entitled to serve.
> BARRINGTON: I accept that.
> PRINGLE: How could a woman say she is discriminated against when she can apply to serve?
> BARRINGTON: In relation to the man. He certainly has a liability imposed on him from which a woman is exempted by virtue of her sex.

When a woman came before the courts as a litigant, he went on, she found herself with a jury of men to try her case, so that in her capacity as a litigant she was deprived of her advantage of a jury, which was a random selection of citizens.

One of the challengers' witnesses was Dr Brendan Walsh, a specialist in demographic statistics, who showed that out of a list of 10,000 jurors who had served in different areas over a certain period, not one woman was on the jury list. Moreover, he said, it had been established from circulars sent to the various county registrars that only six women in the country had in fact applied for jury service. When women did turn up, the court heard, they were invariably 'persons of strong opinions', and the legal teams in a trial, assuming as much, would veto them.

Responding on behalf of the Attorney General, Sheridan told the judge that the Constitution left it to the legislature to determine the yardstick by which juries should be chosen. The 'sheet anchor' of its case was that the courts had 'no concern with the legislative policy of the Oireachtas, and left it to the Oireachtas to legislate'. The plaintiffs had not done enough to show that the act contravened the Constitution. It was unwarranted to suggest that an all-male jury would be prejudiced against women. He argued that there was 'exact equality' in that everyone charged with criminal offences was entitled to the same treatment whether they were male or female. The women's lawyers had not shown that the actual outcomes were discriminatory.

The state had a constitutional obligation to protect the family, Sheridan went on. If, as was being asked by Barrington, women were to be compellable jurors, the 'practical effect' would be that 'a mother who had her housework to do and children to rear would be compelled to come down and sit on a jury, even though there might be a child of tender years involved', as the *Irish Times* paraphrased him.

Pringle was persuaded by the state's arguments and duly ruled against de Búrca and Anderson. The Juries Act did not breach any of the women's fundamental rights, he said, and there was no constitutional right to be tried before a jury drawn from a panel of men and women who had not passed a property test. '[A]s women are not absolutely debarred from serving as jurors, in my opinion it cannot be said that there is any invidious discrimination either in favour of or against them', he said.

The women's legal team got support from some unlikely quarters. In the middle of the saga, Barrington received a letter from a former client who had kept in touch. Barrington had succeeded in getting the man's criminal prosecution quashed some years previously, but in due course his normal activities had resulted in him ending up in Mountjoy. 'Dear Mr Barrington,' he wrote from prison,

> I am delighted to see that you have taken up the cudgels on behalf of the women of Ireland. I think it's a terrible insult to Irish women, the way they are treated in the courts of law. Only the other day, I saw this lovely woman called to serve on my jury only to find her immediately dismissed like some chattel. My blood boiled at this insult to Irish womanhood, but at the same time I could not but feel half-pleased that this lovely, innocent, sensitive creature was not to become involved in man's murky affairs, specifically my own.

De Búrca and Anderson appealed Pringle's decision to the Supreme Court, where the case was heard over a few days in November 1974 by a five-judge court consisting of O'Higgins, Walsh, Budd, Henchy and Griffin. Watching from the public gallery on the opening day was the Chief Justice of the United States, Warren Burger, who was on a visit to Dublin.

Barrington and Sheridan rehearsed the same constitutional points they had fought over in the High Court, but this time it was clear that the plaintiffs were addressing a more receptive audience. De Búrca later recalled Walsh being particularly engaged from the bench. She had seen the same pattern in another case she had been involved in, when a Supreme Court that included Walsh and Cearbhall Ó Dálaigh had overturned a lower court and let her out on bail after being charged with squatting-related offences. 'They would ask really pertinent questions, so that you knew that they were on top of the subject, that they wanted to go down to the very roots of the subject, and they wanted the full argument laid out in front of them', she said. 'Some judges, even on the Supreme Court, would just sit there. They would never ask a question, they would simply listen to the arguments and you don't know whether they are taking them in or whether they are thinking of what time they are going to have their tea.'[24]

De Búrca noted Walsh remarking, during the argument, that the property qualification would mean Wolfe Tone's men of no property would never sit on a jury.

> When he said that I knew – I felt I knew – how he was going to rule . . . It indicated to me straight away that he had a grasp of the argument we were making. That it wasn't simply that we were against property-owners, but that if you exclude women, 50 per cent of the population will have no input into the results of a particular action.[25]

Her hunch turned out to be correct. The Supreme Court decided unanimously that the Juries Act was unconstitutional and therefore invalid.[26] The Chief Justice, whose uncle Kevin O'Higgins was the minister who introduced the 1927 act, did not buy the argument on sex discrimination. However, in his eyes the property qualification meant the act was holed below the waterline.

For Walsh, similarly, the property bar was clearly discriminatory. 'Can it seriously be suggested that a person who is not the rated occupier of any property, or who is not the rated occupier of property of a certain value, is less intelligent or less honest or less impartial than one who is so rated? The answer can only be in the negative', he wrote.

Walsh pointed out that women were actively engaged in all of the professions, in most branches of business, in art and literature and in virtually every human activity. In urban areas, from where most jurors were drawn, there were more women than men. Yet according to figures from the Department of Justice for the ten years immediately preceding the de Búrca and Anderson case, the total number of women whose names were inserted on the jurors list was 'the startlingly low figure of nine'. The numbers who were called for jury service and who served on juries were five and two, respectively. The fact that women could apply to be on juries was beside the point; the effect, as the figures showed, was that very few did, and that as a result juries were completely unrepresentative of society.

Henchy was just as emphatic:

The absence of women from juries means an unconstitutional system
of selection for two reasons. First, it fails the test of representativeness
because it means that some 50% of the adult population will never be
included in the jury lists . . . Secondly, and of even greater importance,
that narrowed choice means that a woman's experience, understanding
and general attitude will form no part in the jury processes leading to a
verdict. Whatever may have been the position at common law or under
statute up to recent times, it is incompatible with the necessary diffu-
sion of rights and duties in a modern democratic society that important
public decisions such as voting, or jury verdicts involving life or liberty, should be made by male citizens only.

Budd and Griffin agreed. The Juries Act was dead. Across the country, judges who were about to empanel all-male juries adjourned the
trials to assess the fallout. De Búrca and Anderson basked in a famous
victory.

Before the Supreme Court decision, in July 1975 the government
had already published the Juries Bill 1975, which was slowly meander-
ing through the Oireachtas. But the court's decision made it 'a matter
of urgency', as Minister for Justice Patrick Cooney said.[27] So the draft
law was then rushed through the Dáil and quickly enacted by the
Oireachtas, with minor changes, as the Juries Act 1976. The property
requirement was gone.

Notwithstanding her success, de Búrca, looking back eleven years
later, was realistic about the obstacles that lay in the path of anyone
seeking to effect social change through the courts. 'They [the courts]
were open to us because of our political involvement', she said.
'Through our political involvement we met certain members of the
legal profession who were liberal-minded, progressive, and who were
willing to take risks to change laws which they saw as anachronisms,
as well as everybody else.'[28]

Yet she also drew great pride from the outcome.

It's immortality of a kind – it's probably the only kind of immortality
which I can hope to achieve. I didn't see it as just women who had the

right to sit on juries and to take part in the legal process, but women – and indeed men – who come before the courts as defendants. I think that they have a better chance of justice because the jury that they will come before is taken from a much wider spectrum of the population than before. I'm proud of that.[29]

Inside the Supreme Court conference room, the result of the juries case was never really in doubt, but the potential fallout from the decision was the subject of extensive debate. If the Juries Act was unconstitutional, did that mean that every jury empanelled since 1927 had been invalid? And did that imply, as alert lawyers would no doubt argue, that every conviction in a jury trial over the previous half-century was in doubt? O'Higgins and Walsh moved to head off the possibility by inserting in their judgments the remark that, though jury panels over the previous fifty years were wrongly restricted, no ineligible individual had served on such a jury. The other three judges – Budd, Henchy and Griffin – did not refer to the issue.

The argument nonetheless made its way back to the Supreme Court relatively soon after *de Búrca*, when a man who had been convicted by a jury in the Circuit Court after the Supreme Court decision in *de Búrca*, but whose jury had been empanelled before the decision, argued that he should be released from jail.[30] This was unanimously rejected by the Supreme Court, although for different reasons. O'Higgins stuck to the reason he had given in the de Búrca judgment. But Henchy, leading a 3-2 majority, was unable to accept O'Higgins's rationale. Pointing out that the unconstitutional provisions of the 1927 act excluded some 80 per cent of adult citizens (women and non-ratepayers) from jury service, he wrote:

> The proposition that juries drawn from the remaining 20% were valid because no ineligible persons served on them I find no more supportable than a proposition that an election would be valid when 80% of those who should have had an opportunity of voting were barred from the polls. The essential spuriousness of such an election would not be overcome by an assertion that no ineligible persons voted.

Instead, the majority held that the convicted individual could be assumed to have waived his right to complain of the jury's invalidity as he had not availed of the opportunity, in the middle of his trial, to object to the jury's composition. (Of course, as O'Higgins pointed out, this assumed the man knew the ins-and-outs of the outcome of de Búrca's case.[31])

In October 1975, a year after O'Higgins became Chief Justice, Walsh was appointed first president of the Law Reform Commission, a new body set up with the task of proposing changes to the State's laws. This meant that he sat only occasionally in the Supreme Court from then on.

In a letter to William Brennan on 2 March 1977, Walsh explained the new arrangement: 'I still sit occasionally in the Supreme Court but I am no longer legally compellable to sit there and I only sit in cases which I think are of particular interest or great importance.' Yet Walsh was keen to stress that he was still involved, and watching developments in the US with a close eye. 'I continue to read the judgments of your Court and your own contributions with very great interest and admiration and I feel that keeps me in reasonably close touch with your fundamental legal developments', he wrote.[32]

Over the years the friendship between Walsh and Brennan had blossomed. The two judges would discuss their families, exchange the occasional novel and correspond on major news events of the day. For instance, in the aftermath of Pope John Paul II's successful visit to Ireland in 1979, Walsh wrote to Brennan:

As you have probably seen on television or read in the papers, we have had a most outstandingly successful visit here from the Pope which was so crowded with events that while in fact he was in the country here for two and a half days it felt like it were two and a half weeks. As I write this letter he has already arrived in the United States so perhaps you will already have met him before I send you this letter. The attendance at the functions were truly colossal. For example, at the Mass in the city of Dublin there was a congregation of 1,250,000 people and at Galway there were about 250,000 to

300,000 young people, at Knock almost half a million and a similar figure at Limerick. When you consider that the total population of the whole island is only 4½ million, and you may write off about a million of those for various political and historical reasons, you will see that about two out of every three people in the whole population have attended the functions.[33]

A couple of weeks later Brennan replied that the success of the Pope's Irish visit 'was I think matched only by the success of his visit here'.[34]

When Walsh took up his position at the Law Reform Commission, the Fine Gael–Labour coalition, using its power to appoint an additional judge, appointed John Kenny to the Supreme Court. Kenny, the son of a building contractor from Rathgar in Dublin, had first come to national prominence as a legal academic in UCD, when in 1959 he had clashed with the university leadership over some of the academic appointments made by the UCD governing body. His proposal to have government appoint someone to investigate the issue was accepted, but it deeply angered Michael Tierney, the prominent UCD president. The tensions between the two men worsened the following year, when Kenny gave legal advice to the college's debating society, the Literary and Historical Society (L&H), in a bitter confrontation with Tierney over college regulations governing membership of student societies.[35] UCD under Tierney was seen as a Fine Gael bastion. (He had been a Cumann na nGaedheal TD for seven years before the party merged with two smaller centre-right parties to became Fine Gael; Tierney came up with the name of the new party.) As one contemporary of Walsh and Kenny puts it, referring to the number of future judges with loose Fianna Fáil links who confronted the authoritarian president, 'a lot of the [early] drama was played out in UCD'. Séamus Henchy, while he was a member of the law faculty, had instituted a judicial visitation in order to challenge the legality of non-law academic staff joining the law faculty. And in 1961 he opposed Tierney's move to suspend the L&H.[36] Similarly, Brian Walsh was seen as a critical internal voice when he was a member of the UCD governing body from 1958 onwards.

Kenny's stand-off with Tierney did him no harm. It may even

have helped him. In the Dáil, he was praised for his courage in standing up against UCD's system of appointments – a stance that, as Gerard Hogan points out, may have endeared him to the Fianna Fáil government, which appointed him to the High Court in 1961.[37]

Kenny belonged to a group of young judges, which included Walsh and Henchy, who were appointed to the High Court in their early to mid-forties and were to lead a creative reappraisal of the Constitution and the courts' place in society.[38] He had left his most significant mark as a High Court judge, where for fourteen years he was considered one of its most authoritative and innovative voices. In the Ryan case his introduction of the concept of unenumerated rights – rights that did not appear in the text of the Constitution but were implied and there for judges to identify – was ground-breaking. With that decision he radically changed the course of Irish constitutional law. Without it, the course of the next thirty years could have been altogether different.

O'Higgins's Supreme Court also showed itself willing to make far-reaching decisions that would have clear financial implications for the government. In June 1974 an eighteen-year-old, John Healy, was brought before the Children's Court charged with breaking into a rugby club in south Dublin and stealing property valued at £18.80. Healy had left school at the age of thirteen and had no money to pay for legal advice. He pleaded guilty to the charge, which was to be tried without a jury. He did not apply for legal aid and was not told that he could do so. He was eventually convicted by a District Court judge and sentenced to three months in jail.

In December 1974 Healy was brought before the same court on a separate charge of stealing a car the previous night. Again he pleaded guilty, but this time he applied for and was granted legal aid. But his solicitor did not turn up for the trial, as solicitors had at the time withdrawn from the legal aid scheme in protest at cutbacks. He asked for an adjournment so that he could find another solicitor, but this was rejected and he was given a six-month sentence.

As this was unfolding, Healy's mother walked into a Free Legal Advice Centre (FLAC) in Tallaght in Dublin. FLAC was a largely voluntary service staffed mostly by young lawyers. She spoke to John Mac Menamin,[39] a student at UCD, who was volunteering in the centre that day. He looked into the case, and contacted his college friend Frank Clarke,[40] who had just finished his training as a barrister at the King's Inns. They agreed it sounded like an interesting case. Clarke got in touch the barrister Ercus Stewart, who in turn approached Rory O'Hanlon, one of the leading constitutional lawyers of the day, who agreed to join the case.

O'Hanlon argued that the District Court judge, by proceeding to convict and sentence Healy while he was not legally represented, was in clear breach of Healy's right to a fair trial and his personal rights under the Constitution. The High Court judge, John Gannon, rejected the constitutional claim. But when it reached the Supreme Court in 1976, the judges unanimously agreed that there was a constitutional right to free legal aid.[41]

'[T]he concept of justice, which is specifically referred to in the preamble [to the Constitution] in relation to the freedom and dignity of the individual, appears again in the provisions of Article 34 which deal with the Courts', O'Higgins said in his judgment. 'It is justice which is to be administered in the Courts and this concept of justice must import not only fairness, and fair procedures, but also regard to the dignity of the individual. No court under the Constitution has jurisdiction to act contrary to justice.'

In a similar vein, Henchy concluded that anyone who was convicted and deprived of his liberty as a result of a prosecution in which, owing to his poverty, he had no legal aid, had good reason to complain 'that he has been meted out less than his constitutional due'. He went on:

> This is particularly true if the absence of legal aid is compounded by factors such as a grave or complex charge; or ignorance, illiteracy, immaturity or other conditions rendering the accused incompetent to cope properly with the prosecution; or an inability, because of detentional restraint, to find and produce witnesses; or simply the fumbling incompetence that may occur when an accused is precipitated into the public glare and alien complexity of courtroom

procedures, and is confronted with the might of a prosecution backed by the State. As the law stands, a legal-aid certificate is the shield provided against such an unjust attack.

It was a far-reaching decision. The court went well beyond the terms of the 1962 law that dealt with legal aid, laying down firmly that anyone facing a possible prison sentence and who had no means to engage a lawyer, must be specifically informed of their right to legal aid. The decision clearly had financial implications for the State, because it meant that public funds for criminal cases could not in future be cut back by the Department of Finance.

If the Healy case caused headaches for government, its financial repercussions paled in comparison with those of a decision that followed a few years later, when the court threw out a pillar of the State's income tax laws and ordered it to tax married men and women separately.

The law, which dated from 1967, had long been seen as unjust towards married women. It stipulated that when a woman got married, her income was deemed to be that of her husband. He was liable for tax on her income, and her income was taxable at her husband's highest marginal rate. In 1974–5, the highest marginal rate was 80 per cent. It was the husband's responsibility to fill in tax forms, and any refunds due to the couple went directly to him.[42]

In June 1977 a group called the Married Persons' Tax Reform Association was set up to campaign for change. Its nucleus was teachers and civil servants, according to the lawyer Yvonne Scannell, who was one of the principal movers.[43] In the face of firm political opposition – only the Labour Party was in favour of tax reform and Fianna Fáil, which had just swept into government, was strongly against it – the association soon concluded that the most effective way of changing the law was through a constitutional challenge in the courts. The group had strong backing from the teaching unions, but it also drew support from women's organizations and a number of female Fine Gael TDs. 'The campaign for fair taxation for married women became a central part of the feminist agenda for the first time in 1977', Scannell writes. 'This was not an objective of the entire committee of the [association], which was anxious not to alienate male and non-feminist support, but it was one of my personal object-ives although I was careful where and when I expressed it.'

The campaign gradually gained momentum, along with much-needed small donations, but it had no hope of finding sufficient money to pay a team of solicitors and barristers. After several lawyers rebuffed their approach, the family law specialist Alan Shatter, whom Scannell had known since college, eventually agreed to take it on, knowing that his prospects of recovering fees were virtually non-existent if the case was lost. Rory O'Hanlon then came aboard, as did Mary Robinson. Neither asked for fees. With the lawyers in place, all the case needed was actual plaintiffs.

The chosen couple were Mary and Francis Murphy, two young national school teachers on modest salaries starting out in their careers. They agreed to take the case, and in July 1979 it opened before Liam Hamilton in the High Court. In an indication of how seriously the State took the challenge, it briefed two senior counsel – Donal Barrington and Tommy Conolly – in addition to the junior John Cooke.

The case was relatively straightforward: the Murphys' barristers argued that the law was unconstitutional because it breached the equal-ity clause as well as the personal rights guarantees in the Constitution. The lawyers also cited Article 41.3, where the State pledges itself to guard with special care the institution of marriage, and to protect it from attack. After a four-day hearing, Hamilton declared the relevant parts of the act unconstitutional on the basis that they were in violation of Articles 41 (the family) and 40.1 (equality). It was a stunning victory for a campaign that had only begun two years earlier.

But the State, facing a huge bill as a result of the judgment, imme-diately appealed to the Supreme Court and briefed a third senior counsel – Frank Murphy – to join its team in an attempt to reverse the High Court decision. The campaigners followed suit by beefing up their own team to two senior counsel, with Kevin Liston and a young Dermot Gleeson replacing O'Hanlon, who had had to with-draw as he was appearing at a lengthy tribunal. Mary Robinson was still in situ, and all were working pro bono.

'I felt that Mr Liston, a somewhat remote person . . . would not be philosophically attuned to the feminist undertones of the case but this proved to be a great advantage,' writes Scannell, 'as he was adept at addressing the all-male Supreme Court in terms which they understood.'[44]

The Supreme Court again ruled against the State, upholding the High Court finding that the act was unconstitutional.[45] 'It was the most important milestone on the road to securing the judicial recognition of equality before the law for women in Ireland', writes Scannell.[46] '*Murphy* was also important in that it provided a focus for the women's movement in the late 1970s, a focus that strengthened and united many Irish women in a common endeavour.'[47]

But the Murphy decision left another vexing puzzle at the Supreme Court's door. If the act was unconstitutional, and had always been so, then the logical consequence was that the State was now facing a huge bill for overpaid taxes dating back to 1967 from women across the country. That sent shockwaves through the system. Asked for clarification on this by the State, four out of the five judges said that any post-1937 act that was declared unconstitutional was invalid as of the date it was enacted. But the court did not go so far as to tell the government it had to repay hundreds of millions of pounds in overpaid tax. Instead, the majority decided that the Murphys could obtain tax refunds from the tax year 1978–9 – the year in which they had begun their case. Other couples would be able to recoup their money only from the tax year 1980–81, which roughly corresponded with the time of the court's decision. It was essentially a piece of judicial improvisation. Henchy's reasoning was that while the court's finding of unconstitutionality meant the act had indeed always been invalid, that did not mean everything done under it was itself invalid. That, he said, was because there had always been 'transcendent considerations' that prevented the re-opening of past events and that courts around the world had rejected such full retroactivity.

'For a variety of reasons, the law recognizes that in certain circumstances, no matter how unfounded in law certain conduct may have been, no matter how unwarranted its operation in a particular case, what has happened has happened and cannot, or should not, be undone.'

It was a puzzle the Supreme Court would face in even more dramatic circumstances in 2006, when its decision to find a section of the law on statutory rape unconstitutional opened the possibility of child sex offenders walking free from jail. In that episode, the judges would lean heavily on the solutions their predecessors on the court came up with to limit the retrospective effects of their decisions on juries and tax.

With decisions such as those on defendants' rights, juries, legal aid and married women's tax the O'Higgins court showed itself every bit as willing as its predecessor to assert itself and to rely on the fundamental rights clauses in the Constitution to throw out legislation when it saw fit. Even many dyed-in-the-wool Fianna Fáil barristers were impressed with O'Higgins, having initially believed that a Fine Gael chief justice would make it his mission to row back on the activism of the Ó Dálaigh years. Yet there were also signs that on social or moral questions there were limits to how far O'Higgins was willing to go in reversing the will of the legislators in Leinster House. It took a 36-year-old gay academic from Trinity College Dublin to show just where those limits lay.

10. The Norris challenge

'Such conduct is, of course, morally wrong, and has been
so regarded by mankind through the centuries.'

Tom O'Higgins

'My client is a congenital, irreversible homosexual.' These were Garret Cooney's opening words on 24 June 1980 as he stood up in the High Court to outline the case of his client, the Joycean scholar David Norris.

The case had been in preparation for years. In the mid-1970s Norris had been one of the founding members of the Campaign for Homosexual Law Reform, a group set up specifically with the aim of mounting a challenge to the laws that made it a crime to engage in homosexual acts. It was a tiny organization – 'four or five members and half a filing cabinet'[1] – but its supporters included politicians and public figures, including Noël Browne, Senator Gemma Hussey, Ruairí Quinn of Labour, the playwright Hugh Leonard, Dean Victor Griffin of the Church of Ireland and the Trinity law professor Mary McAleese, who was co-chair with Norris. The group also counted among its allies a number of practising lawyers, including a leading civil rights solicitor, Garrett Sheehan,[2] who thought the law was unjust and who was happy to represent the people who came to the organization looking for legal representation. 'What was interesting was that many of those people were eminently respectable – architects, clergy, teachers, lawyers and doctors, some of whom were married', Norris recalled.[3]

The group was looking out for an accused man in whose name the constitutional case could be taken, but in the end all eyes fell on Norris himself. 'By that stage both my parents were dead and I had a reasonably tolerant and liberal employer in Trinity College, so could not be pressured from those angles, and I had a passionate sense of the injustice of the law', he writes.[4] They sought a legal opinion from Donal Barrington, and he said they were legally and morally right but that they would have to steel themselves for a long battle, 'because there were political, religious and social aspects to what we sought, and we would have to prepare Irish society for such a significant change'.[5] Barrington also offered Norris a prediction: he would lose in the High Court, he might possibly win in the Supreme Court on a split decision but he would certainly win at the European Court of Human Rights in Strasbourg. 'So don't start unless you're prepared to go right to the end', he said.

Shortly afterwards, Barrington was appointed a judge of the High Court, so he could not take the case himself. Instead the campaign turned to Garret Cooney because, in addition to being a brilliant lawyer, he had a reputation as a conservative Catholic.[6] The two junior counsel were Paul Carney and Mary Robinson, who was an old college friend of Norris's, and the solicitor was John Jay.

Given that the case would centre on Norris's own life experience, Robinson asked him at the outset to put down on paper his account of being a gay man in Ireland. Norris could not type, so he wrote it out in longhand. He wrote about falling in love with a boy in school and about lying in bed listening to the bands playing at the cricket-club dances and how he knew that life was not for him. He wrote:

> As far as the question of sin was concerned, I was, and am a practising member of the Anglican Communion, a church that allows a certain latitude for individual conscience in the relationship between the individual and God, so that while I knew that a number of the clergy despised people like myself, I was confident that my nature was not evil in the sight of the God who had created it.
>
> However, the idea of being a criminal without even knowing it was much more disturbing as it was not a matter of opinion but a political fact. If I expressed myself as my instincts increasingly urged me to, I became de facto apparently a member of the criminal classes liable to arbitrary punishment and disgrace. As I was of a literary

turn of mind even then my attention was jocularly drawn to the facts
of another Irishman – Oscar Wilde. But it was no joke for me, and I
was shocked to discover that the very same laws under which he had
suffered so many years before still applied in Ireland.

. . . I do not ask for mercy, compassion, pity or well-intentioned
advice but for the justice which I believe is enshrined as my right and
entitlement as a citizen under the constitution of this land. I seek the
vindication under law of my right not to be unthinkingly and unfeel-
ingly rejected by my native land, and of my right to conduct my
personal relationships with dignity and decency in accord with my
nature, and without the threat of police intervention or the possibility of blackmail.[7]

Robinson later said that when she read the essay she wept.

Norris had a firm view on how the case should be conducted and
insisted that it not be fought as a dry, technical challenge. 'I wanted
drama and I wanted the case to hit the headlines, to help sway the
public to our side. I believed that one of the things that most crippled
gay people in those days was the complete silence that obscured their
existence.'[8]

In the two and a half years between proceedings being issued and
the case finally coming to court, Norris researched intensively, travelling to the United States to speak to experts and persuade them to give
evidence in his case. Meanwhile, the campaign launched a public
appeal for donations, hoping to raise £10,000 initially and £30,000 over
time to cover the costs of the case, however long it would take.

Under the Offences Against the Person Act 1861 and the Criminal
Law (Amendment) Act 1885, two Victorian-era laws that remained in
force in Ireland, anyone convicted of the crime of buggery could face
a jail sentence. Section 61 of the 1861 law stipulated: 'Whosoever shall
be convicted of the abominable crime of buggery, committed either
with mankind or with any animal, shall . . . be liable to be kept in
penal servitude for life.' The penalty was a jail sentence of not less
than ten years.

Between 1975 and 1979, there had been fifty-eight prosecutions and twenty convictions under the relevant sections of these two laws. Norris sought to have the acts declared unconstitutional, claiming their provisions were not consistent with Article 40.1, which states that 'All citizens shall, as human persons, be held equal before the law', and with Article 40.3, which sets out the guaranteed personal rights of the citizen.

In the witness box, addressing the High Court judge Herbert McWilliam, Norris said he knew the century-old laws he was challenging did not reflect the moral values of the Anglican Church, of which he was a member, and he could not see how they could reflect the moral views of the Irish public in 1980. He told the court that it would be impossible to separate an integral part of his nature and to regard himself as acceptable only when that part of his personality was denied. In cross-examination, Rory O'Hanlon, defending the case for the Attorney General, put it to Norris that nowhere was he liable to criminal penalties for sexual orientation or instinctive feelings.

> NORRIS: I think that is true, because it is not possible to criminalise a state of mind, but it is possible to criminalise an expression of that state of mind and these Acts cover any matters of expression of physical association between males.

Norris argued that the criminal law operated as 'a focus' for the public mind. He pointed out that even in newspaper reports he was often described as 'a self-confessed homosexual', which suggested that anyone who was homosexual was a criminal.

> O'HANLON: Not alone does the criminal law not condemn anyone for instinctive feelings and sexual orientation. Neither does it condemn them for association with other people with the same feeling.
> NORRIS: I have always felt that analogous to the situation in the Penal Laws, in which a person could not be convicted of being a Roman Catholic but could be penalised for attending Mass or for various other expressions of religious conviction. I feel this is precisely the same kind of situation that I am placed in.

o'HANLON: Would you agree that the criminal law is not concerned with persons forming bonds of affection between each other – perhaps living together, perhaps having what could be considered a stable relationship with each other, until they perform certain acts of a sexual nature? Isn't that the way the law is framed?

NORRIS: It is, but it is not clear to me how the State could become aware of some of these acts.

O'Hanlon asked Norris if he was seriously contending that homosexual intercourse would not be regarded as a breach of the moral code. 'I do', Norris replied.

The High Court heard from Dr Thomas McCracken, a partly retired consultant psychiatrist. In 1969, shortly after the death of his mother, Norris had been referred to McCracken after he suffered an anxiety attack while having lunch in Switzer's on Grafton Street and had to be brought to hospital by ambulance. When Norris came to him, McCracken told the court, he advised him that he would have to be very careful in his relationships because homosexuality was illegal. He discussed with him that there were countries, including France, where homosexuality was not an offence.

PAUL CARNEY: Were you advising him to go to one of these countries?

MCCRACKEN: I was leaving it to himself in the light of what he told me.

The court also heard experts from the United States and England on evolving understandings of homosexuality and the effects of changes in law and attitudes in those countries. Professor Donald James West, consultant psychiatrist and professor of clinical criminology at the University of Cambridge, told the judge there had been a considerable change in the medical understanding of homosexuality and it was no longer considered a mental disorder. He also said that the outcome of the legalization of homosexuality in private between consenting adults in the UK had disproved the fears expressed beforehand. He did not think that there was any evidence of homosexuality becoming much more prevalent in England as a result of legalization.[9]

Professor John P. Spiegel, an American psychiatrist, said homosexuality had been removed by the American Psychiatric Association from its list of mental disorders following very thorough research. He told the court that the incidence of homosexuality remained the same whether or not it was forbidden or accepted, and a progressive wave of decriminalization in the United States had resulted in nineteen states having removed homosexual acts as offences on their statute books. He described the effects that the criminalization of homosexuality had on many of his patients, causing them immense stress that led to mental illness. 'We have enough mental illness as it is without society contributing unnecessarily to the number of people suffering from mental illness', he said.[10]

One of the most striking interventions came from two theologians who were called by Norris's side. Micheál Mac Gréil, a priest and lecturer in sociology at St Patrick's College, Maynooth, told the court that the law discriminated against homosexuals and that he would like to see the offences removed so as to help end prejudice and stigmatization. The Rev Joseph O'Leary, chaplain to a convent in Drumcondra, said he had a pastoral concern for those he believed were suffering as a result of the 'confusion and ignorance' about homosexuality. The Catholic approach to the morality of homosexuality had undergone a tremendous change in previous years, he said, and that change was in the direction of a more liberal, more understanding view. The church would never approve of a law that was unjust, and the present law was unjust.

The senior counsel Aidan Browne, for the Attorney General, referred Fr O'Leary to a speech made by Pope John Paul II in the United States the previous year and asked if he accepted that the Pope, in that statement, was saying that homosexual acts were wrong, as distinct from 'homosexual orientation'.

To that Fr O'Leary replied that he did not think anything he said contradicted the Pope. He said the Pope had referred to 'gay' people as his brothers and that was the first time a Pope had ever referred to them in such a way.

BROWNE: He did not refer to them as 'gay'.

FR O'LEARY: We used to refer to tinkers and then they became itinerants and that was an advance. In the same way when homosexuals,

from being called queers, came to be called gay, it was an advance
for us.

BROWNE: For us?

FR O'LEARY: For our society.

The State did not call any witnesses of its own. In his closing
remarks, however, O'Hanlon urged the judge against relying on the
McGee decision. In that case, he said, the judgments were clearly
based on the concept that a right of privacy in marital relations should
be recognized, but it was not an absolute right, O'Hanlon said. He
told the judge that the importance of Christianity in the life of the
people 'received very clear recognition' in the text of the Constitution. The 'preservation of public morality' had always been the
legitimate concern of the criminal law. Sexual relations outside marriage constituted a violation of bodily integrity, and homosexuality
did so 'in a particularly grave manner' as it was against the order of
nature and a perversion of the biological function of the sexual
organs, he said. Moreover, homosexual acts represented a dangerous
or potentially dangerous attack on marriage and the family, and it
was important that the State should do all in its power to discourage
the spread of homosexuality.

Mary Robinson challenged this. Social views that were current
centuries ago ran counter to medical evidence and the modern understanding of homosexuality.

McWilliam, who was the only Protestant judge on the High
Court, took four months to consider his decision. The initial signs
were good for Norris. In the opening sections of his forty-five-minute
address, the judge accepted virtually all the conclusions presented by
the expert witnesses called by the Norris side, including on the nature
of homosexuality, changing social attitudes and the pain and distress
the legal regime caused gay people. It sounded like a manifesto for
gay rights, Norris thought, 'and we began to think that miraculously
we would win'.[11] But then McWilliam changed direction and came
up against what he saw as the legal obstacle standing in Norris's way:
the Christian and democratic nature of the State. 'Although I accept
that the traditional attitudes of the Churches, and of the general body

of citizens, towards homosexuality, are being challenged and may be successfully challenged in the future, it is reasonably clear that current Christian morality in this country does not approve of buggery, or of any sexual activity between persons of the same sex', the judge said. It was not his role to change the law – only to decide whether it was inconsistent with the Constitution. And that he could not find, he said. For Norris, there was a further sting in the tail. The State asked for and was awarded costs against him of £75,000 – three times more than the price Norris had paid for his house on North Great Georges Street not long before.

At a press conference after the decision was handed down, Norris said he was encouraged by aspects of the judgment, including the judge's reference to the statistics on homosexuality and his acceptance of the evidence that gay people had been the victims of prejudice and that they did not molest children. Other aspects left him 'surprised and slightly shocked', however, and he announced immediately that he would appeal to the Supreme Court.

In April 1983 the Supreme Court affirmed McWilliam's decision by a 3-2 vote, with Tom O'Higgins, Tom Finlay and Frank Griffin in the majority and Séamus Henchy and Niall McCarthy dissenting.[12] O'Higgins's majority judgment has a strong claim to be one of the worst the Supreme Court has produced. Not only did it reject Norris's claim on a right to privacy and uphold the constitutionality of the laws on homosexual acts. It did so without citing a single case of the Supreme Court or High Court in support, instead drawing heavily on vague and largely unexplained natural law concepts and the Christian tradition to denounce homosexuality as a suggestible condition that was immoral and wrong. O'Higgins said:

> The preamble to the Constitution proudly asserts the existence of God in the Most Holy Trinity and recites that the people of Ireland humbly acknowledge their obligation to 'our Divine Lord, Jesus Christ'. It cannot be doubted that the people, so asserting and acknowledging their obligations to our Divine Lord Jesus Christ, were proclaiming a deep religious conviction and faith and an

intention to adopt a Constitution consistent with that conviction and faith and with Christian beliefs. Yet it is suggested that, in the very act of so doing, the people rendered inoperative laws which had existed for hundreds of years prohibiting unnatural sexual conduct which Christian teaching held to be gravely sinful. It would require very clear and express provisions in the Constitution itself to convince me that such took place. When one considers that the conduct in question had been condemned consistently in the name of Christ for almost two thousand years and, at the time of the enactment of the Constitution, was prohibited as criminal by the laws in force in England, Wales, Scotland and Northern Ireland, the suggestion becomes more incomprehensible and difficult of acceptance.

A right of privacy could never be absolute, O'Higgins said. There were many acts done in private which the State was entitled to condemn. The law had always condemned abortion, incest, suicide attempts, suicide pacts, euthanasia or mercy killings.

These are prohibited simply because they are morally wrong and regardless of the fact, which may exist in some instances, that no harm or injury to others is involved. With homosexual conduct, the matter is not so simple or clear. Such conduct is, of course, morally wrong, and has been so regarded by mankind through the centuries. It cannot be said of it, however, as the plaintiff seeks to say, that no harm is done if it is conducted in private by consenting males. Very serious harm may in fact be involved. Such conduct, although carried on with full consent, may lead a mildly homosexually orientated person into a way of life from which he may never recover.

In politics, O'Higgins had been regarded as a liberal. When, in 1979, he and the court ruled that an order by the Censorship Board impounding a consignment of family planning leaflets was unlawful,[13] it was seen as an encouraging development by those who hoped that his political instincts broadly tallied with his judicial stance on social and moral issues. Quite apart from *Norris*, however, the court had frequently declined opportunities to introduce social and political reforms. It dismissed an attempt to have postal votes provided to disabled people,[14] for example, and said No to the question of whether illegitimate children should have rights of intestate succession in their fathers' estates.[15]

The kindest interpretation of the majority judgment in *Norris* is that it was a product of the judges' generation and also a reflection of the climate of public discourse in 1983. The ongoing debate about inserting into the Constitution a 'pro-life' amendment to prevent the legalization of abortion in Ireland had thrown up some sharp criticism from anti-abortion groups of the Supreme Court's decision in the McGee case. This may well have put the judges on guard against any perception that they were attempting to legislate from the bench.

Norris may have resulted in one of the poorest majority judgments in the court's history, but it also led to one of the greatest dissents. In the intervening years, Séamus Henchy's powerful text has become one of the most frequently quoted, and has contributed to establishing his reputation as one of the great judges – a verdict that only firmly took hold after his retirement. As Gerard Hogan points out, Henchy was in some ways a traditionalist who recognized the inherent limitations of judicial power and often suggested that change could best be brought about by the Oireachtas rather than through the courts. Yet he had always proved himself willing to give full effect to the fundamental rights protections in the Constitution when he felt the occasion demanded it.[16]

In his Norris dissent, Henchy criticized O'Higgins for relying too heavily on the opinions of the churches about the possible social ill-effects of decriminalizing homosexual acts and not enough on the expert testimony which was heard in the High Court and which the Chief Justice virtually ignored. If the O'Higgins-led majority was correct, Henchy pointed out, then the McGee case could never have been decided the way that it was, given that contraception 'was declared to be morally wrong according to the official teaching of the Church to which about 95% of the citizens belong'. Henchy did not deny the Christian influence in the Constitution but argued that in banning immoral acts the onus was on the State to show that the common good required that ban.

It is not surprising that the repressive and constricting treatment suffered by the plaintiff affected his psychological health. As an involuntary, chronic and irreversible male homosexual he has been cast unwillingly in a role of furtive living, which has involved traumatic feelings of guilt, shame, ridicule and harassment and countless risks to his career as a university lecturer and to his social life generally. Those risks are not the normal lot of the fornicator, the adulterer, the sexually deviant married couple, the drunkard, the habitual gambler, the practising lesbian, and the many other types of people whose propensities or behaviour may be thought to be no less inimical to the upholding of individual moral conduct, or to necessary or desirable standards of public order or morality, or to the needs of a healthy family life, or to social justice, or to other expressed or implied desiderata of the Constitution.

He went on to give a powerful endorsement of pluralistic values and acceptance of difference:

What is deemed necessary to his dignity and freedom by one man may be abhorred by another as an exercise in immorality. The pluralism necessary for the preservation of constitutional requirements in the Christian, democratic State envisaged by the Constitution means that the sanctions of the criminal law may be attached to immoral acts only when the common good requires their proscription as crimes. As the most eminent theologians have conceded, the removal of the sanction of the criminal law from an immoral act does not necessarily imply an approval or condonation of that act. Here the consensus of the evidence was that the sweep of the criminal prohibition contained in the questioned provisions goes beyond the requirements of the common good; indeed, in the opinion of most of the witnesses it is inimical to the common good. Consequently, a finding of unconstitutionality was inescapable on the evidence.

Henchy's judgment was not without its false notes. His passing remark that Norris's public espousal of the cause of male homosexuals was 'tinged with a degree of that affected braggadocio which is said by some to distinguish a "gay" from a mere homosexual', has come in for much criticism. Colm Tóibín called it 'an uncharacteristically stupid comment'.[17] But Henchy's was nonetheless a remarkable and forward-looking judgment.

'It was not even that Henchy was prepared to find for the plaintiff in *Norris* – although that itself was a striking fact in the Ireland of 1983 – but that the language and reasoning of the judgment looked beyond conventional wisdom and inherited assumptions and sought to educate, challenge and enlighten society about the true nature of [human] freedom', writes Gerard Hogan.[18] For Henchy, it was the culmination of what Donal O'Donnell, later a judge of the Supreme Court, called a fascinating intellectual journey that brought him from a childhood in west Clare through University College Galway and a professorship in UCD 'to the point where he delivered his compelling dissenting judgment'.[19] The day after the judgment was delivered, the *Irish Times* predicted correctly that 'it was the view of one of the dissenting judges, Mr Justice Henchy, which at some future time will almost certainly prevail'.[20] Henchy died in 2009, but today a framed extract from his Norris judgment sits on the desk where he worked at home.

For the Supreme Court the judgments in *Norris* crystallized a debate that had been simmering for decades on the subject of natural law – the idea that we have certain rights by virtue of being human, or that a higher law exists above and beyond the Constitution itself. The idea had first surfaced through then Chief Justice Hugh Kennedy in the 1930s, but it did not become a major issue for the courts until 1965, when John Kenny, in the Ryan fluoridation case, discovered in the Constitution an unwritten right to bodily integrity. The notion, which originated in a papal encyclical, followed from what Kenny called 'the Christian and democratic nature of the State'. It arose again in the McGee contraception case, when Brian Walsh explicitly referred to the unspecified personal rights as flowing from natural law. These rights, which included marital privacy, were not created by law, he said, but were 'anterior' to it.[21] In other words, they existed before the Constitution came into force.

A positive side-effect of the judicial debate on natural law, with its close connection to the intellectual traditions of the Catholic Church, was that, in particular in the early days after Independence, it got Irish judges engaging seriously and often in original ways with vital questions about the Constitution and fundamental rights.[22] In the relatively polarized milieu of the Four Courts, the doctrine cut across party lines and provided a way for judges to transcend old Civil War divisions.

Yet as the decades passed and social changes brought rapidly shifting attitudes towards moral questions and the place of religion in society, the problems with reliance on natural law grew increasingly apparent. In his McGee judgment, Walsh acknowledged that there were different views on what natural law meant and alluded to the difficulty in deploying it in an increasingly pluralistic society.[23] The chief problem, however, was that natural law gave judges immense power. 'The judges must . . . as best they can from their training and *their* experience interpret these rights in accordance with *their* ideas of prudence, justice and charity', Walsh wrote (author's italics).[24] It's a highly subjective doctrine, in other words, its content so uncertain that, in the words of John Kelly, it 'affords hardly anything more than the precept of loving justice and hating iniquity, and avoiding evil and doing good'.[25]

The issue came to a head in *Norris*, where O'Higgins argued that the morality of Irish law was essentially Christian and that since Christianity had always condemned sodomy, no law banning it could possibly be unconstitutional. Henchy pushed back strongly against this, but the case against a natural law interpretation was put just as strongly by the second judge in the minority, Niall McCarthy. He wanted to detach the Constitution from any specific version of Christian morality. The Constitution did not stand still, he argued – what was understood in 1937 could not reasonably be held in 1983. For him, the source of the Constitution's unenumerated rights was not God but 'the human personality' itself.

The differences between the judges in *Norris* showed that within the judiciary by the early 1980s there were sharp divisions on the weight and meaning that should be attached to the religious language in the Constitution. The debate had also arisen in the aftermath of the McGee decision a decade earlier. 'How', asked the historian J. H. Whyte, writing in 1980, was *McGee* 'wrung out of a Constitution so specifically Catholic as the 1937 document had been?'[26] For Whyte, the answer lay in the doctrine of unenumerated rights, which left the courts free to discover new rights in the Constitution. But to others there was a much more fundamental explanation. Perhaps Whyte's premise was wrong to begin with: perhaps the Constitution wasn't quite as Catholic as people had always assumed.

That the Constitution was influenced by Catholic social teaching was unremarkable given the historical context of 1937, writes Gerard Hogan. 'What is more remarkable, however, is the extent to which that document also reflected secular – one might almost say "Protestant" – values of liberal democracy, respect for individual rights and the separation of the Church and State and the extent to which it does not reflect Catholic teaching.'[27]

Hogan argues that while the preamble – which is what O'Higgins relied on in his Norris judgment – and other parts of the document were written in a recognizably Catholic tone, in its underlying functioning parts, its deep structure, the document was closer to a secular Constitution in the republican democratic mould. 'One would be hard put to find any Catholic influences whatever in Article 40 [the personal rights provisions], unless it be the anti-abortion provisions of Article 40.3.3 inserted by referendum in 1983.'[28] The historian F. S. L. Lyons, writing in 1985, came to a similar conclusion, describing Article 40 as being 'very much in the liberal, almost one might say, the egalitarian, tradition'.[29]

The O'Higgins view triumphed in *Norris*, but it was clear, through the dissenting judgments of Henchy and McCarthy, that the idea of relying on the natural law, and in particular on the religious language in the preamble, had become bitterly contested ground. (Just twelve years after *Norris*, when adjudicating on the constitutionality of a bill to permit the provision of abortion information for services outside Ireland, the Supreme Court, by then led by Liam Hamilton, would explicitly reject claims about a higher law, thereby bringing down the curtain on natural law as a tool of judicial decision-making.[30])

The majority judgment in *Norris* was not an outlier. Three years later, in *Bowers v. Hardwick*, a majority of the US Supreme Court upheld the constitutionality of similar anti-sodomy laws. In a judgment that had 'remarkable echoes'[31] of O'Higgins's, Chief Justice Warren Burger said condemnation of homosexual acts was 'firmly rooted in Judeo-Christian moral and ethical standards', adding: 'To hold that the act of homosexual sodomy is somehow protected as a fundamental right would be to cast aside millennia of moral teaching.'[32]

After the Supreme Court decision had been handed down in his appeal, Norris was crestfallen. 'Although the verdict was three-two it raises serious questions regarding the value of the Irish Constitution in that it failed to vindicate my rights as a homosexual citizen', he said outside court. 'What use is the Constitution to me?'

The chairman of the National Gay Federation, Eamon Somers, citing research that showed a majority of the population favoured a change in the law, said: 'It would be a pity if the judiciary were to lose touch with Irish society, but it's hard to see that they haven't.'[33]

As he had pledged to do at the outset, Norris responded to the dismissal of his case in the Supreme Court by taking it to the European Court of Human Rights. The Strasbourg court had already, in a case taken by the Belfast gay activist Jeffrey Dudgeon in 1981, examined identical laws in Northern Ireland and found them in breach of the European Convention on Human Rights, so the government knew its chances of winning were slim. (The Strasbourg court decided for Dudgeon by a 15–4 majority; one of the judges in the minority was the Irish representative, Brian Walsh.) According to documents released in 2016 under the thirty-year rule, the Department of Foreign Affairs, through a memo from the then minister, Peter Barry, sought government approval to use Aids as an argument to retain Ireland's laws, but the Department of Health believed this would be 'most unwise' and the government was advised against the idea by the then Attorney General, John Rogers. In a memo to the Cabinet on 8 October 1985, Rogers said there was 'a good chance the State would lose' and that it would be obliged to repeal the law.[34]

The case was argued in Strasbourg by Mary Robinson in April 1988, while Norris and the solicitor John Jay sat in the gallery. 'Jay was great fun, a lugubrious man with a face like a bloodhound, but with a mordant sense of humour', Norris recalls. 'He spent some time in court drawing caricatures of the principals and writing slightly naughty limericks about them. These he would pass to me with a very solemn expression as if they were important legal minutiae. I played the game by maintaining a serious demeanour too, which added to his amusement.'[35]

Six months later, Norris took a call from an RTÉ journalist who told him he had won. Ireland's laws, the court ruled by eight votes to six, were in breach of Article Eight of the Convention on Human Rights, which guarantees the right to privacy. (Once again Brian Walsh was in the minority, although technically the dissent was because he thought Norris had no standing as he was not a 'victim' for the purposes of the Convention.) In 1993, thirteen years after Norris's legal battle began, Ireland became one of the last countries in western Europe to repeal the laws that made homosexual relations between adults a crime.

11. The trouble with extradition

'I fully appreciate that in the present atmosphere this
outlook of mine is political dynamite.'

Billy FitzGerald

The 1970 Arms Crisis was the most dramatic early indication of
how the judiciary would be drawn into the controversies that flowed
from the conflict in Northern Ireland, but there was one particularly
sensitive area in which the judges would be called on to play a central
role throughout the decades of the Troubles – extradition. The issue,
one of the main sources of tension between Dublin and London for
many years, would be the cause of one of the most fraught periods
in the Supreme Court's history.

Up until the mid-1960s, a practice had grown up between An
Garda Síochána and the Royal Ulster Constabulary whereby suspects
were brought to the border and handed over with a minimum of fuss.
That informal way of doing things came to an abrupt end in 1964,
when the Supreme Court, furious that Philip Anthony Quinn had
been arrested just outside the Four Courts and whisked across the
border without having had a chance to bring his case before the Irish
courts, roundly condemned the authorities for having attempted to
bypass the courts and the rule of law and declared the act they were
working with unconstitutional (see Chapter 5).

The government responded to the Supreme Court's decision by
speeding up passage of the Extradition Act 1965, which was to regulate how the State would handle requests from other countries to
hand over citizens facing criminal charges abroad. In it was a short
clause, Section 50, that was at the root of the coming controversies.
That section stipulated that an extradition order could not be made

where the alleged offence was political or connected to a political offence. The precise meaning of the political offence exception as it related to the Troubles was to drive a wedge through the Supreme Court and expose bitter divisions between some of its judges over more than two decades. However, one of the first cases in which the court was confronted with the new law was not connected to the conflict in Northern Ireland at all. Rather, it centred on a KGB spy and the murky world of cold war politics.

On Saturday evening, 22 October 1966, an urbane Dutch-born former MI6 agent, George Blake, executed what would become one of Britain's most famous jailbreaks. With the help of an improvised step-ladder made from rope and knitting needles he scaled the perimeter wall of Wormwood Scrubs prison in London and disappeared. Blake had been serving a forty-two-year sentence for betraying his colleagues and passing details of western operations to Soviet intelligence over a period of nine years. He was one of Britain's most notorious double agents and his sentence, handed down after an *in camera* trial at the Old Bailey in 1961, was then the longest – excluding life terms – in modern British history. The case, said the Lord Chief Justice Hubert Parker, was 'one of the worst that can be envisaged in times of peace'.

Waiting for Blake on the other side of the prison wall was Seán Bourke, a gregarious petty criminal in his early thirties from Limerick. Blake and Bourke had become friends in Wormwood, where the Irishman – a small-time criminal who had gone to England to work on building sites after his release from Daingean reformatory in Co. Offaly – had been serving a seven-year sentence for sending a parcel bomb to a policeman with whom he had fallen out (the officer was not hurt). In prison the two men had hatched Blake's escape plan, and the occasional leave privileges Bourke was allowed towards the end of his sentence gave him the opportunity to begin making arrangements.

Once Bourke had been released the plan was put in motion. The Irishman enlisted the help of two other former prisoners – anti-nuclear activists who had been jailed for acts of civil disobedience – who also knew and liked Blake and believed his forty-two-year sentence was inhuman. According to Bourke's subsequent account of the episode,[1] it was he who sourced the rope and knitting needles and managed to get a walkie-talkie in to Blake so they could communicate across the wall.

When his daring night-time escape set off a massive police man-hunt, the ex-spy was put up in the homes of various peace activists in London for two months before he managed to flee to East Berlin in a camper van that was ostensibly taking a family on holiday. The audacity of the entire plan, and the plotters' ability to elude the security services for weeks after the escape, has in the intervening years given rise to countless conspiracy theories. Was the escape stage-managed? Was it an IRA job on behalf of the KGB? Could it have been an elaborate spy swap engineered by MI6?

A few weeks after Blake reached the Soviet Union, in January 1967, Bourke flew on a false passport to Berlin, where he met a colonel from the KGB and crossed through Checkpoint Charlie into East Berlin. From there he flew to Moscow, where he was warmly welcomed and reunited with Blake.[2] Blake attained hero status in Moscow,[3] but Bourke did not settle in the Soviet Union and in October 1968 he returned to Ireland.

That was where the Irish judiciary came in. Within weeks of Bourke's return to Limerick, he was arrested by gardaí – acting on an English warrant – for helping Blake to escape. A District Court judge ordered that Bourke be delivered to Dublin Airport and handed over to the British police. But Bourke appealed to the High Court under Section 50 of the Extradition Act, claiming that the offence was political in nature. The Limerick man was not a communist, but he told the court that he came to realize that he shared Blake's view as to what constituted a just society. Bourke was also attracted to the idea of embarrassing the British government and establishment and knew that the escape would 'annoy and upset' the British police, towards whom, Bourke told the court, he had a deep and burning hatred.

While Bourke claimed to be broadly sympathetic towards the system of government that existed in eastern Europe, the judge, Andreas O'Keeffe, did not believe that Bourke had helped Blake with a view to furthering the political aims of the Soviet Union. Rather, O'Keeffe believed, Bourke had acted out of a conviction that Blake had been harshly treated and that he had sacrificed a lot for the ideals he believed in. O'Keeffe went on to note that an aversion to the police also spurred Bourke: 'It is quite clear that the plaintiff has strong feelings about police forces in general – in this country, in England and elsewhere – and that something which would cause annoyance to them would give him a certain amount of personal satisfaction, and that this was a factor in his decision to assist in the escape.'

On this analysis, Bourke's actions were not politically motivated. Similarly, the charge the British authorities said they wanted to lay against him – aiding a prisoner in escaping from a prison – was not a political offence. But was it connected to a political offence – the second, and even more vague, exemption under the act?

O'Keeffe admitted that he struggled to understand quite what that 'not very happy' phrase actually meant. The barristers on either side did not really know either. The legislators had come up with the broad language and did not take any steps to qualify or limit its effects. With that in mind, O'Keeffe concluded that since Blake was in prison because he had committed clearly political offences, he was compelled to stop Bourke's extradition.

The judge was admirably upfront about his confusion – 'I am by no means satisfied that my decision is right', he said – as he ordered that Bourke should be immediately released from custody and not conveyed to the British police. There was uproar in England, where the case had garnered huge publicity.[4]

The Attorney General appealed O'Keeffe's decision to halt the extradition, and in July 1970 the case came before a Supreme Court comprising Cearbhall Ó Dálaigh, Brian Walsh, Frederick Budd, Billy FitzGerald and Tommy Teevan, a High Court judge who was called to sit in as a substitute. Having surveyed the case law and the background to the case, the court decided by a 4-1 majority, with FitzGerald occupying his familiar spot in the dissent, that the High Court judge was correct and that Bourke should remain in Ireland. Not only was Blake's original crime of disclosing State secrets to a foreign power a political offence, said Ó Dálaigh. So was his escape, because its purpose was partly to resume work for the Soviet regime and to hand over to them more sensitive information. 'Blake's whole object in getting to Russia was to continue in the service of his Soviet master', Ó Dálaigh said.

> In a world divided by ideological difference, Blake's offence was as political as if in war time he had deserted to the enemy lines and changed his uniform. Therefore, my conclusion is that Blake's offence in escaping was a political offence and that the plaintiff's offence in assisting that escape was connected with Blake's offence in escaping, as has already been shown. Therefore, the plaintiff may not be extradited.

In his judgment, Ó Dálaigh made some broader observations about extradition. He drew a distinction between 'purely' political offences which, of their nature, were political (treason, sedition or espionage, for example) and 'relative' political offences (such as murder) carried out in the course of a rebellion. Crucially, he said that both types were covered by the political exception in the law. This was to have a significant bearing on how the court handled sensitive extradition cases over the following years.

On the same day that the Supreme Court gave its judgment in Bourke's case, it decided another case that for the first time raised the question of how the court would apply the political offence exception to alleged crimes linked to the Northern conflict.

George Magee, a Belfast garage owner and father of five children, fled the North in 1964, when he was wanted on charges of housebreaking, assaulting a police officer, malicious damage and driving without insurance. In January 1968 he was arrested in the Republic on a Northern arrest warrant and the extradition procedure began.

Magee went to the courts to stop it. His concern, he told the High Court, was that something from his past was about to come back to haunt him. After Magee had opened his garage in the early 1960s, he did some work for British soldiers. That gave him access to a number of British military sites in the North, including the barracks at Hollywood, Co. Down. Around 1963 the Hollywood barracks was raided and thieves made off with a haul of arms and explosives. Magee was arrested and brought to Donegall Place police station in Belfast, where he was questioned for twenty-four hours about the raid. The police told him they suspected, given his prior access to the barracks and his knowledge of the complex, that he had something to do with the break-in. But while he was questioned three times in all, he was never charged.

In the High Court in Dublin five years later, Magee claimed that if he was sent back across the border he feared he would be charged in connection with the Hollywood raid. He believed the police had obtained some photographs that would connect him to it, and that that gave him grounds for believing he would be prosecuted for a political offence. Addressing O'Keeffe in the High Court, Magee said he was never a member of the IRA. But he did not deny involvement in the raid. When asked in cross-examination if he had ever engaged in any political activity against the State in Northern Ireland – having been told by O'Keeffe that he was not bound to answer the question if the truthful answer would implicate him in a criminal offence – he replied that he would rather not answer. O'Keeffe then asked if his refusal to answer was for the reason that had just been indicated to him, and Magee replied, 'Yes'. When asked directly if he had had anything to do with the Hollywood raid, he again replied that he would rather not answer. He may not have been in the IRA, Magee told the court, but he was sympathetic towards it and a lot of its members were his friends.

The High Court ordered Magee's release but the gardaí appealed to the Supreme Court. This time the court split 3-2, with the majority – made up of Ó Dálaigh, Walsh and Budd – deciding that Magee should not be extradited. FitzGerald and Teevan dissented. It was a major decision: for the first time, the court was saying it regarded the activities of the IRA as political. Speaking for the majority, Ó Dálaigh said:

> In as clear language as perhaps one could expect in the circumstances, Magee has confessed to being concerned in the preparation of an armed IRA raid on Hollywood military barracks. There can be little room for doubt that his action falls either within the category of 'political offence' or of 'offence connected with a political offence'.[5]

In case after case the courts reiterated their line on political offences. In February 1974 the High Court judge Thomas Finlay gave a detailed judgment in the case of Father Bartholomew Burns, a 38-year-old Kerry-born Catholic priest. While serving as a curate in Glasgow, Fr Burns became friendly with some active supporters of the IRA in the city. In March 1973 he was asked by some acquaintances to look after a suitcase and boxes filled with explosives. Later, Fr Burns would say he knew what was in the boxes but kept them anyway. He had strong views about the injustices faced by nationalists in Northern Ireland.

After the priest returned to Ireland, the Scottish authorities issued a warrant seeking his extradition to face a charge of possessing 130 sticks of gelignite and 150 detonators. Fr Burns was arrested in October 1973. The case made its way to the High Court, where the question for the court to answer was whether Fr Burns's actions were political. Finlay had little doubt: 'The net and only issue raised for determination by me . . . is whether the safekeeping of explosives for an organisation engaged in an attempt to overthrow and change the political structures of a country by the use of violence . . . is either a political offence or an offence connected with a political offence.'

Keeping the explosives was connected with their ultimate use, which was 'intended murder or sabotage'. Noting that a section of the Extradition Act specifically excluded the killing of a head of state or member of his or her family from the category of political offences, Finlay drew the necessary inference that:

> were it not for the exclusion, there is at least one type of murder, or attempted murder, which could or would be a political offence, and it is clear therefore that one starts at least with the basis that a political offence is not necessarily a separate offence from what is described as an ordinary offence . . .

In other words, the implication of the act setting out some murders that could not be considered political was that there were other murders that could be considered political.

> It seems to me that the safekeeping of explosives for an organisation attempting to overthrow the state by violence is . . . an offence of a political character.

He went on: 'It seems again to me impossible to categorise the existing situation in Northern Ireland and Britain . . . as being otherwise than a political disturbance part of and incidental to which is the keeping of explosives for the organisation known as the IRA.'[6]

Finlay was presumably aware of the attention focused on the case, especially in Britain, and of the likelihood that he would be attacked for endorsing terrorism. Perhaps with that in mind, as Michael Farrell has suggested, he added in his judgment that his analysis was a purely legal one and should not be construed as a personal or political comment on the IRA or the conflict more widely.[7]

> I am not entitled or requested to pass any value judgement on the organisation with which the plaintiff says he was in sympathy and for which the plaintiff says he carried out this storage of explosives. I am not required to express any point of view as to whether the activities have any likelihood of success or whether they are wise or justifiable. I am asked a simple question and that is, on the facts as they have been proved, was this a political offence?

In his view, it was.

The positions set out by the Supreme Court in cases such as those of Seán Bourke and George Magee, and that of Finlay in the High Court on Fr Burns, were to be the key judicial pronouncements on the political offence exception for the following decade. They sent a clear signal to the Irish and British authorities that so long as the Extradition Act remained as it was, nobody connected to IRA activities would be handed over to the British.

A pattern took hold. Fugitives wanted by the Northern authorities for their part in IRA activities would flee across the border. The RUC would issue extradition warrants to the gardaí, but the southern authorities showed little enthusiasm for sending them back. Of thirty-two warrants issued by the Northern authorities in connection with subversive activities in 1971 and a further sixteen in 1972, none had been enforced by October 1972.

'Magee's case was to set the trend for the rest of the 1970s', writes Gerard Hogan. 'Nearly every extradition request thereafter in respect of persons charged with paramilitary offences failed on the ground that the offences in question were either political offences or offences connected with a political offence.'[8]

In response to unionist complaints that the Republic was sheltering gunmen the Minister for Justice, Des O'Malley, told the Dáil in December 1971 that extradition for political offences was 'positively forbidden' under international law.[9] That was how the Supreme Court saw it. When extradition cases arrived at its door through the 1970s, it would apply the same broad interpretation.

Naturally, the situation caused fury on the British side. In the background, London put pressure on Dublin to amend its extradition law, 'making clear it was part of the price they would have to pay if they wanted to be consulted about the future of the North'.[10]

A series of bank robberies south of the border, meanwhile, had prompted a crackdown on IRA activity in the Republic. As Farrell points out, O'Malley revived the non-jury Special Criminal Court for subversive crimes in May 1972 and in December the law was changed so as to make it easier to secure convictions on the basis of a garda superintendent's unsupported evidence that he believed someone to be a member of the IRA.[11]

In December 1975, after a Fine Gael–Labour coalition had come to power, the new Minister for Justice, Patrick Cooney, told the Dáil that since 1969, 404 people had been extradited to Britain and 52 to the North under the Extradition Act. But earlier in the year the British Lord Chancellor, Lord Hailsham, had told the House of Lords that not one person had been extradited from the Republic for 'terrorist-type' offences.[12]

Behind the scenes Lord Hailsham found an ally in the one Irish Supreme Court judge who had shown himself in favour of narrowing the interpretation of the extradition law so as to hand over more suspects to the British. Billy FitzGerald had consistently dissented in key extradition cases, often finding himself in a minority of one in arguing for cooperation with the British, but his unexpected elevation to the position of Chief Justice after Ó Dálaigh's departure in December 1972 had put him in a position where he could exert greater influence on how the court dealt with such cases.

In September 1973, three months after meeting him in person,

Hailsham wrote privately to FitzGerald about the extradition issue. The letter was ostensibly about a technicality. In 1971, in the case of Michael Furlong, an alleged thief who was sought by the British police, the Supreme Court had blocked the extradition on the basis that, in order to allow a citizen to be extradited, the offence he was facing in Britain had to have a corresponding offence in Irish law.[13] In that case, the court had broken down 3-2, with Ó Dálaigh, Walsh and Budd in the majority and FitzGerald joined by Richard McLoughlin in dissenting. Lord Hailsham told FitzGerald that the Home Office in London was in touch with the Department of Justice with a view to eliminating the problem that had arisen in the Furlong theft case.

Pointing out that the difficulties could probably only be 'fully and effectively remedied' by amending the Irish extradition law, Lord Hailsham then suggested to FitzGerald that he might use his influence to lobby for a change in the law.

> I need not go into the suggestions which have been made as this is more appropriately a matter for your Minister of Justice. In this and other fields I have no doubt that it is in the interests of both our countries to work towards harmonisation of laws. I will certainly do what I can here to that end, and I hope you may also feel it right to use your influence in Ireland in the same direction.[14]

If the Lord Chancellor's request was unusual, FitzGerald's reply was perhaps even more extraordinary. He first pointed out to Lord Hailsham that their functions were quite different and that his own role as Chief Justice was 'primarily judicial' with certain other statutory duties related to administration, and that he had no function in relation to legislation or advising the government, which was the exclusive duty of the Attorney General. 'Notwithstanding this limitation,' he continued,

> I do, when the occasion arises, urge the Attorney General, when I consider the necessity arises, as to my views on anything which requires to be attended to. I have, in fact, urged the Attorney General of the previous Government, when I held the position of [ordinary] Judge of the Supreme Court, and the present Attorney General, when

I was Chief Justice, to consider what I regarded as the necessary amendments to our Extradition Act of 1965.

FitzGerald told Lord Hailsham that both Attorneys General were aware of the judgments in the cases of Seán Bourke and Furlong, two cases in which FitzGerald dissented. 'I still adhere to the view which I expressed in these cases, that both Furlong and B[o]urke should have been extradited.' He then went beyond the issue of theft cases to distance himself from the political offence exception itself:

It appears to me that notwithstanding the universal reluctance of national governments to define a political offence or an offence connected with a political offence, that the appalling situation now existing in Northern Ireland would justify legislation in this country and in England providing that acts of violence should be deemed not to be political offences. I fully appreciate that in the present atmosphere this outlook of mine is political dynamite.

It was a remarkable exchange: a Chief Justice privately informing a British Cabinet minister that he disagreed fundamentally not only with his own colleagues on the Supreme Court but also with the policy of his own government towards a law that he was charged with interpreting and applying. 'If, as reported in the press,' FitzGerald added, 'the recent negotiations to which you refer have resulted in our Minister for Justice advising the Government that no change should be made in the Extradition Act, I very much regret it.'[15]

With the coming to power of the Fine Gael–Labour government in March 1973, the government took certain steps aimed at making it easier to surrender fugitives. It conferred extra-territorial jurisdiction on the Irish courts to try Irish citizens for murder committed outside the State. It also introduced new court rules in an attempt to speed up extradition decisions – a move that was reported at the time to have been made as a result of British government pressure.[16]

Yet such was the tension between Dublin and London over the issue in the early 1970s that, in the Sunningdale Agreement of December 1973, which set up a power-sharing Northern Ireland executive,[17] the two sides established a commission to look specifically at the bilateral extradition issue. It was seen as a concession to help bring the unionists on board for power-sharing. The two states sent high-powered three-man delegations to the Law Enforcement Commission. On the Irish side were the Supreme Court judges Brian Walsh and Séamus Henchy, Tommy Doyle of the High Court and Declan Quigley, a senior official in the Attorney General's office. Across the table were the Lord Chief Justice of Northern Ireland, Robert Lowry, Lord Justice Scarman, the High Court judge Sir Kenneth Jones and the barrister Brian Hutton QC.[18] The commission was asked to look at several options, including the extension of extradition powers, the establishment of an all-Ireland court and the widening of jurisdiction of courts north and south to cover both parts of the island.

A new all-Ireland court would have required constitutional change in the Republic and would have taken a long time to put into effect, while the idea of giving courts in Dublin and Belfast cross-border jurisdiction was considered somewhat inadequate on the basis that it would be difficult to compel witnesses to travel across the border to give evidence. By far the most contentious issue was extradition, and on this the two sides split evenly along national lines. The major stumbling block was the political offences exception. The two sides differed sharply over whether it would be possible to repeal it.

It was a complex question. There undoubtedly had been a tradition – indeed, a British tradition – of refusing to extradite people on the grounds of a political offence. It was included in the 1957 European Convention on Extradition, which was ratified by Ireland in 1966 and by the UK in 1991. But whether a state could repeal or abolish the political exception was another question. The simple answer was yes, unless there was a constitutional obstacle. During the commission's sessions, the discussions between the judges therefore focused on the Constitution itself.

The Irish delegation, led by Walsh, argued that the non-extradition of political offenders was a generally recognized principle of international law and that any legislation that provided for extradition in such circumstances would be contrary to Article 29.3 of the Constitution, which commits the State to accepting 'generally recognised principles of international law as its rule of conduct in its relations with other States'.

The British had the opposite view. While they accepted non-extradition of political offenders was 'a widespread and well-accepted practice', they rejected the idea that it was a principle of international law. Even if it was, they argued, Article 29.3 was not an absolute restriction on the power of the Oireachtas to legislate.[19]

Somewhat embarrassingly for the Irish delegation, the British judges cited a 1966 Irish High Court judgment that fully endorsed the argument they were making. The judgment held that Article 29.3 was

> not to be interpreted in these Courts as a statement of the absolute restriction of the legislative powers of the State by the generally recognised principles of international law. As the Irish [language] version makes clear, the section merely provides that Ireland accepts the generally recognised principles of international law as a guide (*ina dtreoir*) in its relations with other states.

In other words, the judgment said, the legislators were free to remove or limit the meaning of the political offence exception if they wished to do so.[20] Everyone around the table knew the judgment had been written by none other than Séamus Henchy.

The differences of opinion between Walsh and Henchy on extradition, underlaid by their strained relationship generally, were widely known. In general the judges appointed by Fine Gael tended to be more open to extradition of suspects to Britain and Northern Ireland than Fianna Fáil-appointed judges. But Walsh and Henchy, both appointed by Fianna Fáil, were proof that the divisions within the judiciary were not always along party lines. As their judgments on the issue were to make clear, Henchy did not share Walsh's view that paramilitaries were immune from extradition. He, along with fellow Supreme Court judges who took issue with the court's dominant view on the matter, felt the judges ruling against extradition were providing an intellectual-legal argument for what was essentially a political position.

Walsh, for his part, believed his broad interpretation was justified on a reading of the law and was what the legislators had in mind when they enacted the extradition regime in 1965. He also felt

Henchy had abandoned his republican roots. When Colm Tóibín was researching his *Magill* article on the Supreme Court in 1985, he was told, rather pointedly, that Henchy was a *Daily Telegraph* reader.[21]

On the Law Enforcement Commission, Walsh and Henchy openly disagreed with one another in front of the British judges and the rest of the delegation. It was an awkward situation: the British side was quoting Henchy in support of its view, and as a result the Irish delegation, which was led by Walsh but also included Henchy, was saying Henchy's 1966 judgment was wrong.

The commission reached an impasse. The two sides agreed to a scheme for extra-territorial jurisdiction, which would allow the courts to try people for crimes committed in other states. But there was no glossing over the fact that on the key issue – extradition – the Irish and British judges were on completely different wavelengths.

The commission's final report, which outlined the two sides' positions and acknowledged that they could not agree, stated that the Irish members 'are of the opinion that a change in the extradition laws in the manner already discussed should not be recommended'.[22] This opinion, it noted, was based on four factors: international law, the interaction of international law and Irish law, the European Convention on Extradition and 'the practical difficulties which would follow any such change'.[23] However, those sentences were accompanied by an intriguing footnote which began: 'Mr Justice Henchy's opinion is based solely on the conclusion that if the constitutionality of the proposed legislation [to remove the political offence exception] were challenged in appropriate litigation . . . it is not possible to advise that the legislation would not be held to be repugnant to Article 29.3 and therefore invalid.'

What that meant in plain English was that Henchy was in effect dissenting from the Irish side's position, including its rejection of his 1966 judgment. He was saying: I agree that we should not recommend removing the political offence exception from Irish law – not because I believe that is the right thing to do, but because I cannot guarantee that my colleagues on the Supreme Court would not strike down such a law.

★

The government accepted that the view of the Irish judges on the commission prevented it from abrogating or watering down the political exception, but it was plainly unhappy with the status quo. Introducing the Criminal Law (Jurisdiction) Bill 1975, which was designed to give effect to the recommendation on extra-territorial jurisdiction made by the commission, the Fine Gael Minister for Justice, Patrick Cooney, told the Seanad that there was 'a growing intolerance of and impatience with' the philosophies and activities of paramilitary fugitives. He went on:

> I feel that there is well nigh universal embarrassment in this country at the predicament in which our judges find themselves, being constrained as they are in these extradition applications to release persons accused of the most serious crimes. This widespread embarrassment is compounded by the knowledge that the release of these fugitives is a matter of grave scandal in Northern Ireland where our fellow-Irishmen have suffered so much in their persons and properties at the hands of these people.[24]

Fianna Fáil strongly opposed the extra-territorial jurisdiction plan, claiming it was unworkable and probably unconstitutional, and called instead for all-Ireland courts. Dublin TD Vivion de Valera, son of Éamon de Valera, put it bluntly: 'We are worried about . . . your attempts to sell out to the British.'[25] The bill was passed by the Oireachtas and referred to the Supreme Court, which ruled it was consistent with the Constitution.

The government's hardening stance partly reflected the fact that the South was increasingly being directly affected by the turmoil in the North. During the Ulster Workers' Council general strike that brought down the Belfast power-sharing executive just a month after the Law Enforcement Commission issued its report, loyalist groups had placed bombs in Dublin and Monaghan, killing thirty-three people. IRA members had killed a member of the Seanad, Billy Fox, in March 1974, and a spate of armed robberies had continued unabated.[26] A security crackdown ensued.

Meanwhile, as Michael Farrell points out, the government, led by Liam Cosgrave, appeared to be reversing the position taken by the previous coalition under Taoiseach John A. Costello in 1955, when

Costello argued that IRA violence was the product of partition and the oppression of the minority in the North.[27] Introducing a motion to declare a state of national emergency, so as to enable the government to take tougher measures against the IRA, Cosgrave spelled out this shift: 'The principal element in the conflict is undeniably the armed campaign of violence conducted by the IRA against the security forces and against the economy and life of the area.'[28]

Allegations repeatedly surfaced about a 'heavy gang' within the gardaí, and in June 1977 Amnesty International sent a mission to the Republic which found evidence of maltreatment of suspects by the gardaí.

Nonetheless, on the question of extradition of politically motivated offenders, the coalition accepted that the Supreme Court's interpretation of the Constitution meant the parliament had virtually no room for manoeuvre. In 1977, citing constitutional difficulties, both the Fine Gael–Labour coalition and the Fianna Fáil government that replaced it that year refused to sign the European Convention on the Suppression of Terrorism, which considerably narrowed the scope of the political offence exception. Apart from Malta, Ireland was the only western state not to sign.[29]

By the early 1980s the make-up of the Supreme Court was changing. Walsh, who since 1980 had been juggling his work as a member of the Supreme Court and president of the Law Reform Commission with a new role as the Irish judge on the European Court of Human Rights, was by now only an occasional presence on the bench in Dublin. Séamus Henchy was growing in prominence, meanwhile, and where he went in significant cases Frank Griffin often followed. From an early stage in his stewardship Tom O'Higgins had shown more willingness than Ó Dálaigh or Walsh to relax the effective immunity the court had conferred on political fugitives. Now, with changing personnel alongside O'Higgins, there were signals from the court that it was prepared to shift course on extradition.

The first opportunity to announce that re-orientation came within a year of Walsh taking up his new job in Strasbourg. Maurice Hanlon, a 45-year-old originally from Co. Longford, had fought a long legal battle to block his extradition to England. In 1971 he was arrested and charged at West London Magistrates' Court after police raided his London flat and found nine electric detonators and four ounces of plastic gelatine which the police said he knew had been stolen. Hanlon was released on bail in January 1972, but two months later he broke bail and fled to Ireland. When the British authorities issued a warrant for his extradition, a District Court judge in Dublin issued an order for his transfer to the custody of a British police officer at Dublin Airport. Hanlon went to the High Court to block his return, arguing, first, that the offence was political and, second, that there was no corresponding charge in Ireland to the one he faced in England. After a five-year wait for a judgment, the High Court finally rejected his appeal, so in 1981 he made a final attempt to avoid extradition by going to the Supreme Court.

For the previous decade the Supreme Court had ruled against extradition in a series of cases that presented very similar questions to those central to Hanlon's case. However, this time a three-judge court comprising O'Higgins, Henchy and Griffin unanimously broke the pattern.[30] In a judgment written by Henchy, the court rejected all of Hanlon's claims. It did not accept that his offence was political, not least because the High Court judge had found no acceptable evidence that the detonators and gelatine were for use by the IRA. Henchy said:

> But even if the judge's finding were otherwise, even if it had been found as a fact that the explosive material mentioned in the charge specified in the warrant had been intended for transmission to the IRA, it would not necessarily follow that the accused would be exempt from extradition on the ground that the offence charged is a political offence, or an offence connected with a political offence.

The court also dismissed Hanlon's argument on corresponding offences.

Henchy went on to say that the time had come for new extradition arrangements to be negotiated between Ireland and Britain so as to ensure the claim of non-corresponding offences could not be used to block the surrender of fugitives as a matter of course. The problem had considerably worsened since 1965, Henchy said, because major reform of the criminal law in Britain had reduced the number of matching offences between the two states, with the result that 'the envisaged system of extradition has shrunk to the extent that it now operates only vestigially'. He went on:

> It is not in accordance with the co-operation against crime that should exist between States, particularly neighbouring States, that immunity from prosecution or punishment should be made available by the facile device of the person charged or found guilty transfer-ring himself to another jurisdiction where the law does not contain a corresponding offence.

In the Hanlon case, Henchy may have signalled a shift in thinking on the court, but he did not go as far as saying that a political connec-tion would not necessarily exempt someone from extradition. That question 'must be left open for an appropriate case', he said.

As it happened, that 'appropriate case' was to land at the court's door within a year, when the leader of the Irish National Liberation Army (INLA), Dominic McGlinchey, came before a court compris-ing the same three judges – O'Higgins, Henchy and Griffin – in an attempt to block the gardaí from transferring him to Northern Ireland.

McGlinchey was steeped in republican paramilitarism. Born in South Derry, he joined the IRA in 1971 at the age of seventeen and was interned without trial for a year shortly afterwards. A year later he was jailed for eighteen months for possessing guns. Three of his brothers were also jailed for IRA offences. From 1974 to 1977 McGlinchey was active in the South Derry unit of the IRA, a highly active unit that carried out a large number of attacks on the RUC, UDR and British army. At one stage, the RUC published 'Wanted' posters and leaflets with photographs of McGlinchey and two others. In September 1977 he was arrested in the Republic and jailed for firearms possession and resisting arrest. While in jail he fell out with other IRA members and switched his allegiance to the INLA.[31]

After five years in Portlaoise prison, McGlinchey was released in January 1982 but immediately arrested on a warrant seeking his extradition to the North on a charge of murdering 67-year-old Hester McMullan, a retired postmistress, near Toomebridge, Co. Antrim. One of Mrs McMullan's sons was an RUC reservist, and her daughter worked for the RUC. She was killed in March 1977, when a group of armed men shot and wounded her son and then opened fire on the house. The IRA said it carried out the attack. The extradition warrant sent by the Northern police did not refer to the wounding of Mrs McMullan's son or to the family's connections with the RUC.[32]

McGlinchey did not admit involvement in the murder, but he argued that the offence itself was politically motivated, and that if he was sent across the border he would be charged with other offences that were political. In the background, pressure was increasing on the southern authorities. A month before the High Court hearing on McGlinchey, the Association of Garda Sergeants and Inspectors had added its voice to the rising chorus of calls for members of paramilitary groups to be extradited. A shift was also taking place in the official garda approach to cases that turned on Section 50 – the political offence exception. Through the 1970s it had become the official view that all IRA-related offences were entitled to immunity. Whenever a request for extradition was being processed, lawyers for the Garda Commissioner would either not object to the claim under Section 50 or would not appeal a High Court ruling that Section 50 applied. The result was that the exemption was simply there for the asking. What happened in *McGlinchey* was that this assumption – that Section 50 covered all paramilitary activity – was, for the first time, seriously challenged. The High Court judge, Seán Gannon, duly concluded that McGlinchey had not provided sufficient evidence to show the murder was political and that he should therefore be extradited.

McGlinchey appealed to the Supreme Court, where he abandoned the plea that the murder of Mrs McMullan was politically motivated and focused instead on his claim that he would face other political offence charges if he was handed over to the RUC. That cut no ice with the judges. O'Higgins, Henchy and Griffin now had their chance to adjust the Supreme Court's position. In a judgment written by the Chief Justice and supported by his two colleagues, O'Higgins expressly rejected the line of authority established by the Ó Dálaigh court, saying previous thinking on the scope of political offences was of less relevance in 1982 since modern terrorist violence was 'often the antithesis of what could reasonably be regarded as political, either in itself or in its connections'. He then set out a new test. Whether or not an offence was political in nature 'must depend on the particular circumstances and on whether those particular circumstances showed that the person charged was at the relevant time engaged, either directly or indirectly, in what reasonable civilised people would regard as political activity'. Ó Dálaigh's wide interpretation had, in its way, been political. So too was O'Higgins's attempt to narrow it with his 'reasonable civilised people' test.[33] Yet while that test had an improvisatory air, and the O'Higgins judgment was patchy (it was short and cited no authority), the court arguably had always had more room for manoeuvre than it had previously allowed. The Ó Dálaigh court had never said explicitly that all terrorist activity was entitled to immunity. Increasingly, courts around the world, including in the US, France and Switzerland, were beginning to distinguish terrorism from political offences.[34] But by delivering a poor-quality judgment and failing to cite any authority for its decision, the court left itself wide open to the charge that it had suddenly executed a complete volte-face.

Peter Sutherland, the recently appointed Attorney General to the incoming Fine Gael–Labour coalition, hailed the decision as a landmark that signalled an important – and, from the government's perspective, welcome – shift.

The court would adopt a similar line over the next three years.[35] In one case, the court concluded that the political offence claim could not be used to give immunity from extradition to someone charged with an offence that was intended to facilitate the overthrow by violence of the Constitution and the organs of State – a reversal of the position set out by the Irish delegation at the Law Enforcement Commission a decade earlier.[36] Slowly but unmistakably, the political offence exception was being dismantled by the judiciary.

★

By the time the Supreme Court had taken its decision to allow McGlinchey's extradition, he had jumped bail and was on the run. Now he became the most wanted man in Ireland. Almost a year later, in November 1983, while still in hiding, McGlinchey gave an interview to Vincent Browne, editor of the *Sunday Tribune*, in which he claimed he had killed thirty people and taken part in over 200 bombings and shootings since 1972, though he denied involvement in the McMullan killing. McGlinchey seemed to be taunting the authorities, and the Garda's inability to track him down was becoming a source of acute embarrassment.

In December 1983, McGlinchey and two others overpowered two gardaí who called to a house where he was staying in the east Cork village of Carrigtwohill. They stripped the gardaí of their uniforms, bound and gagged them and fled before the two sergeants managed to raise the alarm and checkpoints were set up all over Co. Cork. McGlinchey's luck finally ran out on St Patrick's Day 1984, however, when at 6.30am twelve garda cars and heavily armed units surrounded a remote cottage where he was holed up in Co. Clare. A ferocious twenty-minute gun battle ensued before McGlinchey eventually surrendered and was taken into custody.[37]

While McGlinchey was being driven from Ennis to Dublin under heavy security a few hours later, his barrister Paddy MacEntee contacted the High Court to seek an injunction restraining the gardaí from sending his client across the border. It was a Saturday and the Four Courts complex was closed, so the emergency High Court hearing took place in the south Dublin home of the judge, Donal Barrington. He granted the injunction so that the issues could be argued in court, and it was assumed that that would buy McGlinchey a few days. But Peter Sutherland immediately appealed Barrington's decision to the Supreme Court. The Chief Justice was in his garden in Sandymount when he heard the news of McGlinchey's capture. O'Higgins decided the State's appeal should be heard as quickly as possible.

What happened next showed how deeply the court's internal divisions on extradition had gone. According to Brian Walsh, who outlined the sequence of events to the then *Magill* editor Colm Tóibín a month or two later, he received a call at home from O'Higgins that

St Patrick's Day. O'Higgins told him that McGlinchey had been captured in a shoot-out and that Barrington had issued an injunction
which was now being appealed by the State. Would Walsh be available, O'Higgins asked, to come to the Four Courts that evening and
sit on a three-judge Supreme Court to hear the appeal? Tóibín
described Walsh's account of what happened next:

> Walsh said that he made it clear to O'Higgins that he would certainly be
> willing to sit on the court, and that he did not believe that McGlinchey
> should be extradited, but should rather be tried for offences allegedly
> committed in the South. He added that if McGlinchey were to be
> extradited it should not be done in any case until Monday morning; the
> reasons were historical, he explained. Kevin Barry had been hanged on
> All Saints' Day, Rory O'Connor and Liam Mellows had been executed
> on the feast of the Immaculate Conception. Dominic McGlinchey
> should not be extradited on St Patrick's Day. O'Higgins, who was in
> favour of the immediate extradition, did not ring back. The two judges
> who came to the court with him that night and extradited McGlinchey
> were Séamus Henchy and Frank Griffin. I was told at the time that of
> the five judges of the court besides Tom O'Higgins, Henchy and Grif-
> fin were considered the two most likely to agree with O'Higgins and
> make the decision unanimous.[38]

The implication was clear: Walsh believed O'Higgins left him off
the court because he knew Walsh would take a different view from
his own and oppose the extradition. Walsh's tone in recounting the
story was one of 'rage', Tóibín wrote.[39]

When the *Irish Times* referred to the incident again fourteen years
later, after Walsh's death, O'Higgins wrote to the paper to deny that
he had excluded his colleague from the McGlinchey case. 'The issue
in McGlinchey (as to whether his alleged offence was political or not)
was decided by a court of three consisting of Henchy J, Griffin J and
myself', O'Higgins wrote (using the lawyers' convention of referring
to judges by the letter J).

> At the time Brian Walsh was President of the Law Reform Commis-
> sion and, as such, could not be required by me to participate in

Supreme Court hearings. While he often did so it was generally with a full court [of five] and always at his request or with his consent. The question of such participation did not arise in McGlinchey which prima facie appeared to be an ordinary extradition appeal. The sitting on March 17th of a court consisting of the same three judges, following the re-arrest of McGlinchey, who had absconded, was merely to give effect to a decision already announced some months previously.[40]

That did not quite explain why O'Higgins called Walsh to ask about his availability but then did not ring back. As Tóibín noted in a response to O'Higgins's letter to the *Irish Times*, he had published the information in *Magill* in 1985 and at the time no one denied the facts as outlined by Walsh.[41]

That prompted another letter from O'Higgins, who said he had not seen the magazine article, probably because by 1985 he was living in Luxembourg as a judge of the European Court of Justice. He then outlined the sequence of events as he saw it.

> When I was informed by my registrar of the development and of the request for an urgent meeting of the court, I had to ascertain – since it was a holiday – what judges would be available. In this regard I certainly spoke to Mr Justice Walsh. I accept that the conversation was probably as outlined by Colm Tóibín. My concern was to have a fall-back situation if the original McGlinchey Court could not be convened. Shortly afterwards it transpired that both Henchy J and Griffin J would be available. This solved my problem.
>
> Colm Tóibín states that Mr Justice Walsh told him that his caller did not phone him back at a later stage. As, presumably, I was the caller in question, I very much regret the oversight, but wish to declare that it was quite unintentional.[42]

Initially, then, O'Higgins had said the question of Walsh sitting on the McGlinchey court 'did not arise', but then accepted, in light of Tóibín's account, that he 'certainly' spoke to Walsh to ask about his availability. It was true that Walsh was only an occasional presence on the Supreme Court in these years, and that he tended mostly to sit in constitutional cases that required a full complement of five judges. O'Higgins never explained why he did not simply check with Henchy and Griffin first. It was at the very least odd not to call Walsh back that Saturday afternoon. Yet, in his defence, others who have sat on the Supreme Court say the practice of a Chief Justice checking all judges' availability for out-of-hours sittings is not unheard of.

Either way, Walsh's conviction that O'Higgins had deliberately excluded him and packed the court, and the fact that he was so angry about it that he wanted the information to get out, speaks volumes not only about his sense of isolation on the court by the mid-1980s but also about the bitter divisions that had emerged as a result of the extradition debates.

The Four Courts was empty and cold that Saturday night when the Supreme Court convened to decide on McGlinchey's fate. The three judges – O'Higgins, Henchy and Griffin – were not wearing their wigs or robes; Henchy was wearing his overcoat. McGlinchey himself remained across the road in the Bridewell Garda Station. The hearing took two hours, but the judges needed just ten minutes to decide that McGlinchey should be extradited. O'Higgins firmly dismissed the INLA man's challenge. 'As far as I'm concerned, it gets from me no sympathy whatsoever', he said.

The McGlinchey decision did not completely shut down the court's internal debates on extradition. A few years later, when O'Higgins had gone to Luxembourg and Henchy had retired, the court – in a judgment written by Walsh – drew a new distinction between terrorism on the one hand and political offences on the other.[43] That enabled it to block the extradition of an escapee from the Maze prison in Belfast in 1990 – a decision Margaret Thatcher called 'deeply offensive and unjustified, offering nothing but encouragement to terrorists'.But by then the court's room for manoeuvre had been severely curtailed by the Oireachtas, which, taking its lead from decisions such as *McGlinchey*, finally felt it constitutionally safe to sign the European Convention on the Suppression of Terrorism. That significantly circumscribed the scope for pleading a political defence exception.

The McGlinchey case, then, was to prove an important turning-point. Within hours of the court's judgment, the INLA leader was taken from the Bridewell and put into a Garda car accompanied by a phalanx of armed detectives. Surrounded by a cavalcade of Garda cars and motorcycle outriders, he was driven at high speed towards Co. Louth. It was almost midnight when he was handed over at the border and became the first republican paramilitary to be extradited since 1922.[44]

12. Replacing O'Higgins

'I have seen so many wheels turn the full circle I intend to
stay around until the wheel turns again.'

Brian Walsh

Tom O'Higgins's decade-long stewardship of the judiciary came to
an end in January 1985, when he accepted a nomination by the Fine
Gael–Labour coalition to become the Irish judge at the European
Court of Justice in Luxembourg. O'Higgins had mixed feelings
about leaving. He did not speak French, the working language of the
court, and it seemed to colleagues that he was enjoying his work on
the Supreme Court. One of the reasons he accepted, he said, was that
the restrictions placed on his life because of the McGlinchey case had
become too much to bear. Even before the case, as a result of the
northern conflict, bullet-proof glass had been installed in the Supreme
Court rooms. For the previous year, gardaí had been stationed per-
manently at the front and back of O'Higgins's house in Sandycove
and the garden was floodlit at night.

'I can't go for a walk on my own. I am not my own man anymore',
he told the *Irish Press* the day the news of his departure was announced.
'At times, you feel like going mad. I never expected this to come into
my life.'[1]

The move also made financial sense. 'It is believed that two presidential elections may have taken their toll on the O'Higgins purse
strings and perks like his chauffeur-driven Rover car were insuffi-
cient to make an impact on his bank balance', the *Irish Independent*
reported.[2] The European job came with a salary of £80,000, with a
maximum tax rate of 45 per cent, whereas the salary of Chief Justice
was £42,000, most of which was taxed at 65 per cent.[3]

At his valedictory sitting – a standard ceremony, that endures to this day, where fellow judges and lawyers pay grossly exaggerated, occasionally sincere, tribute to retiring members of the judiciary – the warmth shown towards O'Higgins was genuine. In his remarks, the departing Chief Justice picked up on a perennial judicial theme by admonishing the media for attempting to pigeon-hole different courts as liberal or conservative. His court had been neither, O'Higgins claimed, but rather 'an objective court' which was composed of judges who applied the law, interpreted the Constitution and respected the rights of the people.[4]

O'Higgins was only partly right. Rarely have the labels liberal and conservative – contested terms that have taken on different meanings at different times – been sufficient to account for the character of a given Supreme Court. The truth has usually been more layered and as a result more interesting. It's also true that one of the keys to understanding Irish judges is the fact that, unlike their counterparts on constitutional courts in many countries, they are all – even those who have also been elected representatives – trained lawyers. Their education and their daily routine on the bench are a diet of relatively mundane legal issues – contract, personal injuries cases and so on – and for the most part they bring the same techniques and the same shared language to bear on constitutional cases. For better or worse, most of them think like lawyers, write like lawyers and reason like lawyers. And for much of the past century, the distinctions between them, perhaps reflecting the small social pool from which most of them are chosen, have been within a relatively narrow spectrum. Moreover, if the labels liberal and conservative were sufficient to understand an entire court, they would have a predictive value and observers would be able to tell at the outset what a given group of judges would decide in each particular case. That has often been possible in the case of the United States Supreme Court (not least in the early twenty-first century) but much less so in the case of its Irish counterpart.

Yet the implication of O'Higgins's claim about his 'objective court' – that the judges' decision-making was not influenced by their backgrounds, their personal views or their prejudices – was clearly wide of the mark. Most cases that come before the Supreme Court suggest a straightforward answer. The judges usually agree on the meaning of a section of a law or a clause in the Constitution. But in key places the language in the Constitution is ambiguous and vague, and the regularity with which the court, not least under O'Higgins, split on key questions is itself proof of the wide room for manoeuvre the judges often enjoy in interpreting it.

O'Higgins, in his eventful ten years as Chief Justice, was himself an example of how individual judges' records could defy neat categorization. Initially dismissed for attempting to row back on the activism of the Ó Dálaigh years, his court actually consolidated and built on some of the key innovations of the 1960s in areas such as criminal procedure and individual rights. In many respects, O'Higgins was himself an activist judge and some of his most important decisions had liberal, progressive results. He joined forces with Walsh to dig in on the rights of defendants, showing a great deal of humanity and compassion in the process.

Asked about his ten years as Chief Justice on the day his departure was announced, O'Higgins said he was pleased to have helped 'establish the rights of the individual over what might be called bureaucracy'.[5] His attachment to the separation of powers, which his critics saw as undue deference to Leinster House and Government Buildings, did not prevent him from finding that free legal aid was a constitutional right, that the Juries Act was unconstitutional because its effect was to exclude women and that the income tax laws were unfair to women – ground-breaking, expansionist decisions in which the court struck important blows for the rights of women and criminal defendants.

Yet the man who was seen as a social liberal when he was a politician was also part of the majority in *Norris*, where he – along with Tom Finlay and Frank Griffin – ruled that the criminal ban on homosexual acts was not inconsistent with the Constitution. His judgment was poorly reasoned, virtually devoid of human empathy and, more to the point, law. To many it sounded 'more like a lecture on traditional Catholic theology than a dissertation on the law'.[6] Years later, in 1991, O'Higgins said he personally favoured decriminalization of homosexuality, suggesting he had changed his mind since the Norris case, but by then his reputation as a conservative on social questions was entrenched.

O'Higgins's period as Chief Justice coincided with some of the worst years of the Troubles, and extradition disputes were to dominate his term in office. His court's move to reverse the long-held position that suspected paramilitaries could not be handed over to the British authorities polarized opinion. Yet, in an editorial on the day O'Higgins announced his departure, even the Fianna Fáil-supporting *Irish Press* was complimentary:

> Cearbhall Ó Dálaigh was a hard act to follow. As Chief Justice he had transformed Irish law, given it a new vibrancy and independence and made the Constitution a real protection for the citizen and not just a set of pious aspirations. The tenure of his immediate successor, Chief Justice FitzGerald, was too short to make for change, but with Tom O'Higgins's arrival many feared that there would be a period of retrenchment. After all, he came from one of the great political dynasties, had been in the thick of political combat for a generation and had fought for the Presidency twice as the Fine Gael standard bearer. Yet, in fact, more constitutional rights were declared in his time than ever before.[7]

Speculation about O'Higgins's possible replacement as Chief Justice began even before he had formally stepped down. The favourite was Tom Finlay, who as President of the High Court was second in seniority after the Chief Justice, but three other names were in the frame: Declan Costello, Niall McCarthy and Brian Walsh.

Finlay, a Jesuit-educated Dubliner, had been a Fine Gael TD between 1954 and 1957. However, his reputation for independence of mind was such that there was not a murmur of dissent when a Fianna Fáil government under Jack Lynch reached across party lines and appointed him to the High Court in 1972. He became president of the court two years later and had produced a corpus of influential

judgments. While more reluctant than O'Higgins to push the boundaries of the judicial role, he was seen as a liberal on the non-jury
Special Criminal Court and turned out to be a strong critic of State
attempts to trample on defendants' rights. In one case at the height of
the Troubles, in 1976, he angrily berated the governors of Mountjoy
and Portlaoise prisons for effectively blocking a young solicitor, Pat
McCartan,[8] from visiting prisoners simply on the grounds that he
was a member of Official Sinn Féin at the time. 'He is more of a law
man, less of a law and order man', one contemporary commentator
remarked.[9]

Finlay was also strong on family law. In what was seen as a radical
judgment when it was delivered in 1978, Finlay ruled that the natural
mother of a baby who had been born outside wedlock should get it
back from the couple who had received it from the adoption board
some years earlier – a decision that was criticized by his ex-party colleague Tom O'Higgins but ultimately upheld by the Supreme Court.[10]
In another case, he held that adultery by a spouse after separation was
no bar to her getting maintenance from her husband, and applied
new equity formulas to give separating spouses their fair share of the
family home, businesses and investments.

Just as importantly, Finlay was seen as a strong administrator as
President of the High Court – a job that in many ways is more onerous than that of Chief Justice. He defused a tense labour dispute
among court staff, oversaw an expansion in court accommodation
and cut the delays for jury trials from eighteen months to eleven.

Widely considered to count against Finlay, however, was an
impression that on social questions he was a traditional conservative.
The Norris case, in which he had gone with the majority, was considered unlikely to endear him to a coalition in which some of the most
influential figures – among them Taoiseach Garret FitzGerald,
Tánaiste Dick Spring, outgoing Attorney General Peter Sutherland
and his successor, John Rogers – were either themselves liberals or
had progressive constituencies to keep happy.

If a liberal outlook was considered an important attribute in a
Chief Justice, that would have enhanced Niall McCarthy's chances.
He, along with Séamus Henchy, had formed the minority in *Norris*,

and his judgment was a tour de force of classic liberalism. 'He plan-gently asserted the right to privacy, at the end of perhaps the most important and influential dissenting judgment for fifty years', accord-ing to the future Supreme Court judge Adrian Hardiman, who revered McCarthy.[11]

Before becoming a judge, the flamboyant, imperious McCarthy had been a star of the law library. He also happened to be a friend of Peter Sutherland since they had worked closely together on a number of cases as barristers. But McCarthy was a long shot: he was at the time the most junior Supreme Court judge, and while judicial inex-perience had not hampered the chances of either of the previous two Chief Justices, Billy FitzGerald or Tom O'Higgins, his politics were a bad fit as well. McCarthy had been retained to defend Charles Haughey in the arms trial and was seen as close to Fianna Fáil. Hav-ing come in for criticism from Fine Gael's own barristers for having just appointed a Labour man, John Rogers, to replace Peter Suther-land as Attorney General, it was difficult for Garret FitzGerald to approve as nominee for Chief Justice someone who had links to the party's old rival.

That fact, combined with his own close links to FitzGerald over many years, was thought to work in Declan Costello's favour. As a former Fine Gael TD and author of the 'Just Society' document that attracted many liberals to the party in the 1960s, Costello had been a leading light in the social democratic faction that counted FitzGerald among its most prominent adherents. He had also served as Attorney General to a Fine Gael-led coalition. He piloted the act that set up the Law Reform Commission and set up the office of the Director of Public Prosecutions, which had gone a long way towards removing political patronage from the process of handing out State briefs in criminal cases.

For a third time, Brian Walsh's name was in the mix. Though he was just sixty-six, he had been on the court for nearly a quarter of a century. If experience and service to the State had been the over-riding considerations, the job would have gone to him, but the fact that he was seen as close to Fianna Fáil no doubt worked against him. In an editorial championing Walsh, under the headline 'Walsh for Chief

Justice', the *Sunday Tribune* argued that the court had failed to regain the stature it enjoyed under Ó Dálaigh.

> There is now an opportunity to put that right. Brian Walsh, who has been a member of the court for over 20 years, is clearly the best man for the job. Furthermore, his liberal and progressive views are more in tune with the policies espoused – at least in his earlier political career – by the present Taoiseach, Dr Garret FitzGerald, than are those of any other judge. There will certainly be no more crucial appointment to be made by the present Government and Taoiseach. The decision should be made without partisanship. The decision should be made in favour of Brian Walsh.[12]

By the mid-1980s, Walsh was feeling increasingly isolated on the court. The line he and Ó Dálaigh had held on extradition was in the process of being reversed. He and Henchy were often at odds,* and he was in effect – owing to his commitments at the European Court of Human Rights and the Law Reform Commission – only a part-time member of the Supreme Court. Moreover, as his anger over what he saw as his exclusion from the hurried McGlinchey hearing demonstrated, he seemed not to trust O'Higgins. A general sense of fatigue comes across from a letter Walsh had written to William Brennan in April 1981, just as he was taking up his new role in Strasbourg.

> As I have been 20 years a member of the Supreme Court here and I have another 9 years to go before I reach retirement age I thought the tedium might be relieved by having my time divided partially between the Supreme Court here and the Court in Strasbourg. As all

---

* Henchy and Walsh clashed on matters other than extradition. It was reported that in 1982 the then Chief Justice, Tom O'Higgins, had to intervene to cool a conflict between the two men in a case over whether the State could appeal an acquittal in the Supreme Court (*The People v. O'Shea* [1982] IR 384). Henchy was convinced that to allow an appeal would infringe the common law principle that an acquitted person should not be put on trial a second time and rejected 'Walsh's highly literalist approach to constitutional interpretation'. Kevin Costello, 'Henchy, Séamus Anthony', in James McGuire and James Quinn (eds.), *Dictionary of Irish Biography*.

domestic remedies must be exhausted in the country from which the complaint originates before the Court in Strasbourg can be invoked it is possible that some day I shall find myself sitting in judgment on my own colleagues in the Supreme Court. My particular sentimental interest in the [Strasbourg] Court is that way back in 1958 I was counsel in the first case that Court ever heard.

In my own case I have been for many years the sole survivor of the Court which I joined in 1961 and I have been more than twice as long in the Court as the next longest serving member of it. I now find myself devoting a lot of my energy to vigorous defences of the more liberal attitudes which prevailed when I joined the Court and to which I was happy to be a party. I suppose this experience may have a familiar ring for you. I have seen so many wheels turn the full circle I intend to stay around until the wheel turns again.[13]

Walsh knew that his chances of succeeding O'Higgins were slim, and confided as much to his friends. On 17 December 1984, just before the government announced its decision, Walsh added a handwritten note to a typed letter to Brennan.

P. S. The Chief Justice is resigning to take office as a judge of the Court of the European Communities at Luxembourg. For political reasons my chances of succeeding are nil and in fact I was twice passed over before, although the most senior member of the Court, for the same reasons. However I am quite philosophical about it. You may be amused by the enclosed newspaper comment. I'm sure you've experienced the same so I feel I am in excellent company![14]

He enclosed a photocopy of the 'Walsh for Chief Justice' editorial from the *Sunday Tribune*.

In a reply written on St Stephen's Day, Brennan offered Walsh some encouragement and consolation: 'I was not the least surprised to read the "Walsh for Chief Justice" reports . . . But you must remember that the very great ones somehow miss – Holmes, Brandeis and Cardozo are among the outstanding examples. However, if your government has any sense it will follow the newspaper's advice.' Oliver Wendell Holmes, Louis Brandeis and Benjamin Cardozo were three of the most influential justices in the history of the US Supreme Court. None had been Chief Justice. As Brennan did not need to spell out, it was also a post that had eluded him.[15]

In the event, when the government chose O'Higgins's replacement as Chief Justice, it opted for Finlay. Into his former position as President of the High Court went Liam Hamilton, who was seen as close to Labour. The spoils of senior legal appointments had thus been divided between the two parties: Fine Gael got its favoured candidate into the office of Chief Justice while Labour, having had its say on the appointment of the Attorney General, also had the final say on the President of the High Court.

If O'Higgins had served out his time and stayed on for another two years, Fianna Fáil, led by Charles Haughey, would have been back in government and Walsh would almost certainly have been appointed Chief Justice. But it was not to be: he had been overlooked for the third and final time.

A year after Finlay took over, when Walsh was still on the court, he told the Australian lawyer Garry Sturgess that he was not upset at having lost out. 'From a personal point of view really it didn't affect me in any way whether I was Chief Justice or not because one is judged by what one does, not the capacity in which you do it', he said.[16] Walsh was putting a brave face on it. A colleague who knew him well says that while he did not dwell on it too long he was clearly disappointed at the time. 'Brian Walsh had great regard for Finlay – Finlay was a barrister he always recommended to people – but at the same time he was very disappointed, I remember, for about a week. He was rather crestfallen. He got over it.'

The appointments of Finlay and Hamilton were widely welcomed. But, as the *Irish Times* noted in an editorial, Finlay was taking the helm in the Supreme Court 'at a time of acute sensitivity in the relationship between the law, the Government and the People'. It went on:

Criminal justice, personal rights and liberties, perhaps even the very nature of the State's sovereignty are all coming under review and reassessment. The Supreme Court's role in helping to determine the sort of society which will operate here is, and will remain, pivotal. The era of the part-time judge, coasting along to retirement after a lucrative career at the bar, is over.[17]

The leader-writer's warning that the court would soon be confronted with questions that went to the heart of Irish sovereignty turned out to be prescient, although the case that raised those questions was perhaps not what the paper had in mind.

13. Putting it to the people

'We can see the consequences but it doesn't mean we are going
to be deterred from what we think is right.'

Brian Walsh

Just after 6pm on Christmas Eve 1986, as shoppers were finishing
their Christmas errands and Dublin was winding down for the holiday, a smattering of people gathered in Court No. 4 in a deserted
Four Courts. Neither the duty judge in the High Court, Donal Barrington, nor the barristers were wearing their wigs or gowns. A few
gardaí stood at the back of the courtroom, having been called in to
help track down court officials so that the out-of-term hearing could
take place at short notice.

At the outset the proceedings hit an obstacle: shorthand typists
were on Christmas leave, but Barrington was insistent that he would
not make a judgment in a case of this importance without a record
being kept. Lawyers for the plaintiff asked for a short adjournment,
whereupon a junior counsel got on his bike and cycled to Capel
Street, where he found one of the last remaining tape recorders as
stock vanished in the last hour before closing time. He rushed back to
court, placed it in front of Barrington and pressed 'record'. As Barrington began to speak he was setting in train a process that would
have a dramatic effect on Irish democracy for decades to come.

Raymond Crotty, a lecturer in Trinity College's Department of
Economics, was making a last-minute attempt to block the government from ratifying the Single European Act. The act, the first major
revision of the Treaty of Rome which established the European Economic Community (EEC) in 1957, was a significant step in the process
of European integration. It aimed to establish closer economic

and political cooperation among member states, in particular by creating a single market for goods and services, with a significant extension of qualified majority voting. It also expanded EEC powers, notably in the fields of research and development, the environment and common foreign policy.

Earlier in December the Oireachtas had passed the European Communities (Amendment) Act 1986 – a law that would bring the treaty's provisions into Irish law. The treaty itself was due to come into force throughout the EEC (now the European Union) on 1 January 1987. But in order for that to happen, two final steps were required. First, President Patrick Hillery had to sign the Single European Act into Irish law. And second, Ireland, along with every other member state, had to lodge an 'instrument of ratification' – a short statement that said Ireland, having met all the constitutional and legal requirements, formally ratified the treaty – with the government of Italy, the designated country for ratification.

President Hillery signed the act on Christmas Eve just as Raymond Crotty's team was arguing his case seeking an injunction to stop the government taking any further steps to ratify the treaty without first holding a referendum. It was reported that the government had an aircraft on standby to bring the signed document to Rome before the 1 January deadline.[1]

The core of Crotty's argument was that the treaty gave new powers to the European institutions that went beyond the powers that the people of Ireland permitted when they voted to join the EEC in 1972. He argued that the government's method of ratification – a vote of the Oireachtas – was unconstitutional in that only the people themselves could surrender sovereignty through a referendum and that he, Crotty, had a right as a citizen to that referendum. Variations on the same point had been doing the rounds among lawyers and activists for months. The previous month, thirteen lawyers – including figures like the veteran senior counsel Seán MacBride, and two high-profile members of Trinity College's law faculty, Professor Mary McAleese and lecturer Kader Asmal[2] – had argued in a letter to the *Irish Times* that, quite apart from any view they might hold as individuals about the treaty itself, they were convinced that it gave

'novel and additional legislative and executive competence' to the
European institutions 'over and above that possessed by the European
Communities we agreed to join in 1972'. The Oireachtas would be
'acting invalidly', the signatories said, by passing the act without first
adopting a constitutional amendment that would give it the proper
authority. In other words: a referendum was required.[3]

The letter had been drafted by Anthony Coughlan, who was
senior lecturer in social policy at Trinity College and had been
a long-time critic of the EEC. As a student in University College
Cork, Coughlan had briefly been a member of the Labour Party,
where he was a contemporary of future Labour figures Michael
O'Leary and Barry Desmond, but his chief political involvement
since then had been through a small think-tank, the Common Market Study Group, which argued for a No vote in the referendum on
EEC membership in 1972.

When the letter was published, the government was already coming in for severe criticism for having delayed the passage of the act
until the last minute, enacting it only in December despite the treaty
itself having been signed by Ireland and other member states in Luxembourg the previous February.

Yet the Fine Gael–Labour coalition, keen not to hold up the ratification process and scarred by its loss of a referendum on divorce just
seven months earlier, was in no mood to put the treaty to a vote –
especially not given that there was a general election in prospect the
following spring.

The plan for the Crotty case had come together at the last minute.
In the law library in mid-November, a few days after the letter from
the thirteen lawyers appeared in the *Irish Times*, the senior counsel
Paul Callan had bumped into one of the signatories, junior counsel
Séamus Ó Tuathail, and complimented him on it. Ó Tuathail mentioned the exchange to Coughlan, who was an old friend. Coughlan,
Ó Tuathail and others had over the previous weeks and months been
discussing the idea of a legal challenge to the Single European Act. A
diverse coalition was coming together, including the solicitor TC
Gerard O'Mahoney, known as Gerry, and the husband-and-wife
team of Joe Noonan and Mary Lenihan, Cork solicitors who were

active in the Campaign for Nuclear Disarmament and were concerned about the foreign policy aspects of the treaty.

Though the campaign was gaining momentum, those involved knew that to pursue a court challenge they would need a senior counsel willing to take on the case pro bono. Together, Coughlan and Ó Tuathail approached Callan, himself an unsuccessful Labour Party candidate in the 1969 election, and explained their thinking. At first he was not convinced they had much of a case. For two or three weeks they worked on persuading him. Night after night, joined by the junior counsel Antonia O'Callaghan, the group would meet in Gerry O'Mahoney's house on Merrion Square from around 9pm and talk early into the morning, teasing out the legal points and debating them for hours on end. Finally, Callan was convinced there was a strong case. 'Now,' he said, 'where is the plaintiff?'

'There was no one to take the case', Coughlan recalls. 'I remember going back to Trinity College after this meeting and thinking, "Maybe I should offer myself as a plaintiff." Then I thought, "Maybe Raymond would do it."'

Raymond Crotty was a 61-year-old Kilkenny farmer turned economist who had lectured widely and become a leading agricultural economist. He was also something of a maverick; his advocacy of land taxes as a means to improve agricultural efficiency did little to endear him to the Irish farming lobby. During the debate leading to the referendum on Ireland's EEC membership in the early 1970s, he and Coughlan had been joint secretaries of the anti-EEC Common Market Study Group. After the 1972 campaign, Coughlan had been involved in setting up the Irish Sovereignty Movement, but Crotty had drifted away from the group and focused on his academic writing.

The two men's scepticism towards the EEC came from somewhat different perspectives. Crotty's sprang from his conviction that the EEC's strategy for agriculture, the Common Agricultural Policy, would benefit big farmers and, by pushing up prices, hinder the revolution he believed was needed in Irish agricultural output. Coughlan opposed the EEC on democratic grounds, arguing that handing over law-making powers to institutions that Irish citizens had little control over entailed an unwelcome loss of sovereignty or national autonomy. Nothing that had happened in the thirteen years since Ireland's accession had changed their view.

The more he thought of it, the more it made sense to Coughlan that Crotty was the ideal person to challenge the Single European Act:

> I was a long-standing critic of the EU. I had been so in 1972 and even further back than that. While Raymond was known as a critic, he was much less prominent than I was. Raymond was older. He was more established. He was married. He had a family. He was an international economist. He had worked for the World Bank. He had written a major book on Irish history.

After Callan came on board as senior counsel, Coughlan phoned Crotty, who was confined to bed after wrenching a muscle. He readily agreed, so the next day Coughlan, O'Mahoney and a notary public were at his bedside to witness his formal instructions to initiate proceedings in the High Court.

The Crotty side had few resources and no public backing from any of the mainstream political parties, although it did have support from the neutrality lobby and had informal contact with a senior figure in Fianna Fáil, which was then the main opposition party. Its leader, Charles Haughey, was alive to the damage a legal defeat would inflict on Garret FitzGerald and his coalition, and one of his key advisers, Martin Mansergh, discussed the case with Coughlan on several occasions. 'There was certainly no money or anything like that', says Coughlan. 'They weren't privy to the court case at all, but they were politically interested in anything that might cause embarrassment to the coalition.'

The government was convinced it would see off the legal challenge, but it briefed a formidable team of barristers, led by the senior counsel Eoghan Fitzsimons. Urging Barrington not to grant the injunction, Fitzsimons said Crotty's attempt was an abuse of judicial process and that the court had no power to interfere in the executive process that was now in train. He said Greece was about to deposit its ratification papers in Rome, which would leave Ireland alone among twelve member states not to have adopted the treaty before the agreed deadline of New Year's Day. If the courts were to injunct Ireland, Fitzsimons said, it would be 'a major international embarrassment' to Ireland in the eyes of its European partners. The State's legal team also argued, as they would throughout the saga, that when Irish voters approved EEC membership in 1972 they were signing up for an evolving community and implicitly accepting that it would grow and develop down the road.

Barrington was aware of the significance of Crotty's move. It was, he said in court on Christmas Eve, 'an extremely difficult case' and what Crotty was seeking – to restrain the government from ratifying an international treaty – was 'quite unusual and, as far as I know, without precedent'. Barrington said he found the issues 'very trouble-some' but concluded that Crotty had raised 'an issue of such substance and importance as to warrant preserving the status quo until the issue has been resolved in these courts'.

The government's claim about potential international embarrass-ment got short shrift. It would be even more embarrassing, Barrington remarked, to have ratified an international treaty and then have to withdraw from parts of it which might be found to be unconstitu-tional at a later date. The judge was careful not to venture an opinion on the constitutional question, but he granted Crotty the injunction and said the constitutional question should go to a full High Court hearing.

Crotty was jubilant. 'In the funereal gloom of the foyer of the locked Four Courts on Christmas Eve, a few of us jigged a few steps', he later wrote in his memoir.[4] He was also amazed at how quickly Barrington had absorbed the details of a large and dense treaty and several days of legal argument, then managed to summarize it after just one hour's adjournment. 'It was one of the most impressive intel-lectual performances I have witnessed. It induced in me a new and higher regard for the legal profession; and especially for those at the apex of it in this country's judiciary.'[5]

On Christmas Eve, shortly after Barrington had granted the injunction, Crotty was walking home when he passed Leinster House and suddenly came face to face with Peter Barry, who was leaving the building late. Barry, the Minister for Foreign Affairs, was one of the architects of the Single European Act and one of Crotty's named opponents in court. The two men had never met but they recognized one another immediately on the street. 'Quite spontaneously we grinned at each other and wished one another a happy Christmas!'[6]

When Ireland awoke on Christmas morning, the injunction was the lead item on the RTÉ news. The decision left the government reeling. Garret FitzGerald and Peter Barry discussed it when they met at a funeral on St Stephen's Day, but they differed on how to respond. Barry wanted to appeal Barrington's decision to the Supreme Court immediately, but FitzGerald was inclined to let the High Court action take its course. The result was that contradictory statements were issued by the government spokesman and by Barry himself, heightening the impression of disarray within the Cabinet.

Meanwhile, the leader of the opposition felt he had reason to be pleased. A barrister on the Crotty side, Aidan Browne, had close Fianna Fáil connections and when the decision came through, he phoned Haughey with the news. Haughey was delighted. At that stage, the widespread assumption was that the case would eventually be rejected, either at the full High Court hearing or in the Supreme Court.

The government's initial legal advice was that it would almost certainly win in the High Court but that it would not be a good idea to 'push the courts around during the holiday period'. It was also told that failing to deposit the instrument of ratification in Rome by the 1 January deadline for ratification would not necessarily be damaging to Ireland, but that if it was not done before a European Council summit in March it would, in the words of one somewhat excitable source, be 'crisis stuff'.[7] FitzGerald's view won out: the Cabinet would sit tight and see what the High Court would do. Ministers were agreed on one thing: if only President Hillery had referred the act to the Supreme Court before signing it, doubts about its constitutionality could have been headed off and this mess could have been avoided. But the government was far from blameless: as commentators were quick to point out, it had delayed the ratification process for almost a year.

Meanwhile, lawyers on both sides were working round the clock to prepare their cases. The Crotty team worked from Callan's flat in Ballsbridge. Joe Noonan and Mary Lenihan brought their word processor up from Cork – it was the first computer most of those in the room had seen. There was a break-in over Christmas at the offices of Crotty's solicitors, Moylan Whitaker, so 'with memories of Watergate still fresh and with a healthy respect for our own Special Branch, the risk that the offices might have been bugged seemed sufficiently real to make us move to somewhere we could be sure no-one could eavesdrop on what I soon realised were very sensitive discussions', Crotty wrote.[8] Everyone was concerned about the mounting costs; at one point Aidan Browne jokingly reminded Crotty that he still had a couple of hours in which to transfer the family home into his wife's name.[9]

On St Stephen's Day, Callan called at Barrington's house to get the judge to sign a copy of the judgment and thereby make it official. Barrington's wife, Eileen, told him the judge had gone for a walk in the Dublin mountains. 'Where exactly?' Callan asked. So he drove to the mountains, tracked Barrington down and eventually got his signed copy.

The full High Court hearing took place over ten days in January 1987 and on 12 February a three-judge court comprising Barrington, Liam Hamilton and Mella Carroll emphatically rejected Crotty's case. In a judgment written by Barrington, the court found that Crotty was not entitled to make such a case, because he was not personally affected by the provisions of the act and that ratification of the treaty would not make it immune from future constitutional challenge, as Crotty's side had claimed.

Government ministers breathed a sigh of relief. Crotty was dejected, not least as he now faced a legal bill estimated at around £50,000 (around €120,000 at today's values). His backers had set up a fund-raising group called the Constitutional Rights Campaign, co-chaired by Mary McAleese and the trade unionist John Carroll, but there seemed little hope of pulling in enough money to cover costs of that scale.

For Crotty's team there was little time to dwell on the defeat in the

High Court, however, because the drama immediately shifted to the Supreme Court, where Crotty got a temporary extension of the injunction preventing the government from depositing the treaty with the Italian government. By now the instrument of ratification was sitting in the Irish embassy in Rome, waiting to be dispatched across the city. It was to sit there for some time, because after a full hearing of its own, the Supreme Court, on 9 April, delivered a judgment that was to reverberate across Europe.

The court, which for this case comprised Finlay, Walsh, Séamus Henchy, Frank Griffin and Tony Hederman, had two questions to answer. First, was the European Communities (Amendment) Act – the law the government had enacted to give effect to its ratification of the European treaty in domestic law – unconstitutional? Second, should the government be restrained from ratifying the European treaty itself?

The first question came under the so-called one judgment rule, as it related to the constitutionality of a post-1937 act of the Oireachtas. That meant the court had to speak with one voice and not issue any dissenting judgments. On this question – the standing of the European Communities (Amendment) Act – the court found that it was constitutional. Crotty, sitting in the public gallery, assumed he had lost the whole case. He thought: 'Everything was lost: the case; all my material assets, which would not be nearly adequate to cover what I imagined the costs would be; and a good hunk of whatever reputation I had.'[10]

But Finlay and the other judges continued to speak. The government had urged the court not to stick its nose into the question of how an international treaty should be agreed, telling it that the executive function of agreeing to such treaties could never be up for judicial scrutiny. On this second and more significant question the court was split. While the judges were unanimous in agreeing that if the government signed up to a single European foreign policy – a treaty that went beyond the 'essential scope and objectives' of the EEC, as Finlay put it – that would indeed be inconsistent with the constitution, they differed on whether this treaty crossed the line. Finlay and Griffin found that it did not, and as a result concluded that the government could go ahead and ratify it without first asking the people for an amendment to the Constitution. But they found themselves in a minority. Walsh, Henchy and Hederman saw it differently. For them, the Single European Act was a significant and decisive step along the path to a single European foreign policy. And that meant it could only be ratified by referendum.[11]

Crotty and his team were elated, but the nature of the decision was something of a surprise. Their principal argument – and the one they thought had the best chance of winning – was that signing up to the single market involved extending a range of new powers to the EEC and allowing majority voting on many of them, with the result that Ireland's sovereignty was diluted beyond what the people had agreed to with EEC membership in 1972. While Crotty's lawyers had argued the foreign policy point, they felt it was of relatively marginal importance. Internally all the credit for the foreign policy argument went to Joe Noonan and his wife, Mary Lenihan, the anti-nuclear activists who had drafted the original memorandum on that angle.

Now, of course, the manner of the victory was academic. Crotty, Coughlan and their team had scored a major victory, and their supporters cheered the outcome as a milestone for the power of the people over the elites.

The impact of the Crotty decision was felt across Europe. The European Commission called it 'regrettable'. Ireland's European commissioner, Peter Sutherland, called for 'urgent clarification' of Ireland's position and said the country faced 'an acid test of our commitment to Europe'. Back in Dublin, Taoiseach Charles Haughey, who had become Taoiseach in March (after the High Court decision but before that of the Supreme Court), now had to deal with the fallout from a case he had quietly encouraged while in opposition. He worked the phones for a few days, briefing heads of government on the dilemma the government now faced. He then recalled the Dáil a week early from its Easter recess to approve legislation allowing for a referendum.

Haughey's position on the treaty had shifted almost as soon as he came to power. As leader of the opposition, he had told the Dáil it was 'dishonest and misleading' for FitzGerald and his ministers to portray ratification as being of great benefit to the country. He said changes to EEC voting procedures, by widespread abolition of national vetoes, would disadvantage Ireland and that the claim that the treaty protected Irish neutrality 'cannot be sustained'.[12] Then, when he was in power the following April, he said the government had a responsibility to its European partners to 'take expeditious steps' to enable the treaty to come into force.[13] 'Haughey wasn't a person who was overly bothered about consistency between opposition and government', says one former colleague.

As politicians struggled to work out the long-term implications, Labour leader Dick Spring told Haughey that the Anglo-Irish Agreement and all binding international agreements entered into by the government since 1937 could now be challenged as unconstitutional. Another Labour politician, Barry Desmond, said the Supreme Court's ruling on the conduct of foreign relations had highlighted a 'black hole' in the Constitution which he said proved the need for a new Constitution to meet the needs of the late twentieth century.[14] Garret FitzGerald called the Supreme Court's decision 'abnormal, complex, damaging and dangerous'.[15]

Some of the initial claims about the potential scope of *Crotty* may have been exaggerated, but it was a decision that was to have a huge bearing on the country's relationship with the European Union. 'The Supreme Court's decision in *Crotty v. An Taoiseach* will probably rank as one of the most extraordinary ever delivered by that court', Gerard Hogan wrote later that year. It was, he added, 'a remarkable display of judicial activism' by the three-man majority.[16]

While Crotty's supporters hailed the result as a victory for democracy, others saw it as an excessive encroachment on political terrain by the judiciary. In the fraught aftermath of the decision, Progressive Democrats leader Des O'Malley said it was unsatisfactory that the government did not now 'have the same normal power that any democratic state has to make international treaties and to ratify them and put them into effect'. Arguably, he said, the court had 'stepped beyond its normal bounds' by becoming embroiled in policy.[17] That view was widely shared within the (largely pro-European) circles in which politicians and officials moved, and if anything it has hardened in the intervening years, as the impact of *Crotty* has become clearer.

Since 1987 every European treaty has been put to a referendum, and two – the Nice and Lisbon treaties – have been defeated before being approved at the second attempt. Even though many lawyers believe the Crotty decision left governments more room for manoeuvre than they have allowed – and a later Supreme Court decision in 2012 clearly hinted that it agreed with that analysis[18] – the political reality is that Irish people have come to expect referenda on European treaties. To deny them one would be politically damaging. To deny them one and then have the treaty in question declared unconstitutional by the Supreme Court is a scenario no government has been willing even to contemplate.

'Overall, the effect of the Crotty ruling on the nature of Irish democracy is not to be underestimated', wrote Gavin Barrett, associate professor in law at UCD, in a critique of the decision in 2011. The effect was that *Crotty* had led to 'the deployment in Ireland of direct democracy in the place of representative democracy to an extent unparalleled in any other state in the European Union'. Referenda were now held independently of the will of both democratically elected branches of government, Barrett wrote, and not because it had been called for in any citizen initiative but purely because 'the Supreme Court in *Crotty* asserted that this is what the Constitution implicitly requires, the Constitution making no express provision on the point'.[19]

On 26 May 1987, a referendum on the Single European Act was passed with the support of 70 per cent of Irish voters. But while the result came as a relief to the government, enabling it finally to ratify the treaty, the campaign itself was to lay the ground for future legal challenges that would constrain governments even further in fighting European referenda. That was because in the run-up to the vote, for the first time, the government ran its own campaign, using public money, to advocate a Yes vote. The group around Coughlan and Crotty were furious and thought of taking another constitutional challenge against the move, but they were so drained after the original case that they let it go.

A new opportunity presented itself in 1992, when the government held a referendum on the Maastricht Treaty, which was to lead to the creation of the single currency. Again the government used taxpayers' money to fund its Yes campaign, and this time a challenge was mounted. Patricia McKenna, an art teacher and Green Party activist who had been active in the group that included Coughlan and Crotty, agreed to be the plaintiff. The legal team was again led by Paul Callan and Séamus Ó Tuathail, who took the case on the same pro bono basis as they had fought *Crotty* five years earlier.

McKenna's case fell at the first hurdle. The High Court judge, Declan Costello, dismissed McKenna's argument as an attempt to draw the judiciary into a political question where it had no remit. 'Should the Government decide that the national interest required that an advertising campaign be mounted which was confined to extolling forcibly the benefits of an affirmative vote, it would be improper for the courts to express any view on such a decision', Costello said.[20]

McKenna could have appealed Costello's decision to the Supreme Court, but the referendum was fast approaching and the group thought she would have little chance of success in the circumstances, so she took the case no further. Instead the campaign group waited for its next opportunity, which came along in 1995, when a referendum to remove the constitutional prohibition on divorce was called.[21] McKenna – by now a Green Party MEP with a greater profile – initiated a virtually identical legal challenge. As it happened, both she and her party were in favour of divorce and were campaigning for a Yes vote, but she still believed in the principle that a government should not use taxpayers' money to try to achieve a referendum result favourable to one side. In the High Court, Ronan Keane rejected her claim. He pointed out that the Constitution had nothing to say about how referendum campaigns should be run and decided that the issue was one for the executive rather than the judiciary.

That deference towards the government and the Oireachtas was not shared by the Supreme Court, which decided in McKenna's favour by a 4-1 majority. Of the judges, Séamus Egan alone felt the government was free to use public money on a campaign, as in his view there was no constitutional or legislative impediment. But for the majority, made up of Liam Hamilton, Hugh O'Flaherty, John Blayney and Susan Denham, the requirements of equality, democracy and fairness meant otherwise.[22] It was another landmark. The judgment was delivered just a week before polling, and the government was forced to cancel its plans for blanket advertising over the last week of the campaign. And while the case was specifically about the divorce referendum, its effects were to be felt in all future referenda, including those on European integration.

Crotty had in effect required the government to put European treaties that entailed a surrender of sovereignty to a referendum and *McKenna* had blocked the government from spending public money to campaign on one side. The next angle to come in for judicial scrutiny was the broadcast media. While Coughlan had not been involved in the divorce campaign, he felt the media coverage of the campaign had been one-sided. He brought the issue to the Broadcasting Complaints Commission, maintaining that the public service broadcaster RTÉ was in breach of its statutory obligation under the Broadcasting Acts to be objective, fair and balanced in its coverage of matters of public controversy. (Because all the Dáil's main parties supported the proposal to remove the prohibition on divorce the usual time allotted by RTÉ for party political broadcasts in advance of a vote had been skewed, with forty minutes going to the Yes side and ten to the No side.)

In March 1997 the commission rejected his complaint. Coughlan challenged that finding as an error in law in the High Court, where the judge, Paul Carney, ruled in his favour. That decision was upheld by the Supreme Court in January 2000, again by a 4-1 margin, with Hamilton, Denham, Keane and Henry Barron in the majority and Donal Barrington – by now a Supreme Court judge – writing a solitary dissenting judgment. From now on all broadcasters were obliged to allow equal air-time for political broadcasts for the two sides of the argument in a referendum campaign.

★

All three of these decisions – *Crotty, McKenna* and *Coughlan* – have had a huge impact on the way referenda are run but also more broadly on Ireland's relationship with the process of European integration and the practice of Irish democracy itself. Behind all three was the same nucleus of activists and lawyers, demonstrating more than any other sequence of constitutional cases the immense impact that committed private citizens could exert when they came before receptive judges.*

Anthony Coughlan was the key figure behind the scenes in all three Supreme Court challenges. In his memoir, published in 1988, Raymond Crotty would point to Coughlan as the driving force behind the anti-EEC campaigns. 'It was he more than anyone else who opened up the debate on the [Single European Act] and placed it centre-stage in Irish politics where it could not possibly get through on a nod-and-a-wink', he wrote.[23]

'All these cases stemmed from concern about undemocratic practices', Coughlan remarks. 'If the Single European Act in 1986 had been allowed to go through without legal challenge, there is absolutely no reason why there should have been a referendum on Maastricht or Amsterdam or Nice or Lisbon.'

Looking back on them thirty years after *Crotty*, he and others who were involved feel fully vindicated. 'It was a contribution to establishing fair practices and procedures in all referenda', Coughlan says. 'It was a useful thing to do.'

Yet the legacy of those cases, *Crotty* in particular, remains contested. What for their champions were examples of the judiciary's strength in upholding citizens' rights to equality and fair procedures were, for opponents, case studies in how judicial activism could lead the courts to overstep the mark and interfere in the political domain with far-reaching negative results. To many of those critics, the decisions have distorted democracy.

In a speech in 2013, Peter Sutherland said the effects of *Crotty* had

---

* A fourth case was taken in 2012, when Donegal TD Thomas Pringle challenged the constitutionality of the European Stability Mechanism. Anthony Coughlan was again a key figure in developing Pringle's case. The challenge was rejected by a 6-1 majority in the Supreme Court, *Pringle v. Ireland* (2012).

been 'considerable and damaging for the State' in that Irish negotiators ever since had taken minimalist positions on foreign affairs
and justice out of fear of having to call a referendum.[24] *McKenna* has
been denounced, by former Chief Justice Tom O'Higgins, among
others, for taking the biggest, democratically elected player – the
government – off the pitch in referendum campaigns and allowing
privately funded individuals or groups with no democratic mandate
to influence campaigns.

The Coughlan ruling has also been blamed for skewing debate.
Though it originally applied to party political broadcasts, it has sometimes been interpreted – both by nervous broadcasters and by wily
campaign strategists – as a requirement to allocate mathematically
equal amounts of air-time to each side of an argument in referendum
debates. In the absence of firm guidance from the courts as to what
balanced coverage means, broadcasters have interpreted it cautiously
as meaning a 50:50 approach.

According to Gavin Barrett, the result has been to nullify any
advantage that elected leaders or parties enjoy compared to those
who have no mandate or support. When there is no real opposition to
a referendum proposal, broadcasters find themselves in the surreal
position of being unable to interview those who wish to argue its
merits. In practice, Barrett writes, 'the "50-50" rule creates a perverse
political incentive to oppose Constitutional amendments on European treaties'.[25]

The Supreme Court judges in the *Crotty* majority were no doubt
well aware of the uproar that their decision would cause within
mainstream politics. In a letter to William Brennan on 11 May 1987,
a month after the decision had been announced, Walsh sent copies of
the judgments to his US counterpart and told him about the political
fallout.

In our own Court we have been pretty busy recently. You may have
heard of our decision in what is called the Single European Act case,
which is really a Treaty between ourselves and eleven other countries. The Court accepted part and rejected part, which has caused
great fuss among politicians. It is the first time ever that the Court has

been asked to intervene and did in fact prevent the Government ratifying a Treaty. The decision was a majority one, 3-2, with, I am afraid, myself leading the majority. I enclose herewith a special newspaper supplement which will give you the terms of the Treaty concerned and all the opinions. I hope you will find it interesting. In the result there now has to be a referendum towards the end of this month to amend the Constitution by writing into it a specific reference to this Treaty alongside the reference to the Treaties of the Common Market, which were put in by a constitutional amendment at the end of 1972.

The political argument has very much accused the Court or the majority of the Court of interfering with the Government's foreign policy, but I think when you read the judgments you will see that that is not sustainable. In fact in my own opinion I went out of my way to state the complete freedom of the Government to pursue any foreign policy it liked, but what I said was unconstitutional was giving away that freedom. In the meanwhile the other eleven countries (some of whom accept the Treaty with certain misgivings) are held up because the Treaty cannot come into force until all twelve ratifications are in.[26]

Brennan thanked Walsh for the judgments, telling him they would make 'wonderful reading' for an upcoming flight to California, where he was due to give the commencement speech at his nephew's graduation ceremony. As it happened, Brennan had indeed heard about the Single European Act case. At the Irish embassy in Washington on St Patrick's Day, which was after the High Court decision but before that of the Supreme Court, he told Walsh, he had heard 'much unfavourable reaction from the diplomatic genre'. But Brennan reassured Walsh: 'Bureaucrats always cry, but it's more crocodile tears than not, I've found.'[27]

At least some members of the Supreme Court felt the government could have played its hand better. In a remarkable interview with the *Irish Times* on 4 March, the final day of the Supreme Court hearing of Crotty's case, Walsh, notwithstanding the fact that the case was still going on, was happy to share his annoyance at the claim by the State's lawyers that it would be diplomatically embarrassing for Ireland if the court ruled with Crotty. The Department of Foreign Affairs had put in an affidavit, he told the paper, which said that other EEC member states 'were very cross with us', which he found 'totally irrelevant'. Walsh told the paper: 'Certainly we're not concerned about what other people think, and if they think badly of us, they should think badly of the Dáil or the Government which kept us hanging round for nearly two years and then enacted at the last moment.'

'We don't think of these things. We can see the consequences but it doesn't mean we are going to be deterred from what we think is right.'[28]

The Crotty case was a legal milestone. For close Supreme Court-watchers it was significant for another reason: it was one of the last major cases involving Brian Walsh and Séamus Henchy, two of the great Supreme Court judges in the twentieth century.

The following year, when the Fianna Fáil administration was looking for a head for the new Independent Radio and Television Commission, a litany of recent examples of cronyism meant it had to be seen to choose someone whose integrity and independence were above reproach. The government approached Henchy about resigning from the Supreme Court to take up the new role, and he duly agreed, bringing his sixteen-year tenure on the court to an end a year before he was due to retire.

In the *Irish Times*, Fintan O'Toole regretted Henchy's appointment as 'a bad day's work for Ireland' by Fianna Fáil – not because Henchy lacked the probity, intelligence and clear-sightedness for the job but, on the contrary, because the government was removing from a far more important body, the Supreme Court, 'probably the most consistent progressive force over the last two decades'.[29]

Fianna Fáil's one 'indisputably great contribution to Irish intellectual life' had been in its appointment of Supreme Court judges, O'Toole said. Brian Walsh, Cearbhall Ó Dálaigh, Niall McCarthy and Séamus Henchy had 'not only pushed back the limits on individual freedom in Ireland since the early 1960s, they have done so with a combination of energy and reforming zeal with rigour and erudition that is rare in Irish public life'.[30]

Henchy left an immeasurable legacy and, to a large extent, shaped the current generation of judges, who came of age when he was at the height of his powers in the late 1970s and early 1980s. He was in some ways a traditionalist, recognizing 'the inherent limitations of judicial power, often advocating that change could best be brought about by the Oireachtas rather than through the courts'.[31] But he was also an ardent defender of individual freedoms, and was capable of looking beyond the conventional legal wisdom to make ground-breaking decisions in areas where the politicians lacked either the moral courage or the energy to act.

He was not without his blind spots and his weaknesses. He could be difficult to appear before. He was part of the three-judge High Court that threw out the Nicolaou adoption case. Yet his main judgment in the McGee case on contraception was an audacious, imaginative sweep of the Constitution that, by finding that the document, taken as a whole, implied a zone of individual freedom to do things of which others might not approve, was a radical advance.

Ironically, given that he was appointed by a Fianna Fáil administration that wished to calm the Supreme Court down, he was pivotal to some of its most far-reaching decisions. His powerful, angry denunciation of the ban on homosexual acts in *Norris*, which put him on the right side of history, is probably the most commonly cited of the court's dissents. And through his decisions in the de Búrca case on juries, Crotty's challenge against the Single European Act and Mary and Francis Murphy's successful attempt to make the tax laws fairer, he contributed to major changes in Irish public life and society in the second half of the twentieth century.

Yet recognition was relatively slow in coming Henchy's way. He was a private and reserved man who drew little attention to himself; when he stepped down in 1988, the tributes – a few notable exceptions, such as O'Toole's column, notwithstanding – were respectful rather than laudatory. A number of factors caused that to change after his retirement and, particularly, after his death in 2009. Although Henchy had originally been close to Fianna Fáil, he was later

identified with the anti-Haughey wing of the party – an impression
that gained weight through his stewardship of the Arms Trial and his
stance on issues such as extradition, which went against the dominant
Fianna Fáil view under Haughey. As the scale of Haughey's corrupt
conduct became clear in the 2000s, in the public mind it vindicated
further those who had stood against him. Henchy may have said next
to nothing in public about Haughey during his lifetime, but he was
seen as one of those who had always regarded him with a wary eye.
Above all, perhaps, the quality of Henchy's writing – he is now considered one of the great prose stylists of the judiciary – helped his
work endure.

Having stayed on for two years after Henchy's departure, Walsh
retired in 1990 after a remarkable twenty-nine years on the Supreme
Court. Unlike Henchy, Walsh's status as a judicial colossus was firmly
established by the time he retired. It was no accident that his time on
the court coincided with a legal revolution in Ireland – one that elevated the Constitution and the protections it afforded citizens and, as
a consequence, turned the Supreme Court into a major force that was
to have a profound effect on Irish society.

With his close collaborator Cearbhall Ó Dálaigh, Walsh injected
life and vitality into an institution that, in general, had struggled to
assert itself or even begin seriously to grapple with the potential the
Constitution offered. The two men were cosmopolitans, and in many
ways they were visionaries. Walsh was the driving force behind
the attempt to use that Constitution to forge a distinctly Irish legal
system that broke with the traditional reliance on English law and
practice and opened itself up to new international influences. As his
long friendship with William Brennan demonstrated, the principal
influence was the United States, where a written Constitution and a
set of expansionist-minded liberal judges – led by Brennan himself –
seemed to Walsh to offer an ideal template for the project he and
Ó Dálaigh were undertaking. Walsh too had his blind spots, of
course. He was ill advised to allow himself to be identified so much
with Haughey. Some of his judgments on criminal law went so far
that they were quickly repudiated by subsequent courts.

Walsh was a staunch conservative on moral issues, as his positions on homosexuality, adoption and abortion made clear, but on criminal law he was liberal, and the insistence on the rights of defendants against the State was a constant theme over his thirty years as a judge. In the 1960s, that stance infuriated the government, yet, to Walsh's credit, grumbling from Merrion Street did not seem to bother him in the slightest. The result was a series of judgments – from *Byrne v. Ireland*, which gave ordinary citizens the right to sue the State, through *McGee* on contraception and *de Búrca* on women jurors – that accelerated social change, nudged the government into action and pressed the Constitution into service as a real force in the life of the State and its citizens.

In subsequent years, it became a parlour game among lawyers to choose between Walsh, Henchy and Ó Dálaigh. But that was to miss the point. Collegiate courts such as the Supreme Court by design militate against dominance by single individuals. Even the Chief Justice is only one voice among up to seven, and as Billy FitzGerald showed in the early 1970s, even the most senior judge can have next to no impact on the direction of the court if he is an isolated voice. The result is that no major shifts can take place without a majority of like-minded judges.

Individually, people such as Ó Dálaigh, Walsh and Henchy could have achieved very little. Yet they came along at a time when propitious conditions – including wider social and generational changes and a cluster of innovative senior judges such as O'Higgins, Kingsmill Moore, Budd and Kenny – gave them the opportunity to effect a dramatic judicial departure. Their achievement is that everyone now takes their achievements for granted. As Walsh himself observed, 'things that nobody thought could happen did happen'. And when they did, everyone soon wondered why they hadn't happened earlier.

Walsh and William Brennan retired within months of one another in 1990. On 20 March of that year, Walsh wrote to his American colleague. 'Dear Bill,' he began,

> By the time you receive this letter I shall have retired from the Supreme Court at the compulsory retirement age of 72 which I shall

have received on the 23rd March. As I told you I shall continue on in the European Court of Human Rights until 1998 and as the work of that Court is continuously increasing in volume I shall certainly not be idle.

With his new-found free time, Walsh wrote, he hoped to have the opportunity to visit the US more frequently, and he was looking forward to seeing Brennan in the very near future.[32]

'I know that retiring from your court can't be too easy', Brennan responded a week later. 'You certainly leave a remarkable record of accomplishment. It's a volume of work that will always be remembered.'[33] By October, Brennan himself had retired after thirty-four years on the US Supreme Court.

The two men remained in frequent contact as they adjusted to and then settled into retirement, exchanging birthday and Christmas cards and occasionally visiting one another.

Almost three years later, in February 1993, Walsh wrote to Brennan from his home in Clontarf. He congratulated his friend on a recent award, wished him a speedy recovery from a recent illness and told him he looked forward to their next meeting. 'Don't forget that we have a date for a drink on New Year's Eve 1999', Walsh wrote.[34] Brennan replied quickly, assuring his friend that he was 'on the road to almost full recovery' and sending his 'affectionate best' to Walsh's wife, Noreen, and their children.[35]

They were to be the last letters between Walsh and Brennan. The two men, whose careers had followed such similar paths and intersected in a way that allowed them to forge a thirty-year friendship across the Atlantic, were growing old and increasingly frail. They would not get to share that drink on the eve of the new Millennium. Brennan died in July 1997. Walsh passed away in Dublin eight months later.

14. X

'. . . the failure by the legislature to enact the appropriate legislation is no longer just unfortunate; it is inexcusable.'

Niall McCarthy

It passed largely unnoticed at the time, but on 24 January 1981 a meeting took place at Mount Carmel Hospital in Dublin that was to set off one of the most bitter and protracted social debates to convulse Ireland since the foundation of the State. Gathered in the room were delegates from over a dozen Catholic, medical and anti-abortion associations, from the Irish Catholic Doctors' Guild to the Society for the Protection of Unborn Children (SPUC). Other groups, including the Irish Nurses' Organisation and Pax Christi (a Catholic peace and reconciliation movement), sent messages of support.[1]

At this, the inaugural meeting of the Pro-Life Amendment Campaign (PLAC), the objective was set out simply by Denis Barror, a solicitor and member of the Responsible Society, an organization that had been set up the previous year after a meeting organized by the Catholic laymen's organization the Knights of St Columbanus.

'The issue which concerns this meeting is abortion', Barror told delegates. As he explained, abortion was made illegal in Ireland by the Offences Against the Person Act of 1861, but there was nothing in the Constitution explicitly banning it. In his view, that meant there was no obstacle to prevent abortion being introduced, either by the Oireachtas simply changing the law or by the courts declaring that the prohibition was inconsistent with the Constitution. The only way to make sure neither of those things could happen, he argued, was to write an express ban into the Constitution.

If no steps are taken to amend the Constitution in this respect, there is a danger that someone may take an action requesting the courts to declare that the present legislative prohibition of abortion is itself unconstitutional in that it inhibits personal rights in some respect. It is unlikely that such an action would succeed at the present time but it could conceivably succeed three or four or seven years hence. A constitutional amendment enacted now prohibiting abortion would forestall and out-manoeuvre anyone thinking of taking such an action.[2]

As Tom Hesketh points out in his book on the saga, *The Second Partitioning of Ireland?*, the Irish debate on abortion in the early 1980s was unusual in that initially groups seeking a more restrictive legal regime set the terms of the discussion. In the United States and most of Europe, it was the other way around: the momentum was generated by pro-choice lobbies who created a dynamic in favour of a more liberal legal regime, often with successful results.[3] In Ireland the perceived threat to traditional Catholic values represented by that liberalizing current, both at home and abroad, was one of the chief reasons the anti-abortion lobby began to organize and coalesce around the demand for a constitutional amendment.

For many in the anti-abortion lobby, concern about what an activist Supreme Court might do was a central plank of the case for putting the issue to a referendum. Ever since the court had found, in May McGee's landmark case on contraception, that there was in the Constitution an implicit right to marital privacy, lawyers had been debating whether that decision could prove a stepping-stone to a general right to privacy that would encompass a right to abortion. In 1965, the US Supreme Court, in *Griswold v. Connecticut*, had identified an unwritten right to privacy in the US Constitution. Eight years later, in *Roe v. Wade*, it famously extended that right to privacy to include a woman's decision to have an abortion. When the Irish court made the McGee decision in 1973, the same year that *Roe v. Wade* was delivered in the US, two of the judges in the majority, Séamus Henchy and Frank Griffin, cited *Griswold v. Connecticut* as authority for their finding. As the anti-abortion lobby saw it, if there was a straight line from *Griswold* to *Roe v. Wade*, what was to stop *McGee* paving the way for an Irish *Roe v. Wade*?

In 1977, a short but significant debate took place between constitutional lawyers in the pages of the Jesuit academic journal *Studies*. James O'Reilly, who was a lecturer in law at UCD, dismissed the 'prophets of doom' who claimed that *McGee* could open up a route to abortion. 'Nothing could be further from the truth', O'Reilly wrote. In Ireland, 'whatever else privacy may mean, it does not mean abortion.' He based his argument primarily on statements made in Walsh's judgment, including the judge's observation that, unlike contraception, 'any action on the part of either the husband and wife or of the State to limit family sizes by endangering or destroying human life must necessarily not only be an offence against the common good but also against the guaranteed personal rights of the human life in question'. He also noted Griffin's observation that on abortion 'entirely different considerations may arise'. All of that put clear blue water between contraception and abortion, in O'Reilly's opinion. Abortion clearly did not come within the protected zone of privacy around the family. And in any case, he added, a right to abortion would run counter to the 'whole ethos of the Irish system'.[4]

This drew a response from William Binchy, who was then research counsellor at the Law Reform Commission and who would become an influential figure in the anti-abortion movement. Binchy saw a clear path from *McGee* to abortion. O'Reilly had underplayed the importance of the social context, he argued, in particular the trend towards rapidly changing attitudes on abortion in the western world.

> The Supreme Court in *McGee* was quite probably in advance of general public opinion. In the foreseeable event of some change in attitudes in this country on the question of abortion, the McGee decision ... constitutes live ammunition in the hands of a Court which might again be ahead of public opinion.[5]

Yes, the McGee case was not concerned with abortion, but that was precisely why it was not a legal precedent against abortion, he wrote:

> The concept of marital privacy which *McGee* has imported into this country from the United States, with little analysis, is of such a pliable nature that it may readily be bent, as has happened in the United

States, to accommodate the recognition of the 'right' to abortion. Without such a concept, it is difficult to see how the Constitutional argument in favour of abortion could get off the ground. Once such a concept has been accepted, this is no longer the case.[6]

Reflecting on the issue in the mid-1980s, Brian Walsh, who himself was anti-abortion, was of the view that an amendment had not been necessary because the constitutional protection for the right to life encompassed that of the unborn. Nor did he believe that the Supreme Court would have found a right to abortion, although he did acknowledge that in theory a future court could do so. Asked by the Australian lawyer Garry Sturgess if it alarmed him that the Supreme Court had been drawn into a major political controversy – the amendment debate – in this way, he said:

> It didn't alarm me at all, in the sense that I didn't think there was any possibility in the foreseeable future of it happening. But secondly, it didn't alarm me for a different reason, because the Supreme Court has exercised a very powerful influence on the framing of certain types of [legislative interpretation]. So I think the fears expressed were not so much a distrust of the Supreme Court as a recognition of the power of the Supreme Court. That it might come some day that, perhaps with a different personnel, they might get themselves into the position of saying 'this is purely a private matter and that there isn't a public interest in it, therefore people can more or less do as they wish'. I thought that was highly unlikely, but it was possible at some stage. Because big changes like that are brought about not overnight but by a certain process, if you like, of inch-by-inch [movement] until one can rationalise the situation into the final change-over.[7]

The meeting at Mount Carmel may have fired the starting gun on the organized campaign to change the Constitution, but for more than a year leading up to it advocates on both sides of the debate had been preparing to do battle. As Gene Kerrigan points out, the focus of the women's movement had splintered somewhat after Charles Haughey's 'Irish solution' had taken the heat out of the contraception issue, but in late 1979 and early 1980 a small group of women came together to form the Women's Right to Choose Group.[8] That in turn led to the establishment of the Irish Pregnancy Counselling Centre, which would provide non-directional counselling for women with unwanted pregnancies. If a woman said she wanted an abortion, the centre would refer her to a clinic in England. A similar service was offered by the Well Woman Centre, run by Anne Connolly in Dublin.

. The existence of these referral services was a reminder – an uncomfortable one for the anti-abortion lobby – that while the law had stood still for more than a century, by the mid-1980s thousands of Irish women were travelling to Britain every year for abortions. In February 1981, when all of the Republic's MEPs voted against a pro-choice motion at the European Parliament, an editorial in the *Irish Times* pointed to the disjunction between politicians' rhetoric and the reality for many Irish women. At least 3,000 Irish women travelled to Britain for abortions every year, it said, and by some estimates the real figure was closer to 10,000. '[H]ave those who mark out Ireland's abhorrence of abortion any plans to prevent abortion or to help those who are contemplating abortions for reasons of their own?'[9]

In parallel with the liberalization of abortion laws elsewhere and the increasing focus of the Irish women's movement on the issue, local anti-abortion groups had been growing increasingly organized from early 1980. The most significant was SPUC, an offshoot of a British group of the same name, whose posters advertising public meetings on opposition to abortion began to appear in shopping centres from September 1980. 'SPUC's initial steps were taken on the periphery of media consciousness, but in the heartland of Catholicism – the parish halls, presbyteries and pulpits. It was a genuine grassroots movement', writes Kerrigan. 'Its problem was that it was all dressed up, in its Sunday best, with nowhere to go. Abortion was already illegal.'[10]

It was for that reason that SPUC and about a dozen other anti-abortion forces were to consolidate around the demand, first proposed by the Irish Catholic Doctors' Guild (set up ten years earlier as a reaction to what its founders identified as a growing 'decline in ethical values'), for a constitutional amendment. The academic and pro-choice activist Linda Connolly has written that this nascent anti-abortion movement made itself visible and became mobilized 'by diverting the abortion debate into the legal/constitutional arena – an area which required extensive resources and legal expertise'.[11]

The debate that followed was, in historian Diarmaid Ferriter's words, 'one of the most poisonous witnessed in twentieth-century Ireland'.[12] A sense of the atmosphere can be gleaned from reports of an event organized by SPUC on Christmas Eve 1981, when about 2,000 people carrying flowers and lighted candles marched through the streets of Dublin demanding an amendment. 'A handful of women from the Women's Right to Choose Group staged a counter-demonstration at the GPO', the following day's paper reported. 'They stood in silence behind a banner giving the name and the Dublin phone number of the group. Most of the marchers ignored the women; a few jeered, a man shouted that if they had their way no children would be born in Ireland at all; and others tried to press anti-abortion leaflets into their hands.'[13]

The march, the organizers said, was timed to take place in the run-up to the Feast of the Holy Innocents, 'in memory of the 3,800 Irish babies killed in British abortion clinics during the past year'. Outside Leinster House, the crowd cheered when the president of SPUC, Wexford journalist Billy Quirke, said that the 'atheistic trend-setters who are in public life today and who control the media' gave disproportionate air-time and newspaper space to those trying to undermine the traditional morality of Ireland. 'We are the great silent majority of Ireland', he told the crowd.

By June 1981, PLAC had produced a draft amendment wording, largely written by one of its legal advisers, senior counsel John Blayney.[14] It did not refer to the pregnant woman and adopted the Catholic view that the foetus was entitled to the status of personhood from the moment of conception.[15]

> The State recognises the absolute right to life of every unborn child from conception and accordingly guarantees to respect and protect such right by law.

It was PLAC's good fortune that it appeared on the scene at a moment of acute political instability, when party leaders, ever conscious that another election was around the corner, were vulnerable to pressure and receptive to the claims of interest groups – not least one that had been assiduously developing a grassroots network across the country and had the backing of the Catholic Church. The group managed the situation skilfully, playing political leaders off against one another in a way that worked to its advantage. After its first meetings with Taoiseach Charles Haughey and Fine Gael leader Garret FitzGerald in April and May 1981 PLAC's representatives had declarations of support for a referendum from the leaders of the two major parties (the Labour Party was more equivocal).

According to Kerrigan, some of FitzGerald's advisers felt many voters perceived him as remote and insufficiently in tune with traditional Catholic values. 'It was felt that some of the electorate didn't even know he was a Catholic. The PLAC demand was an opportunity to get into line.'[16]

Fine Gael included the commitment to a referendum in its manifesto for the June 1981 election, although there was no mention of it in the programme for government subsequently agreed with the Labour Party. FitzGerald reassured PLAC representatives that they should not read too much into the omission, but they could see he had growing doubts about the idea. It was a stroke of good fortune for the anti-abortion lobby, therefore, that when a general election was called in February 1982 FitzGerald was replaced as Taoiseach by Haughey, who had remained steadfast in his commitment to a referendum. Haughey duly acted on the pledge by announcing his plan for a bill within a month of his arrival in Government Buildings.

Until then, pro-choice voices had been somewhat diffuse, but Haughey's move galvanized liberal opponents and forced them to unite around a common purpose they could all agree on: the imperative to block an abortion ban being written into the Constitution. The result was the Anti-Amendment Campaign (AAC), which emerged in early 1982 and acted as a fulcrum for liberal opposition to Haughey's plan. The AAC was an umbrella group that drew its members from the Protestant churches, medicine, law, the women's movement and mainstream politics. Among its most prominent figures were: Dr George Henry, Master of the Rotunda; the Labour politicians Michael D. Higgins, Jim Kemmy, Ruairí Quinn and

Barry Desmond; Trinity senators Mary Robinson, Shane Ross and Trevor West; Noel Browne, David Norris and Christy Moore. All the key women's rights organizations, including the Irish Pregnancy Counselling Centre, the Dublin Well Woman Centre and the Women's Right to Choose Group, were involved.

From the law library, where the amendment had exposed sharp divisions, the barristers Adrian Hardiman, John Mac Menamin and Frank Clarke joined the AAC steering committee and persuaded fellow lawyers to join. In February 1983, when the campaign was at its height, ninety-eight barristers – almost a quarter of all the barristers practising in the country at the time – made a statement from the Four Courts in which they denounced the proposed amendment. 'It was never intended that the Constitution should enshrine a specific viewpoint on a highly controversial issue; especially when that specific viewpoint reflects not the general consensus of all citizens, but more the beliefs of some members of one particular denomination', they said in the statement. 'This principle applies no less strongly where a majority of citizens are adherents to one particular creed.'[17] The list of signatories included some of the most prominent lawyers in the country, among them the future judges Michael Moriarty, Barry White, Brian McCracken, Séamus Egan, Nial Fennelly, Paul Gilligan, Kevin Haugh, Mary Irvine, Seán Ryan, Ray Fullam, Adrian Hardiman, Frank Clarke, Elizabeth Dunne, John Mac Menamin, Catherine McGuinness, Brian McGovern and Patrick McCarthy.

By July 1982, Labour leader Michael O'Leary finally came out against the idea of an amendment, putting more pressure on Garret FitzGerald to follow suit. FitzGerald's reservations were by now well known, and the involvement in the AAC of some Fine Gael members showed that the issue had opened up wider fissures within FitzGerald's party.[18]

The Fianna Fáil government published its amendment wording on 2 November 1982. Two days later, Haughey's administration lost its slim majority in a key vote, resulting in the dissolution of the Dáil and the calling of an election that had been expected for some time.

To Haughey's opponents, the proximity of the two developments – the publication of the draft amendment and the calling of an election – seemed to confirm their suspicions about his advocacy for constitutional change: that it had less to do with moral conviction than with pure politics. The previous July, Conor Cruise O'Brien had spelled it out when he wrote that a referendum offered Fianna Fáil 'marvellous possibilities' to reveal the extent of the split in Fine Gael.

> The real reason why we are likely to get this Bill has nothing to do with the right to life, except the right of politicians to political life. Moral issues, in contemporary conditions, are splendid hunting terrain, for the hungry wild dogs of Fianna Fáil. Moral issues don't split Fianna Fáil. It is a robust and disciplined party. It knows a moral issue when it sees one, and it knows what you do about a thing like that. What you do is, you find out what is the electorally rewarding approach to the moral issue in question, and you adopt that approach forthwith.[19]

Cruise O'Brien was not alone in seeing an ulterior motive behind Fianna Fáil's enthusiastic embrace of the amendment project. As the election campaign got under way, an *Irish Independent* editorial took Haughey to task over his handling of the issue:

> That an Attorney General and a Government had the nerve to issue such a proposal is indicative either of bankruptcy or of political advantage seeking. It was done in a rush. It was done at a time when no rational debate was possible. And it was done with both the distinct possibility of a general election being in the air, but also with the definite intention of an election within weeks.[20]

On the other hand, Hesketh points out that Haughey's commitment to PLAC had been 'consistent and unmistakable' from Day One and that work on the amendment wording, drafted by Attorney General John Murray, had been under way from the earliest days of the February–November 1982 administration.[21]

The task of formulating the wording had been a difficult and drawn-out process involving multiple drafts over the lifetime of two Fianna Fáil governments and a series of meetings between Martin Mansergh, Haughey's special adviser, and senior figures in the Catholic and Protestant churches. After a rush to get it finalized in advance of the Dáil being dissolved, the final draft, which was shown to the church leaders in advance of publication, was as follows:

> The State acknowledges the right to life of the unborn and, with due regard to the equal right to life of the mother, guarantees in its laws to respect, and, as far as practicable, by its laws to defend and vindicate that right.

For its advocates, the draft was a compromise. The wording was certainly an attempt to marry PLAC's position with that of the churches and the legal opinions provided to government. It did not refer to an 'absolute' right to life or to rights kicking in at the point of conception, as some within PLAC wanted, and made no attempt to define when life began. It also referred to the rights of the mother – one of the criteria set down by Dr Henry McAdoo, the Church of Ireland Archbishop of Dublin, at a meeting with Mansergh earlier that autumn. But PLAC was content that it met its essential demands.

In critics' eyes, however, the wording was a confused hotchpotch that stored up trouble for the future. The fundamental problem was plain to see. By setting the equal right to life of the mother and the unborn against one another, the government was leaving it open as to how those two rights were to be weighed. As Mary Robinson observed, the formula 'would throw the entire matter into the lap of the courts'. Above all, the AAC argued, the amendment would have severe repercussions for medics and would raise doubts over the legality of certain forms of contraception – not to mention embedding in the Constitution a view it believed had no place there.

Hardiman, who was later to become AAC chairman, denounced the proposal as an encroachment by the State on the private lives of citizens. 'I believe that the general tendency of the amendment would be to increase the role of the State and the law in the area of sexuality and specifically to bring within the ambit of the law many areas which are now . . . private', he said.[22]

Garret FitzGerald initially welcomed Haughey's wording and went into the November 1982 election pledging to put it to the people in a referendum if Fine Gael was in government. Partly as a result of the

apparent consensus between the two parties, abortion was a marginal
issue during the election campaign, and when FitzGerald returned as
Taoiseach at the head of a Fine Gael–Labour coalition the pledge was
duly included in the Programme for Government.

By early 1983, however, amid signs of increasing unease within
government over the Haughey wording, FitzGerald began to waver.
The key factor was legal advice provided by the Attorney General,
Peter Sutherland, who wrote a memo setting out grave reservations
about the wording. In Sutherland's view, the text was so ambiguous
that it would in effect hand over to the judiciary the job of figuring
out when abortion was or was not allowed. Did 'unborn' mean the
right to life began at conception or viability? If it was the former,
what medical advice was available, and would that mean certain
forms of contraception would be affected? What did the text mean by
'with due regard' to the right to life of the mother? How were doctors to weigh these two rights to life – that of the mother and the
unborn – if a given medical emergency demanded it?

'The proposed Amendment will in my view tend to confuse a doctor
as to his responsibilities rather than assist him and the consequences may
well be to inhibit him in making decisions as to whether treatment
should be given in a particular case', Sutherland wrote. 'In these circumstances,' he concluded, 'I cannot approve of the wording proposed.'[23]

With FitzGerald's support, Sutherland drafted an alternative:

> Nothing in this Constitution shall be invoked to invalidate, or to
> deprive of force or effect, any provision of a law on the ground that it
> prohibits abortion.

That would have closed off the possibility of the Supreme Court
finding a right to abortion, but it would not have blocked a future,
more liberal Oireachtas from changing the law. For that reason, among
others, the anti-abortion lobby distanced itself from Sutherland's
proposal. Even Fine Gael members of Cabinet were split. Minister
for Justice Michael Noonan argued that public opinion would never
accept Sutherland's suggestion and put officials in his department
to work on a different wording that would explicitly protect the
right to life of the unborn. Noonan lost the argument, but when

FitzGerald's government tabled the Sutherland wording in the Dáil it was defeated by 87 to 65.

And so it was the original Haughey draft, now publicly opposed by FitzGerald, that went before the people in a referendum. It passed on 7 September 1983 with 67 per cent of the vote.

In a televised debate on the eve of the referendum, by which time the passage of the proposal looked virtually guaranteed, FitzGerald warned that – contrary to the explicit aim with which the anti-abortion lobby began its campaign three years earlier – the amendment would give the Supreme Court a bigger role than ever in interpreting the law on abortion.[24]

It would take less than a decade for events to bear that out, when the judges were confronted with arguably the most controversial case to come to the Four Courts since the Constitution came into force.

In early December 1991, a fourteen-year-old middle-class convent schoolgirl was raped by her friend's father. The two families knew each other well and the girl was a regular visitor to her friend's house. The friend's father had begun molesting her in June 1990, a month before her thirteenth birthday. In August 1990, while she was staying with her friend's family when her parents were in Lourdes, he raped her for the first time. The abuse had been getting worse in the year leading up to the December 1991 rape.

The girl did not tell anyone of the abuse she was suffering until 27 January 1992. She had been unwell for a number of days and on that day it emerged that she was in the early stages of pregnancy. She told her parents everything that had been happening. Later, the girl confided in her mother that when she found out she was pregnant she had wanted to kill herself by throwing herself downstairs.

The girl was referred to a hospital, and on 30 January the crime was reported to the gardaí. The distraught girl and her family were in a harrowing situation. After discussing it together they decided the best course was for her to have an abortion. Given the Irish legal ban, that meant leaving the country. They opted for England.

As the garda investigation got under way, the parents told a member of the force that they were considering travelling for an abortion and raised the possibility that someone could be present with them in England to carry out a DNA test on the foetus so that the identity of the father could be confirmed. The garda was not sure whether such evidence would be admissible in court but promised to make inquiries. Gardaí sought an opinion from the office of the Director of Public Prosecutions, and on 5 February the parents were informed that the DNA evidence could not be used in court. They were distressed to hear this, but in the same conversation they confirmed that they and their daughter would still go to England the next day. They travelled as planned, and on arrival they made arrangements for the abortion.

Meanwhile, back in Dublin, word of the case had reached the offices of the most senior legal officers in the country. The Director of Public Prosecutions, Eamonn Barnes, heard about it as a result of the garda query to his office. Barnes wondered whether the case raised a constitutional issue, given the 1983 'right to life' amendment, so he phoned the Attorney General, Harry Whelehan, and briefed him. Whelehan thought about it and, without consulting the government, instructed lawyers to seek a High Court injunction to prevent the girl from travelling. In doing so he was using his powers to take independent action as 'guardian of the public interest'. Whelehan was granted an interim injunction at a private, *in camera* hearing at the High Court. From then on, to protect her anonymity, the girl would be known as Miss X.

Once they were informed of the injunction, the girl and her parents cancelled the arrangements for an abortion and returned to Ireland. On the journey home, the girl told her mother that she had wanted to throw herself under a train when she was in London. Later, in the presence of a garda, when her father said the situation 'was worse than a death in the family', she added: 'Not if it was me.'

Although the injunction hearing was closed to journalists (at the time cases involving minors were automatically held in private), the news appeared in a short, 230-word story on the front page of the *Irish Times* on 12 February under the headline 'State Attempts to Stop Girl's Abortion'. It was a busy news day: the surrounding headlines were about Albert Reynolds's dramatic first days as Taoiseach, when he sacked eight of twelve serving ministers. But the case of the fourteen-year-old schoolgirl shunted everything else to one side that day. In his first hours as Taoiseach, Reynolds had a crisis on his hands.

Years later, the press secretary to that government, Seán Duignan, recalled the moment Reynolds learned about the case. 'On my very first day as government press secretary, I walked into the Taoiseach's office and he said "Welcome Diggy, you're not going to believe what just landed on my desk." I said, "Something called the X case?" He said, "I don't believe it. How could this happen to me on my very first day in office?"'

In private, the prevailing view in government was that Whelehan should have delayed or turned a blind eye until the girl was out of the country and had had her abortion. But Whelehan maintained he had had a constitutional duty to act. 'I am not prepared to say I regret having to do my duty. I do, of course, regret the upset, the sadness and the trauma which was visited on everybody involved but that is something which I can't do anything more about', he told the *Scannal* programme on RTÉ in 2012. 'I don't want this to sound harsh but where the mother of the child who is entitled to have its life protected decided to seek an abortion the only mechanism in our system is for the Attorney General to intervene and to make a case for the child to be born alive.' (In the High Court, judge Declan Costello had backed up Whelehan's view of where his responsibilities lay, saying the duty of the Attorney General in the circumstances 'cannot be in doubt'.)

Politicians, whether in government or opposition, struggled to understand Whelehan's thinking, Duignan wrote in his memoirs.

> [B]ecause when it comes right down to it, Irish politicians of whatever stripe, including the great moralisers, approach these kind [*sic*] of issues in enthusiastic conformity with Charles Haughey's much derided dictum that there are Irish solutions to Irish problems. So, on both sides of the House, they muttered that Harry and his people should have sought advice, i.e. deferred action until it was too late – 'let the file fall behind a radiator' – or at least dawdled until the deed was done, so as to keep them out of the whole embarrassing mess, while the young rape victim underwent an abortion somewhere outside the jurisdiction.[25]

On the day of her return from London, Miss X's parents brought her to a clinical psychologist. She was emotionally withdrawn, with a 'vacant expressionless manner' that indicated to the psychologist that she was in shock and coping with the appalling crisis she faced 'by a denial of her emotions'. In Costello's summary of the psychologist's evidence, he noted:

> She did not seem depressed but he said that she 'coldly expressed a desire to solve matters by ending her life'. In his opinion, in her withdrawn state 'she was capable of such an act, not so much because she is depressed but because she could calculatingly reach the conclusion that death is the best solution'. He considered that the psychological damage to her of carrying a child would be considerable and that the damage to her mental health would be devastating. His report was supplemented by oral testimony. He explained that in the course of his consultation with the defendant she had said to him: 'It is hard at fourteen to go through the nine months,' and that she said: 'It's better to end it now than in nine months' time.' The psychologist understood this to mean that by ending her life she would end the problems through which she was putting her parents, with whom she has a very strong and loving relationship.[26]

When the debate over the abortion amendment was at its height in 1983, the Pro-Life Amendment Campaign had confidently asserted that a situation such as this would never arise. One of PLAC's lawyers, Iarfhlaith O'Neill, stated at the time that a court would never grant an injunction to stop an Irish woman going to England for an abortion, because it would be 'totally impracticable'.[27] It turned out he was wrong, except that in the event it was not a woman who was stopped but a girl.

Costello presided over a full High Court hearing, where evidence was given by both sides and on 17 February, in a judgment that wrestled with the virtually impossible task of weighing two equal constitutional rights to life – a pregnant woman's and that of the unborn – he felt he was left with no option but to make the injunction permanent. Miss X was legally barred from leaving the country. The grotesque, surreal situation was captured by the *Irish Times* cartoonist Martyn Turner. He drew Ireland surrounded by a barbed-wire fence, with a little girl clutching a teddy bear standing behind it. The caption read: 'The introduction of internment in Ireland . . . for 14-year-old girls.' The cartoon was instrumental in the family's decision to fight the High Court decision. (The girl and her mother later visited Turner and asked for the original, which was subsequently used to raise funds for the Rape Crisis Centre.[28])

The High Court decision provoked outrage. Within hours of Costello's judgment, 700 people marched to Government Buildings, some of them calling for Whelehan's resignation. 'Not the Church, not the State, women must decide their fate', the protesters chanted.[29] For their part, the anti-abortion lobby accused politicians of exploiting Miss X's situation for their own ideological ends. Bernadette Bonar, a leading anti-abortion activist, suggested that the rape investigation might have been 'a set-up' by opponents of the Eighth Amendment.

In the Dáil and on the airwaves the controversy was the only topic of discussion. Gardaí seized thousands of copies of the *Guardian* at Dublin Airport on the basis that it contained an advertisement for abortion services, and there were reports of Garda plans to block the airports and watch the ferries. Further afield, marches and vigils took place at Irish embassies and consulates in Britain and the United States. The French daily *Libération* said it put a question mark over Ireland's membership of the European Community, while the King and Queen of Sweden came under pressure to cancel a planned visit to Dublin.

Into this maelstrom, just over a week later, stepped the five judges of the Supreme Court. By 1992, the court had considered the meaning of Article 40.3.3 – the Eighth Amendment – on three occasions. The interpretation was strict in all three: the court had granted injunctions against two counselling agencies and various students' union magazines so as to block Irish women obtaining information about legal abortion services in Britain.

The Supreme Court in early 1992 comprised Chief Justice Tom Finlay, Tony Hederman, Niall McCarthy, Hugh O'Flaherty and Séamus Egan. All five men were practising Catholics. All except O'Flaherty were in their sixties or seventies. Only one, Niall McCarthy, was seen as a liberal on social questions. Another, Hederman, was considered particularly conservative on moral issues. When the appeal by Miss X was lodged, Finlay approached O'Flaherty and asked him if he felt he should recuse himself from the case given that, as a barrister, in 1988, O'Flaherty had represented SPUC in a case against a counselling service. O'Flaherty felt there was no need and said he was happy to take part. (Later he wondered whether he would have been better off stepping aside – not because he felt they decided the X case wrongly, but because he and other members of the court always felt a little uncomfortable with both the applause and the criticism that came their way from different sides of the abortion debate afterwards. Never in their careers would they preside in a case that attracted greater scrutiny.)

Representing Miss X were the former Attorney General John Rogers with Mary O'Toole and Séamus Woulfe. Opposite them, for the State, were Peter Shanley, James O'Reilly and Éanna Mulloy. At the outset, barristers for several media organizations brought an application to be allowed to cover the Supreme Court appeal given the public interest questions it raised, but the government objected and the media request was quickly refused by Finlay. Instead, he said that an edited transcript – edited by the court itself – would be made available with the decision.

So one of the most significant Supreme Court appeals since the court's establishment – one with profound constitutional and political implications – took place behind closed doors. For three days the public waited for news and the papers filled their pages with speculation about what might be going on.

On the afternoon of the third and final day of the hearing, when both sides had wrapped up their arguments, the judges retired to the conference room directly behind the court. In the courtroom, the lawyers sat back and began their wait. It was now out of their hands. The judges sat around the long table in the conference room, Finlay at the head and two judges on either side. They placed their wigs on the table.

Usually, at the judges' conference, the outcome of a case becomes clear immediately. But on occasion, if the group is badly split or some judges want more time to think about it, the process can be drawn out. In *X* there was not much time, and the judges knew it.

The discussion was calm. On the one hand, it was just another case, and the exchanges followed a familiar pattern. Yet the judges were aware that this was anything but an ordinary case.

In keeping with court tradition, Finlay invited the most junior judge – meaning the most recent appointee – to speak first. All eyes turned to Egan. Egan, a popular 69-year-old with a dry wit, had a reputation as a strong advocate for defendants' rights and a defender on the bench of traditional Catholic values. He briefly sketched out his thoughts. It quickly became clear that he was in favour of allowing the girl's appeal.

It was 1-0.

Next up was O'Flaherty. By far the youngest member of the court – he was fifty-three – O'Flaherty had been a high-flying barrister who appeared in some major cases, often for the State, before joining a select group of lawyers to be appointed directly from the law library to the Supreme Court. That was just two years previously, in 1990. He had been a Fianna Fáil barrister and idolized Cearbhall Ó Dálaigh and the breakthroughs of the 1960s. His views on social issues were considered mainstream Fianna Fáil, which meant he would not have been in favour of abortion. Although he loved the law, he was far from dogmatic; to him, a judge without common sense was no judge at all. And where some of his colleagues were stand-offish and distant, he was every bit the warm, gregarious Kerryman, with a store of anecdotes on everything from Daniel O'Connell to the latest law library gossip. When Justice Antonin Scalia, the leading conservative on the US Supreme Court, would visit Dublin in later years, he would invariably end up at O'Flaherty's house near Herbert Park in Ballsbridge for a sing-song with a group that also included Adrian Hardiman, who had devilled with O'Flaherty. In 1992, O'Flaherty's star was on the rise. Everyone knew that he was a future Chief Justice.

As soon as he began to speak at the X case conference, it was clear where he was going. The appeal should be granted, he said.

2-0.

Finlay turned to McCarthy. If a barrister in the case had ranked the judges by their likelihood to grant Miss X the right to travel, McCarthy would have been at the top of the list. McCarthy was a big presence: flamboyant, charismatic, hyper-articulate. He was probably the leading barrister in the country for well over a decade, famous for his style as a cross-examiner and his ability to zone in on the essentials of a case. 'As such he earned a huge income and lived, and looked, like a grandee', Adrian Hardiman later wrote. 'Though not unusually tall, he gave the impression of massivity.'

Like O'Flaherty, McCarthy had been close to Fianna Fáil (he represented Charles Haughey at the arms trial) and had been appointed directly from the law library to the Supreme Court, in 1982. As a judge, McCarthy was consistently liberal. His dissent in *Norris*, which was one of the first big cases after his appointment, was a trenchant and powerful argument for the right to be left alone. It and the judgment of his colleague in the dissent in that case, Séamus Henchy, would go on to become probably the most influential minority judgments the court ever produced.

Among judges there is a decision-making spectrum that runs from pragmatism to principle; McCarthy liked to think he was closer to the latter. On one occasion, not long after O'Flaherty joined the court in the early 1990s, McCarthy gently upbraided him for what he, McCarthy, saw as 'a result-oriented judgment', suggesting O'Flaherty had made up his mind and then rationalized backwards. O'Flaherty went away with his tail between his legs. About a week later, in O'Flaherty's presence, McCarthy said exactly the same thing to the Chief Justice, Tom Finlay, about one of his judgments. 'Oh', O'Flaherty said. 'Everyone is giving result-oriented judgments except yourself, and yours have to be treated as if they're the Ten Commandments.' They laughed; McCarthy loved people to fight back at him.

In the X case, some of the others around the table were clearly uncomfortable to find themselves in this position. Not McCarthy. He had been intensely engaged with the case; in argument he spoke more than anyone else, pressing counsel again and again to clarify their points and think through the implications of their positions.

When it was his turn to speak, McCarthy confirmed that he would allow the appeal. The injunction should be lifted.

3-0.

Fourth in line was Hederman, perhaps the quietest of the group. The 71-year-old, the son of a draper from Naas, Co. Kildare, had been Attorney General to a Fianna Fáil government led by Jack Lynch from 1977 to 1981. He was conservative on social questions. Hederman disagreed with Egan. In his view the meaning of the Eighth Amendment was clear, and the court could not allow Miss X to travel for an abortion.

It was 3-1.

By the time Finlay got to speak, the outcome was clear – even if he sided with the State, Miss X's side had won. In the event Finlay told the room that he agreed with Egan, O'Flaherty and McCarthy.

That was it: 4-1 for Miss X.

Together the judges agreed that, given the urgency of the situation, they should return to court immediately and announce their decision. They would write and deliver their judgments later.

At 3pm, the Supreme Court registrar went to the press room and told journalists that the court would give its decision in public in a few minutes. Reporters ran down the corridor with notebooks in hand. Newsdesks were alerted so that they could begin planning the pages. Lawyers quickly returned to their seats; the speed of the decision had taken everyone by surprise. When the judges returned, Finlay needed just two sentences to deliver their ruling.

'The Court is satisfied that the appeal should be allowed. Reasons will be given later and counsel will be notified.'

The significance of what the Supreme Court had done was lost on no one. Words such as 'momentous' and 'watershed' appeared on nearly every front page the next morning. For Miss X, there was relief and vindication. That relief was shared by politicians, although to the dismay of a great many of them they were well aware that the abortion debate was now firmly back on the agenda. Not only that, but it was feared within government that the outcome could have implications for the upcoming referendum on the Maastricht Treaty. Inserted in that treaty, at the insistence of the previous Haughey-led administration, was a protocol that stated that nothing in Maastricht should affect the application in Ireland of Article 40.3.3. The protocol had been designed to ensure abortion could never be introduced in Ireland. But if the Supreme Court was now saying abortion was legal in certain circumstances, the protocol would actually copper-fasten that. And given that the Supreme Court had several years earlier declared that Article 40.3.3 prohibited the supply of information to Irish women on legal abortion services in Britain, both liberals and conservatives could have grounds for opposing Maastricht. For government ministers, that raised the prospect of a European treaty being defeated over abortion.

When the Supreme Court decision was announced, Reynolds was in a motorcade on his way to a meeting with his British counterpart, John Major, in Downing Street. The news came first to Duignan, who called the carphone in the lead car and conveyed to Reynolds the message from the Four Courts. The line went silent; Duignan thought Reynolds hadn't heard him. Eventually the Taoiseach spoke up: 'We're up to our necks in it now, Diggy. They're all out to get us.'

In public, Reynolds welcomed the decision and focused on the one aspect he was genuinely relieved about. 'The family is now free to take whatever action they wish', he said. (Given the all-clear by the Supreme Court, Miss X and her parents again travelled to England, although she miscarried before having the termination.)

However, as Reynolds and the rest of the political class knew, the brief announcement from the court left big questions unanswered. Was the court split? How had it come to its decision? What did it all mean for the Eighth Amendment?

The judges returned to their chambers and worked flat-out for a week to prepare their judgments, which were delivered on 5 March. It was widely assumed that the court had decided merely to allow the girl to travel for an abortion, but when the judgments were read in their entirety over two-and-a-half hours by the judges, this time in order of seniority, it became clear that four out of the five judges had interpreted Article 40.3.3 – the Eighth Amendment – as meaning there was a right to have an abortion in Ireland, albeit in limited circumstances.

Finlay argued that the Constitution had to be interpreted in accordance with concepts of prudence, justice and charity – all mentioned in the preamble. For him there was a clear risk that the girl would take her own life. He distanced himself from Costello's attempt to balance the degree of threat to the lives of the mother and the unborn and came up with an alternative:

> If it is established as a matter of probability that there is a real and substantial risk to the life as distinct from the health of the mother which can only be avoided by the termination of the pregnancy, such termination is permissible.

That was the key line. It meant that the Eighth Amendment was unravelling. An article inserted into the Constitution in 1983 with the aim of closing down any possibility that the courts would allow abortion had actually opened the door to it, albeit in very narrow circumstances.

Finlay was not going on a solo run here. During argument in the case, he and McCarthy had extracted an important acknowledgement from the State's senior counsel, Peter Shanley, that the amendment did not block abortion in all circumstances:

MCCARTHY: Are you saying that there is only one answer: the child must be aborted if the mother is in imminent danger of death? If this is so, where does 'as far as practicable' enter the equation? Do you accept that the Eighth Amendment envisages a 'lawful abortion' in Ireland?

SHANLEY: Yes, I accept that. For example, a mother suffering from a cancerous condition which requires chemotherapy has the right to have her pregnancy terminated. The pregnancy may be terminated if, but only if, there is an inevitable danger to the right to life of the mother.

FINLAY: Your formula is not a formula of absolute equality. It allows for tolerance. It is an equality until imminence of death. Who should survive?

SHANLEY: The mother.

Hederman's lengthy dissenting judgment centred on his belief that in order for the constitutional right to life of the unborn to be set aside, there would need to be cogent evidence of a genuine threat to the mother's life. He said that no threats of a medical nature had been presented by counsel for X and instead the court was being asked to rely on the assessment of a psychologist whose evidence was that there was a 'serious threat to the life of the first defendant [Miss X] by an act of self-destruction by reason of the fact of being pregnant'. He went on:

> If this young person without being pregnant had suicidal tendencies due to some other cause then nobody would doubt that the proper course would be to put her in such care and under such supervision as would counteract such tendency and do everything possible to prevent suicide. I do not think the terms of the Eighth Amendment or indeed the terms of the Constitution before amendment would absolve the State from its obligation to vindicate, and protect the life of a person who had expressed the intention of self-destruction. This young girl clearly requires loving and sympathetic care and professional counselling and all the protection which the State agencies can provide or furnish. There could be no question whatsoever of permitting another life to be taken to deal with the situation even if the intent to self-destruct could be traced directly to the activities or the existence of another person.

Particularly stinging for the politicians was the judgment given by McCarthy, who felt the failure of the Oireachtas to enact laws to give effect to the Eighth Amendment was at the heart of this constitutional crisis. Several of his colleagues did not agree with McCarthy's strong language, but he was adamant. When he delivered the key lines in court, his voice deliberately slowed down.

> In the context of the eight years that have passed since the Amendment was adopted . . . the failure by the legislature to enact the appropriate legislation is no longer just unfortunate; it is inexcusable. What are pregnant women to do? What are the parents of a pregnant girl under age to do? What are the medical profession to do? They have no guidelines save what may be gleaned from the judgments in this case. What additional considerations are there? Is the victim of rape, statutory or otherwise, or the victim of incest, finding herself pregnant, to be assessed in a manner different from others? The Amendment, born of public disquiet, historically divisive of our people, guaranteeing in its laws to respect and by its laws to defend the right to life of the unborn, remains bare of legislative direction.

★

The extent of the court's decision may have disappointed the anti-abortion lobby, but those who campaigned for a right to abortion were similarly disheartened by the restrictive regime it left in place. As Ivana Bacik points out, 'the corollary of the Chief Justice's test was that where a woman was not facing a threat to life, then not only would it be illegal for her to have an abortion in Ireland, but she could also be prevented from travelling abroad to avail of legal abortion elsewhere.'[30]

Questions about abortion have been put to the people four times since the X case. In November 1992, eight months after the Supreme Court gave its decision, the government held a referendum on the proposal to partially reverse the decision by explicitly excluding suicide as a ground for abortion. That was rejected by 65 per cent of the votes cast.

On the same day, two other proposals were approved: the Thirteenth Amendment guaranteed freedom to travel abroad for an abortion, while the Fourteenth enshrined the right of access to information on abortion. Ten years later, in 2002, a Fianna Fáil–Progressive Democrats coalition attempted to amend the Constitution so as to tighten the ban by removing the threat of suicide as a ground for abortion. The proposal was narrowly defeated.

Niall McCarthy's excoriating words for the legislature went unheeded by successive governments, each one seemingly more wary – or, in critics' eyes, more cowardly – than the last to touch such a sensitive and divisive issue. Women continued to travel to Britain for abortions through the 1990s, but politicians were determined to keep the issue at arm's length. Yet, in the 1990s alone, there were a number of further abortion cases, some of which were heard *in camera*, that raised critical questions about Article 40.3.3 and its implications. The rule of automatic exclusion of journalists and members of the public from such cases meant that even the fact that they took place did not emerge at the time.

A case that occurred in late 1999 showed how sensitive the issue remained. That autumn, an asylum seeker who had been in Ireland just a few months told the Department of Justice that she wanted to travel to Britain for an abortion. For that, as an asylum seeker, she would need a re-entry visa issued by the department. However, after being interviewed by officials, the woman's request was refused on the basis, she was told, that she did not meet the criteria set down by the X case. Unnoticed by the media, the woman's solicitor went to the Four Courts on a Friday night and secured permission to seek judicial review in the High Court. The case was scheduled to be heard the following Monday.

When the news reached Government Buildings, it set off alarm bells immediately. The decision to refuse to issue travel documents had been taken without any political involvement and threatened to revive the fraught debate over the right to travel to procure termination of a pregnancy. When the question had been put to the electorate seven years earlier, voters had agreed – by a margin of nearly two-to-one – to add to 40.3.3 a subsection stating that the article 'shall not limit freedom to travel between the State and another state'. In other words, pregnant women were free to travel abroad even if it was to have an abortion. However, there were differing views within the system on whether the amendment required the authorities to issue travel papers in situations such as had arisen with this asylum seeker. Did it impose a positive obligation on the state (to issue documents, for example) or simply require it not to intervene to stop women travelling? That was the sort of question that preoccupied government figures on the frantic weekend leading up to the asylum seeker's court hearing. Once the hearing started on Monday, it would cause a sensation.

According to senior political sources, the Department of Justice had, in the period 1992–9, issued at least two re-entry visas for other asylum seekers who said they wished to travel for abortions in Britain. But on this occasion department officials had taken the opposite stance. It meant the issue nearly every politician feared most was about to hit the headlines again. This was the last thing Bertie Ahern's government needed. On a weekend of anxious discussions among senior government ministers and officials, the message came down from the highest levels: there was not to be another X case. On Sunday night, just hours before the case was to begin in open court, the department reversed its decision and a re-entry visa was issued to the woman.

In the following decade, in May 2007, the High Court granted a 17-year-old girl with an anencephalic pregnancy the right to travel to the UK for an abortion.[31] The girl brought the case against the Health

Service Executive (HSE) when it tried to stop her travelling to Britain to have an abortion. She was four months pregnant at the time of the hearing, and had learned that the foetus had anencephaly, a neural tube defect resulting in the absence of a major portion of the brain, which is usually fatal within three days of birth. The girl, 'Miss D', had been in the care of the HSE for some months, but was refused permission to leave the state to have an abortion and was told that the HSE had notified the gardaí that she was not permitted to leave the state. Miss D said she was not suicidal, although she was deeply traumatized by the fact that her baby had no chance of survival.

The court ruled that there was no law or constitutional impediment to stop Miss D from travelling for an abortion, and said that the actions of the HSE social worker in telling the gardaí that Miss D must be prevented from travelling were without foundation in law.[32]

On 21 October 2013, Savita Halappanavar, a 31-year-old seventeen-weeks pregnant woman, arrived at University Hospital Galway because she was in pain. The following day she was told that she was miscarrying. On her second day in hospital, in considerable distress and knowing that her baby would not survive, she asked for and was refused an abortion. On 28 October, just under a week after going into hospital, she died due to complications arising from a septic miscarriage.

Whether the refusal to terminate her pregnancy determined Savita Halappanavar's fate remains contested. But public outrage after the story broke in mid-November resulted in a Fine Gael–Labour coalition enacting a law the following July, the Protection of Life During Pregnancy Act, to finally give effect to the judgment in the X case and set out the circumstances in which abortions could be carried out in Ireland.

The Eighth Amendment remains in place, leaving Ireland with one of the most restrictive abortion regimes in the western world. The amendment may have turned out to be far more ambiguous than the anti-abortion lobby believed in 1983, but it remains firmly opposed to the demand of an increasingly organized campaign – invigorated since the 2013 law was enacted – for repeal. Among the most prominent voices on both sides of the debate are activists who were not even born when the Eighth Amendment convulsed Ireland in the early 1980s.

15. The Whelehan affair

'We have come for a head, Harry's or yours – it doesn't look like
we're getting Harry's.'

Ruairí Quinn

Finding the right person to sit on the bench is one of the most important tasks a government undertakes. Judges are virtually unsackable.
A bad one can do damage. A great one can enhance the entire democratic system and improve people's lives in profound ways. Yet
the selection of judges is one of the most secretive processes in
government – one so informal, unregulated and tightly guarded that
even most ministers have no idea how it works.

The system of appointments was designed to be opaque, if it can be
said to have been designed at all. The Free State Constitution said
that judges were to be appointed by the Governor General on the
advice of the Executive Council. The 1937 Constitution adopted the
same system, with the President making appointments on the advice
of the government. There were basic minimum requirements. No
lawyer with less than ten to twelve years of experience in practice
was eligible, for example, and through the twentieth century vacancies on the Circuit, High and Supreme Courts were open only to
barristers (the process was opened up to solicitors in 2002) or sitting
judges.

But that was it. Beyond those two principles – the government
chooses, and it can only choose barristers – the law was silent. That
left government with almost total discretion to appoint whatever
barrister it wished without having to justify the decision or explain
why it was taken. Government and departmental records from the
1920s to the 1980s are conspicuously silent on the internal debates

about candidates or the rationale for choosing certain individuals over others. (That secrecy endured into the late twentieth and early twenty-first centuries. One senior politician who was involved in appointing a number of judges kept a special drawer, where he would leave all lobbying letters on behalf of would-be judges so that they would not get mixed up with official correspondence and therefore be accessible under the Freedom of Information Act.)

While there was little correlation between judicial appointments and party allegiance in the early decades of the State, by the 1960s that had changed. By then a barrister's political affiliations were clearly a factor in appointment to the bench. At the end of the '60s, when the American academic Paul C. Bartholomew found that those appointed to the bench in Ireland tended to be accomplished and respected lawyers, he also found that they were invariably people who were 'favourably regarded' by the government. And where a cross-party appointment was made, it was generally a question of optics – it made the process look non-partisan.[1]

But political allegiance was not the only influence on appointments. Another factor was – and remains – arguably even more important than any other: personal relationships. For those who move in establishment circles, Dublin is small. The legal world is smaller still. Over the years those who were appointed, whether or not they had links to the governing party, tended to be acquainted, at least to some degree, with the people who appointed them.

'Politics matters in judicial selection, but it is not the full story', writes Jennifer Carroll MacNeill in her recent book on the politics of judicial appointments. 'It is neither necessary nor sufficient for judicial appointments in Ireland. For those candidates who are eligible and suitable for appointment . . . being politically sympathetic to the government of the day is very helpful in securing a judicial appointment, but being personally known to the decision makers of the day is crucial.'[2]

For most of the twentieth century, the appointments system remained as it had been since 1924: secretive, informal and so mysterious that it rarely impinged on the public consciousness. But in the mid-1990s, the process was thrust into public view when disputes over two senior vacancies on the bench became so acrimonious that they helped bring down a government.

In July 1994, when Tom Finlay was coming up to retirement as Chief Justice after nine years in the job, Taoiseach Albert Reynolds's preferred successor was Liam Hamilton. As President of the High Court, Hamilton was the second most senior member of the judiciary after the Chief Justice and thus would have been seen as a leading candidate. Indeed, Tom Finlay had been President of the High Court before his appointment. Hamilton had chaired the long-running Beef Tribunal, an inquiry into alleged malpractice in the Irish beef processing industry, and delivered his final report to government on the same day Finlay took his leave from the Supreme Court. The report, published in early August, cleared Reynolds of wrong-doing in his dealings with the firm at the heart of the investigation, Goodman International, when he was Minister for Industry and Commerce. A different finding could have finished Reynolds's career and caused the Fianna Fáil–Labour coalition government to collapse. There was considerable muttering in political circles after the report was published that Hamilton, knowing that the delivery of his report would coincide with the retirement of the Chief Justice, had somehow managed to produce a 900-page report that cleverly evaded dealing with the questions about Reynolds. At worst, it was described as 'the longest job application in history'.[3]

Although Hamilton had been a Labour supporter and had connections with the trade union movement, the party had gone off him. While in his account of the background to appointing the new Chief Justice Tánaiste Dick Spring's adviser Fergus Finlay does not hint at disappointment about Hamilton's conclusions in the tribunal report there is no doubt that many in Labour considered it a whitewash. Rather, Finlay writes that Spring thought Hamilton should remain as President of the High Court, where he was seen as 'an excellent manager of the busiest court'.[4] Spring thought the Chief Justice appointment was an opportunity to modernize and reform the courts and wanted the job to go to Donal Barrington, who at the time was a judge on the European Court in Luxembourg. Spring felt that

Barrington would be a 'forward-looking and progressive' Chief Justice.[5] However, the government learned from the Attorney General, Harry Whelehan, that Barrington was technically disqualified, as the law required an appointee to the Supreme Court to be either a serving domestic judge or a practising barrister – a status Barrington had given up to go to Europe.* So, even though Labour were annoyed by how quickly Reynolds pushed the matter through Cabinet, as soon as the problem with Barrington's eligibility became clear, Hamilton's appointment went ahead.

In the loveless Fianna Fáil–Labour cohabitation, a union marked by constant bickering and mutual suspicion, the tensions over Hamilton's appointment were as nothing compared to the stand-off over who would replace him at the head of the High Court. It emerged that as the discussions about the next Chief Justice had been going on, Harry Whelehan had let Reynolds know that he would be interested in the presidency of the High Court if Hamilton got the top job. Reynolds was supportive and told Whelehan as much. In his memoir, Reynolds explained his thinking as follows:

> As far as I was concerned, it was traditional that if the chief constitutional officer of the state and legal adviser to the government indicated an interest in a major position, it was normal that the request should be acceded to, if the Taoiseach was so minded. The Attorney General had indicated his strong interest in being appointed president of the High Court, I had agreed and given him my word, and that was that.[6]

That was not that. The problem was that the Labour leadership was decidedly cool on the idea. They regarded Whelehan as a Fianna Fáil man and a conservative Catholic. Memories of his key role in the X case were still fresh in Labour minds. They also felt that Whelehan had given an excessively cautious legal opinion on Cabinet confidentiality during the Beef Tribunal – one that favoured Fianna Fáil (the Supreme Court subsequently upheld Whelehan's view).

In early September, Spring told his special adviser, Fergus Finlay,

---

* This rule was subsequently changed by an amendment one insider christened 'the Barrington Retrieval Clause'.

that Whelehan had approached him to seek his support for the job. Finlay asked his boss whether he had given any commitment. 'You must be joking!' was Spring's reply.[7]

Spring's preferred candidate was Susan Denham, a young, liberal judge who had become the first woman ever on the Supreme Court when she was promoted from the High Court two years earlier. Denham was not consulted before her name was put forward, and almost as soon as it emerged that she was being touted as a candidate she told the government, through Hamilton, that she would prefer to stay in the Supreme Court.

Suddenly Whelehan's name was the only one on the table. Spring felt he was being bounced into an unsuitable appointment and was determined to resist. Reynolds, instinctively resentful of having to deal with a coalition partner, but also bruised and sore at what he saw as Labour condescension towards (and briefing against) him in recent controversies, was equally determined that he would have his way.

The row over the appointment simmered for weeks – not helped by the profound distrust between Spring and Reynolds and the two men's absence abroad on government business and them not actually speaking 'for a couple of weeks on end'.[8] Inevitably word of what was going on reached the media, making the situation an even bigger headache for a coalition that was coming apart in the public glare.

The controversy had been rumbling on for over a month when, in late October, the *Sunday Independent* ran an explosive story. Picking up on a detail contained in a UTV current affairs programme, it reported that a Northern Ireland police warrant seeking the extradition of a priest, Brendan Smyth, who had fled to the Republic in 1991 after being charged with the sexual abuse of children, had lain unattended in the Attorney General's office for seven months. Spring, who had been prepared to concede defeat on Whelehan's appointment, once again resolved to block it.

Reynolds and Fianna Fáil appear not to have grasped the danger to the government from this turn of events. Reynolds reacted by digging in further. But by now the crisis was only tangentially connected to Whelehan. 'I think Albert saw it as a kind of . . . macho political wrestling match with Spring', says one party figure. To Labour, too, the judicial vacancy became a proxy for every dispute that had been simmering between the two sides for months.

At the next Cabinet meeting, on 11 November, when Whelehan had outlined his office's report on the Smyth debacle, the Attorney General left the room and the Taoiseach, to Labour's astonishment, immediately proposed him for the High Court post. Every Fianna Fáil minister agreed. Spring led the Labour ministers out of the room in silence. That afternoon, without telling Spring, Reynolds and Whelehan, accompanied by Minister for Justice Máire Geoghegan-Quinn, went to Áras an Uachtaráin, where President Mary Robinson formally made the appointment.

Duignan recalls Reynolds telling him at the Áras: 'No Taoiseach ever sacrificed so much for an Attorney General.'[9] Though they had loyally supported their leader, some Fianna Fáil ministers were amazed that it had reached this point. The saga seemed to confirm what politicians had suspected of Whelehan since the X case: he was a good lawyer and a man of integrity but he seemed to have no political antennae whatsoever. Independence of mind is an asset in an Attorney General, but to be effective the holder of the office has to be able to read the politics of a situation. To many it was perplexing that Whelehan had not simply withdrawn his name from the running. At the Áras that afternoon, Geoghegan-Quinn approached Whelehan and said as much to his face: 'When I'm out in the snow on the election trail in Galway and people on the doorsteps ask me, "What about Harry Whelehan?" I'm going to reply, "Fuck Harry Whelehan".'[10] But now Harry Whelehan was the second most senior judge in the State. And the coalition was on the brink.

What saved the government from falling that day was a U-turn from Reynolds. The new Attorney General, Eoghan Fitzsimons, briefed Reynolds and the Fianna Fáil ministers about a situation he had discovered that seemed to echo the Smyth case. Another paedophile priest, John Anthony Duggan, had fled to Ireland and the British authorities had requested his extradition, but there had been delays in dealing with that situation as well. Senior figures in government believed the revelations about the Duggan case undermined Whelehan's account of the delay in the Brendan Smyth case. Fitzsimons was dispatched to see Whelehan. He asked him to delay his swearing in at the Supreme Court and to consider his position, but Whelehan refused. He felt it was 'inappropriate and constitutionally incorrect and improper' that a government would pressure him to resign.[11]

A few days later, on the suggestion of Minister for Social Welfare Michael Woods, who Fitzsimons understood was acting at Reynolds's instigation, Fitzsimons called at Whelehan's house at 10.30pm. Woods had said that there was a 'grave danger' that the peace process would break down if the Taoiseach had to resign. Whelehan was being invited to step down to save the peace process. Again he refused.

Labour presented Fianna Fáil an ultimatum: Spring and his party would stay in government only if Reynolds went into the Dáil and acknowledged he had been wrong to appoint Whelehan against Spring's wishes. Senior figures from both parties, including ministers Brendan Howlin, Ruairí Quinn, Brian Cowen and Noel Dempsey, worked late into the night on an agreed wording. Labour agreed to the key sections of the script, but trust between the two parties was now so shattered that Fianna Fáil insisted on having the commitment in writing from Spring. He duly signed: 'Dick Spring, 16th November, 10.22 a.m.'[12]

Everyone was aware that Reynolds was about to do an extraordinary thing: publicly attack the second-highest-ranking judge in the State. When he heard of the plan, Fergus Finlay was amazed.

> It was not that I felt sympathy for Harry Whelehan – I didn't – but rather that I could not see how the damage that was about to be done to important institutions could be undone. The Office of the Taoiseach, the Office of Attorney General, the second highest judicial post in the land – all were about to be dragged through the mud. Nothing like that had ever happened in my memory – it reminded me of the book *The Final Days* about Richard Nixon.[13]

Later that day, as agreed, Reynolds went into the Dáil and delivered a speech in which he flagellated himself and finally threw Whelehan under the bus:

> I now accept that the reservations voiced by the Tánaiste are well founded and I regret the appointment of the former Attorney General

as President of the High Court . . . I also regret my decision to proceed with the appointment against the expressed opposition of the
Labour Party. I guarantee that this breach of trust, a trust on which
the partnership Government was founded, will not be repeated.[14]

By giving the speech as agreed, Reynolds appeared to have saved
the coalition from collapse. Spring came to his office and there were
'handshakes and backslaps all round', Reynolds recalled.[15]

Their new-found bonhomie was to last less than an hour. An
anonymous phone call to Spring revealed that Reynolds had known
about the Duggan case earlier than he had admitted – and, crucially,
that he had known about it before he gave a Dáil speech defending
the Whelehan appointment earlier in the week. Labour ministers
believed Reynolds had not only withheld vital information from
Spring but had misled the Dáil as well. They were furious, as Reynolds recalled:

> They came to confront me – Dick Spring, Howlin, Quinn and Mervyn
> Taylor – and accused me of lying, of deliberately withholding informa-
> tion about the Duggan case and of deceiving the house. Of course I
> denied it vehemently; but all my explanations – that I had not wilfully
> misled the house but had been waiting for the Attorney General's
> definitive advice, as was correct procedure – fell on deaf ears.[16]

At one point in the meeting, Quinn told Reynolds: 'We have come for
a head, Harry's or yours – it doesn't look like we're getting Harry's.'[17]

The game was finally up. Whelehan's position was untenable and the
government was about to fall. The next day, 17 November, Reynolds
resigned as Taoiseach and leader of Fianna Fáil. A month later Fianna Fáil
was out of office and Labour had entered a new coalition government.

Within twenty-four hours of the Taoiseach's resignation, Whelehan called the High Court press corps into his chambers and gave
them his resignation statement. He was stepping down, Whelehan
said, to prevent his office being 'further embroiled in public controversy'. It was the shortest judgeship ever: he had been a judge for six
days, and had sat in court for just one of them.

★

The Whelehan appointment was unlikely to be the first time senior politicians had differed over a judicial vacancy, but it was the first time that such a dispute had spilled out in all its unedifying colour. For outsiders, it cast light on the political dimension of the appointments process, prone as it was to becoming bound up with party rivalry and political calculation. However, revealing as the dispute was, a critical aspect escaped scrutiny – presumably because it occurred during a fast-moving, multi-pronged scandal. Reynolds's extraordinary decision to approach – twice, albeit via intermediaries – a High Court judge and ask him to resign so as to avert a government collapse was a clear breach of the separation of powers between the executive and the judiciary.

One of the chief by-products of the crisis was a new system for selecting judges. At the height of the stand-off between Fianna Fáil and Labour in late 1994, Reynolds and Spring set up a ministerial sub-committee comprising Quinn, Cowen, Howlin and Dempsey. Its task was to work out a compromise that would enable Labour to stay in government and restore trust between the key players so as to put the coalition on a more stable footing. In early October, the four men met at Tinakilly House Hotel in Co. Wicklow and hammered out a deal that sketched out a set of key principles. Chief among them was the outline of a new way of making judicial appointments that the negotiators hoped would make the process more transparent and avert another Whelehan-style episode. Labour had pushed hard for this, and Reynolds accepted it on condition that the Whelehan appointment would be waved through.

The 'Tinakilly Treaty', as it was mockingly christened by the opposition, envisaged a system where the final decision on selecting a judge would remain with the government – as the Constitution required – but that a new body, known as the Judicial Appointments Advisory Board (JAAB), would be set up to advertise vacancies, consider applications and then make recommendations to government.

The JAAB was a short-term fix to get the government out of a hole. Cowen, one of the Tinakilly Four, admitted as much a year later with the abandon of a man liberated from the conventions of ministerial discretion. Still smarting over the collapse of the Fianna

Fáil–Labour coalition, Cowen told the Dáil that the reform of the appointments system, which he helped design, was 'a charade' that amounted to little more than 'a political response to a temporary political problem that had nothing to do with the proper administration of the courts'.[18]

The JAAB plan was enacted by the Fine Gael–Labour–Democratic Left coalition in 1995. It would comprise: the Chief Justice and the presidents of each court; one nominee each from the Law Society and Bar Council, the representative groups for solicitors and barristers; the Attorney General; and three individuals nominated by the Minister for Justice.

The new system required the JAAB to recommend at least seven names for each vacancy, and in theory reduced the scope for government meddling by requiring it to have 'due regard' to the JAAB list. But at the same time the government retained ample discretion, as it could choose a name that did not appear on the JAAB list so long as it publicized the fact that it had done so. Moreover, the JAAB had no role in the selection of the Chief Justice, the presidents of each court or the promotions of serving judges. So if it had existed at the time of the Whelehan selection it would have made no difference at all.

As Carroll MacNeill points out, the JAAB system was created not as a result of any serious policy discussion or research. It was a rushed fix for a political problem.[19] That fitted into a general pattern. Politicians may have shown a keen interest in selecting judges, but they rarely if ever gave any thought to how the judiciary should be organized or run. The result, by the 1990s, was a courts system that was badly in need of reform.

New judges were greeted with a work environment that had changed little in seventy years. They were given an office and provided with some bound black notebooks to use in court, but not much else. They were allocated a crier or tipstaff who would accompany them to court and function as a type of personal assistant, but otherwise they were left entirely to their own devices. They received no training or professional guidance.

The government of the day controlled the funding and day-to-day operations of the courts, yet communications between the judiciary and senior ministers were a grey area. The judges nominally belonged to a single class of public sector employee – the judiciary – but in practice they worked alone, dozens of little independent republics spread across the country, and had no organization to represent them as a group. Even at the apex of the system, there was no official forum for discussion between the government and the senior judges. That worked fine when individuals on each side got along and could work out their own informal ways of communicating, but the weaknesses of that ad hoc arrangement would be at the root of some of the most bitter disputes between the two sides over pay and pensions in the early twenty-first century.

On the issue of judicial conduct and ethics, the law was virtually silent and successive governments had shown little interest in the topic. Judges were accountable in the sense that they heard cases in public, swore an oath on taking office and could, under the Constitution, be removed from office for 'stated misbehaviour or incapacity' by resolutions of both the Dáil and Seanad. By the 1990s, however, momentum was gathering within the judiciary and government behind the idea that a new body should be set up to contribute to high standards in the judiciary and to handle allegations of judicial misconduct. In 1996, a working group was set up, chaired by Susan Denham, to look into how other countries dealt with the issue and to make recommendations. The report was presented to the Chief Justice, Liam Hamilton, and the Minister for Justice, John O'Donoghue, in November 1998.

That was the same month that a young Kildare man, Philip Sheedy, was given early release from prison, setting off a chain of events that led to the most serious crisis the judiciary had ever faced.

16. In the eye of a hurricane

'. . . as my last duty and so that confidence can be restored in the
administration of justice, I have decided to offer my resignation
as judge of the Supreme Court.'

Hugh O'Flaherty

On 15 March 1996, Philip Sheedy, a young architect from Leixlip,
Co. Kildare, was involved in a crash at the Glenview roundabout in
Tallaght, a suburb in south-west Dublin. Witnesses described his
sports car, which he had bought just twenty-four hours earlier, taking off 'like a missile' before it hit the roundabout, then travelling
sixty feet in the air before landing on another car. In that second car
were Anne and John Ryan, a married couple who had known each
other since they were teenagers. They were heading home with their
two children from a local swimming pool in Tallaght. Anne, who
was driving, was killed. John and the children were badly injured.
Sheedy escaped with minor injuries and was arrested and charged
with dangerous driving causing death. He was over the legal blood/
alcohol limit. The following year, in October 1997, when the case
came before the Circuit Court, Sheedy pleaded guilty. The court
heard he became suicidal after the crash and ended his relationship
with his girlfriend because he thought he was too bad a person to
marry.

Among the character references available to the judge – though
not used, according to the court record – was one from the Dublin
West TD, Brian Lenihan jnr, stating that the accused was 'from a
very good family. He is in his occupation an architect. He is a
respected member of the local community in Coolmine. I know him
to be of good character.' The reference had come about because Philip

Sheedy's mother, Anna, played bridge with Kathleen Tunney, wife of the former Fianna Fáil TD and party chairman Jim Tunney. Tunney recommended that the Sheedys get a character reference from a local TD and arranged a meeting between Philip Sheedy and his father (also Philip) and Lenihan in the Dáil.

The Sheedys did not achieve their aim of avoiding a custodial sentence. Philip Sheedy was sentenced to four years in prison, with a review after two years, in October 1999. In November, acting on a request from Sheedy himself, the judge, Joseph Matthews, dropped the review date. Had the review date stood, Sheedy could not have been considered eligible for any kind of early release before it.

Anne Ryan's death at the age of thirty-six was an unspeakable tragedy that left her husband, John, and their two children distraught. The newspapers carried reports on the court case, but once the sentence was handed down the story faded from the news pages and the Ryans were left to go about trying to reassemble their lives.

Sixteen months had passed when, on a mid-week morning in February 1999, the Attorney General, David Byrne, came to visit the Chief Justice, Liam Hamilton, at his chambers in the Four Courts.

The two men knew each other well. In his years as Chief Justice, Hamilton was a regular visitor to Government Buildings and the Department of Justice, where he would come to chat about everything from court reform to work practices. Sometimes he would just 'drop by and shoot the breeze', in the words of one former justice minister, Nora Owen. He became so familiar to people in government that he was widely known simply as 'Hammo'. 'While he was conscious of the separation of powers and the dignity of his office, he was a remarkably unbuttoned and relaxed character', says another government insider.

Hamilton had an atypical background for a judge. From Mitchelstown, Co. Cork, he was the son of a garda who had been educated by the Christian Brothers and, because his family did not have the money to send him to university, on leaving school he entered the civil service. He was posted to the Department of Justice and through that ended up working in the central office of the High Court in Dublin. Encouraged by some of the barristers who used the central office, he successfully applied for a civil service scheme that covered the costs of studying law. He did so at UCD and then at the King's Inns before becoming a barrister in the mid-1950s.

Hamilton was gregarious and easy-going. Ministers and officials admired how he never stood on ceremony – they noticed that he always introduced himself at receptions simply as 'Liam Hamilton' without mentioning his title – and Cabinet members felt he was among the few judges who had any understanding of what made politicians tick. Like them, he was a fixer, a problem-solver rather than a theorist. Some fellow lawyers saw his result-oriented pragmatism as a weakness, but he saw it as a strength, and politicians could relate to it. The only thing that exasperated them about Hamilton was his chain-smoking: whenever he left a room he would leave behind an overflowing ashtray and a thick white smoky cloud.

But when David Byrne came to visit Hamilton in the Four Courts that February morning, the pleasantries were brief. Both men knew this was serious. Under the Attorney's arm was a sensational memorandum.

The previous day, Byrne had been contacted by the Director of Public Prosecutions, Eamonn Barnes. He told Byrne that a young architect named Philip Sheedy, who was serving a four-year sentence for dangerous driving causing death, had been granted early release after a Circuit Court hearing the previous November, just thirteen months after he had been convicted. Apparently the judge, Cyril Kelly, citing a psychological report, said he had 'grave concerns' about Sheedy's mental condition and suspended the remainder of his sentence there and then. The strange thing, Barnes had explained to Byrne, was that the hearing had taken place without the State, which was responsible for prosecuting Sheedy in the first place, receiving any advance notice.

Even before Byrne had been alerted, the Four Courts was abuzz with rumour. It always is. But this time the rumours were very serious, suggesting that the failure to notify the gardaí or the DPP's office was not due to error or oversight but was a deliberate move from somewhere within the court system. If the stories were true, the two men immediately realized, this was a very big deal.

That night, Byrne called the Minister for Justice, John O'Donoghue, who was attending an EU meeting in Berlin, and filled him in on the conversation with the DPP. O'Donoghue was not aware of it at the time, but just a few days earlier his private secretary had received a letter from John Ryan, Anne's widower. A friend of the Ryan family had spotted Sheedy in Tallaght, and when inquiries were made to the gardaí it turned out they were unaware of his early release. Ryan was writing to the minister to protest that he and his family had not been notified that Sheedy was out.

On the phone from Berlin, O'Donoghue told Byrne there would have to be an inquiry. The following morning, while the Attorney was at the Four Courts briefing the Chief Justice, O'Donoghue contacted the Secretary General of his Department, Tim Dalton, and asked that the Garda Commissioner should investigate (plans for a criminal investigation were later dropped). By this point, all the key players – Byrne, Barnes, Dalton and O'Donoghue – were in constant contact with one another.

The re-listing of the Sheedy case was unusual even on its own terms. The normal procedure, when someone who was convicted wished to appeal the severity of a sentence, was for their lawyers to take a case to the Court of Criminal Appeal. Only in exceptional circumstances could a case be re-opened in the Circuit Court after sentencing. But that was one of the least remarkable things about the Sheedy case. At their meeting in the Four Courts, Byrne showed Hamilton a memorandum which contained the allegation that a Supreme Court judge, Hugh O'Flaherty, had played a part in re-opening the case.

When Byrne left, Hamilton went to O'Flaherty and told him the gist of the claims. O'Flaherty responded with a vehement denial but told Hamilton that, the previous October, he had spoken to the County Registrar, a senior Circuit Court official, about the possibility of re-listing the case and the procedures that would be involved. O'Flaherty said that he gave the registrar, Michael Quinlan, a copy of a judgment he had delivered in the Court of Criminal Appeal the previous July. O'Flaherty said the case, *DPP v. McDonald*, had similarities to the Sheedy case.[1]

Hamilton knew the State was going to go to the High Court to challenge Cyril Kelly's decision to release Sheedy, so he decided to hold off on any further inquiries in case that challenge eventually made its way to the Supreme Court on appeal. The State duly went to the High Court, but Sheedy withdrew his opposition and voluntarily returned to prison.

In the Four Courts, however, the drama was only beginning.

When Liam Hamilton resumed his inquiries in late March, he met the president of the Circuit Court, Esmond Smyth, and his counterpart in the High Court, Frederick Morris. Cyril Kelly had been promoted to the High Court in November the previous year, a few weeks after he had released Sheedy, so Morris was now his line manager.

O'Flaherty was in the United States for some speaking engagements, but Hamilton spoke to him by phone on 31 March and told him that the story was about to go public and that it was possible he would be named by O'Donoghue in the Dáil the next day. O'Flaherty cut short his trip and returned to Dublin a few days later. In a statement he handed to Hamilton on his return, O'Flaherty emphatically denied 'any suggestion of improper interference' by him in the course of justice in this or any other case and said he was not responsible for the Sheedy case being re-listed before Judge Kelly.

O'Flaherty told Hamilton that he did not know Sheedy. In his version of events, some time in late 1998, probably October, while out walking his dog he casually bumped into a young man called Ken Anderson, 'a son of family friends and neighbours', who was accompanied by a sister of Philip Sheedy.

'This encounter was entirely by chance. They gave me an outline of the facts in Mr Sheedy's case', he wrote. Those facts seemed to O'Flaherty 'somewhat similar' to *DPP v. McDonald*, a case he had dealt with in the Court of Criminal Appeal the previous summer. 'In any event, I suggested that it might be possible for the case to be re-listed so that the Circuit Judge could have another look at it in the light of the McDonald decision and in the light of the defendant's deteriorating health situation. If that was an error – and I am prepared to accept that it was – it was an erroneous view of the law but did not involve any wrongdoing.'

His reason for asking Quinlan, the County Registrar, to visit him in his chambers was to confirm in his own mind that such a course was feasible, O'Flaherty said:

> I mentioned the Sheedy case to him indicating that the case had been mentioned to me and that I had suggested that it might be possible to have it re-listed in the Circuit court. I made it clear to Mr Quinlan that my only interest in the matter arose from the fact that I had expressed a view outlined above and I gave him a copy of the decision in the McDonald case. Mr Quinlan said he would look into the matter. He later contacted me and said that the case would be re-listed.

O'Flaherty said that in speaking to Quinlan he was 'acting in a private capacity' as he had no official status in the matter and never sought to suggest the contrary.

> I made no request of Mr Quinlan concerning the handling of this case. I did not ask him to have the case listed. Still less did I ask him to have the case listed before a particular judge or to have the case handled in a manner that might preclude the Director of Public Prosecutions from being represented in the case.

He added:

> I acted out of a spirit of humanitarian interest in relation to this matter. If I am to be faulted for that, let it be so. However, I had no other motive. In so far as this case has brought undue and skewered focus on the judiciary, I deeply regret it.

Quinlan agreed with O'Flaherty's account of their conversation, which he said lasted less than two minutes. After the conversation, Quinlan got hold of the Circuit Court file on the Sheedy case and contacted the solicitor Michael Staines, who Quinlan had been told had taken over from Sheedy's previous solicitor. As it happened, Staines had not even met Sheedy yet and had no formal instructions to act for him. Quinlan said he informed Staines that, if he received instructions from his client to do so, he could bring an application to a Circuit

Court judge, who might or might not be willing to hear it. If Staines did that, Quinlan said he suggested, he should go before the judge in Court No. 24 – who happened to be Judge Kelly – as Judge Matthews, who had previously dealt with the case, was not in Dublin.

About a week later, according to Quinlan, Staines contacted him and said he had instructions to bring an application to court.

Quinlan said he told Staines that the other side, the Chief State Solicitor, should be notified as it was not the normal practice for the Circuit Court office to notify the State – that was the applicant's responsibility. Quinlan said he then handed the file to an official in the Circuit Court and requested that the case be listed for the date chosen by Staines.

Staines's version of events was very different. In a letter to the Chief Justice, he explained that the call from Quinlan the previous October came out of the blue. 'He asked me when I was going to put in an application to review the sentence of Philip Sheedy. I explained to him that I knew nothing whatsoever about such an application. He informed me that Judge Cyril Kelly was awaiting an application for review.'

Staines told the Chief Justice he asked Michael Quinlan what this was all about, 'and he indicated to me that, "You don't want to know."' Staines told the Chief Justice he was 'bemused' when he received the call from Quinlan. 'This was the first time in my twenty years of practice that I received such a phone call from a Court official', he said.

After Staines had got instructions from Sheedy, he spoke again with Quinlan, who, he said, referred him to *DPP v. McDonald* and suggested Staines should base his application on that. Staines strongly denied Quinlan's claim that he had told Staines it was the solicitor's responsibility to inform the State of the listing of the case.

> I would like to say here and now that under no circumstances did Michael Quinlan or any other member of the Circuit Court ever inform me, either in that conversation or in any other conversation, that I should inform the State . . . Furthermore, I would like to reiterate that at no stage did I pick the particular date nor did I suggest to anybody that I wanted Judge Cyril Kelly to hear the application.

Indeed, Staines added, it was his view that the only judge who would hear an application to re-instate a review date was the original judge – in this case, Joseph Matthews.

When Esmond Smyth, who was assisting the Chief Justice in gathering testimony, put that very question to Judge Kelly – why had he presided in the Sheedy review when it was Judge Matthews who had handed down the sentence? – Kelly said it was 'not an unusual practice for a Criminal Circuit Judge to make orders where another Circuit Judge had previously made an Order'.

Smyth, as the Chief Justice noted in his report, did not agree with this assessment, but Kelly maintained it was correct.

The accounts given by the two Circuit Court judges, Kelly and Matthews, were in direct conflict. Recounting the circumstances that led to him presiding in the initial Sheedy sentencing hearing, Matthews said he got a call from Judge Kelly at lunchtime one day in October 1997 asking him to hear the case. Judge Kelly had had the barristers from both sides in his chambers on various occasions to discuss aspects of the case and he now felt he was too close to it, Matthews recalled.

> He told me the accused had no previous convictions and came from a good family. He said he felt it was a suitable case for a suspended sentence. He said he would send the file over.
>
> I read the file. I formed the view that this particular case, on the facts on file at least, could not on any basis be a case for a suspended sentence. I wondered was Judge Cyril Kelly actually familiar with the facts or was he so busy that he might have missed the gravity of the case on the facts as they appeared in the Book of Evidence.

Judge Matthews said he was 'puzzled and concerned'. In his eyes the Sheedy file showed 'recklessness of an extraordinary degree'. He had to speak to Judge Kelly in person. He walked to his colleague's office with the case file under his arm. In his office, Judge Kelly was sitting at his desk. He nodded but did not say anything, Judge Matthews recalled.

'Cyril,' Judge Matthews recalled saying,

> I've read the file in the case that you asked me to deal with. So there's absolutely no misunderstanding over this I just wanted to say two

things. One: I can't impose a suspended sentence in this case, and, two, it's not a case in which, in my view, a suspended sentence could be imposed. Even if I could, this is not a suitable case, in my view, in which to do so.

Judge Kelly did not speak, his colleague recalled.

By gesture he indicated to me with both hands out at arm's length and made a face, which I took as a gesture meaning, 'If that's what you think, then that's what you must do.' I felt absolutely happy that he knew I disagreed with his view and I was completely free to do as I felt was appropriate under the law and sentencing policy. I left immediately and returned to my chambers.

Asked about Matthews's account, Kelly denied ever saying that he believed the case was suitable for a suspended sentence. He denied that the exchange in his chambers ever took place. He never said he was too close to the case and had no recollection of having met both sets of barristers, according to Kelly.

As Gene Kerrigan later pointed out in the *Sunday Independent*, it may have been possible to find out who was right: Matthews said the meeting with Kelly was arranged by his crier talking to Kelly's crier. But the Chief Justice appears not to have spoken to either crier.[2]

One of the key questions was whether O'Flaherty and Kelly had actually discussed the case between themselves. 'If that was so, justice minister John O'Donoghue told one of his colleagues at lunch one day, "Neither of them can ever admit it because it's a criminal offence"', writes Pat Leahy. The suggestion that they had discussed the case was denied by both judges.[3]

The critical date was 12 November 1998. On that day, after a hearing in Court No. 24 that lasted no more than a few minutes, Judge Kelly ordered the immediate release of Philip Sheedy. The only representative of the State in the courtroom was a clerk in the Chief State Solicitor's office who saw a listing for the case and brought the file to court but did not know what it was about.

The transcript of that hearing fitted onto a single page. It showed that Judge Kelly did not call on lawyers for either side to say anything to him. He did not refer to *DPP v. McDonald*. Luigi Rea, Sheedy's barrister, told the judge he had a number of witnesses who would testify as to his client's good character. The judge ignored him. He said this was a case where he had had 'the benefit of a psychology report and . . . I have grave concerns in relation to his [Sheedy's] mental condition at the moment'. That was that. 'OK', said the judge, unprompted. 'I will suspend the balance of his sentence, own bond of three years to be of good behaviour.'

There was then a brief pause in the transcript before Judge Kelly resumed the hearing, just to put something on the record.

'Mr Rea, that last matter: as usual, I read my papers; just the various reports give concern in my mind in relation to his mental stability.'

'Yes, my Lord, that is my concern', Rea replied.

'That is for the record, anyway', said the judge.

The Hamilton report zoned in on the issue of a psychology report. In the file on the case, there was no new psychology report. There were two old reports – both drawn up by the Fianna Fáil senator Don Lydon, a senior psychologist at St John of God Hospital, that had been used by Judge Matthews when he imposed the original sentence, yet Judge Kelly in court had said he had seen a psychology report and had concerns about Sheedy's state 'at the moment'.

In his account, Staines said that, a few days after Judge Kelly ordered Sheedy's release, he – Staines – was informed by Luigi Rea that the judge had requested

> that I would obtain from a psychiatrist a medical report which would set out Philip Sheedy's psychiatric/psychological condition as of the 12th November 1998 as the medical report on the court was from a psychologist and also out of date. This new report was then going to be put on the Court file. I indicated that I was not prepared to do this.

It was a startling statement. To have inserted a new medical report into the court file after the hearing would have been to falsify the record. Esmond Smyth went back to Judge Kelly and put the point to him. What psychological report had he been referring to in court? In an account of their conversation, Smyth summarized Kelly's response:

Judge Kelly is unable to remember what expert reports were before him on the 12th November 1998, when he dealt with this case, but he believes that any expert reports that he relied upon would be contained in the court file and he is satisfied that it was such expert reports that enabled him to form the view which he expressed in court.

In Staines's account of the exchange with Rea, Judge Kelly said: 'I recollect that I subsequently met Mr Rea B.L. informally, who commented to me that the expert report on file was not up-to-date. I suggested to Mr Rea B.L. that he should consider obtaining an up-to-date medical report.'

In his report, the Chief Justice concluded bluntly that whatever the motive for that suggestion may have been, it was 'manifestly improper'.

By asking him to make his own inquiries into the judges' actions – the first time ever that the judiciary had had to respond to a request from the government about its internal affairs – the government had put Hamilton in a difficult position. It was awkward having to sit in judgment on his own colleagues, including one – O'Flaherty – whom he knew, liked and had worked closely with for many years. In addition, he was not given the tools to carry out a thorough investigation. By the time he had collected written statements from everyone involved, it was clear that a number of key facts about the episode were in dispute. To resolve them would have required a very different type of inquiry.

Hamilton did not have much time. The Sheedy Affair, as it had become known, was now a burning public controversy. The government, under ferocious pressure from the opposition and the media, was eager to have the report out as soon as possible. In the Dáil, the Fine Gael deputy leader, Nora Owen, raised the possibility of invoking the impeachment procedures under Article 35 of the Constitution, which stated: 'A judge of the Supreme Court or the High Court shall not be removed from office except for stated misbehaviour or incapacity, and then only upon resolutions passed by Dáil Éireann and Seanad Éireann calling for his removal.' The provision had never been used before; that senior politicians were even mentioning it showed that the establishment was in uncharted waters.

When he had gathered all the material, Hamilton went away and prepared a draft report. He then showed it to his colleagues on the Supreme Court: Ronan Keane, Susan Denham, Kevin Lynch, Donal Barrington and Frank Murphy. O'Flaherty, as one of those at the centre of the controversy, was excluded.

The first draft did not go down well. Its conclusions were soft. Hamilton's instinct seemed to be to chart a way carefully out of the mess without being the one to wield the axe. The group wrestled with it. O'Flaherty was liked and admired by everyone in the room. His approach to cases gave the court an important dimension that his colleagues valued. They had all known each other for decades, soldiering in the trenches of the law library when it was a much smaller place, where everyone knew everyone. They had sat alongside one another in court, pored over cases in the conference room, shared gossip and generally built up a strong rapport. The closest the group had ever come to a row was an impassioned disagreement between Keane and Barrington on an obscure point of European law. They were also aware that O'Flaherty's star was on the rise. Everyone in the Four Courts and Government Buildings knew that he was a future Chief Justice. Across the judiciary, many people looked at O'Flaherty and thought, 'There but for the grace of God . . .'

Yet at the same time the members of the court were shocked by what Hamilton had uncovered and felt firm action had to be taken if public confidence in the judiciary was to be maintained. Some were furious over what had happened. In the 1990s, some of the major institutions in Irish life, including the Dáil, the banks and the Catholic Church, had been discredited by revelations emanating from a series of tribunals and public inquiries. The judiciary had suffered no such damage; opinion polls showed that it was consistently the most trusted branch of government. Everyone on the court was aware that it now found itself at a critical juncture.

Several members struggled to believe how O'Flaherty could have put himself in this situation. Notwithstanding personal sympathy for a colleague, it was clear that at the very least O'Flaherty, based on his own account, had done something they considered he should not have done, and that the sequence of events it had set in train had had serious consequences. That was even more true of Kelly. To avoid saying so in clear terms, it was argued within the court, would discredit the institution. Several meetings were held, some in small groups, some as a group of six. The atmosphere grew tense, at times emotional. Voices were raised. When the atmosphere grew particularly fraught, Barrington and Lynch separately indicated to Hamilton that they would resign unless the conclusions were hardened. That clinched it. In effect, it meant: *they go or we go*. It would be sensational and extremely damaging.

Denham tried to calm the situation. Since joining the court in 1992, she had come to be seen as a skilful diplomat. The appointment of a relatively young woman to the highest court had initially put some noses out of joint in the rigidly hierarchical and overwhelmingly male world of the law library and the senior judiciary (she was a regular attendee at the monthly lunches that Mella Carroll, the first ever female High Court judge, used to organize in her chambers for fellow women on the bench), and in her early days in the group Hamilton, a man's man, seemed not quite sure how to deal with her. At conference, when the group was discussing a case, Hamilton had been in the habit of taking out a cigarette and lighting up. 'Liam, put that away', Denham would say. 'It's bad for you and it's bad for us.' And he'd comply.

Ultimately, the report was substantially rewritten. The final version, notably in its conclusions, was much more direct and sharp-edged than Hamilton's initial draft.

The report was particularly critical of Judge Kelly. It found that there was no practice in the Circuit Court whereby a Circuit judge could review, in a criminal case, a final decision of a colleague in the same court who was available or likely to be available: 'Insofar as Judge Kelly thought that such a practice existed he was mistaken. Insofar as he followed such an alleged practice himself, he was wrong.'

The unanswered questions over the psychological reports were highlighted in the report. 'There was no up-to-date psychological report on the file and no information on the file from which the learned trial judge could have deduced the mental condition of the accused "at the moment" ', the report concluded. By announcing his decision without allowing either side to make submissions about the case, Kelly deprived himself of any opportunity to learn from proper sources what Sheedy's present condition was.

'I take the view that Judge Kelly should not, in the circumstances of this case, have entered on a review of a sentence imposed by one of his colleagues', the Hamilton report stated.

'I conclude moreover that, having entered on the review, he failed to conduct the case in a manner befitting a judge. In these circumstances, I conclude that Judge Kelly's handling of this matter compromised the administration of justice.'

The conclusions on O'Flaherty were less severe but blunt nonetheless. The report accepted that he became involved in the case 'in a spirit of humanitarian interest'. But it did not share O'Flaherty's belief that a Supreme Court judge, having called the County Registrar, 'could expect that anything said by him would be received by the said official as if it had come from a private individual'.

Hamilton was 'satisfied' that had O'Flaherty not spoken to the County Registrar, he – the registrar – would not have phoned Sheedy's solicitor and opened the possibility of the case being re-listed. Once that possibility was opened, it was 'natural, and proper' that Sheedy's solicitor should do anything, consistent with the law and his professional duties, to exploit that possibility in the interests of his client. And then the key lines:

> I therefore conclude that this case might not have been re-listed in the way it was but for the intervention of Mr Justice O'Flaherty. I also conclude that Mr Justice O'Flaherty's intervention was inappropriate and unwise, that it left his motives and action open to misinterpretation and that it was therefore damaging to the administration of justice.

The conclusions, as Hamilton and everyone else was well aware, made the positions of both Kelly and O'Flaherty untenable. At an event at the Law Society shortly after he completed his report, Hamilton was visibly shaken.

From there, events moved quickly. On 15 April, Hamilton presented his report to the Attorney General, David Byrne. The
following day, Cabinet agreed that the government would write to
Kelly and O'Flaherty underlining to them the gravity of the findings
and indicating that if they did not voluntarily step down the government would move to initiate the procedure for removing them from
office.

Kelly remained silent. O'Flaherty went on the defensive. In a letter
to the Oireachtas Joint Committee on Justice, in which he asked for
permission to address members, O'Flaherty expressed 'deep regret'
for his 'inappropriate and unwise action' in the Sheedy case.

Outside his home in Ballsbridge, O'Flaherty told the RTÉ reporter
Charlie Bird that he would not resign because he had done nothing
wrong, and a judge could not be removed from office 'simply by hyp-
ing something up, spreading rumours and hoping he'll go quietly'.
Asked if it had been a difficult period for himself and his family,
O'Flaherty replied: 'Even judges are human, to some extent.'[4] As
photographers waited outside O'Flaherty's house they watched some
of the judge's friends, including the entertainer Kathleen Watkins
and Taoiseach Bertie Ahern's partner, Celia Larkin, come and go.

An unprecedented confrontation was looming. Government
sources were briefing that work was about to begin on resolutions of
impeachment in the Oireachtas. But on the eve of a Cabinet meeting
where this was to be on the agenda, O'Flaherty finally bowed to the
inevitable. 'The highest duty of a judge is impartiality, as well as the
appearance of impartiality, and as my last duty and so that confidence
can be restored in the administration of justice, I have decided to
offer my resignation as judge of the Supreme Court', he stated. Within
a few days Kelly and Michael Quinlan had also stepped down.★

★ While the resignations averted the prospect of impeachment, the pressure
merely shifted from the judiciary to the government. It emerged that a friend of
the Taoiseach's, Joe Burke, had visited Sheedy in prison in October 1998. On foot
of a call from the Department of Justice, who had come across a July 1998 representation from the Taoiseach on Sheedy's behalf (asking that Sheedy be allowed
out on day release), officials in the Taoiseach's office reminded Ahern that he had
been contacted by Sheedy's father and that he had passed on the representation.

In the weeks after the judges' resignations, the atmosphere in the Four Courts was funereal. What Hamilton had uncovered left many judges shocked, though some took solace that the institution had confounded sceptics by producing a report that was anything but a whitewash by the proverbial old boys' club. At a personal level, life-long friendships were sundered. Anger at the fact that they were made to sit in judgment on their colleagues was mixed with sadness and a general sense of disbelief at the whole thing. The speed of it all – just two months had elapsed from the moment the Chief Justice was first told of the allegations to the day the two judges and the court official resigned – left people dazed. The episode also drove home the urgency of a Judicial Council that would handle allegations of judicial misconduct – an idea that had been first proposed in a report that landed on the Minister for Justice's desk around the same time that Sheedy was being given early release in the Circuit Court.

A year after the resignations, Susan Denham gave a speech in Australia in which she outlined the course of the Sheedy controversy and its aftermath. These were rare public comments from within the senior judiciary about an episode that still haunted the bench. Denham did not play down its significance. It was, she recalled, 'the most serious constitutional crisis involving the judiciary since the foundation of the State'.[5]

As a group, the judges of the Supreme Court never spoke about it again.

When the story of Ahern's representation appeared on the front page of the *Sunday Tribune*, Tánaiste Mary Harney was livid. While saying there was nothing improper in his conduct, Ahern, reluctantly, publicly apologized to Harney for not revealing his intervention in a timely way. A year later finance minister Charlie McCreevy re-ignited the political storm around O'Flaherty by proposing him to fill a vacancy at the European Investment Bank. There was a public outcry at the idea that someone who had been forced to resign as a Supreme Court judge was now deemed worthy of one of the most lucrative posts in Europe. The controversy simmered through the summer of 2000 until O'Flaherty brought it to an end by withdrawing his name.

17. New judges, new ideas

'Judges have become legislators and have the advantage that
they do not have to face an opposition.'

John Kenny

'What about you for the Supreme Court', Mary Harney said.

'You're not serious', Adrian Hardiman replied.

'I am.'

At first the idea surprised Hardiman as much as anyone. It was not
that he lacked the credentials. He was perhaps the best-known barrister in the country, with a formidable courtroom style and sharp
legal mind. But he was only forty-nine – young for any judge, let
alone a member of the Supreme Court, where the average age of the
group can hit the mid-sixties. To go there straight from the law
library – a leap made by just a handful of lawyers in the court's
eighty-year history – would be a big change of direction. Plus, he was
Adrian Hardiman – the trenchant, pugnacious, outspoken bon viveur
who could be found every weekend at the popular haunts of the chattering classes, the Unicorn restaurant and Doheny & Nesbitt's pub,
drinking and arguing late into the night with his old group of friends
from politics, journalism and his student days at UCD. Few lawyers
conformed less to the stereotype of the judge as an austere and distant
ascetic.

In UCD in the early 1970s, where he moved in a circle of friends
that centred on the history faculty and the debating chamber of the
Literary and Historical Society (L&H), Hardiman was considered
more likely to end up a politician than a judge. An accomplished
orator and a punchy debater, he hit all the usual milestones of an
ambitious politico in the making, first becoming auditor of the L&H

(where he beat his future Supreme Court colleague Frank Clarke to the post) and then winning election as head of the Student Representative Council (SRC), the forerunner to the Students' Union.

For a man who even then saw himself as a proud nineteenth-century liberal, striding around campus in a jacket and tie and with the thrusting self-confidence of a Jesuit private-school (Belvedere) education, the SRC megaphone was an unlikely accessory. Hardiman's election caused consternation in the SRC's left-wing faction; when the result of the student ballot was announced in a UCD lecture theatre, some of the leftists promptly commandeered the fire hose and the meeting ended in chaos.

His new role required him to make some unexpected alliances. In early summer 1973, a huge row erupted in the English faculty, where the head of department unilaterally decided to re-structure the final exam paper. It threw the students, and many of them ended up with worse degrees than they should have got. There was uproar on campus. Protests broke out. Hardiman was in the front line of the revolt, along with the representative of the English students: Joe Higgins, the future leader of the Socialist Party. Two more unlikely political bedfellows it would be hard to imagine. 'They were amazing', one contemporary recalls. 'There were mass meetings with Hardiman and Higgins addressing the crowds. They came very close to closing down the English department.' Hardiman loved it.

He might have had a political philosophy, but he hadn't yet found a party. Many in his group of college friends, which included Clarke, Michael McDowell, John Mac Menamin, Kevin Cross, Alison Lindsay, Paul O'Higgins and Brian McGovern – all of whom are today senior judges or barristers – gravitated towards Fine Gael. At first Hardiman followed suit, but while the 'Just Society' rhetoric chimed with his social attitudes, Fine Gael never quite felt like a natural fit (his father, Patrick, was a schoolteacher with republican leanings and his mother, Lucy Colley, was related to the former Fianna Fáil Tánaiste George Colley). So he crossed the divide and joined Fianna Fáil. He advised and canvassed for Síle de Valera in the early 1980s and in June 1985 local elections stood himself for the party in Dún Laoghaire but was not elected.

By the time he dipped his toe into local politics Hardiman already had a national profile. He had taken a leading role in the main umbrella group for opponents of the 1983 abortion amendment, the Anti-Amendment Campaign, when he had thrown himself into the fraught television debates. He had framed his opposition around what was to become a familiar Hardiman critique: the amendment, he argued, was an unacceptable encroachment by the State, encouraged by the Catholic hierarchy, into the private lives of Irish women. That won him many friends on the left.

In late 1985 he joined his friend Michael McDowell in the formation of a new political party led by the former Fianna Fáil minister Des O'Malley. In the Progressive Democrats he was one of a number of future judges and barristers – a group that included Paul Carney, Gerard Hogan, Nicholas Kearns and Paul O'Higgins – who worked on policy and offered legal advice. It was through the PDs that Hardiman struck up a lifelong friendship with the future Tánaiste Mary Harney. He never stood as a PD candidate – he was asked to stand in Dublin South-East but declined.

Towards the end of the '80s, Hardiman drifted away from politics and focused increasingly on his work in the Four Courts, where he was in heavy demand. He rarely did any work for the big corporate law firms; instead he specialized in defamation and, in particular, criminal law, usually representing the accused against the State. He took defamation cases on behalf of members of the Guildford Four, former MEP Proinsias de Rossa and the broadcaster Marian Finucane. He liked a challenge, taking on hopeless criminal cases and at one time agreeing to represent the well-known Dublin criminal Martin 'The General' Cahill. When he got that brief, he returned to the law library, slammed the files down on a table and declared with relish: 'Look what I've got!'

Once the Fianna Fáil–PD coalition offered him a place on the Supreme Court in early 2000, however, Hardiman was never going to turn it down. While he had a lucrative practice, it was also a stressful one. Becoming a judge would entail a pay cut, but it would give him more time to indulge his interests in history and literature.

Also, he was well aware that while barristers' work may live on in the oral history of the law library, judges can leave a legacy that long outlives them. Judges get to shape the law and influence society. He was flattered by the offer, and he knew the chance might never come along again. He said yes.

The court Hardiman joined was in transition. In the space of eight months in 1999 and 2000, four judges – Donal Barrington, Kevin Lynch, Henry Barron and the Chief Justice, Liam Hamilton – had all stepped down on reaching the then mandatory retirement age of seventy-two. Three new ordinary members of the court joined in the same period: Nial Fennelly, Catherine McGuinness and Hugh Geoghegan.

Fennelly, who had connections to Fine Gael as a young barrister, had been a leading barrister and the first Irishman to serve in the key role of Advocate General at the European Court of Justice in Luxembourg, and his return to Dublin gave the court much-needed European law expertise after Barrington's departure. Fennelly would emerge as a pivotal figure on the court over the next decade and a half.

The Belfast-born McGuinness, only the second woman ever to be appointed to the Supreme Court, was the daughter of a Church of Ireland rector, Canon Robert Ellis. After graduating from Trinity College she worked for the Labour Party and served three terms as an independent senator before, as her time in the upper house was coming to an end, becoming a barrister at the relatively mature age of forty-two. When she was appointed to the Supreme Court on the same day as Hardiman in early 2000, by which time she had built a reputation as an expert in family law, McGuinness became one of very few judges to have presided in all three of the Circuit, High and Supreme Courts.

Geoghegan, the third of the new judges, belonged to a family steeped in Irish legal and political history. His father, James Geoghegan, was Éamon de Valera's first Minister for Justice and sat on the Supreme Court between 1936 and 1950. His father-in-law was Tom Finlay, the former Chief Justice (and former Fine Gael TD), who had retired in 1994 after almost a decade at the head of the judiciary.

The big question in early 2000 was who would succeed Hamilton, who was due to retire as Chief Justice at the end of January. For both court and government there was a lot riding on the decision. Even though by the spring of 2000 there would be just three survivors, Ronan Keane, Frank Murphy and Susan Denham, of the Supreme Court from which Hugh O'Flaherty had resigned the previous year, the scars from the Sheedy Affair were still raw. Senior figures in Government Buildings knew the appointment of a new Chief Justice, coinciding with the arrival of a clutch of new judges on the court, was an opportunity to settle the court and give it a clean break after all the upheaval. The government was alive to the danger of getting it wrong. The post-Albert Reynolds Fianna Fáil leadership, from Bertie Ahern down, had been traumatized by the debacle surrounding the appointment of Harry Whelehan as President of the High Court six years earlier. That it had led to the collapse of a Fianna Fáil–Labour coalition they were convinced should never have fallen, and to the party's exit from power, was still an open wound. They were determined not to be undone like Reynolds had been over a judicial appointment. One senior figure believes it made them more determined to tread carefully with senior appointments. 'After the problems we had with Harry Whelehan, that coloured the judgment of our generation . . . '

The timing was symbolic in other ways; the dawn of the new millennium was a time of public introspection about the successes and failures of the State since Independence. Changes were afoot in the Four Courts, where the volume of litigation was increasing, the workload was getting heavier and the setting up of the Courts Service in 1999, which involved the transfer of responsibility for the day-to-day running of the courts from the Department of Justice to the new body, nominally gave the Chief Justice ultimate oversight of the whole creaking system. The Sheedy Affair was not the only festering sore; the public standing of the legal profession had been severely undermined by the inflated fees lawyers had been paid for their work in a series of public tribunals into suspected planning and political corruption whose value and usefulness were still contested.

In the media, the appointment was portrayed as an opportunity to set the tone for the judiciary as it embarked on a period of major change. 'Seldom has the anticipated appointment of a Chief Justice been weighted with such significance', wrote Justine McCarthy in the *Irish Independent*. 'When the Government announces the name of the new incumbent next week, the decision will signal the future direction of the country's highest court and, some would argue, by extension, the future of the country itself.'[1]

Rising wealth, rapid social change and the increasing volume of cases going through the High Court were bound to throw up major questions for the Supreme Court in the coming decade. Everyone knew it was eventually going to have to deal with the fallout from the tribunals and confront new questions posed by the internet, the rise of the ecological movement, advances in reproductive science, the expansion in European law and growing agitation for reform of family law. 'As a new Ireland emerges into the 21st century, a young, modern, confident country embracing peace and prosperity, the seminal influence of the Supreme Court will substantially shape its destiny', McCarthy wrote.[2]

So who was in the running for Chief Justice?

If the vacancy had arisen a year earlier, there would have been no contest. Hugh O'Flaherty was virtually assured of the prize. But O'Flaherty's resignation the previous year left the field wide open. Of the possible candidates, Susan Denham had her supporters within Cabinet, some of whom had got to know and admire her through her leading role on the Courts Commission, which had paved the way for the establishment of the Courts Service. Denham was widely touted as a favourite in the press, where it was noted that she would be the first ever woman (and Protestant) to become Chief Justice. But even though she had been on the court for eight years, she was, at fifty-four, still considered relatively young for the position.

Also in the running was High Court President Frederick Morris. In addition to his experience and organizational ability, honed in the demanding High Court position, it was also thought to work in his favour that appointing him would open up a plum vacancy for the government to fill. In the weeks after Christmas, Morris was considered a front-runner. Working against him was the fact that he was only two years from retirement.

Within the small group of senior government figures who had any say in the matter, the shortlist in the final weeks was cut to two candidates: Ronan Keane and John Murray.

To commuters on the early-morning DART, Keane was the tall man with the black Crombie hat who would get on at Monkstown with the London *Times* under his arm and then stride purposefully up the quays to the Four Courts every morning. To lawyers, he was one of the leading judges in the country.

Keane had been on the Supreme Court for four years and before that had been a High Court judge for almost two decades, having become the youngest member of that court when he was appointed by Jack Lynch in 1979. Some judges enjoy working in the High Court more than the Supreme Court; they relish the cut-and-thrust, the exchanges with witnesses, not knowing what they'll have to deal with each day. Keane was temperamentally more suited to the Supreme Court; he was a thinker, a prolific author of legal books, essays and reviews. He was not quite an introvert – he had dabbled in acting in UCD. He had joined Fianna Fáil as a barrister but soon lost interest and drifted away from the party. His wife, the social diarist and fashion journalist Terry Keane, from whom he was separated, had a very high profile,[3] but he was the sort of person who didn't mind having to sit on his own in his chambers all day reading through boxes of case files. Although his public persona was that of the genial, bookish intellectual, he was seen as quite a practical man. Ministers remembered that when he became a judge he made a point of visiting every prison in the country to see conditions for himself.

Murray, the second name on the shortlist, did not belong to the same Dublin milieu as most judges of his generation. From a middle-class family in Limerick, his father was a civil servant and later a builder, and his mother was a teacher, though she had to give up her job on marriage. Educated at Crescent College in Limerick and Rockwell College in Co. Tipperary before going on to UCD, he was twice elected president of the Union of Students in Ireland (slogan: 'Hurry, hurry, vote for Murray!'), in which capacity he attended a conference of the communist-led international Union of Students in Ulan Bator. According to the journalist Vincent Browne, who was in UCD at the same time, Murray was 'believed to have been the first Jesuit-educated Fianna Fáil Limerick man ever to have visited Outer Mongolia on a travel grant. Unknown to him, it was almost certainly paid for by the KGB.'[4]

The Fianna Fáil connection also made Murray something of an outsider at the Bar, which was dominated by Fine Gael supporters. Married to Gabrielle Walsh, daughter of the late Supreme Court judge Brian Walsh, Murray was Attorney General twice in governments led by Charles Haughey, and in that role he wrote the 1983 anti-abortion amendment that Hardiman, Fennelly, McGuinness and others had so implacably opposed. Murray spent much of the 1990s in Luxembourg as a judge on the European Court of Justice, but had been on the Supreme Court for about a year by the time the vacancy for Chief Justice came up in early 2000.

Keane and Murray both had their champions in government, but by the time it came to making a decision it broke down roughly along party lines. Fianna Fáil wanted Murray, the PDs wanted Keane. The key players kept the discussion tight – most Cabinet members knew nothing about it and the detail never got out – and both sides pushed hard for the man they wanted. In the end the cases for the two candidates were sent to the Taoiseach and Tánaiste for a final decision. From Ahern and Harney a deal emerged: Keane would be Chief Justice, but on the tacit and private understanding that, if the parties were still in government when he retired in 2004, Murray would replace him. The appointment was widely welcomed. 'He is everything a judge should be', one senior counsel told the *Irish Examiner*.[5]

Shifts in the Supreme Court's thinking do not occur overnight. Change occurs gradually, by a slow, almost imperceptible process of accretion that can take years or even decades to become apparent. At times nobody outside the Four Courts, and few within the building itself, will even notice until the process has been completed and the wheel has fully turned. That's partly because no single judge, no matter how firm their views or persuasive their arguments, can effect much change unless they have a majority who share the same view.

Jack Lynch appointed Billy FitzGerald as Chief Justice in the early

1970s to douse the activist flame lit by Cearbhall Ó Dálaigh and Brian Walsh, but in the absence of a majority of his own, FitzGerald's role in the major constitutional cases was that of the indignant dissenter shouting soundlessly from the wilderness. Similarly, several years passed under Chief Justice Tom O'Higgins before, facilitated by a turnover in membership of the court and a hardening of public opinion against republican paramilitaries, his court rewrote its position on the political offences exception in extradition cases.

The other reason for gradual evolution is that, until 2014, with the establishment of a Court of Appeal, the Supreme Court had no power to pick and choose the cases it heard. That meant it had to wait for the right cases to come along. Even if the judges had completely changed their view on a topic, they could not announce it until someone stood before them and asked the right question.

By the early 2000s, it was clear that one of the most influential doctrines in Irish constitutional law in the twentieth century – unenumerated rights – was drifting out of favour. The idea that the Constitution contained these implicit rights, which were not explicitly mentioned in the Constitution but which judges could identify, was first articulated by the then High Court judge John Kenny, when, in Gladys Ryan's seminal case on water fluoridation in 1965, he found a constitutional right to bodily integrity. The Ó Dálaigh-era Supreme Court, heavily influenced by a similar trend in the United States, enthusiastically embraced the idea and went on to use it as the basis for some of the most important decisions the court ever took.

The impact of the unenumerated rights doctrine on Irish law – and, indirectly, on Irish society – is difficult to overstate. Between the mid-1960s and the early 1990s it resulted in the discovery of almost twenty new, constitutionally protected rights, including rights to marital and individual privacy, to earn a living, to have access to the courts, not to be tortured or ill treated, to travel outside and within the State, to marry, to procreate, and to justice and fair procedures.

For decades, there had been vigorous debate among lawyers on the wisdom of the doctrine. Influential constitutional lawyers such as John Kelly, Gerard Hogan and Gerard Casey, while acknowledging that a document as open-textured as the 1937 Constitution would mean that a form of implied rights would always be necessary, wrote critiques in which they questioned the open-ended nature of the doctrine and the space it gave judges to bring simple value judgments to bear on the decision-making. In 1979, more than a decade after he inaugurated the era of unenumerated rights, John Kenny had happily acknowledged that the judiciary had taken on the function of the politicians:

> To most people this would seem to be a function of the legislature only and, in many ways, this exciting feature is the most unusual aspect of the Constitution. Judges have become legislators and have the advantage that they do not have to face an opposition.[6]

To many judges, that was anathema – a complete inversion of the judicial function.

Hogan argued that unenumerated rights were having a distorting effect on constitutional law in that judges, by basing their decisions on implied rights, were ignoring the potential that lay within the actual text of the Constitution.[7] For example, why create a right to bodily integrity when the Constitution itself required the State to vindicate and protect from unjust attack 'the life, person, good name, and property rights of every citizen'? Could May McGee not have been granted the right to import contraceptives by simply invoking the guarantee of the inviolability of the dwelling when this implied a right of privacy within the home and, by extension, the marital bedroom? In this analysis, the Irish judiciary ended up taking the US inspiration too far; whereas the US Supreme Court was working with a relatively short and pithy Constitution, Bunreacht na hÉireann, which was almost four times longer, offered the judges far more explicit avenues through which to protect individual rights and apply them to a changing society.

As the years passed, and the grip of natural law and religion generally on mainstream legal thinking in the law faculties and the Four Courts began to weaken, judges grew increasingly uncomfortable with the implications of the unenumerated rights doctrine. Most of the new rights that had been 'discovered' were fully accepted – the right to privacy, for example, was clearly derived from bringing different parts of the Constitution together – but others were more tenuous. A new generation of judges, taught in many cases by advocates of judicial restraint, were instinctively uncomfortable with the power it conferred on them. A great many cases left room for judicial subjectivity, but, according to this view, finding an unwritten right made subjectivity the guiding tool of judicial interpretation. If they could invent rights from whatever source they liked – be it a papal encyclical or a personal view – cases would come dangerously close to being about one question: do the judges think something should happen or not?

That changing attitude percolated from the Supreme Court down through the High Court, the lower courts and the law library. As constitutional lawyer Oran Doyle points out, the rate of judicially discovered rights had slowed down significantly in the late 1980s and early 1990s. In 1997, under Chief Justice Liam Hamilton, a majority of the Supreme Court identified a new right – that of an adopted person to know the identity of his or her mother.[8] But the decision was accompanied by a sharply worded dissenting judgment from Ronan Keane, who urged restraint on the court. (That Keane had long harboured doubts about unenumerated rights was acknowledged explicitly in 2004, the year he retired as Chief Justice, when he wrote that he shared the 'unease' of others about the 'somewhat dubious premises on which the doctrine of unenumerated rights rests and the dangers for democracy of unrestrained judicial activism in this area'.[9])

As it turned out, the discovery of the right of adoptees to know their parents – and Keane's dissent in the same case – were to be among the last serious judicial pronouncements on the topic of unenumerated rights. The doctrine has never been formally disowned. The court continues to tease out the meaning of several unenumerated rights – the right to privacy, for example – but rarely since the late 1990s has the doctrine been invoked in a case and not since the late 1990s has a new right been found. The Supreme Court under Keane did not need to stick a notice on its door one day advising barristers not to come looking for unenumerated rights. Everyone just knew.[10]

18. Hitting the brakes

'What happens when you have a series of rights all of which are
competing for the limited financial resources of the State?'

Rory Brady

Jamie Sinnott was born in October 1977, the third of nine children
born to Kathy and Declan Sinnott. He developed normally until the
age of four months. Then his behaviour changed. He would scream
incessantly as though in acute pain. He only seemed happy when he
was in bed, away from all sound and light, the curtains closed and no
one touching him. Within months he lost control of his jaw, which
had started to clamp. As his condition worsened, Kathy was told by a
professor of paediatrics that he probably had autism and that she
should go home and 'watch the autism develop'.[1]

When he was almost one, Kathy brought him to her native America, where he was diagnosed as suffering from a psycho-motor
problem that affected the sending of messages from his brain to his
muscles and limbs. She was advised by a specialist in Chicago that
intensive intervention was required in the form of occupational therapy, physiotherapy and speech and language training. The treatment
brought major improvements in Jamie's condition. He stopped most
of his repetitive movements. He would make eye contact and interact
with people around him. He stopped crying and even smiled.

Kathy and Jamie returned to Ireland after a few months, on the
understanding that similar treatment would be available in Cork,
where the Sinnotts lived. But she was fobbed off at nearly every
turn — not quite told that there was no help available, but not provided with it or told how to access it. One doctor told Kathy autism
in children was the result of cold, unloving mothers — a theory

advanced in the 1950s (the term used was 'refrigerator mothers') that had been discredited for decades.

For the first ten years of his life, Jamie Sinnott was given access to what amounted to little more than a baby-sitting service provided by nurses who were not teachers or therapists, and with no element of formal education. At the age of eleven he briefly took part in a course of education with a trained physiotherapist, and made some progress, but the project was discontinued after a trial period.

Jamie's education as a teenager was sporadic and truncated. It was only when he was seventeen that he first attended an appropriate school, St Paul's, a special needs school in Cork run by the autism and intellectual disability support charity the Cope Foundation. St Paul's sought to have Jamie leave when he was eighteen, but his mother protested that his education was only beginning and secured another year. But that was it; the school refused to teach him for a third year and he was removed to another Cope centre, which Kathy considered inappropriate because the teachers were not qualified to deal with people like her son and there was no occupational or speech therapy.

For two decades, Kathy Sinnott fought a forlorn battle to persuade the authorities to recognize the distinct educational needs of children with autism and to provide appropriate education and training for those who had the condition, particularly those who, like Jamie, had severe physical and mental disabilities. In time her efforts developed into a campaign on behalf of autistic children generally, but notwithstanding documented international progress in the area, she continually came up against official ignorance of autism and struggled to be heard. For Jamie, the problem was compounded by misleading professional advice that set back his education and training for years.

In 2000, when he was twenty-three, Jamie and Kathy Sinnott sued the Department of Education. Article 42.4 of the Constitution requires the state to provide for free primary education. In going to the Four Courts in 2000, lawyers for the Sinnotts argued that the state, by insisting that that obligation ended when a child turned eighteen, was denying Jamie his constitutional rights. This was the nub of the case: was the right to primary education based on age or need?

Except for the right to free primary education, the explicit rights set out in the 1937 Constitution are all civil and political rights, including personal liberty, freedom of expression and freedom of religion. To some lawyers, however, the document also gave the judiciary ample scope to identify implied socio-economic rights. Sinnott's case was the first major attempt to persuade the court to do so.

Every judge who dealt with the case was appalled by Sinnott's treatment at the hands of the State. In the High Court, where he ruled in favour of Sinnott after a month-long hearing, Judge Robert Barr was scathing:

> Anyone who heard [Kathy Sinnott's] evidence in court and witnessed her demeanour must have been moved by her account of intelligent, selfless dedication and heroism in contending over the years with so much official indifference and persistent procrastination which has continued up to and through this trial. It is a sad commentary that even at this late stage the State has failed to address realistically its constitutional obligation to provide for the on-going education of the first plaintiff.

Barr found that Jamie Sinnott had a right to free primary education for 'as long as he might benefit from it', and awarded mother and son £225,000 for the breach of their constitutional rights. It was a landmark moment. 'The decision that the State's responsibility to provide free primary education for the severely handicapped does not stop at the age of 18 has massive implications for hundreds of disabled people and could lead to multimillion pound costs for the State', the *Irish Times* reported the next morning.[2] Already more than 100 cases were before the High Court aimed at compelling the State to provide appropriate education for other children with autism or other special needs.

At first the government appeared to accept the judgment. 'There is no doubt that, over many decades, the State failed to provide the sort of education for children with special needs which they have a right to receive', the Taoiseach, Bertie Ahern, told the Dáil, adding: 'The case is over and the judgment is made. We are doing things differently now.'[3]

It was not over at all. Around the Cabinet table, opinion was split on whether to appeal Barr's decision to the Supreme Court. Some ministers argued strongly against pursuing the case; they were uneasy about prolonging a confrontation with a profoundly disabled man and feared the inevitable public backlash. Already, in anticipation of an appeal being lodged, the opposition had ratcheted up its attacks over the Sinnott case.

Yet others in government were convinced they had to appeal. The Sinnott judgment had implications that went beyond this very sad situation, they argued. It might mean that people who had no recognized physical or mental disabilities but who were, for example, functionally illiterate, could claim the right to free primary education. More significantly, they believed, the judiciary, by in effect ordering the government to spend taxpayers' money in a certain way, had crossed a 'red line' into the executive's domain, and it set a dangerous precedent. 'Suddenly the thing was in sharp focus', says one source with knowledge of government deliberations – the 'thing' being the relationship between the executive and the judiciary.

The compromise was that the government would agree to pay the £225,000 in damages, as well as legal costs, to the Sinnotts, but that it would challenge the substance of Barr's decision in the Supreme Court (in fact the State appealed that portion of the damages – £55,000 – that had been awarded to Kathy Sinnott). They would insist that the right to free primary education ended at eighteen.

Eight months later, in the spring of 2001, a Supreme Court comprising Keane, Denham, Murray, Murphy, Hardiman, Geoghegan and Fennelly heard the appeal. It was the first time that the Supreme Court had ever sat as a court of seven (five was the required minimum for constitutional cases) – an indication of how significant they viewed the case to be – and photographers were given rare access to the courtroom to capture the novel sight of seven wigged judges lined up on the dais as the hearing began.

The court took more than three months to prepare its decision, and in July 2001 it announced that the State's appeal had been upheld by a 6-1 majority.[4] Alone in agreeing with the High Court judge's conclusion that free primary education was based on need was the Chief Justice himself. Keane argued that to see eighteen as the cut-off point in all cases was arbitrary and overly rigid. In the vast majority of cases, primary education denoted the stage of a child's education lasting from ages six to twelve. But, at the age of twenty-three, Sinnott's skills did not extend much beyond those most children acquired in the home between birth and age four, he said. Sinnott was one of a small category of people who, because of their mental disability, could never enjoy life in all its diversity and richness but to whom at least a measure of happiness might be available. The uncontested evidence in the case was that, to attain even that low plateau, Sinnott required continuing access to education.

Keane was heavily outnumbered. For the majority, the right to free education in Article 42.4 specifically applied to children, not citizens or persons. The question then was when someone ceased to be a child and reached adulthood. The unanimous answer of the six judges was eighteen. They were not saying that Sinnott was not entitled to have his needs met after that age, Hardiman pointed out, just that those needs could not compulsorily be met after eighteen on the basis of Article 42.4.

An important thread in the majority judgment was a sense that Barr had strayed too far beyond a judge's remit. The separation of powers, Hardiman wrote,

> is a vital constituent of the sovereign independent republican and democratic State envisaged by the Constitution. It is not a mere administrative arrangement: it is itself a high constitutional value. It exists to prevent the accumulation of excessive power in any one of the organs of government or its members, and to allow each to check and balance the others. It is an essential part of the democratic procedures of the State, not inferior in importance to any article of the Constitution.

The majority judgment in *Sinnott* was the most significant statement on the separation of powers in many years – until, just a few months later, the court was presented with another case that again raised the question of how far the judiciary could go on socio-economic rights.

In the late 1990s, a raft of cases had come through to the High Court concerning the State's obligations to provide secure educational facilities for children with severe behavioural disorders who posed a risk to themselves and to others. A number of times the government told the courts that it was committed to making more secure places available and that it was working on it. In the early cases, High Court judges agreed to give the government more time. But with each passing month, and with little evidence that the government was acting on its pledges to the court, the judges were growing increasingly exasperated. In a case in 1995, Hugh Geoghegan, then a High Court judge, declared that the State had a constitutional obligation to provide 'as soon as reasonably practicable . . . suitable arrangements of containment with treatment' for troubled children.[5] But the judges were careful not to go beyond that point.

As the High Court judge in charge of the minors' list, Peter Kelly saw at first hand the distress and misery the lack of suitable facilities was causing. Week after week, his court was presented with some of the worst cases of disturbed and vulnerable children for whom no suitable services were available. In one case, Kelly felt he had no option but to send a seventeen-year-old girl to the Central Mental Hospital, a hospital for the criminally insane, because the State's failures had left him with no other option. The child, who fantasized that her recently dead father would come and rescue her, subsequently wrote to Kelly, including poetry on one occasion. He read some of her letters in court: 'You probably think I've gone mad,' she wrote, 'but I have not . . . All I want is people who are really going to be there for me, no matter what.'

As the cases continued to pile up through 1999, Kelly finally ran out of patience. He had been assured by the State for more than a year that plans for new facilities were advancing, but when he was told that progress had stalled and plans had changed without the court being notified, he took grave exception. The judge described the situation as a 'scandal' and bemoaned how addressing the rights of troubled young people was 'bogged down in a bureaucratic and administrative quagmire'.[6] He took the unusual step of making an order compelling the Minister for Justice to act on the plans for a facility within a specified timescale. He was not getting involved in policy, Kelly was careful to say; the order would 'merely ensure that the Minister who has already decided on the policy lives up to his word and carries it into effect'.

A year later, when a similar case, *TD v. Minister for Education*, came before him, Kelly did much the same thing. In his view, the tool was working. The only case in which the State had met its constitutional obligations was the one the previous year in which he had made an order compelling the government to act. Perhaps keen to show that he was only resorting to this method in particularly egregious circumstances, Kelly set out a list of criteria to be considered by the court when deciding whether or not to grant such orders. They pressed home the message that the orders should be used sparingly, and only in exceptional circumstances after the government had been given an opportunity to put things right. 'It is no exaggeration to characterise what has gone on as a scandal', Kelly said.[7]

The government had been keeping a close eye on what Kelly was doing. Views at Cabinet differed. Some members were livid, convinced that the High Court was tearing up the separation of powers by in effect telling ministers how to spend public money (though Kelly's argument was that they themselves had already decided to spend it; he was only telling them to make good on their promises).

'That was a key period', recalls a former minister. 'Did it mean we could be told to start building schools or hospitals?'

But there were contrary views: 'I tended to agree with him sticking in the boot', says another senior Cabinet figure. 'I wouldn't have had much sympathy for the department or the agencies not providing the places. He might have ripped governments over the years, but I always felt he knew what he was talking about. He was fighting for the guy at the bottom.'

The stand-off over places for vulnerable children escalated when, in another case, Kelly went as far as to threaten to hold the Ministers for Health, Justice and Education in contempt of court if they failed to provide a secure place for a young girl who had absconded from a therapeutic unit. The girl was extremely disturbed, having been sexually abused at the age of ten, and had twice tried to take her own life, once by hanging and another time by setting herself alight. The State complied with Kelly's order, so the threat of contempt was lifted, but the government, feeling the courts had crossed a line by threatening to jail ministers, was by now determined to put a stop to what many ministers saw as Kelly's excessive encroachment on executive terrain.

It appealed the decision in *TD v. Minister for Education* to the Supreme Court, where in December 2001 Kelly's decision was overturned by 4-1, with Keane, Murphy, Murray and Hardiman making up the majority. Denham alone agreed with Kelly and accepted that there could be exceptional cases in which the courts could direct the executive to spend public money.

Once again, however, the majority found that the High Court judge had taken too lax a view of the separation of powers. In Keane's words,

> I am satisfied that the granting of an order of this nature is inconsistent with the distribution of powers between the legislative, executive and judicial arms of government mandated by the Constitution. It follows that, as a matter of principle, it should not have been granted by the trial judge, however much one may sympathise with his obvious concern and exasperation at the manner in which this problem had been addressed at the legislative and executive level.

Taken together, *Sinnott v. Minister for Education* and *TD v. Minister for Education* were seen as putting a brake on incipient moves towards judicial recognition of socio-economic rights. Although there was a clear majority in both cases, the judgments were subsequently associated strongly with Hardiman. This was to be a pattern of his years on the court: because he wrote so colourfully, journalists tended often to reach first for his judgment, even when the main one was written by someone else. But it was also widely known that the separation of powers was a topic close to Hardiman's heart.

Unusually among judges, Hardiman was quite happy to defend his decisions in other fora. If the court had decided those two cases differently, he told the MacGill Summer School in 2004, it would have 'significantly extended its own powers to the applause of many, at least in the so-called "chattering classes" and the media'. But it would also have represented 'a further very significant transfer of power to an unelected judiciary already very powerful by the standards of most European countries'.[8] It was a position firmly rooted in his conception of liberalism: that there were certain decisions that only democratically elected institutions could take.

The cases ignited a lively debate about whether the Constitution has within it implied socio-economic rights such as a right to housing or healthcare. Constitutional lawyer Gerry Whyte argues that by reading the Constitution as a whole, with its endorsement of values such as social solidarity and social inclusion, manifested in clauses such as the pledge 'to safeguard with especial care the economic interests of the weaker sections of the community', it becomes clear that the Constitution endorses the position that judicially enforceable socio-economic rights can be said to exist.[9] At the very least, the argument goes, the judiciary should be able to insist, in egregious cases, on what law professor Donncha O'Connell calls a 'bottom line of constitutional justice' that must be met by the other branches of government.[10]

From the outset the idea faced fierce resistance, however, from those who felt it was not the role of unelected judges to get involved in policy or to tell the government how to spend taxpayers' money. To do so would be completely at odds with the separation of powers. Politician and former Attorney General Michael McDowell said decisions on how to apportion scarce resources were 'the stuff of politics, and not at all appropriate to be decided by the court'.[11] 'What happens when you have a series of rights all of which are competing for the limited financial resources of the state?' asked the Attorney General, Rory Brady, in 2004.[12]

Fifteen years on, the position set down in *Sinnott* and *TD* holds firm. To their critics, the judges were overly dogmatic; the Constitution gave them far more room for creativity than they allowed. Two years after the judgments were given, Hogan and Whyte wrote that 'it might be contended' that those decisions 'signal the ascendancy of classical liberal democracy over more communitarian values in the judicial interpretation of the Constitution, while at the same time reflecting an excessive judicial conservatism on the question of whether the judiciary could ever command the other branches of government to take certain positive steps'.[13]

Yet while the court of the 2000s generally baulked at the sight of anything that it felt resembled legislating, the judges jealously guarded their judicial prerogative to fit their reasoning to the circumstances of each case, even if that made their thinking appear inconsistent and contradictory.

In 2004, it emerged that, over a period of thirty years, the State had unlawfully charged medical card-holders for the cost of their stay in nursing homes. When the issue came to light, the government passed a bill to make this unlawful practice lawful. In effect, it was retrospectively justifying the taking of pensions from old people while taking away the right of those people to take action to recover the money. When President Mary McAleese referred the bill – the Health (Amendment) Bill 2004 – to the Supreme Court, the judges found the key parts of it unconstitutional and told the State to pay the money back.

The decision was to have huge financial implications – the cost to the state was ultimately €484 million, more than the annual current budget of the Department of Justice[14] – yet inside the court the decision to strike down the nursing homes bill was one of the easiest the judges made that year; they were all in absolutely no doubt about it. And this from a court that refused to tell the political branches how to spend taxpayers' money? Within the court, however, they drew an important distinction: the court was not telling the government to give money to these elderly people; it was telling the government it could not take money away from them.[15] It was, they said, about respecting people's property rights, even those of the most vulnerable.

The court's restraint on the separation of powers gave rise to a left-wing critique that accused it of undue deference to the government. Those who saw the court as a tool of social change were dismayed, for example, when it rejected a claim by the Equality Authority that Portmarnock Golf Club, by banning women from full membership, was a 'discriminating club' under the Equal Status Act. Hardiman, Geoghegan and Fidelma Macken, who joined the court in 2005, made up the majority, with Denham and Fennelly in dissent. In an excoriating 20,000-word judgment, Hardiman tore the authority's case to shreds with the sort of trenchant rhetorical flourishes and stream-of-consciousness digressions (at one point he described Googling 'all-women book clubs', which, he declared, yielded 1,400,000 results) that were becoming his trademark. 'You just imagine how he picked up the Dictaphone and screamed into it for two hours', said a High Court judge with a mixture of amusement and resignation.

Hardiman's judgment notwithstanding, the case was actually decided on quite technical grounds. Under the Equal Status Act exemptions are made for clubs established to cater for the 'needs of members of a particular gender'. The case boiled down to whether the purpose of the club was solely golf or the golfing needs of men (having established that playing golf was indeed a 'need'). The court accepted the latter argument and so ruled the club was exempt from the provisions of the Equal Status Act.

The case had been taken by the Equality Authority in the hope of making a wider point and laying down a marker. The authority was under immense pressure from the Department of Justice, which was flatly opposed to its spending public money on a case such as this, which officials saw as a frivolous indulgence. Similarly, within a certain milieu in the law library, which counted many Portmarnock members in its ranks, the case was treated with disdain.

'A victory there would have been a breakthrough', says one supporter of the authority. 'It would have shattered some people's preconceptions beyond the parameters of the case. That there are old institutions here that could be taken down, that there are old practices that could be challenged, that you could get judges to lay down markers – in terms of modernizing, pushing out an equality agenda.'

Yet, like all attempts to categorize a Supreme Court in any era, the

claim that it was defined by deference to the executive was a simpli-
fication. The court was noticeably strong on the rights of defendants –
a stance that never endears a court to the Department of Justice and
the wider bureaucracy but one that many of the judges felt strongly
about. It took a strong line against any attempts to deny individuals
due process or fair procedures – a line of thinking that has run
through the court for decades and has resulted in Ireland having some
of the highest standards of due process in criminal and civil cases of
any common law country.

Within the court in the 2000s, there were sharply divergent
views among the judges. Fennelly was as sympathetic to arguments
about freedom of the press as Hardiman was hostile. There was clear
ideological blue water between Hardiman and McGuinness on socio-
economic rights, and between Murray and Denham on social issues.
As they grappled with the legal questions thrown up by the significant numbers of asylum seekers who began to arrive in Ireland by the
late 1990s, interesting tensions emerged within the group. In 2003,
the court decided by a 5-2 majority that the non-Irish parents of
Irish-born children were not entitled to live in the country by virtue
of having an Irish-born child. Fennelly and McGuinness dissented,
relying on the strong constitutional protection for the family and the
inherent rights of the child, and their stance was fully endorsed by
the European Court of Justice in 2011.

In the Abbeylara case the court had to decide on the right of
Oireachtas committees to hold inquiries. The case arose following
a tragic incident in April 2000. Members of the Garda Emergency
Response Unit shot dead an armed mentally ill young man, John
Carthy, in Abbeylara, Co. Longford, following a twenty-five-hour
siege at his home. In response to calls for an independent public
inquiry to investigate the shooting, politicians proposed to hold an
inquiry at which they would question the gardaí involved. The gardaí
challenged their right to do so and to make findings about the gardaí's
actions. In its judgment the court split 5-2, with the ruling holding
that the parliament had no right to conduct an inquiry that could
lead to adverse findings of fact against an individual (Keane and

Murphy dissented). That decision in effect prevented the Oireachtas holding meaningful inquiries of its own. The decision was in keeping with a principle the court had long upheld: that any attempt by any other arm of the state to take on anything that resembled judicial power would be firmly resisted.[16] (When a referendum was held in 2011 to change the Constitution so as to get around the roadblock the Supreme Court had erected with its Abbeylara decision, the people rejected the proposal.)

There were an awful lot of lawyers in the Abbeylara case. The Attorney General, Michael McDowell, argued for the State, but the Oireachtas committee was also represented. The Fine Gael TD Alan Shatter, one of its members, who was a high-profile solicitor and his party's spokesperson on justice, law reform and defence, chose to represent himself. At one point in the ten-day hearing, Shatter addressed the court, left and returned to Leinster House. When the case resumed after lunch, however, the judges said they would not begin until Shatter was back in court. A message was sent to the Dáil, and Shatter returned to the court to be present for the afternoon's business.

When the charge was levelled at the High Court and Supreme Court in the mid-2000s that they were too cautious, that they were too slow to push the boundaries of the judicial role, the private response from the judges and their advocates was that the environment had changed. The society and the world the courts faced in the mid-2000s were infinitely more complex than the ones the judges surveyed in the 1960s. Ó Dálaigh and Walsh were working with a Constitution that had scarcely begun to be mined, the argument went, and the questions they were asked reflected that. Who now thought a papal encyclical was a valid source for a judicial decision? By the twenty-first century, the huge volume of European laws, regulations and conventions emanating from Brussels and Strasbourg had added huge complexity to the legal environment in which they functioned. The judges also fretted about unintended consequences; all they knew were the facts in the case before them, and they had neither the skills nor the resources to investigate wider ramifications.

All of this was underpinned by an intellectual conviction that to have judges meddling in policy-making would be anti-democratic and bad for society. They looked across the Atlantic and observed how the decision of the United States Supreme Court to legalize abortion through *Roe v. Wade* had always left a question mark over the democratic legitimacy of abortion in the eyes of opponents. Even forty years on, the issue was at the top of the political agenda and had the ability to mobilize huge demonstrations.

When Irish voters overwhelmingly approved a referendum proposal to introduce same-sex marriage in 2015, advocates of judicial restraint in the Four Courts saw it as a vindication of sorts. Had the courts recognized a right to same-sex marriage, as they had been invited to do some years earlier, the theory went, the decision would have been bitterly argued over for decades. And the country would never have had the benefit of knowing that a clear majority of citizens favoured extending marriage rights to their gay compatriots through the ballot box. Of course, stepping back in this way was itself an ideological position on the part of the judges.

In any case, the idea that the court had backed off entirely from conflict with the executive was not the full picture. In the 2000s, the Supreme Court and High Court together made fourteen findings of unconstitutionality – the nuclear weapon in the judicial arsenal. The figure included the decision to strike down the law on statutory rape in the CC case (see Introduction) and to declare unconstitutional the nursing homes bill. That figure of fourteen was slightly less than in the 1970s, when seventeen laws were struck down, but it was around the average for the second half of the twentieth century.[17] The figures for the 2000s show a focus on ensuring rights are upheld in the political, criminal and broader legal processes of the State, with an emphasis on fair procedures and access to the courts.[18]

Case by case, year by year, the post-2000 court was staking out and refining its positions. In the conference room, the seven judges spanned the full spectrum on most of the big cases, but although there were occasional tensions – there was, as always on the court, irritation and resentment over those who shirked their share of the judgment-writing burden – voices were never raised and the judges generally got along well together.

Adrian Hardiman had settled into the court better than many expected. With hindsight, it's clear that these were some of his most influential years. 'Adrian's going to have fun with this one', colleagues would say when a case that hit on one of his favourite topics – defendants' rights, the media, the separation of powers or political correctness – came up. Yet his mannerisms on the bench were so similar to his style as an advocate that many of his colleagues wondered whether his heart always remained in the law library. He would cheerfully pummel barristers to extract concessions that he would triumphantly highlight when unpicking their case in his excoriating judgment. On the bench, he would raise his thick eyebrows over his glasses with a look that conveyed a combination of pity and wonder that the person before him could come out with such idiotic thoughts. 'Could you repeat that, please', he would say to counsel, leaning forward in his chair, his pen poised over his notebook. That was when a barrister knew Hardiman had won.

A few years after he joined the court, an official asked all the judges to write short biographies that could be posted online and distributed with official material. Hardiman wrote down the standard list of achievements – degrees earned, articles published and so on – before adding a reference to how he had 'withdrawn from all vivid and controversial scenes' since 2000. Not quite.

At the Justice Media Awards, an annual event held by the Law Society, in 2008, Hardiman gave an address in which he sharply criticized media coverage of the courts – one of his pet peeves – saying journalists' work on the Supreme Court was confusing, uninformative and often wrong. He said he looked with envy at the highly skilled press corps attached to the US Supreme Court, and lamented that legal reporting in Ireland had 'yet to find its Des Cahill or Joshua Rozenberg.'[19] Warming to his theme, Hardiman said the proverbial farmer and the cowman – lawyers and journalists – should be on better terms. He then referred to female legal journalists as 'cowgirls'.

Hardiman's fellow judges were annoyed with him. Not a word was spoken about it at the conference table, but judges complained about it in small groups and discussed how they could distance themselves from what Hardiman had said. The next time the court was in session, Susan Denham turned and addressed the press bench. 'I'm delighted to see the exceptionally high standard of reporting we normally have in this court', she said. 'Thank you.'

19. Supreme conflict

'This was the worst of all worlds.'

Anonymous

If the law library was a Fine Gael citadel, then by the 2000s Fianna Fáil had begun to breach the ramparts. Or at least to some it felt that way. As Taoiseach since 1997, Bertie Ahern was unassailable. An unprecedented economic boom sent his popularity and that of his party soaring, leaving its traditional rival, riven by internal fractures and struggling to assert itself, trailing in the slipstream of Bertie's electoral juggernaut.

The mood in the Four Courts can be sensitive to shifts in the balance of power in Leinster House. The party with the keys to Merrion Street not only controls judicial appointments but also chooses which barristers to brief in State cases, from the small road traffic charge that might earn a practitioner €100 to the long-running blockbuster case worth hundreds of thousands of euros.

The economic boom caused an explosion in litigation and sent vast amounts of money sloshing through the legal system. The highest-earning barristers, who built practices working exclusively for big corporations and financial institutions, could pull in €2 million a year. Judicial salaries rose. Barristers' fees rocketed. At the top of the earnings tree, some people grew very wealthy indeed.

The litigation bonanza also had a wider, if less frequently noticed, effect. Because there was only so much more work that the big names or the sons and daughters of legal bigwigs could take on, it enabled more young practitioners to break into a profession in which it was notoriously difficult to gain a foothold. That helped to dilute the social homogeneity of the law library, dominated as it had been for so long by middle-class men who had gone to the same schools and universities. The shift was slow – it was still virtually impossible to survive in the first years in practice without a part-time job on the side – but it was noticeable nonetheless.[1]

In the 1970s, when the law library was a relatively small place, it had been possible to identify almost everyone's party affiliation. As the numbers of practising barristers rose – by the 2000s there were about 2,000 members – that became much more difficult. Yet, while many barristers had no party links at all, the party in power still mattered. Older practitioners in particular took their party politics very seriously. In the early 2000s the Fianna Fáil barristers were exultant. They got a Fianna Fáil Attorney General, Rory Brady. Several of their number made their way onto the bench. Briefs were coming their way and their men were elected to senior roles in the Bar Council, the body that represents barristers.

Naturally, they took every opportunity to rub their Fine Gael colleagues' noses in it. Plaques and statues of Fianna Fáil grandees started to appear around the place. 'They rejoiced', recalls one lawyer, sitting at a desk in the law library.

> If you go out the door there, you'll see a plaque on the wall that this extension was opened by Bertie Ahern. If you go downstairs, you'll see there's a wing dedicated to Eamon Leahy [a senior counsel who died young in 2003].[2] They were never done putting up fucking plaques around here, Fianna Fáil. They loved to put them in the faces of Fine Gael. Every time another plaque went up, the Fine Gaelers fumed. It was ridiculous.
>
> There's one upstairs in a corridor. Who the fuck passes there? But there are Fine Gael barristers who will be annoyed to see it – that's who. So get it up.

By the mid-2000s, the impact – or lack of impact – of the judicial selection system introduced in the wake of the Whelehan affair was becoming clear. The Judicial Appointments Advisory Board (JAAB), made up of senior judges, representatives of the legal profession, the Attorney General and a number of lay members, would receive applications and send government a list of recommended names. It was not allowed to rank the individuals or identify particular lawyers as outstanding candidates. Its function in practice, then, was to weed out the unsuitable.

Although all members of the board were nominally equal, the presidents of each court had particular influence. It was not quite a veto, but if the president of the Circuit Court, for example, was strongly opposed to a particular applicant's name being recommended, that carried a lot of weight. Names would be scratched from the list due to lack of experience or a patchy track record, but the board also came up with informal codes to weed out unsuitable names. "'Temperament" was code for "bonkers", "drink problem", "issues at home"', recalls one former member. Therefore, the mere mention of 'temperament' was enough to result in an application being discreetly put aside.

An important change took place in the early 2000s, as Jennifer Carroll MacNeill points out.[3] The law setting up the JAAB required the board to recommend at least seven names for each vacancy. In the early years after it was set up in 1995, the board as a general rule put seven names forward each time, provided there were that many applicants. That limited the government's room for discretion, because even though Cabinet could in theory pick someone who did not appear on the JAAB list, the fact that it had to reveal publicly that it had done so was a strong political disincentive. But in the early 2000s, the JAAB received legal advice that suggested it was being too selective in limiting itself to just seven names. So, apparently on its own initiative, it began to send government long lists of names, excluding only those who did not meet the minimum eligibility requirements. The result was that the Attorney General and the Minister for Justice – two of the key players in the selection process – began to receive lists of more than a hundred names for a District Court vacancy and more than seventy for each opening on the Circuit Court (there were far fewer applicants for the High and Supreme Courts).

Suddenly, thanks to the JAAB's own change of policy, the government had virtually limitless discretion to appoint whomever it liked, so long as he or she had submitted an application. 'The decision fundamentally changed the role of the JAAB from being a quasi-selection body to being a purely screening body', writes Carroll MacNeill.[4] A senior counsel puts it more bluntly. 'It's a fig leaf', he says. 'It's a filter to make sure you're not an axe murderer or a child abuser, but that's it.'

Political patronage was less of a factor the higher up the courts chain a vacancy arose, but at the lower courts, in particular the District Court, lobbying was intense. Local solicitors would contact their TDs, who would call or write to ministers or their advisers to convey the message. Candidates' election agents would seek preferment on the basis of their service to the party. Family members of would-be judges would turn up at weekend hurling matches, where they would, supposedly by accident, bump into a TD or a minister.

'At District Court you'd be driven mad', says one former minister. 'There would be intensive lobbying at District Court level', another minister agrees. 'At Circuit level, a bit less. At High Court level, very little. If there was any lobbying at Circuit Court and High Court level in my time, it would have been counter-productive. I would not have appointed people who lobbied.' Not every politician took the same stance. 'It's very hard to get away with saying there's absolutely no politics in it, because we have to be truthful', says a former senior minister. 'There is politics in it. But that's partly the size of Ireland . . . it's very hard to get away from it.'

There was one place in which the JAAB has had no effect at all: the Supreme Court. In all but two cases since 1995, appointees to the court have been selected from within the ranks of the High Court, a route in which the JAAB has no involvement. The two who were not already serving judges – Adrian Hardiman and Donal O'Donnell – were outstanding barristers who were appointed directly from the law library and whose elevations were universally welcomed. High Court judges occasionally lobbied for promotion, but it was usually frowned upon. And although party politics could still play a role, it was less significant a factor than it was further down the chain.

In the 2000s and early 2010s, Fianna Fáil-led governments appointed a majority of lawyers who had no connections to the party to senior legal and judicial positions. In 2004, Frank Clarke and John

Mac Menamin, both of whom had close connections to Fine Gael, were made High Court judges. Paul Gallagher, a star at the Bar, and one with no party history, was appointed Attorney General in 2007. Similarly, Donal O'Donnell was one of the leading constitutional lawyers in the country when he was appointed to the Supreme Court in 2010 and had no links to any party.

If a Taoiseach had little interest in appointments, it could give the Attorney General and the Minister for Justice huge power, but other ministers were not told until they arrived for the weekly Cabinet meeting. 'I wouldn't tell anyone until the last minute', says a former Minister for Justice. 'I used to ring up [the Taoiseach] the night before the Cabinet meeting. I would leave it very late – about 10.30pm – and ring and say, "By the way, I'm bringing an appointment to the Cabinet tomorrow".'

Perhaps more than for any other appointments in the government's control, names for appointments to the Supreme Court were kept extremely tight. There were four·people whose opinions counted: the Taoiseach, Tánaiste, Attorney General and Minister for Justice. Beyond that group, nobody else in Cabinet had any say or even any knowledge of the process until the names were presented at Cabinet for formal approval, by which time the decision had been made. But among the decision-makers the dynamic shifted from government to government. As Taoiseach, John Bruton had more interest in the process than Bertie Ahern or Enda Kenny, neither of whom was plugged into legal networks. Ministers who were also lawyers – Brian Cowen, Michael McDowell and Dermot Ahern, for example – got more involved than those who rarely if ever met a lawyer. Certain Chief Justices let the government know if they objected to a name; the government listened, though – much to the Chief's chagrin – it often did not take the view on board. 'I wouldn't accord a Chief Justice that function', says one former minister. 'It's none of their fucking business.'

What were governments looking for in a Supreme Court judge? 'Generally what is being sought is somebody with a low centre of gravity, sound judgment and a high intellectual capacity', says one ex-minister with knowledge of the process. 'It's an act of faith, in some respects. And when you're taking a decision that carries risk, you have to be cautious.' Politics clearly plays a part, but it can be trumped by other factors. 'Sometimes you have a star [on the list], and you want that person in there', says a former Attorney. 'That would dislodge political affiliation, I think.'

According to another former decision-maker, a record of well-reasoned judgments, 'even if you don't always agree with the outcome', was one of the most important factors.

> I would regard as important that they're an individual whose judgments indicate some general level of common sense and understanding of the human condition, and who has the capacity while sitting in that court to intellectually engage with lawyers, to put the hard questions to those lawyers and to engage constructively with lay litigants whilst not insulting those who come before the court, not barracking people who come before the court. People who have the personality to work with and be respectful of their colleagues.

Yet others bristle at the suggestion that previous party affiliation should as a rule work against a candidate. 'The Constitution is where law and politics meet, and really you want to make sure that whoever is on the Supreme Court is a good constitutional lawyer. And that by implication requires some feel for political science, some kind of a sense of big-picture politics', says a former Cabinet member who selected several judges.

> I'm not saying that you want somebody who is always going to play the game, but it would be inappropriate to appoint somebody who for instance didn't have much interest in current affairs, didn't read the newspapers, was very much in an ivory tower. I'm not entirely sure that's the kind of person you want in the Supreme Court. I know the other point can be made – it's a prize, it's a 'thank you'. But I don't think we have had appointments to the Supreme Court where the people involved have been duffers. I just don't think that has happened. It would be subject to too much comment.

And yet, while the appointments system was political, all the evidence suggested it was impossible to identify any general correlation between the party that selected a judge and that judge's decision-making record. For the most part, voting patterns on a given Supreme Court were a mix of overlapping lines and shifting blocks that varied with each case. To test the hypothesis, the Dublin City University academics Robert Elgie, Adam McAuley and Eoin O'Malley analysed all Supreme Court judgments between 1963 and 2006 in order to observe whether judges appointed under Fianna Fáil-led governments systematically dissented from decisions made by judges appointed under Fine Gael governments, and vice versa. Their conclusion was no. 'Contrary to expectations,' the authors write, 'we find that there is no evidence to suggest that the partisan heritage of judicial appointments affects the decision-making of justices once they have been appointed to the Supreme Court.'[5]

'One of the great things about our judiciary and the way they conduct themselves is that no matter what government appoints them, no matter whether they do or don't have political backgrounds, it's very difficult to discern any political bias in any judgments that I have ever read', says one lawyer who has served in government.

Once a judge was appointed, however, the shutters came down. Official communications, mainly on administrative business, went between the Chief Justice or the presidents of each court and either the Attorney General or the Department of Justice. Ministers would occasionally bump into judges at social or sports events. ('You would not meet the judiciary at Croke Park, and less again Lansdowne Road for soccer matches', says one disgruntled minister. 'But rugby matches, they would be there in strength.')

Through much of the 2000s, notwithstanding the controversy over the statutory rape law, there was little to strain the relationship between the judges and the politicians. Fianna Fáil-led governments were riding high in the polls, the economy was booming, judicial salaries were rising in line with other public sector incomes and the Courts Service was benefiting from increased funding to overhaul the country's creaking court infrastructure. When a new €600 million criminal courts complex was built near Phoenix Park – the largest court-building project since Gandon's Four Courts was completed at the end of the eighteenth century – it was to symbolize a new beginning.

By the time the complex opened in November 2009, however, it already seemed like a monument to another era. By then the economy had suffered a spectacular collapse. Anglo Irish Bank had been nationalized while the State was giving multi-billion euro cash injections to the Bank of Ireland and Allied Irish Bank to keep them afloat. Unemployment was hitting double figures in percentage terms, public spending was being drastically cut and, the previous February, 100,000 people had taken to the streets of Dublin to protest at the government's handling of the economic crisis.

The Fianna Fáil–Green Party coalition led by Brian Cowen was struggling to grasp the scale of the cataclysm, let alone contain it. In February 2009, it had announced a recovery plan that required €2 billion in savings – a figure so large that it involved deep incisions into spending across virtually all government activity. The bulk of the savings, €1.4 billion, was to come from a pension levy on all public servants, ranging from 3 per cent for the lowest-earners to 9.6 per cent for those on an annual income of €300,000 or more. But was it actually going to be imposed on all public servants? This was a question the opposition, through the Fine Gael frontbencher Alan Shatter, was quick to ask. Shatter had one category of public servant in mind – the judges.

Alan Shatter was re-igniting an issue that had been a source of tension between generations of politicians and judges, right back to the foundation of the courts system. When the new State was founded in 1922, judicial salaries were reduced and were pegged at about half those of their English counterparts. That remained the position in the early decades after Independence, with the judges getting no significant increase. In January 1932, at a time when the public finances were in dire straits, Ernest Blythe, the Minister for Finance, wrote to Chief Justice Hugh Kennedy asking the judges of the High and Supreme Courts to follow the example set by government ministers by taking a voluntary 10 per cent pay cut as 'a gesture and a contribution on their part towards solving a national problem'.

Blythe said the government was not proposing to 'interfere' with the judges' rights; in the Free State Constitution Supreme and High Court judges' salaries were protected against reductions by the government. Instead he was, initially at least, relying on moral pressure to encourage compliance: 'You are probably familiar with the fact that in many countries action of the kind I suggest has been taken, the nearest analogy being Great Britain, where the highest judicial salaries have been abated by as much as 20 per cent and those next below by 10 per cent.'[6]

Kennedy convened a meeting of the senior judges, where the proposal met strong resistance. In his reply to Blythe the Chief Justice said that given their financial commitments it would be 'impossible' for the judges to take a voluntary pay cut. This was 'not attributable to any extravagance', he wrote, the judges' salaries 'not being in any degree excessive'. He also took issue with the comparison with England, where, he pointed out, High Court judges earned twice as much as their Irish counterparts. 'Indeed the salaries of the Saorstát Judges are confidently believed to be much less than the annual incomes of many of the leaders of the Bar practising before them, earnings at the Bar having grown in recent years, as it is believed, in correspondence with the increased cost of a professional man's standard of life.'[7]

The government did not take kindly to the rebuff. Responding to Kennedy, Blythe said he was 'very disappointed' at the judges' 'unreasonable' attitude, pointing out that the cost of living had fallen considerably since their salaries had been fixed. He then put the threat of an enforced cut, which would require a constitutional amendment, on the table: 'If the financial position does not speedily improve I fear that what would not be given will have to be taken. I am anxious for many reasons that the Government should not be forced to such a course and I propose (when a little less busy) to ask the Judges to reconsider their attitude.'[8]

The stand-off rumbled on. The government continued to apply

pressure, and Kennedy continued to resist. In the Four Courts, he was urged by colleagues to hold the line. In March his Supreme Court colleague Gerald Fitzgibbon wrote to Kennedy urging him not to give in. He said that making a voluntary cut would be 'an admission that our salaries are too high'. It was an insult, Fitzgibbon argued, to ask for a voluntary concession under a threat of compulsion if it was not granted. By resisting the government's move the judiciary would be

> upholding a vital principle, not in our own selfish interest, but in that of the whole nation. The independence of the Judges is of vital importance to the liberty of every individual citizen, and it is secured only by the provisions that a Judge cannot be removed, except for good cause, and then by the legislature alone, and that he is not dependent for the amount or payment of his salary upon the will of the Executive or of the Legislature, once he has been appointed to his office. Our Constitution is not alone in providing an independent Judiciary as a bulwark to protect the nation from the tyranny either of an individual despot or of a democratic executive. In my humble submission we should refuse to surrender rights which were given to us, not for our own aggrandisement, but to guarantee to the nation, whose servants we are, our independence from all executive influence or control . . .

Ultimately the government did not act on its threat. Five years later the 1937 Constitution extended the bar on reducing judicial pay to judges of all courts. Article 35.5 stated: 'The remuneration of a judge shall not be reduced during his continuance in office.' The article was intended to be a declaration of the independence of the judiciary from the other branches of government and a bulwark against any attempt to challenge that independence. Judges should feel free to administer justice as they saw fit without fearing that the government could punish them for a judgment ministers did not like by cutting their pay.

The pay issue did not go away. Almost every decade it arose in some form, raised either by the government or by the judges themselves. In the early 1950s, the judges tried a new approach. In October 1950, Chief Justice Conor Maguire sent Taoiseach John A. Costello a memo outlining a claim by the judges that, on their reading of the Constitution, with its bar on reducing judges' salaries, they were constitutionally immune from having to pay income tax or any other tax on their salaries. Accompanying the memo was a threat that the judges were prepared to take legal action to press the point. He was writing, Maguire told Costello, 'in the hope that it may be possible to reach some solution without the necessity for an appeal to the Courts by some individual judge'.[9]

You cannot be serious! was the essence of the government's reply. It rejected the claim out of hand. In a letter to Maguire, Costello said the government had carefully considered the judges' position and felt unable to accept it. While he did not consider it appropriate for the government to enter into a detailed discussion with the judges about it – presumably because Maguire had threatened legal action – Costello pointed out that for the quarter-century since the State's foundation the judges had accepted appointment 'in the knowledge that their salaries would, in fact, be taxed on the same basis as any other salaries and have received their salaries and paid the tax without (so far as we are aware) any protest or any suggestion to the Government during all that time, that their salaries should be immune from taxation under Constitutional provisions'.[10]

Minister for Finance Seán MacEntee followed up in response to further correspondence from Maguire later in 1951, saying he too was constrained in what he could say by the threat of legal action but felt 'bound to say that I do not think [the claim] is well-founded'.

It is, of course, for the judges to decide on their future course of action in relation to the question, but it would seem to me ill-advised that they should sit in judgment on their own cause. A decision that they were free from income tax or other similar charge would scarcely be accepted by the public who, in my opinion, will be disposed to take the view that, as citizens, the Judges should be prepared to share the tax burdens which the duty of maintaining the State and its services imposes on the community and would probably demand that the existing position and current practice should be appropriately confirmed.[11]

In 1954, shortly after the death of the former Supreme Court judge John O'Byrne, his widow, Marjorie, began proceedings in the High Court seeking a declaration that the salary her late husband received as a judge was exempt from income tax and that any tax deduction from his salary was illegal and contrary to the Constitution. In the High Court, judge Kevin Dixon rejected the claim, finding there was nothing in the Constitution to place judges in a class apart on liability to income tax. This was upheld by the Supreme Court, in a 3-2 decision led by Maguire himself in the majority. The court rejected the claim that income tax was an attack on judicial independence, finding that the Constitution did not preclude the deduction of income tax from the gross salary of a judge provided the deductions were similar to those applied to others on the same income level.[12]

While the O'Byrne judgment put an end to the dispute over income tax, the broader question of judicial pay persisted. Judges had been given modest increases in 1947 and 1953, and again in 1968 and 1971. By the 1980s, however, it was 'accepted that these salaries had fallen well behind what was appropriate, with the potential effect this might have on attracting people of high calibre to these positions'.[13] Significant increases were granted in 1989 and 1990, and from 1990 to 2008 the salaries of the judiciary, as with most higher civil servants and politicians, almost tripled.

When, in 2009, the Cowen government sought advice as to whether the pension levy could be imposed on the judges, the Attorney General, Paul Gallagher, was of the view that it could not be done. Alan Shatter took issue with this and pressed Cowen in the Dáil on whether any approach had been made to members of the judiciary to suggest they voluntarily reduce their salaries by an equivalent of the levy. The government hadn't done that, but the idea was now on the public agenda. At the time, judges' salaries ranged from €295,000 for the Chief Justice to €147,000 for a District Court judge, with High Court judges earning €243,000 a year. At those salary levels, constitutional clause or not, it was difficult to argue that this one category of worker should be insulated from the pain. Public pressure for a voluntary cut began to grow. Doing so 'would send a clear message that they (the judges) understand the crisis the State is in, and that they wish to contribute to its solution along with everyone else', wrote Carol Coulter, legal affairs editor of the *Irish Times*.[14]

Cowen, wary of crossing a constitutional line, was reluctant to ask the judges to make a voluntary contribution. But within weeks of the government's plan, on 31 March, it was announced that arrangements had been made for judges to pay their contribution towards the pension levy directly to the Revenue Commissioners. The move had been instigated by John Murray, Chief Justice since 2004, as a way for judges to show solidarity by making a voluntary payment without the government having to impose the levy. The gesture would be voluntary and confidential; it would be for each individual judge to deal directly with Revenue.

From the outside, it looked like the plan had been agreed without too much trouble. But it had not been quite that smooth. While most judges accepted the plan, some were concerned that the information on who had or had not paid would get out. That was why the judiciary insisted that the process had to be confidential: to avoid a perception that individual judges were seeking public approval or career advancement by publicly paying the levy, and to make sure a storm of vitriol did not come down upon those who did not pay.

If the government and judiciary hoped the controversy would end there, they were in for a shock. In the Four Courts, the atmosphere was growing tense. The judges had more than six months to make the payment for that year, and many decided to wait until October, when they always did their tax returns, to do it. But several of the savvier judges paid it immediately, knowing journalists would be sniffing around for the information. At one of the Supreme Court's weekly lunches in June 2009, Murray asked whether everyone had paid and said it was always possible that Revenue would release a figure for the amount it had received. That caused consternation. Did that mean the process was not confidential after all? some judges asked.

Similar conversations were taking place in the other courts. When one senior judge told a more junior colleague it was important to pay, because worse could follow if they didn't, the second judge accused him of behaving like Stalin, prompting the more senior man to threaten to resign if the remark was not retracted. Many more such threats were to follow. Senior figures in government knew the judges were beginning to split. Word reached Brian Lenihan, the Minister for Finance, that one senior judge had been heard, as he left Mass in Donnybrook one Sunday morning, telling people that it was disgraceful that judges were being asked to pay.

As the storm clouds were gathering, senior judges were preoccupied with something else: gowns. Murray had wanted for some time to introduce new, European-style judicial attire to replace the old British-influenced garb the judges had been wearing since Chief Justice Hugh Kennedy's abortive attempt to replace it in the 1920s. The designer Louise Kennedy was commissioned to do the job, and she made several visits to the Supreme Court conference room in early to mid-2009 to demonstrate different options. This too got back to government. 'They're down there talking about new wigs and gowns, or no wigs and new gowns. I was thinking, "Jesus, Mary and Joseph!"', says one former minister. 'I just felt, some of these people didn't live in the real world, as regards what was coming down the tracks.'

The atmosphere was relatively calm in July 2009, when the judges of the High and Supreme Courts met for their annual conference in Adare, Co. Limerick. The agenda was the standard list of topics related to the administration of the courts. 'It's always like a residents' association meeting, where all the usual cranks stand up and complain about litter on the streets. It's indistinguishable from that', says one reluctant participant. But on this occasion the agenda also included the gowns, which were to be shown to the judges for the first time. To much hilarity, two High Court judges, Mary Irvine and Peter Charleton, paraded around the room modelling the new designs before it was agreed that there should be further consultation before a final decision was made at the conference of the entire judiciary that November.

As the meeting was wrapping up, Murray went to take a call from

Gerry Curran, the media adviser to the Courts Service. When he returned, the Chief Justice informed the judges that a story was about to break on the RTÉ evening news that only nineteen judges out of 148 had to date paid the pension levy. At first the room went silent. Those around the table felt aggrieved; they had until the end of the year to make the voluntary payment, and many of them had planned to do so when they filed their tax return in October. A statement making that point was hurriedly issued. But the judges knew that for all they might argue about the unfairness of the story, this was going to look terrible.

They were right on that score. The story dominated the news agenda the next day. Mary Harney, the Minister for Health, said she was disappointed at the low take-up rate and said she believed the judiciary would respond and 'show solidarity with those people that are losing their jobs and people who had to take a big hit in their incomes'. Her Cabinet colleague Willie O'Dea, the Minister for Defence, said the judges were setting a 'poor example'.

Government ministers were not just trying to channel the public mood. They needed the judiciary to play ball if they were not to stand accused of having gone too easy on the high-earners in the Four Courts. Now the government was in the line of fire. 'God love the poor judges', wrote Miriam Lord, capturing the general mood in the *Irish Times*. 'According to the Taoiseach, they have been battling "constitutional inhibitions" since the levy was introduced. In fact, all they want to do is cast off those inhibitions and pay up. Mind you, only 19 of them have managed so far. Good news is, they have until the end of the year. Unlike everyone else.'

Amid the clamour, the Fianna Fáil TD Niall Collins stepped forward and made a proposal: if the Constitution blocked the government from imposing the pension levy on the judges, why not hold a referendum to change it? At that stage it was an isolated call.

On the Monday after the Adare conference, a tense meeting was held in the Supreme Court conference room. Murray brought in a sheaf of negative press clippings and, following some complaints around the table about how unfair the coverage was, the group discussed what to do. Ultimately it was agreed that Murray would put out a statement correcting the more egregious misrepresentations. He spent the day working on it. Later, at lunch, the group discussed an email Hardiman had circulated earlier in the day suggesting that the judges should hire a PR consultant like P. J. Mara or Terry Prone to make their case in public. The idea fell like a lead balloon.

In his statement, Murray took issue with 'unfair and misleading' statements about the issue, adding that he felt there would be 'a strong and continuous participation' in the scheme. Cowen then came to the judges' aid, welcoming Murray's statement and saying it was 'not correct' to say that judges who had not yet made a contribution 'have refused to do so'. It was 'essential to protect the independence of the judiciary', Cowen said. 'Were it otherwise governments and legislatures could pressurise the judiciary and undermine their independence.'

But the criticism did not abate; it grew louder. Judges visited each other's chambers to exchange stories about the abuse they were getting: one had fruit thrown at his car in the judges' yard by someone who yelled that he should 'pay your fucking pension levy'. A story emerged from the criminal courts on Parkgate Street, where a judge, when he apologized to a jury about the absence of some facility, was told: 'If you judges had paid your pension levy, this mightn't have happened.' Increasingly, the judges were of one mind on one point at least: if only the government had just imposed the pension levy on them, it would have saved everyone a lot of grief. 'No judge would have dared challenge that view in the current climate', one said. 'This was the worst of all worlds. We had a confidential, non-transparent arrangement for payment of the pension levy. There was speculation as to who was paying and who wasn't. You had judges openly boasting that they weren't going to pay and would never pay . . . It was a huge own-goal by the judiciary.'

The general air of gloom in judges' chambers grew darker still when, within days of the news of the low take-up emerging, Dearbhail McDonald, the *Irish Independent*'s legal affairs editor, broke the story about the gowns. 'Fashion guru Louise Kennedy has been commissioned by the Chief Justice to create an unprecedented new range of designer robes for the country's judges', it began.[15] The timing could scarcely have been worse. Several judges listened in funereal silence as the story was discussed on the *Pat Kenny Show* on radio that morning. Another meeting was called to discuss whether to put out another statement (they decided against). Now the judges were pre-occupied with a new concern: what if the cost of the gowns got out? Nobody was to talk about the gowns.[16]

Meanwhile, the press was keeping a running tab on the judicial sign-up rate for the voluntary contribution. By September, just half of all serving judges – 72 out of 144 – had paid. By January the figure was at 111. In private, the judiciary was split into two camps. A small minority, led by lower-earning judges in the District Court but including a number from the High Court, complained that they were under financial strain and could not afford to take the hit. At the same time, the Chief Justice and the presidents of the various courts were in turn coming under intense pressure from within their ranks to take a stronger stance against the hold-outs. 'There was a lack of leadership', says one judge from the time.

> [They] were more preoccupied with the gowns than getting pension levy compliance from the judges. Had that been done, I think the judges might have been left alone. You couldn't have a situation where judges were sitting in the High Court, not paying any pension levy while their registrars were suffering a 10 per cent deduction in their salary. How could you possibly justify that? There was no way. They wouldn't put the boot in. They didn't feel confident enough to put the boot in.

The High Court judges met for lunch twice a week – one known as 'the picnic' every Wednesday, where everyone brought their own sandwiches, and a more formal gathering on Fridays which used to be catered before funding was withdrawn during the recession. Through late 2009, the pension levy and the public opprobrium being heaped on the judiciary was the only topic of conversation at the lunches. The mood worsened in December, when the *Irish Times* published an opinion piece by Alan Shatter in which he called for a referendum on judicial pay. This was the worst-case scenario in the judges' eyes. But they were reassured by Shatter's apparent marginalization under Enda Kenny's leadership of Fine Gael. At the time, the party's justice spokesman was the emollient Charlie Flanagan. It was assumed that even if Fine Gael got into government after the next election, Shatter was unlikely to become Minister for Justice and therefore have any chance to act on his idea.

20. Détente

'In a world of instant communication and commentary, the
concept of silence may seem unusual.'

Susan Denham

Tensions over the judges' voluntary contribution simmered through
2010. While the public line was that the decision to pay was each
judge's alone, in private pressure was now being applied on those
who had not stumped up. High Court President Nicholas Kearns
confirmed as much in an interview with the *Irish Times* in October of
that year, when he said the presidents of the four courts – the Supreme,
High, Circuit and District – had sent joint letters to all judges remind-
ing them of the need to pay the contribution. 'It is important to
remember that the judges themselves did not seek any special treatment to insulate themselves from the pain being felt across the public
service', he said.[1]

Eventually, 85 per cent of judges signed up, including everyone in
the Supreme Court and all but one in the High Court. But by then it
was too late. The slow initial take-up rate was all people remembered, and it enabled politicians to go on the offensive.

One politician in particular, or so it seemed to the judges.

By now Alan Shatter had produced a private member's bill to
allow for a referendum to cut judicial pay. He was proposing that it
should be put to the people on the day of the next election. In order
to maintain confidence in the judiciary, he said, 'it is important they
should be seen as part of the community and not an elite set apart'.
Thanks to a significant shift in the political landscape, Shatter's voice
now carried much more weight. In June 2010, Enda Kenny's opponents had mounted a botched heave to remove him from the party

leadership. Charlie Flanagan threw his weight behind Kenny's challenger, Richard Bruton, but Shatter remained loyal to the leader. When a victorious Kenny announced his front bench reshuffle in early July, Flanagan was demoted and Shatter became justice spokesman. That put him first in line for the Department of Justice if Fine Gael won the next election.

The Cowen government was disinclined to take up Shatter's referendum idea, but everything except pay was being slashed. The Courts Service budget was cut, a proposal circulated to do away with judges' ushers and there was talk of longer court sitting times. The budget announced in late 2010 brought two further pieces of bad news for the judges. The first was unintentional. In order to clamp down on high-earning company executives who were given multi-million euro pension pots as a tax-efficient way to effectively top up their pay, the budget limited tax relief to pension funds worth up to €2.3 million. While the measure was aimed mainly at senior executives in the private sector, it caught two other categories of people with a mix of public and private pensions: judges and hospital consultants. The result was that a large portion of judges' pensions would end up being taxed at 73 per cent – enough to virtually wipe out the private pension pots they had been building up since their time at the Bar.

The second budgetary measure was very much deliberate: new appointees to the judiciary would be paid 10 per cent less than incumbents. The idea of a two-tier judiciary (some of those who joined later referred to themselves as 'the yellow-packs') left senior judges angry. An emergency general meeting of the entire judiciary was called. These meetings were always difficult to control; getting three judges to agree on something is difficult enough, but looking for a common position among 140 of them is an impossible task. By now voices were being raised. The judges were at sea. There was open talk of strikes and mass resignations.

In the spring of 2011, Fine Gael and Labour swept to power with the biggest majority of any government in the history of the State. Kenny became Taoiseach, Labour leader Eamon Gilmore was installed as Tánaiste, Shatter took over at the Department of Justice and Brendan Howlin was Minister for Public Expenditure and Reform.

Another key figure, and the chief interlocutor for the judiciary from then on, was the Attorney General, Máire Whelan, a senior counsel with links to the Labour Party. The Programme for Government committed the coalition to holding a referendum on judges' pay.

Relationships got off to a bad start. 'We were amazed at the dys-functionality of the judiciary – how disunited they were', says one government source. Groups of judges would adopt a single stance at meetings with ministers and their officials, and then afterwards individual judges would call 'and tell you they disagreed with the official [judges'] position'.

In April, more than six weeks after the new government took office, Murray paid a routine visit to Kenny at Government Build-ings. He raised the implications of the pension lump sum issue and briefed Kenny in detail on the gown situation. The meeting ended amicably and Murray returned to the Four Courts. A few days later, the newspapers carried reports of the meeting, including the fact that Murray had raised the pensions question. Politicians and columnists were indignant over what was portrayed as judges looking for a spe-cial deal. When Kenny was door-stepped about it, he immediately made clear that there would be no special deal for the judges.

'If Enda gives in to any special pleading on behalf of this pam-pered, privileged elite, we are doomed as a government because we won't have a leg to stand on when we ask ordinary hard-pressed tax-payers to take more pain in the years ahead', one senior Fine Gael TD told the *Irish Times*. Murray, who was already coming under pressure in the judiciary to take a more assertive stance, was rattled by the leak and the public criticism that ensued. At first the judges were con-vinced the government had leaked it. Then rumours circulated that a journalist had overheard a judge talking about it at a reception. Others saw ministers' fingerprints all over the leak. Barrister, for-mer Fianna Fáil strategist and political commentator Noel Whelan observed:

When they [the government] needed a further popular challenge on which to show their political virility, they gave a public lash to the judiciary. As political strategy, it was brilliant. Leak the details of a private conversation between the Chief Justice and the Taoiseach and then put your own construction on it knowing the judges would never be able to spin back. The Government then renewed a promise of a popular referendum on judges' pay and even the usually more sedate media got stuck in with criticism of the judiciary and positive comment for the Government.[2]

Kenny himself was generally quite bemused by the judges. He had a small number of acquaintances in the legal profession but, like Bertie Ahern before him, he tended not to mix in legal circles and had a generally low opinion of the Bar. He also knew that many of the Fine Gael barristers had supported Richard Bruton in the 2010 heave. 'I don't know what to make of them', he told advisers about the judges when tensions were at their height.

With the government making it clear that the referendum would go ahead, positions hardened in the Four Courts. 'This Government came in with a clear agenda', one judge complained. 'This wasn't a level playing field.'

While it might have helped the judges' case if there had been 100 per cent payment of the voluntary contribution, since there hadn't been, there was little realistic chance that the referendum would be dropped. The judges found themselves at a loss as to how to play the situation.

> None of us had ever gone into a scenario like this. Judges' incomes had risen over the preceding decade . . . It was happy days. Nobody wanted to give up what had taken so long to bring about. But we needed to give something up, because the ultimate menace was about to descend on us in the form of Shatter, with his loathing of judges and barristers.

In the Four Courts, Shatter's proposals for an overhaul of the legal profession were meeting stiff resistance. For their part, ministers thought the judges overplayed the Shatter factor; after all, his plans had wide support in government, notably from the powerful Department of Public Expenditure and Reform under Howlin. The general sense was that judges were pampered and complacent. Ministers were also surprised by how bad the judges were at lobbying. At one meeting, a senior judge told a Cabinet member that many of his colleagues simply could not take a hit on their incomes because they had their children in private schools. 'It became clear that they had no real intention of changing anything', says one senior figure.

The government duly published the proposed wording of the referendum in June, and at around the same time Shatter emailed Murray to inform him that, if the vote was carried, pay rates for new judges would be cut by 31 per cent. Again, the judges went into panic mode. At a hastily convened joint meeting of High and Supreme Court members – around forty-five judges – in Room 15, a courtroom converted for meetings on the first floor of the Four Courts, there was fury around the table over the fact that they had to read about the amendment wording in the newspapers. Whelan and Howlin came in for criticism, but Shatter was the focus of the judges' ire. Many of them were convinced he had a vendetta against them. The upshot of the meeting was that a sub-committee would be set up to draft a submission for government. It would comprise two Supreme Court judges, Nial Fennelly and Adrian Hardiman, and two from the High Court, George Birmingham and Gerard Hogan.[3]

The anger was still palpable when the same group of judges convened for their summer conference in Farmleigh in the Phoenix Park a few days later. By then the sub-committee had drafted a statement setting out the judges' position, with the intention of issuing it to the media on behalf of the judiciary. It was a relatively innocuous text. It complained about a lack of contact from government and argued that the amendment as proposed would not protect judicial independence or comply with Ireland's international obligations. It said the judiciary was keen to engage in dialogue with the government on the issue. By now the judges were not objecting to a referendum, but they wanted the proposal to include an independent body that would set pay rates, thereby taking that power away from government, which they felt would threaten judicial independence.

This was a key point. In the public mind, judges' objections to the referendum came down to one thing: money. For some of them, that was undoubtedly true. In the Supreme and High Courts, many judges had taken big pay cuts to join the bench and watched their old colleagues in the Bar earning multiples of what they earned. But the judges are a diverse group; attitudes varied. Some were in severe financial trouble, having made bad property investments during the boom and lost big as a result. Government ministers wondered privately whether one or two senior judges might be close to being insolvent. Other judges were particularly put out by what they saw as the unfairness of the pension lump sum reform, which was designed to change behaviour in the private sector but as a largely unintended consequence hit judges in such a way that, for some at least, the vast bulk of their pension pots had been emptied at the stroke of a pen.

But there was also a deeper reason for many judges' anger: the government's moves hit them right where they have always felt most exposed. One of America's founding fathers, Alexander Hamilton, said that while in theory the three branches of government were equal, in practice the judiciary was the weakest, because it controlled 'neither sword nor purse'. It's a commonly heard axiom among Irish judges. For all their bravado and self-importance, many judges have an acute sense of their own vulnerability. They have always clung dearly to the two protections the Constitution provides: the guarantee of independence and the ban on government reducing their pay. In 2011 the State was involved in almost half the cases that went through the courts. The judges took their decisions – often decisions that cost the State huge amounts of money or caused headaches for ministers and their officials – knowing that, short of impeachment and long-term reconfiguration of the judiciary through the appointments system, there was no way for the government of the day to punish them. Now, as they saw it, one of those two protections was about to be removed. That was why they wanted an independent salary-setting body to stand between them and the government.

At Farmleigh, pressure on the leadership was intense. Those gathered were aware that a number of Circuit Court judges were threatening legal action. One judge told the meeting they couldn't go on 'like seal pups being clubbed to death on pack ice'. A senior judge warned darkly that 'all hell will break loose' unless a statement went out.

In a small drawing room on the ground floor at Farmleigh, the four members of the sub-committee were joined by Murray and Kearns. They went through the text line by line. But just as the meeting was about to sign off on it, a question was raised: in whose name was it to be issued? Did they need the unanimous agreement of all judges? That was impossible: already one High Court judge had indicated he wanted to dissent. Hardiman had been threatening to publish a newspaper article under his own name, but colleagues had talked him out of it. Now he was adamant that the statement should go out and suggested it be issued under the names of Murray and Kearns. Murray wasn't keen on that.

Murray told the group that Susan Denham also had reservations about a statement. That was significant, because, as they all knew, she was the front-runner to succeed Murray, who was due to retire as Chief Justice the following month. And as the succession date came closer she was steadily gaining in authority.

The judges of the Supreme Court and the High Court were split on whether to issue the statement or go through the traditional lines of communication. Eventually the Farmleigh meeting ended with no decision other than that the statement should be given to the Attorney General.

A few days later, when Shatter gave an interview in which he seemed to rule out any change in the proposed policy, the judges were again up in arms. In a flurry of emails, the call went up: the statement had to be released. An extremely tense meeting of its judges took place in the Supreme Court that morning – one of the most difficult anyone could remember. Murray and Denham were against issuing the statement. Hardiman was in favour, and had support from others. Several judges shouted at each other across the conference table. The problem was that the court literally did not know how to take a decision about what to do. As a collegiate court, did it have to be unanimous or by majority? The exchanges became so heated that one judge threatened to resign there and then, before being talked down.

Eventually the Supreme Court said no to putting the court's name on the statement but agreed instead to post it on the Courts Service website, a move to which Shatter strenuously objected. Brendan Ryan, the chief executive of the Courts Service, received a call telling him to take it down. This put him in an invidious position; the Courts Service receives its funding from the Department of Justice. The text was removed from the site but published almost immediately by newspaper websites.

The dispute over how to issue the statement was symptomatic of the situation in which the judges found themselves. They were being criticized almost daily by politicians and journalists, but they had no formal way of responding and were hopelessly split on whether it was appropriate for them to say anything at all. Ministers, who were privately receiving updates on the bitter split in the Four Cours, looked on with a mixture of bemusement and alarm.

As the end of Murray's term as Chief Justice approached in July 2011, the government's attention turned to possible replacements. There were three names considered: Susan Denham, Nial Fennelly and Nicholas Kearns, whose efficient running of the fast-growing High Court had won plaudits. Another judge lobbied hard for the job. He canvassed ministers, knocked on TDs' doors at night and went to Mayo to approach several people whom he had never met but who happened to be acquainted with the Taoiseach. One day, in the run-up to the government's decision, the wife of a senior minister was pushing a trolley along a supermarket aisle when a woman approached her, introduced herself as this judge's wife and said he would make a great Chief Justice. 'His modus operandi was so outrageous that it disqualified him', says a source. Another judge approached a government adviser and complained that his name had not been mentioned in an *Irish Times* report about contenders for the post.

Denham was the clear favourite. Since her appointment to the Supreme Court at the age of forty-six, she had shown herself a shrewd diplomat and a key player behind a series of major reforms, notably the establishment of the Courts Service. For that reason she had already been seriously considered for the role in 2000. The eldest child of the former editor of the *Irish Times*, Douglas Gageby, Denham came from a family with a tradition of both non-conformism and public service. Her speeches and judgments framed reform of the courts as being in the service of society, and stressed a view of the Constitution not as a narrow rulebook but as the expression of principles that guide the community. In her two decades on the bench she had built up a reputation for liberal judgments. She gave the sole dissenting judgment in an abortion case in 1993, when the court rejected an application from a Dublin clinic to overturn a previous order that prevented it from assisting pregnant women to travel abroad for abortions or giving information on overseas clinics.[4] She also dissented in *TD v. Minister for Education* in 2001, where a majority on the court held the High Court had been wrong to direct the State to act on a pledge to build and open a number of secure units for vulnerable children.

In July, the Cabinet formally signed off on Denham's appointment as Chief Justice. Within government, Denham was widely liked and respected. 'There was a general positive feeling about her', says one well-placed source. When she had joined the Supreme Court in 1992, she had been its first female member. Now, nineteen years on, she was to become the first woman (and the first Protestant) to lead the Irish judiciary.

One of the new Chief Justice's first acts was to announce she would not be taking the €38,000 salary increase that came with the job.

Susan Denham's preference was for engagement over confrontation. She believed the judiciary could better influence decisions by quiet, behind-the-scenes contacts than by public rows. She hinted at this in her first statement as Chief Justice, when she stressed the importance of the 'constitutional convention' that judges refrain from engaging in matters of public controversy or political debate:

> In a world of instant communication and commentary, the concept of silence may seem unusual, but it is an inherent part of our democratic tripartite system of government. Indeed, in these difficult times the need for an institution of independence and thoughtfulness, with an obligation to maintain the rule of law, is greater than ever.

Denham's problem was that morale was on the floor and by now there was a sizeable group of judges, which included Kearns,

Hardiman and Peter Kelly, who were convinced the soft approach wasn't working. They now had what one critic called the worst of both worlds: 'we got a huge amount of adverse publicity and we were going to end up with all the cuts that came anyway.' Some judges were critical of Denham for getting too close to Alan Shatter. It drove them crazy that she always referred to him as 'Alan'.

In late summer, ministers were told that Hardiman was threatening to resign if the referendum was passed. The government was well aware of the judges' strong views about the referendum and their belief that Shatter had it in for them. Yet while Shatter may have been to the fore in making the case for the referendum, the judges' focus on him obscured the fact that the proposal was fully supported across government. 'I don't think Alan was motivated by malice towards the judiciary', says a Cabinet colleague. 'He really was of the view that they should pay their fair share. But it wasn't his exclusive idea. DPER [Howlin's department] was the line department.'

Another Cabinet minister argues that the referendum was in the judges' own interest. 'I was concerned that if the same salary reductions that had impacted right across the public service didn't ultimately apply to the judiciary at a time when so many people were [being made unemployed], that public respect for the judiciary would collapse. It would damage the judiciary as an institution', the minister says. He adds that at no point did the judges suggest taking a voluntary pay cut – as distinct from making a contribution in lieu of the pension levy.

On 27 October 2011, a proposal to remove the bar on reducing judges' pay was approved by referendum with 80 per cent support. 'We were beaten into the ground', says one judge. 'Twenty per cent [against]', says another. 'We didn't know we had that many friends.'

By the time of the referendum, the government had passed four laws affecting judges' pay and pensions. By the end of 2012, the salary of an existing judge of the High or Supreme Court had fallen by 33 per cent; for new entrants the reduction was 45 per cent. In addition, a new rule was introduced whereby judges had to serve twenty years – previously it had been fifteen – before they could retire on a full pension. That meant that for a generation of lawyers in their early to mid-fifties, who would normally have been expected to apply for places on the bench, the window had closed.

It was abundantly clear that one of the judiciary's biggest problems was that it was struggling to speak with one voice. Instead, various factions had opened up separate lines of communication with the government. Three weeks after the referendum, a group of judges including Peter Kelly, Kearns, George Birmingham, John Edwards and others set up the Association of Judges of Ireland (AJI), which was to act as a collective mouthpiece. Kelly was elected chair, with an executive committee including representatives from each court. One of the intriguing side-effects of the dispute was a rapprochement between Hardiman and Kelly, who had had a cool relationship since Hardiman's unsparing judgment overturning Kelly in *TD v. Minister for Education* in 2001 but who now found common purpose in the battle against government.

In time, key Cabinet members came to see Kelly as the most impressive negotiator they had met from within the judiciary. 'The meetings between Howlin and Kelly went very well because they were both straight talkers, very clear, very direct', one source recalls. 'Peter understood Government, I think. He understood the need for equity and burden-sharing. What he wanted were other concessions. He was someone who had all the skills of a SIPTU organizer. "If you want that, then I want these four things, and this one I really want." There was a good dynamic.' When Kearns retired in 2015, the government chose Kelly to replace him as President of the High Court.

The referendum and the creation of the AJI took some of the heat out of the relationship between ministers and judges, but it took longer to restore trust. Issues continued to simmer in the background and then boil over. Both sides blamed the other, for example, for the delay in introducing a Judicial Council that would be responsible for judicial conduct, education and training. The idea had been in circulation for almost a decade without any sign of a bill being passed. The judges claimed the government was holding up the plan; Cabinet members believed the judges were resisting because they feared a proposal to have judges make public declarations of their financial interests. Whatever the reason, the absence of such a body came into sharp focus in 2011, when a complaint was made about a judge behaving inappropriately in a hotel. Some British tourists complained when the man, who was only later identified as a judge, emerged semi-naked from his hotel room one night and began to yell abuse and swear at them for making noise. He was also alleged to have angrily told them he had relatives in the old IRA who had fought the British. The incident was first reported to the hotel management and then to the courts. All the senior judges could do was to sit down with the judge over a cup of tea and suggest that he take a rest.

Behind the scenes, in early 2013, discussions were taking place within the judiciary on whether to sue the State. The two suggested grounds for action were, first, the new differential in pay between judges of the same courts and, second, the reductions in judicial pay generally after the referendum was passed. According to the constitutional amendment, judges' pay was subject to taxes, levies and charges that were imposed on 'persons generally' or 'persons belonging to a particular class'. In the view of some judges, the government had not shown how the scale of the cuts to judicial pay was directly referable to another group in the public service. Legal advice was sought from a senior counsel, and the view emerged that the judiciary should write to the government asking it to identify another group that had taken a hit of the same scale. But the letter was never sent. Instead, the executive committee of the AJI decided to negotiate with ministers, and ultimately they won a pledge to the effect that the difference in pay between old and new judges would be eroded with the passage of time. 'In the end nobody wanted to send the letter threatening legal action', says one. 'Even if it emerged that the Government had acted illegally, no judge was going to take legal action.'

In this fraught climate, every move by government was seen in the Four Courts as an aggressive act. The judges were particularly upset about the treatment of Judge Kevin O'Higgins when his term at the European Court of Justice in Luxembourg came to an end in early 2013. Since Ireland had joined the European Union it had been the practice for governments to renew an Irish judge's term at the court if the judge wished to stay on. But when O'Higgins's renewable six-year term came to an end in early 2013, he was informed by a government official that the government would not be re-nominating him. On top of that, although there were two vacancies on the High Court at the time, he was not offered a position there. Shatter was unapologetic. He said there was no 'usual convention' of offering a judge coming back from a posting abroad a position in the domestic courts, spelled out O'Higgins's existing pension arrangements and said that the replacement to the European courts as well as the High and Supreme Courts was 'a matter for the Government'.⁵ The same pattern held in the case of the two other Irish judges in European courts: neither was re-appointed. 'To me that was worse than the amendment', says one judge. Members of the Irish judiciary hold their position until retirement and cannot be removed by a minister, but the O'Higgins decision upset many judges. 'There was no reason for the non-reappointment other than that they could. It felt like another salvo in the war', says one judge.

Tensions between the Four Courts and Government Buildings hit the headlines again in April 2013, when the *Sunday Business Post* reported that Peter Kelly had told a gathering of business leaders that the government was demolishing judicial independence 'brick by brick'. Kelly reportedly criticized the government's handling of a range of issues, including judges' pay, the creation of new family courts and the appointment of new specialist insolvency judges drawn from the ranks of county registrars. All had been done without con-sultation, he said. Perhaps most damagingly, Kelly suggested that communication between the two sides had completely broken down.

Kelly's remarks were made at a private gathering of business people; and they remained as private as could be expected of anything said in front of hundreds of people in a city as small as Dublin. The story caused a furore. Shatter swiftly issued a response, saying it could do 'great damage' to the State if the message was given that there was political interference in court proceedings. It was 'a matter of some seriousness', he said, to have a question mark hanging over judicial independence.

As politicians from across the divide weighed in and the media began referring to a constitutional crisis, the AJI rushed out a state-ment of support for its president, confirming the essence of the story. It said that Kelly had pointed out that for almost ninety years of the

State's existence there had been no need for an association of judges, given the 'mutual respect' demonstrated by the executive and judicial branches. 'All structures, both formal and informal, which existed for communication between these two branches of government have ceased.' That evening, at an event at the Law Reform Commission, Hardiman gave his full support to Kelly, saying he spoke for the judges: 'The notion that judicial appointments should continue to be entirely political while there is a zero protection, from a financial point of view, for the judges, against the executive, is one not consistent with the maintenance of an independent judiciary as it's understood in the common law world.'

Behind the scenes, frantic efforts were being made to calm the situation. As senior figures in government saw it, there had been no breakdown in communications. All the senior judges had mobile numbers for Shatter and Whelan. Only a few weeks previously, Shatter had met Denham for lunch at the Cliff House restaurant on St Stephen's Green, and a month earlier letters had been exchanged with Whelan's office. Several judges knew about the contacts, but Kelly, it appeared, did not. When he found out, he felt undermined. Key AJI figures felt he should have been told. It was extremely tense; at different times that week, ministers worried that they could have to deal with one and maybe even two resignations from the highest levels of the judiciary.

Views among senior judges were divided. Some believed Denham should have kept the wider judiciary informed of every contact she had with Shatter since the pay referendum. 'On the other hand,' said another, 'if you tell 200 people, is it likely not to be in the paper the next week? If you're involved in difficult discussions, you certainly don't want them, while they're being conducted, to be in the public domain, because that can affect the discussions.'

When even President Michael D. Higgins was being asked for his view on the stand-off, both sides realized the fallout from Kelly's speech was getting out of hand. In Merrion Street and the Department of Justice, they were adamant that it was for the judges to fix the problem. A clear message was sent to the Four Courts: either you go public with our contacts or we will.

Denham was due to give a speech at Griffith College. As she worked on the script that afternoon, the atmosphere was fraught. Kelly and Denham spoke to each other and to senior figures in government. The Taoiseach was kept informed. Denham indicated she would include some paragraphs in her speech aimed at calming things down. The choreography was agreed. That evening, reporters and television cameras turned out in big numbers at Griffith College to hear Denham, visibly nervous, say that she had had 'many constructive meetings with the Minister for Justice' on plans for a new Court of Appeal as well as contact with the Taoiseach and the Attorney. But a new structure for dialogue was clearly needed, she said, so both sides had agreed to form what would be known as a Working Group for Renewal.

As Denham spoke, Kelly was in Government Buildings, where he was drafting a short statement on behalf of the AJI after a meeting with Whelan. 'The meeting was cordial and fruitful', the statement said. 'As a result, the AJI is satisfied that its concerns are fully understood and that progress will be made by mutual co-operation in resolving issues.' It concluded: 'The AJI is grateful to the Attorney General for her assistance in this regard.'

The public messages, timed to be out before the six o'clock news, immediately defused the situation. Denham got the credit. To her supporters, she had shown mettle when she had to. To her critics, she had had to backtrack. That weekend, an influential AJI figure was at a concert in Dublin when a woman leaned over and said to him: 'There you are. It took a woman to sort out that mess during the week.' (The fact that Denham was the only woman ministers encountered at meetings with the judiciary, and that ministers felt she was isolated as the only woman on the Supreme Court, was one of the reasons the government made a point of preferring women for future vacancies. Between 2013 and 2016, the number of women on the Supreme Court jumped from one to four.*)

---

*Catherine McGuinness and Fidelma Macken, who also served on the Supreme Court, had retired in 2006 and 2012 respectively. It went unnoticed at the time, but one day during the legal year 2005–6 the court reached a milestone when a

Some internal voices, bruised and sore after the disputes with government, continued to argue that the senior judiciary, led by Denham, should have taken a more publicly confrontational position. But to others it would have been an unwinnable battle. 'I think she showed extraordinarily good judgment not to do that', says one Cabinet member. In government circles, her stock rose, enabling her to secure support and ultimately approval for the new Court of Appeal – an intermediate court that would sit between the High and the Supreme Courts – in 2014.

The public stand-off that followed Kelly's speech was to be the last major confrontation in the saga. A year later, Shatter resigned and was replaced by Frances Fitzgerald, whose conciliatory, consensual style – similar to that of Denham herself – brought a radical shift in tone to the relationship with the judges. It helped that the worst of the economic crisis appeared by then to have passed. Conversations between the two sides were no longer dominated by discussion about cuts to the courts' budget.

All through those tense years, the Supreme Court itself had been busier than ever, struggling with a backlog of hundreds of cases that made the argument for a Court of Appeal more pressing than ever. Even government ministers admired how the superior courts never seemed to let the behind-the-scenes tensions intrude on their work – 'one of the great things about our judiciary', says one minister who took a tough public stance against the judges on pay and pensions. The same compartmentalization could be seen at case conferences, where even on difficult cases where opinion was divided the atmosphere, in contrast to the rows over the relationship with government, rarely grew tense.

The make-up of the court was changing. By mid-2013, as relations with government were on the mend, the court consisted of Denham, Murray, Hardiman, Fennelly, O'Donnell, Liam McKechnie, Frank Clarke and John Mac Menamin.

---

three-judge court comprising Denham, McGuinness and Macken became the first all-female Supreme Court to hear a case.

O'Donnell, the youngest member of the court, had been a star constitutional lawyer at the Bar when he was appointed directly to the Supreme Court in 2010; his record as a senior counsel showed that there was scarcely a high-profile constitutional case involving the State where he was not involved. Born in Belfast and educated at UCD, O'Donnell was a son of Turlough O'Donnell, a member of the Northern Ireland High Court and the Court of Appeal between 1971 and 1990. He was already emerging as one of the most influential figures on the court.

McKechnie, who also joined the court in 2010, came from a modest background in Cork and had been a High Court judge for a decade before his elevation to the Supreme Court. One of his most prominent cases in the High Court was that of Lydia Foy, a transsexual woman. McKechnie ruled that the Civil Registration Act 2004, which did not permit the issuing of a new birth certificate to Foy, was incompatible with the European Convention on Human Rights.

The careers of the two newest appointees to the court – Frank Clarke and John Mac Menamin – had followed strikingly similar trajectories since they met in UCD in the early 1970s. Like O'Donnell and McKechnie, Clarke did not come from the Dublin middle-class private-school background that was typical of most judges. Born in Walkinstown and educated at Drimnagh Castle CBS, Clarke was the first member of his family to go to university. In college, where he studied maths and economics, he joined Fine Gael, eventually becoming an occasional speech-writer for Garret FitzGerald and an election agent for the Fine Gael TD George Birmingham in the 1980s. Having himself run unsuccessfully for the Seanad in the 1980s, Clarke turned his focus to the law library and built a big practice in commercial and constitutional law. As a High Court judge since 2004, Clarke – a horse-racing fanatic and a Leinster rugby season-ticket holder – was known for his skilful handling of complex commercial cases and dealt with some of the biggest cases linked to the economic collapse.

Like Clarke, Mac Menamin went to UCD, got involved in the debating society the L&H and worked for Fine Gael politicians before being called to the Bar in the early 1970s. The two men were then appointed to the High Court by a Fianna Fáil–PD coalition on the same day in 2004, and to the Supreme Court, again on the same day, by the government in March 2012. Mac Menamin is a cousin of Michael McDowell. As a barrister, Mac Menamin had a wide practice that included commercial law, insurance and defamation. He represented the *Sunday Independent* in the Proinsias De Rossa libel trial, was legal adviser to the Medical Council and appeared for a number of clients before the Flood/Mahon Tribunal. Mac Menamin wrote speeches for a number of senior Fine Gael figures, including Garret FitzGerald, and many believed that, had Michael Noonan become Taoiseach after leading Fine Gael into the 2002 general election, Mac Menamin would have been a front-runner for the post of Attorney General.

The Denham Supreme Court is a high-powered court, not without its internal intellectual tensions. Its lines of thought are only beginning to become clear, but in a number of areas the court has begun to refine its thinking on key issues. In the Pringle case in 2012, for example, it took a more nuanced view of sovereignty than it had in *Crotty* in 1987, in the process narrowing the scope of that influential judgment.[6]

In keeping with a trend set by other courts, it jealously guarded its judicial prerogative, using its power to strike down laws each year since 2011, but at the same time showed itself reluctant to trample on what it saw as executive or legislative terrain by itself ushering in major social change. When the terminally ill multiple sclerosis sufferer Marie Fleming challenged the blanket ban on assisted suicide in 2013, the court rejected her claim, finding that the right to life did not mean there was a right to die. But the court also made it clear that the Oireachtas was free to allow a form of assisted dying if it wished, noting that nothing in its judgment 'should be taken as necessarily implying it would not be open to the State, in the event the Oireachtas were satisfied that measures with appropriate safeguards could be introduced, to deal with a case such as that of Ms Fleming'.

The court was more than willing to admonish government inaction or inertia. It did so on asylum law and procedures, which it saw as overly complex and cumbersome. Particularly severe was its criticism of the legislature for failing to keep up with scientific advances in assisted human reproduction. In 2014, the court ruled by a 6-1 majority, with Clarke dissenting, that the genetic mother of twins born to a surrogate mother was not entitled to be registered as their legal mother on their birth certificates.[7] Each of the judgments showed deep discomfort at the courts having been put in this situation, facing the ethical and moral fallout from what the State had tacitly allowed to develop but not bothered to regulate. In judgments that echoed Niall McCarthy's stinging criticism of the legislature's inaction in the X case over two decades earlier, the judges described a 'legal half-world' that 'cries out for legislation', a world where couples struggling with 'the pain of infertility' face the prospect of having to become a 'vociferous pressure group' to agitate for a proper legal regime.[8]

The case also revealed internal differences on the court's role. In the one dissenting judgment out of seven, Clarke remarked that 'there may be circumstances where the courts are required to develop common law principles to meet new scientific circumstances'. Hardiman, echoing his views in cases such as *Sinnott v. Minister for Education* more than a decade earlier, distanced himself from Clarke's 'expansive attitude to the courts' power' and warned that if the court did take up the invitation to 'overrule the established understanding of "mother"', it would 'dangerously approach illegitimacy'.

A fault-line also arose over criminal law, in particular the balance to be struck between the rights of the accused and the need to enable the authorities to investigate and prosecute crime. In a series of cases, the court made strong statements on civil liberties, standing on the side of the accused and adopting a strict line on garda lapses. In 2011, for example, the court ruled that a key section on search warrants in the Offences Against the State Act was unconstitutional, a ruling that infuriated gardaí.[9] Three years later, the court quashed a rape conviction on the ground that suspects who requested a lawyer could not be questioned by gardaí until they got that advice. The decision had very significant implications for garda investigations.[10]

In a landmark case in 2015, the court revisited a question that had exercised it for decades: when, if ever, can evidence that was obtained by the authorities in breach of a constitutional right be used in court? By a narrow majority – four to three – the court came up with a new test: evidence taken in 'deliberate and conscious' violation of a constitutional right should be excluded except in exceptional circumstances.[11] Up until then, in line with a judgment of the court in 1990, all evidence obtained in breach of a constitutional right was excluded, whether or not the breach was deliberate or due to a mistake.

In one of the three dissenting judgments, Adrian Hardiman said he was 'gravely apprehensive' about the majority decision. Taking up one of the themes of his fifteen years on the court, he accused his colleagues of over-ruling 'one of the monuments of Irish constitutional jurisprudence' and giving gardaí 'effective immunity from judicial oversight'. It was to be one of the last major judgments he wrote.

Afterword

First-time visitors to the Four Courts are struck by the grandeur and the noise. Barristers weighed down by lurching stacks of box-files hurry through the labyrinthine network of corridors and passageways on their way to court. Doors slam and shoe leather screeches on the tiles. In the Round Hall, the throbbing heart of the building, solicitors and their clients huddle together for last-minute confabs while anxious-looking witnesses walk past. For much of the twentieth century, bewigged lawyers spilling out of court would light up in the Round Hall, sending a fug of smoke rising towards the high ceiling beneath the famous dome. Now the cigarettes have disappeared, and the horsehair wigs are nearly gone too.

All of human life has passed through the doors of the High Courts that open onto the Round Hall. Lines of barristers in black gowns and white collars squeeze into long benches, packed so tight they look like penguins huddling against the wind. In front of them, with their backs to the bench, are the solicitors. To their side are the court reporters, hunched over their notebooks and laptops and straining to hear. Amid all of this are those for whom this is the last place they want to be: the businessman, the victim of a serious car crash, the distraught couple trying to stop their home being repossessed. Witnesses break down and cry. Onlookers occasionally shout from the public gallery.

The Supreme Court is different. Although just a few metres north of the bustling Round Hall, the court of final appeal is quiet and austere. There are no witnesses, less human drama, fewer comings-and-goings. And it's small – so small that just a few metres separate the lawyers from the row of up to seven judges lined up on brown-leather swivel chairs on their walnut dais. The room reeks of history. Its décor may have changed over the decades, but otherwise it has altered little since Hugh Kennedy or Cearbhall Ó Dálaigh presided.

It doesn't take much imagination to picture a young, hopeful David Norris in the public gallery, or a determined May McGee doing her knitting as she waits for the judges to announce their decision.

The ordinary business of the court – long, involved exchanges on the finer points of law – can feel rarefied, at a remove from the world outside. Yet amid the rigid conventions and high formality, significant moments in the life of the court have a way of announcing themselves as such.

The 7th of March 2016 was one of those days. It was still dark that morning when Chief Justice Susan Denham got a call to tell her that Adrian Hardiman was dead.

The Supreme Court as a physical space may be largely unchanged in its ninety-two-year history, but the institution itself is a fluid, constantly evolving organism. Judges come and judges go, currents of thinking drift in and out of favour and judicial approaches have a way of reflecting changes taking place in the world outside. Yet the timing of Adrian Hardiman's death felt like the end of an era. Relations with the government were back on an even keel and the bitter rows of recent years were fading memories.* In early 2016 the court was on the cusp of big changes. Throughout its history, and unlike many equivalent courts around the world, the Supreme Court had been unable to select its cases. So it heard everything. One day it

---

* It was a measure of how relationships were returning to normal after the bitter pay disputes that communications between the Chief Justice and the government were growing increasingly mundane. In January 2015, Denham wrote to Simon Harris, the Minister of State with responsibility for the Office of Public Works, to complain about the lack of heating in the Supreme Court. Having taken daily temperature readings for twenty-five days, she sent the results to Harris and warned that she would have to cancel court sittings unless adequate heating could be provided. Heating problems in the Supreme Court were as old as the State itself. In 1933, the then Chief Justice Hugh Kennedy complained to the Supreme Court registrar about the 'arctic conditions imposed by the Board of Works on the Supreme Court judiciary', adding: 'We shall eventually have to ask to be supplied with Lap-landers' suits and a supply of whale oil for internal consumption to keep the fires burning and our impoverished blood brought to a proper warmth' (letter from Hugh Kennedy to James O'Brien, 18 October 1933, NAI 2011/21/25).

might be asked to decide at what point life began and the next to hear an irate pensioner complaining that her neighbour's extension was blocking her light. A dramatic increase in the volume of cases going through the High Court had created a bottleneck and left the Supreme Court with a four-year waiting list. In order to help ease the pressure, the government had increased the membership of the court to ten and established a Court of Appeal, a proposal that had been endorsed by voters in a referendum in October 2013. The new court, occupying a position just below the Supreme Court, had begun to hear more routine appeals and to free up the Supreme Court to focus on the major cases.

For the first time the Supreme Court was positioned to become an institution more akin to a constitutional court, with the power to pick and choose its cases, to spend more time deliberating on them and, potentially, to become an even more influential force in Irish public life. Significant judicial turnover was also changing the profile of the court. Apart from Denham, at the time of his death Hardiman was the only link to the court of the previous decade. The Chief Justice herself was within a year of retirement after almost a quarter of a century on the court.

By the early twenty-first century, some of the state's major institutions – the Catholic Church, the banks, the political class – stood discredited in the eyes of the public. The judiciary had been badly damaged by the disputes over pay and pensions, but surveys suggested the cost to its public reputation was relatively limited. When the Council of Europe published an audit of its member states' parliamentary, judicial and prosecution systems in 2014, it found Ireland's judiciary to be one of the most trusted institutions in the country.

With the centenary of the court's establishment on the horizon, it was a measure of its success as an institution that its greatest achievement was taken for granted: that a citizen could stand before the court in the expectation that the judges would decide his or her case independent of the other arms of government – or, as their constitutional declaration committed them to doing, 'without fear or favour, affection or ill-will towards any man'.

At the same time, in many respects, access to justice remained an ideal far from being fulfilled. The judges presided at the apex of a creaking, antiquated courts system where the cost of taking legal action was prohibitively high for all but the country's wealthiest citizens. The courts system lacked transparency and was designed around the interests of those who worked in it rather than those who needed to use it.

In addition, the senior judiciary still had a long way to go to reflect the diversity of the country its members served. The process by which the judges were selected – an opaque and mysterious arrangement fully understood only by the few who controlled it – did neither politicians nor judges any favours and fell far short of what an advanced democracy should expect.

By 9am on 7 March Adrian Hardiman's death was the lead item on the radio news. He was just sixty-four when he died, but he was the second most senior member of the Supreme Court. He had been one of the country's most prominent lawyers for over three decades, and though his influence had declined over time, he was one of the court's biggest personalities.

His fellow judges were in shock when they arrived at the Four Courts. Some were in tears. The disagreements on law between him and his colleagues were in their judgments for everyone to see, but that was business. Most of the judges had been friends long before they joined the bench.

When they met in the conference room that morning, the judges' conversations were hushed. Susan Denham took her place at the head of the table and they sat down. Around her were Donal O'Donnell, Liam McKechnie, Frank Clarke, John Mac Menamin, Mary Laffoy, Elizabeth Dunne, Peter Charleton and Iseult O'Malley. They were joined by the two ex officio members: Seán Ryan, the President of the Court of Appeal, and Peter Kelly, President of the High Court.

An official asked whether the tricolour on the Four Courts should be lowered to half-mast. Nobody was sure what the protocol was; it had been so long since a sitting Supreme Court judge had died.

It was decided to mark the occasion with a public sitting. So the judges around the conference table sketched out a brief appreciation for their late colleague. While it described Hardiman as 'a colossus', it included a simple human tribute: 'It is as a colleague and a friend that the members of the court will miss him. His eloquence in conference, his depth of knowledge, his humour but most of all his friendship will be sorely missed by each member of this court.'

As 2pm approached, barristers piled in from across the building, filling the small courtroom to capacity and leaving a trail of people snaking out the door. Photographers and television cameramen – allowed in as a one-off – set up at the back of the court.

In the courtroom, the judges took their positions in order of seniority: Denham in the middle, Ryan and Kelly to her left and right and the remaining judges to either side. The chair immediately to Denham's right, the one Hardiman would normally take, was left empty in his honour.

The sitting lasted less than two minutes. Tribute delivered, Denham and her colleagues rose and filed out silently. Once they had left, the doors at the back of the court swung open and the room emptied as quickly as it had filled. The crowd fanned out into the bustle and hum of another day in the Four Courts.

Appendix: Judges of the Supreme Court

Chief Justices

Hugh Kennedy (1924–1936)
Timothy Sullivan (1936–1946)
Conor Maguire (1946–1961)
Cearbhall Ó Dálaigh (1961–1972)
William FitzGerald (1973–1974)
Thomas O'Higgins (1974–1985)
Thomas Finlay (1985–1994)
Liam Hamilton (1994–2000)
Ronan Keane (2000–2004)
John Murray (2004–2011)
Susan Denham (2011–present)

Ordinary judges of the Supreme Court

Charles O'Connor (1924–1925)
Gerald Fitzgibbon (1924–1938)
James Murnaghan (1925–1953)
James Creed Meredith (1936–1942)
James Geoghegan (1936–1950)
William Johnston (1939–1940)
John O'Byrne (1940–1954)
William Black (1942–1951)
Cecil Lavery (1950–1966)
Theodore Conyngham Kingsmill Moore (1951–1966)
Cearbhall Ó Dálaigh (appt. 1953; appt. Chief Justice December 1961)
Martin Maguire (1954–1961)
Kevin Haugh (1961–1969)
Brian Walsh (1961–1990)
Andreas O'Keeffe (appt. 1965; appt. President of the High Court October 1966)
Frederick Budd (1966–1975)

William FitzGerald (appt. 1966; appt. Chief Justice January 1973)
Richard McLoughlin (1969–1972)
Séamus Henchy (1972–1988)
Frank Griffin (1973–1991)
John Kenny (1975–1982)
Weldon Parke (1976–1981)
Anthony Hederman (1981–1993)
Niall McCarthy (1982–1992)
Hugh O'Flaherty (1990–1999)
Séamus Egan (1991–1995)
Susan Denham (appt. 1992; appt. Chief Justice July 2011)
John Blayney (1992–1997)
Donal Barrington (1996–2000)
Ronan Keane (appt. 1996; appt. Chief Justice January 2000)
Frank Murphy (1996–2002)
Kevin Lynch (1996–1999)
Henry Barron (1997–2000)
John Murray (appt. 1999–2015; appt. Chief Justice July 2004)
Nial Fennelly (2000–2014)
Hugh Geoghegan (2000–2010)
Adrian Hardiman (2000–2016)
Catherine McGuinness (2000–2006)
Brian McCracken (2002–2006)
Fidelma Macken (2005–2012)
Joseph Finnegan (2006–2012)
Donal O'Donnell (2010–present)
Liam McKechnie (2010–present)
Frank Clarke (2012–present)
John Mac Menamin (2012–present)
Mary Laffoy (2013–present)
Elizabeth Dunne (2013–present)
Peter Charleton (2014–present)
Iseult O'Malley (2015–present)

Presidents of the High Court
(ex-officio members of the Supreme Court)

Timothy Sullivan (appt. 1924; appt. Chief Justice December 1936)
Conor Maguire (appt. 1936; appt. Chief Justice April 1946)
George Gavan Duffy (1946–1951)

Cahir Davitt (1951–1966)

Andreas O'Keeffe (appt. 1966; appt. to European Court of Justice December 1974)

Thomas Finlay (appt. 1974; appt. Chief Justice January 1985)

Liam Hamilton (appt. 1985; appt. Chief Justice July 1994)

Harry Whelehan (appt. 15 November 1994; resigned 17 November 1994)

Declan Costello (1995–1998)

Frederick Morris (1998–2001)

Joseph Finnegan (appt. 2001; appt. Supreme Court December 2006)

Richard Johnson (December 2006–October 2009)

Nicholas Kearns (2009–2015)

Peter Kelly (2015–present)

Presidents of the Court of Appeal
(ex-officio members of the Supreme Court)

Seán Ryan (2014–present)

Bibliography

Archives

National Archives of Ireland (NAI), Dublin

Chief Justice
Dept of An Taoiseach
Dept of Justice

University College Dublin Archives (UCD)

Papers of Hugh Kennedy (1879–1936), IE UCDA P4
Papers of Cearbhall Ó Dálaigh (1911–1978), IE UCDA P51
Papers of Declan Costello (1926–2011), IE UCDA P237
Papers of Richie Ryan (1929–), IE UCDA P272

Manuscript Division, Library of Congress, Washington DC

William J. Brennan Papers, Box II: 62/103

Newspapers

Freeman's Journal
Irish Independent
Irish Mirror
Irish Press
Irish Times
Nenagh Guardian
New York World
Sunday Business Post

Sunday Independent
Sunday Times
Sunday Tribune

Periodicals

Dublin University Law Journal
Irish Law Times and Solicitors' Journal
Judicial Studies Institute Journal
Magill
Northern Ireland Legal Quarterly
Studies
The Bar Review
The Dublin Review
The Dublin Review of Books
The Irish Jurist

Radio/Television

Altered State, RTÉ television series, Autumn 2010
Primetime, RTÉ television, 1 June 2006
The Law Makers, RTÉ radio series, Autumn 2012, presented by Peter Ward
    SC. Interviews with Donal Barrington, Ronan Keane, Catherine
    McGuinness, Bryan McMahon, Mary Robinson and John Rogers
What If, RTÉ Radio 1, 2006–8

Private recordings

Sturgess, Garry, three interviews with Brian Walsh, recorded in Dublin
    and Strasbourg, 1986
Sturgess, Garry, interview with Máirín de Búrca, recorded in Dublin, 1986

Reports

Judicial Appointments Review Committee, 'Preliminary Submission to the Department of Justice and Equality's Public Consultation on the Judicial Appointments Process' (Dublin, 2014)

Law Enforcement Commission, 'Report to the Minister for Justice of Ireland and the Secretary of State for Northern Ireland' (Dublin, 1974)

Law Reform Commission, 'Report on Jury Service' (Dublin, 2013)

Report of the Chief Justice into the Circumstances Leading to the Early Release from Prison of Philip Sheedy (Dublin, April 1999)

Books/Articles/Chapters/Papers

Ahern, Bertie, *The Autobiography* (London, 2009)

Bacik, Ivana, *Kicking and Screaming: Dragging Ireland into the 21st Century* (Dublin, 2004)

Barrett, Gavin, 'Building a Swiss Chalet in an Irish Legal Landscape? Referendums on European Union Treaties in Ireland & the Impact of Supreme Court Jurisprudence', *European Constitutional Law Review*, vol. 5, no. 1 (2009), pp. 32–70

Barrett, Gavin, *A Road Less Travelled: Reflections on the Supreme Court Rulings in Crotty, Coughlan and McKenna (No.2)* (Dublin, 2011)

Barrett, Max, *The Law Lords: An Account of the Workings of Britain's Highest Judicial Body and the Men Who Preside over It* (London, 2001)

Barrington, Donal, 'The Constitution in the Courts', *Administration*, vol. 35 (1987), pp. 110–27

Barrington, Donal, 'The North and the Constitution', in Brian Farrell (ed.), *De Valera's Constitution and Ours* (Dublin, 1988)

Bartholomew, Paul C., *The Irish Judiciary* (Dublin, 1971)

Beth, Loren P., *The Development of Judicial Review in Ireland, 1937–66* (Dublin, 1967)

Beytagh, Francis X., *Constitutionalism in Contemporary Ireland: An American Perspective* (Dublin, 1997)

Binchy, William, 'Marital Privacy and Family Law: A Reply to Mr. O'Reilly', *Studies*, vol. 66, no. 264 (1977), pp. 330–35

Bodkin, M. McDonnell, *Recollections of an Irish Judge* (London, 1914)

Brennan, William J., jnr, 'The Ninth Amendment and Fundamental Rights', in James O'Reilly (ed.), *Human Rights and Constitutional Law: Essays in Honour of Brian Walsh* (Dublin, 1992)

Brown, Terence, *Ireland: A Social and Cultural History, 1922–2002* (London, 2004)

Byrne, Raymond, and McCutcheon, Paul, *The Irish Legal System* (Dublin, 2001)

Carolan, Eoin and Doyle, Oran, *The Irish Constitution: Governance and Values* (Dublin, 2008)

Carroll MacNeill, Jennifer, *The Politics of Judicial Selection in Ireland* (Dublin, 2016)

Casey, J. P., 'The Development of Constitutional Law under Chief Justice Ó Dálaigh', *Dublin University Law Journal*, vol. 3 (1978), pp. 3–20

Casey, J. P., *The Office of the Attorney General in Ireland* (Dublin, 1980)

Casey, J. P., 'The Development of Constitutional Law under Chief Justice O'Higgins', *The Irish Jurist*, vol. 21 (1986), pp. 7–34

Casey, J. P., '*Crotty v An Taoiseach*: A Comparative Perspective', in James O'Reilly (ed.), *Human Rights and Constitutional Law: Essays in Honour of Brian Walsh* (Dublin, 1992)

Casey, J. P., *Constitutional Law in Ireland* (Dublin, 2000)

Chubb, Basil, *The Constitution and Constitutional Change in Ireland* (Dublin, 1978)

Clarke, Desmond, 'The Role of Natural Law in Irish Constitutional Law', *The Irish Jurist*, vol. 17 (1982), pp. 187–220

Clarke, Desmond, 'Unenumerated Rights in Constitutional Law', *Dublin University Law Journal*, vol. 34 (2011), pp. 101–26

Clarke, Frank, 'Mr Justice Declan Costello: A View from the Bar', *The Bar Review,* vol. 3, no. 4 (1998), pp. 170–71

Clarke, Frank, 'The Constitution: Nationality, Identity and Language' (Paper delivered at the Burren Law School, 2013)

Clarke, Frank, 'Union and Common Law: Harmony or Tension', in Kieran Bradley, Noel Travers and Anthony Whelan (eds.), *Of Courts and Constitutions: Liber Amicorum in Honour of Nial Fennelly* (Dublin, 2014)

Coffey, Donal K., 'The Judiciary of the Irish Free State', *Dublin University Law Journal*, vol. 33 (2011), pp. 61–74

Collins, Stephen, *The Power Game* (Dublin, 2001)

Connelly, Alpha, 'Ireland and the Political Offence: Exception to Extradition', *Journal of Law and Society*, vol. 12, no. 2 (1985), pp. 153–82

Connolly, Linda, *The Irish Women's Movement: From Revolution to Devolution* (Dublin, 2003)

Conway, Kieran, 'Views from the National Archives on Judicial Appointments', *Irish Law Times* (April 1996), pp. 95–7

Coogan, Tim Pat, *De Valera: Long Fellow, Long Shadow* (London, 1993)

Costello, Declan, 'The Natural Law and the Irish Constitution', *Studies*, vol. 45, no. 180 (1956), pp. 403–14

Costello, Kevin, *The Law of Habeas Corpus in Ireland* (Dublin, 2006)

Cox, Neville, 'Judicial Activism, Constitutional Interpretation and the Problem of Abortion: Roe v Wade and X v AG', in Eoin O'Dell (ed.), *Leading Cases of the Twentieth Century* (Dublin, 2000)

Creed Meredith, James, *The Rainbow in the Valley* (Dublin, 1939)

Cronin, Anthony, *No Laughing Matter: The Life and Times of Flann O'Brien* (London, 1989)

Cross, Kevin, 'Fiat Justitia', in *Dublin Review of Books* (April 2014): http://www.drb.ie/essays/fiat-justitia

Crotty, Raymond, *A Radical's Response* (Dublin, 1988)

Curran, C. P., 'Figures in the Hall', in Caroline Costello (ed.), *The Four Courts: 200 Years* (Dublin, 1996)

Curtin, Deirdre, and O'Keefe, David (eds.), *Constitutional Adjudication in European Community and National Law: Essays for the Hon. Mr. Justice T. F. O'Higgins* (Dublin, 1992)

Daly, Paul, '"Political Questions" and Judicial Review in Ireland', *Judicial Studies Institute Journal*, vol. 8, no. 2 (2008), pp. 116–46

Davis, Fergal F., *The History and Development of the Special Criminal Court, 1922–2005* (Dublin, 2007)

De Bhaldraithe Marsh, Clíona, 'Introductory address, on the occasion of the conferring of the Degree of Doctor of Laws *honoris causa* by the National University of Ireland on Donal Barrington', Royal Hospital Kilmainham, Dublin, 2 December 2009

Delany, Hilary, and Hogan, Gerard, 'Anglo Irish Extradition Viewed from an Irish Perspective', *Public Law*, vol. 93 (Spring 1993), pp. 93–120

Denham, Susan, 'The Diamond in a Democracy', keynote address to the annual conference of the Australian Institute of Judicial Administration, Darwin, Northern Territory, Australia, July 2000

Denham, Susan, 'Some Thoughts on the Constitution of Ireland at 75', delivered at the conference 'The Irish Constitution: Past, Present and Future', organized by UCD School of Law, Royal Irish Academy, Dublin, 28 June 2012: http://cdn.thejournal.ie/media/2012/06/20120629cj-speech.pdf

Denham, Susan, Chief Justice's Address to Griffith College Law Society, Griffith College Dublin, 17 April 2013

Dickson, Brice (ed.), *Judicial Activism in Common Law Supreme Courts* (Oxford, 2007)

Doolan, Brian, *Constitutional Law and Constitutional Rights in Ireland* (Dublin, 1994)

Doyle, Oran, *Constitutional Equality Law* (Dublin, 2004)

Doyle, Oran, 'Conventional Constitutional Law', *Dublin University Law Journal*, vol. 38, no. 2 (2015), pp. 311–30

Duignan, Séan, *One Spin on the Merry-Go-Round* (Dublin, 1995)

Earner-Byrne, Lindsey, *Mother and Child: Maternity and Child Welfare in Dublin, 1922–60* (Manchester, 2007)

Elgie, Robert, McAuley, Adam, and O'Malley, Eoin, 'The (Surprising) Non-Partisanship of the Irish Supreme Court', *Irish Political Studies*, vol. 31 (2016, forthcoming)

Ellmann, Richard, *James Joyce* (Oxford, 1982)

Fanning, Bryan, *The Quest for Modern Ireland: The Battle of Ideas 1912–1986* (Dublin, 2008)

Fanning, Ronan, *Independent Ireland* (Dublin, 1983)

Fanning, Rossa, 'Hard Case, Bad Law? The Supreme Court decision in *A v The Governor of Arbour Hill Prison*', *The Irish Jurist*, vol. 40 (2005), pp. 188–219

Farrell, Brian, 'The First Dáil and its Constitutional Documents', in Brian Farrell (ed.), *The Creation of the Dáil* (Dublin, 1994)

Farrell, Michael, *Sheltering the Fugitive? The Extradition of Irish Political Offenders* (Dublin, 1985)

Farry, Michael, *Education and the Constitution* (Dublin, 1996)

Fennelly, Nial, 'The Dangerous Idea of Europe? Van Gend en Loos (1963)', in Eoin O'Dell (ed.), *Leading Cases of the Twentieth Century* (Dublin, 2000)

Ferguson, K. (ed.), *King's Inns Barristers, 1868–2004* (Dublin, 2005)

Ferriter, Diarmaid, *The Transformation of Ireland 1900–2000* (London, 2004)

Ferriter, Diarmaid, *Occasions of Sin: Sex and Society in Modern Ireland* (London, 2009)

Ferriter, Diarmaid, *Ambiguous Republic: Ireland in the 1970s* (London, 2012)

Finlay, Fergus, *Snakes and Ladders* (Dublin, 1998)

Finlay, Thomas A., 'Mr Justice Brian Walsh', in James O'Reilly (ed.), *Human Rights and Constitutional Law: Essays in Honour of Brian Walsh* (Dublin, 1992)

Finn, Tomás, *Tuairim, Intellectual Debate and Policy Formation: Rethinking Ireland, 1954–1975* (Manchester, 2012)

FitzGerald, Garret, *All in a Life: An Autobiography* (Dublin, 1991)

Forde, Michael, *Extradition Law in Ireland* (Dublin, 1995)

Forde, Michael, *Constitutional Law* (Dublin, 2004)

Forester, Margery, *Michael Collins* (Dublin, 1989)

Foster, Roy, *Vivid Faces: The Revolutionary Generation in Ireland 1890–1923* (London, 2014)

Gallagher, Michael, 'The Constitution and the Judiciary', in John Coakley and Michael Gallagher (eds.), *Politics in the Republic of Ireland* (London, 2005)

Garvin, Tom, *1922: The Birth of Irish Democracy* (Dublin, 1996)

Geoghegan, Hugh, 'The Three Judges of the Supreme Court of the Irish Free State, 1925–36: Their Backgrounds, Personalities and Mindsets', in F.M. Larkin and N.M. Dawson (eds.), *Lawyers, the Law, and History: Irish Legal History Society Discourses and Other Papers, 2005–2011* (Dublin, 2013), pp. 29–53

Geoghegan, Hugh, '*Crotty* Put to Sleep by *Pringle*', in Kieran Bradley, Noel Travers and Anthony Whelan (eds.), *Of Courts and Constitutions: Liber Amicorum in Honour of Nial Fennelly* (Dublin, 2014)

'G. H', 'Case and Comment: Mr Justice Brian Walsh', *Dublin University Law Journal*, vol. 12 (1990), pp. 106–14

Golding, G. M., *George Gavan Duffy* (Dublin, 1982)

Gwynn, Denis, *The Irish Free State 1922–1927* (London, 1928)

Gwynn Morgan, David, *The Separation of Powers in the Irish Constitution* (Dublin, 1997)

Gwynn Morgan, David, *A Judgment too Far? Judicial Activism and the Constitution* (Cork, 2001)

Gwynn Morgan, David, '"Judicial-o-centric" Separation of Powers on the Wane?', *The Irish Jurist*, vol. 39 (2004), pp. 142–60

Hale, Brenda (Baroness Hale of Richmond), 'Women in the Judiciary', Fiona Woolf Lecture for the Women Lawyers' Division of the Law Society, 27 June 2014

Hardiman, Adrian, 'The Role of the Supreme Court in our Democracy', in Joe Mulholland, (ed.), *Political Choice and Democratic Freedom in Ireland* (Dublin, 2004)

Hardiman, Adrian, 'Weasel Words and Doubtful Meanings: A Study in the Language of Law "Reform"', *Judicial Studies Institute Journal*, vol. 7, no. 2 (2007), pp. 1–16

Healy, Maurice, *The Old Munster Circuit* (Dublin, 1939)

Henchy, Seamus, 'Precedent in the Irish Supreme Court', *The Modern Law Review*, vol. 25, no. 5 (September 1962), pp. 544–58

Hesketh, Tom, *The Second Partitioning of Ireland?* (Dublin, 1990)

Hogan, Gerard, 'Irish Nationalism as a Legal Ideology', *Studies*, vol. 75, no. 300 (Winter 1986), pp. 528–38

Hogan, Gerard, 'The Supreme Court and the Single European Act', *The Irish Jurist*, vol. 22, no. 1 (1987), pp. 55–70

Hogan, Gerard, 'Chief Justice Kennedy and Sir James O'Connor's Application', *The Irish Jurist*, vol. 23 (1988), pp. 144–58

Hogan, Gerard, 'Constitutional Interpretation', in Frank Litton (ed.), *The Constitution of Ireland 1937–1987* (Dublin, 1988), pp. 173–91

Hogan, Gerard, 'Unenumerated Personal Rights: Ryan's Case Re-Evaluated', *The Irish Jurist*, vols. 25–7 (1990–92), pp. 95–116

Hogan, Gerard, 'The Early Judgments of Mr Justice Brian Walsh', in James O'Reilly (ed.), *Human Rights and Constitutional Law: Essays in Honour of Brian Walsh* (Dublin, 1992)

Hogan, Gerard, 'Hugh Kennedy, the Childers Habeas Corpus Application and the Return to the Four Courts', in Caroline Costello (ed.), *The Four Courts: 200 Years* (Dublin, 1996)

Hogan, Gerard, 'The Constitution Review Committee of 1934', in Fionán Ó Muircheartaigh (ed.), *Ireland in the Coming Time: Essays to Celebrate T. K. Whitaker's 80 Years* (Dublin, 1997)

Hogan, Gerard, 'The Sinn Féin Funds Judgment Fifty Years On', *The Bar Review*, vol. 2, no. 9 (July 1997), pp. 375–82

Hogan, Gerard, 'The Supreme Court and the Reference of the Offences Against the State (Amendment) Bill 1940', *The Irish Jurist*, vol. 35 (2000), pp. 238–79

Hogan, Gerard, 'Directive Principles, Socio-Economic Rights and the Constitution', *The Irish Jurist*, vol. 36 (2001), pp. 174–98

Hogan, Gerard, 'De Valera, the Constitution and the Historians', *The Irish Jurist*, vol. 40 (2005), pp. 293–320

Hogan, Gerard, 'John Hearne and the Plan for a Constitutional Court', *Dublin University Law Journal*, vol. 33, no. 1 (2011), pp. 75–85

Hogan, Gerard, 'The Judicial Thought and Prose of Mr. Justice Seamus Henchy', *The Irish Jurist*, vol. 46 (2011), pp. 96–116

Hogan, Gerard, *The Origins of the Irish Constitution* (Dublin, 2012)

Hogan, Gerard, 'Unenumerated Personal Rights: The Legacy of *Ryan v. Attorney General*', Paper delivered at the conference 'Judges, Politics and the Constitution', Dublin City University, 4 September 2014

Hogan, Gerard, '*Elegantia juris*: Mr. Justice Seamus Henchy: Some Thoughts on Two Leading Judgments', School of Law, University of Limerick, School of Law, NUI, Galway, Mr Justice Henchy Memorial Lecture, Corofin, Co. Clare, 23 October 2014

Hogan, Gerard, 'Mr Justice Brian Walsh: The Legacy of Experiment and the Triumph of Judicial Imagination', Address given at UCD Sutherland School of Law, 5 November 2014

Hogan, Gerard, Kenny, David, and Walsh, Rachael, 'An Anthology of Declarations of Unconstitutionality', *The Irish Jurist*, vol. 54 (2015), pp. 1–35

Hogan, Gerard, and Walker, Clive, *Political Violence and the Law in Ireland* (Manchester, 1989)

Hogan, Gerard, and Whelan, Anthony, *Ireland and the European Union: Constitutional and Statutory Texts and Commentary* (London, 1995)

Hogan, Gerard, and Whyte, Gerard (eds.), *J. M. Kelly: The Irish Constitution* (London, 2003)

Holland, Ailsa C., 'The Papers of Hugh Kennedy: A Research Legacy for the Foundation of the State', *The Irish Jurist*, vol. 24 (1989), pp. 279–304

Horgan, John, *Seán Lemass: The Enigmatic Patriot* (Dublin, 1997)

Horgan, John, *Noel Browne: Passionate Outsider* (Dublin, 2000)

Horgan, John, 'Death by Respectability?', *Dublin Review of Books* (1 February 2015)

Humphreys, Richard, 'Constitutional Law: Reflections on the Role and Functioning of the Supreme Court', *Dublin University Law Journal*, vol. 12 (1990), pp. 127–37

Humphreys, Richard, 'Constitutional Interpretation', *Dublin University Law Journal*, vol. 15 (1993), pp. 59–77

Humphreys, Richard, 'Interpreting Natural Rights', *The Irish Jurist*, vols. 28–30 (1993–5), pp. 221–30

Keane, Ronan, 'The Voice of the Gael: Chief Justice Kennedy and the Emergence of the New Irish Court System, 1921–1936', *The Irish Jurist*, vol. 31 (1996), pp. 205–25

Keane, Ronan, 'Across the Cherokee Frontier of Irish Constitutional Jurisprudence. The Sinn Féin Funds Case: Buckley v. Attorney General (1950)', in Eoin O'Dell (ed.), *Leading Cases of the Twentieth Century* (Dublin, 2000)

Keane, Ronan, 'Judges as Lawmakers: The Irish Experience', *Judicial Studies Institute Journal*, vol. 4, no. 2 (2004), pp. 1–18

Keane, Ronan, 'Reflections on the Irish Constitution', *Radharc: A Journal of Irish and Irish-American Studies*, vols. 5–7 (2004–6), pp. 135–53

Keane, Ronan, 'The One Judgment Rule in the Supreme Court', in N. M. Dawson, (ed.), *Reflections on Law and History* (Dublin, 2006)

Keane, Ronan, 'Reconciling Ireland's Sovereignty with Membership of the European Union – The Lessons of *Crotty* and *Pringle*', in Kieran Bradley, Noel Travers and Anthony Whelan (eds.), *Of Courts and Constitutions: Liber Amicorum in Honour of Nial Fennelly* (Dublin, 2014)

Kelly, J. M., *Fundamental Rights in the Irish Law and Constitution* (Dublin, 1967)

Kennedy, Hugh, 'Character and Sources of the Constitution of the Irish Free State', *American Bar Association Journal*, vol. 14 (August–September 1928), pp. 337–445

Kennedy, Ronan, *The Supreme Court of Ireland: A History* (Dublin, 2004)

Kennedy, Ronan, 'Extra-Judicial Comment by Judges', *Judicial Studies Institute Journal*, vol. 5, no. 1 (2005), pp. 199–212

Kenny, John, 'The Advantages of a Written Constitution Incorporating a Bill of Rights', *Northern Ireland Legal Quarterly*, vol. 30 (Autumn 1979), pp. 189–206

Keogh, Dermot, *The Making of the Irish Constitution* (Cork, 2007)

Kerrigan, Gene, 'The Moral Civil War', in John Horgan (ed.), *Great Irish Reportage* (Dublin, 2013)

Kingston, James, Whelan, Anthony, and Bacik, Ivana, *Abortion and the Law* (Dublin, 1997)

Kohn, Leo, *The Constitution of the Irish Free State* (London, 1932)

Kotsonouris, Mary, *Retreat from Revolution: The Dáil Courts, 1920–1924* (Dublin, 1994)

Laffan, Michael, *Judging W. T. Cosgrave: The Foundation of the Irish State* (Dublin, 2014)

Larkin, Felix M., and Dawson, N. M. (eds.), *Lawyers, the Law and History* (Dublin, 2013)

Leahy, Pat, *Showtime* (Dublin, 2009)

Lee, Joseph J., *Ireland 1912–1985: Politics and Society* (Cambridge, 1989)

Lewis, Anthony, 'Law and the Press: A Deadly Embrace', *The Irish Jurist*, vol. 33 (1998), pp. 34–46

Lewis, V. Bradley, 'Natural Law in Irish Constitutional Jurisprudence', *Catholic Social Science Review*, vol. 2 (1997), pp. 171–82

Lyons, F. S. L., *Ireland since the Famine* (London, 1985)

Lysaght, Charles, 'The Life of Cecil Lavery', *The Bar Review*, vol. 17, no. 4 (July 2012), pp. 83–4

McAndrew, Martin John, 'Revisiting the Courts of Justice Act, 1924, from a Political Perspective', Conference Paper, Dubin City University, September 2014

McCafferty, Nell, *Nell* (Dublin, 2004)

McCarthy, Niall, 'Una Voce Poco Fa', in James O'Reilly (ed.), *Human Rights and Constitutional Law: Essays in Honour of Brian Walsh* (Dublin, 1992)

McCartney, Donal, *UCD: A National Idea* (Dublin, 1999)

McDermott, Paul Anthony, 'The Separation of Powers and the Doctrine of Non-Justiciability', *The Irish Jurist*, vol. 35 (2000), pp. 280–304

MacGuckian, Sile, 'Judge or Politician? The Political Role of the Judiciary in Society', *Dublin University Law Journal*, vol. 27 (2005), pp. 302–29

McGuire, James, and Quinn, James (eds.), *Dictionary of Irish Biography*, vols. 1–9 (Cambridge, 2009)

Mac Intyre, Tom, *Through the Bridewell Gate: A Diary of the Dublin Arms Trial* (London, 1971)

McMahon, Bryan, 'Developments in the Irish Legal System since 1945', in
    J. J. Lee (ed.), *Ireland 1945–70* (Dublin, 1979)

McMahon, Deirdre, 'The Chief Justice and the Governor General Contro-
    versy in 1932', *The Irish Jurist*, vol. 17 (1982), pp. 145–67

Mac Menamin, John, '"Imperfect Obligations" – Constitutional Principles
    and the Charter of Fundamental Rights', in Kieran Bradley, Noel Trav-
    ers and Anthony Whelan (eds.), *Of Courts and Constitutions: Liber
    Amicorum in Honour of Nial Fennelly* (Dublin, 2014)

Manning, Maurice, *The Blueshirts* (Dublin, 2006)

Mansergh, Nicholas, *The Irish Free State: Its Government and Politics* (Lon-
    don, 1934)

Marrinan, Patrick, 'Review: *Lies in a Mirror: An Essay on Evil and Deceit* by
    Peter Charleton', *The Bar Review*, vol. 11, no. 5 (November 2006), p. 180

Mathews, Aidan Carl, *Immediate Man: Cuimhní ar Cearbhall Ó Dálaigh* (Dub-
    lin, 1983)

Meehan, Ciara, *The Cosgrave Party: A History of Cumann na nGaedheal,
    1923–33* (Dublin, 2010)

Millen, Cynthia, *The Right to Privacy in the United States and Ireland* (Dublin,
    1998)

Milotte, Mike, *Banished Babies: The Secret History of Ireland's Baby Export
    Business* (Dublin, 1997)

Mohr, Thomas, 'The Rights of Women under the Constitution of the Irish
    Free State', *The Irish Jurist*, vol. 41 (2006), pp. 20–59

Montesquieu, Charles Louis de Secondat, Baron de, *The Spirit of the Laws*,
    trans. Anne M. Cohler, Basia Carolyn Miller and Harold Samuel Stone
    (Cambridge, 1989)

Murphy, Tim, and Twomey, Patrick (eds.), *Ireland's Evolving Constitution,
    1937–1997: Collected Essays* (Oxford, 1999)

Murray, Brian, 'The Supreme Court and the Constitution in the Nineteen
    Eighties', *Studies*, vol. 79, no. 314 (Summer 1990), pp. 160–75

Neuberger, David (Lord) '"Judge not, that ye be not judged": Judging Judi-
    cial Decision-Making', F. A. Mann Lecture 2015

Ní Loinsigh, Nóra, 'Judicial Dissent in Ireland: Theory, Practice and the
    Constraints of the Single Opinion Rule', *The Irish Jurist*, vol. 51 (2014),
    pp. 123–48

Norris, David, *A Kick against the Pricks: The Autobiography* (London, 2013)

Ó Cearúil, Micheál, *Bunreacht na hÉireann: A Study of the Irish Text* (Dublin, 1999)

Ó Cearúil, Micheál, *Bunreacht na hÉireann: Two Texts or Two Constitutions?* (Dublin, 2002)

O'Donnell, Donal, 'James Joyce, Boss Croker, Oliver Wendell Holmes and the Influence of America on Irish Constitutional Law', *The Bar Review*, vol. 13, no. 1 (February 2008), pp. 2–7

O'Donnell, Donal, 'Nial Fennelly: *Mallak* and the Rule of Reasons', in Kieran Bradley, Noel Travers and Anotney Whelan (eds.), *Of Courts and Constitutions: Liber Amicorum in Honour of Nial Fennelly* (Dublin, 2014)

O'Donnell, Donal, 'A Partial or Uneven Administration of the Law: Lawyers, the Law and the Importation of Arms into Ireland, 1914', *The Irish Jurist*, vol. 53 (2015), pp. 100–24

O'Donnell, Donal, 'Irish Legal History of the Twentieth Century', *Studies*, vol. 105, no. 417 (Spring 2016), pp. 98–120

O'Dowd, John, 'Review of David Gwynn Morgan, *The Separation of Powers in the Irish Constitution*', *The Irish Jurist* (Dublin, 1997)

O'Dowd, John, 'The Sheedy Affair', in Robert Clark and Joseph McMahon (eds.), *Contemporary Issues in Irish Law and Politics*, vol. 3 (Dublin, 2000)

O'Dowd, John, 'Judges in Whose Cause? The Irish Bench after the Judges' Pay Referendum', *The Irish Jurist*, vol. 48 (2012), pp. 102–31

O'Flaherty, Hugh, 'The Independent Bar and the Defence of Human Rights', in James O'Reilly (ed.), *Human Rights and Constitutional Law: Essays in Honour of Brian Walsh* (Dublin, 1992)

O'Halpin, Eunan, *Defending Ireland: The Irish State and Its Enemies since 1922* (Oxford, 1999)

O'Halpin, Eunan, 'Politics and the State, 1922–1932', in J. R. Hill (ed.), *A New History of Ireland*, vol. 7, *Ireland, 1921–84* (Oxford, 2003)

O'Hanlon, Rory, 'A Court in Session', in Aidan Carl Mathews (ed.), *Immediate Man: Cuimhní ar Chearbhall Ó Dálaigh* (Dublin, 1983)

O'Higgins, Thomas F., 'The Constitution and the Communities – Scope for Stress?', in James O'Reilly (ed.), *Human Rights and Constitutional Law: Essays in Honour of Brian Walsh* (Dublin, 1992)

O'Higgins, Tom, *A Double Life* (Dublin, 1996)

O'Mahony, Conor, 'Societal Changes and Constitutional Interpretation', *Irish Journal of Legal Studies*, vol. 1, no. 1 (2010), pp. 71–115

O'Malley, Des, *Conduct Unbecoming: A Memoir* (Dublin, 2014)

O'Malley, Ernie, *The Singing Flame* (Dublin, 1978)

O'Malley, Thomas, *Sexual Offences: Law, Policy and Punishment* (Dublin, 1996)

O'Reilly, James, 'Marital Privacy and Family Law', *Studies*, vol. 66, no. 261 (Spring 1977), pp. 8–24

O'Toole, Fintan, *The Irish Times Book of the Century* (Dublin, 1999)

Osborough, W. N., 'Constitutional Law – A Waning of Judicial Activism?', *Dublin University Law Journal*, vol. 2 (1979–80), pp. 101–3

Osborough, W. N., *The Law School of University College Dublin* (Dublin, 2014)

Phelan, Diarmuid Rossa, *Revolt or Revolution: The Constitutional Boundaries of the European Community* (Dublin, 1997)

Quinn, Gerard, 'The Judging Process and the Personality of the Judge: The Contribution of Jerome Frank', *Judicial Studies Institute Journal*, vol. 2, no. 2 (2002), pp. 141–62

Reid, Madeleine, *The Impact of Community Law on the Irish Constitution* (Dublin, 1990)

Reynolds, Albert, *My Autobiography* (Dublin, 2010)

Robinson, Mary, *Everybody Matters: My Life Giving Voice* (London, 2014)

Ross, Shane, and Webb, Nick, *The Untouchables* (Dublin, 2012)

Ruane, Blathna, 'Regime Change: The Fate of the Senior Crown Judiciary Following the Anglo-Irish Treaty 1921', *The Irish Jurist*, vol. 54 (2015), pp. 96–114

Ruane, Blathna, and others (eds.), *Law and Government: A Tribute to Rory Brady* (Dublin, 2014)

Ryssdal, Rolv, 'Brian Walsh and the European Court of Human Rights', in James O'Reilly (ed.), *Human Rights and Constitutional Law: Essays in Honour of Brian Walsh* (Dublin, 1992)

Sarkin, Jeremy, and Binchy, William, *Human Rights, the Citizen and the State: South African and Irish Perspectives* (Dublin, 2001)

Scannell, Yvonne, 'The Taxation of Married Women: Murphy v Attorney General (1982)', in Eoin O'Dell (ed.), *Leading Cases of the Twentieth Century* (Dublin, 2000)

Simpson, A. W. B. (ed.), *Biographical Dictionary of the Common Law* (London, 1984)

Stern, Seth, and Wermiel, Stephen, *Justice Brennan: Liberal Champion* (Boston, MA, and New York, 2010)

Sturgess, Garry, and Chubb, Philip, *Judging the World: Law and Politics in the World's Leading Courts* (Sydney, 1988)

Sutherland, Peter, 'The Constitution, the Courts and the Legislature', Second Brian Lenihan Memorial Address, Trinity College Dublin, 16 February 2013

Tobin, Fergal, *The Best of Decades: Ireland in the Sixties* (Dublin, 1996)

Tóibín, Colm, 'Inside the Supreme Court', *Magill* (Feburary 1985)

Tóibín, Colm, 'A Brush with the Law', *Dublin Review*, no. 28 (Autumn 2007)

Towey, Thomas, 'Hugh Kennedy and the Constitutional Development of the Irish Free State, 1922–1923', *The Irish Jurist*, vol. 12 (1977), pp. 355–70

Twomey, Adrian F., 'The Death of Natural Law?', *Irish Law Times* (November 1995), pp. 270–73

Walsh, Brian, 'The Constitution and Constitutional Rights', in Frank Litton (ed.), *The Constitution of Ireland 1937–1987* (Dublin, 1988)

Walsh, Brian, 'The Constitution: A View from the Bench', in Brian Farrell (ed.), *De Valera's Constitution and Ours* (Dublin, 1988)

Ward, Tanya, *Justice Matters: Independence, Accountability and the Irish Judiciary* (Dublin, 2007)

Whelan, Noel, *Fianna Fáil: A Biography of the Party* (Dublin, 2011)

Whyte, Gerard, 'Natural Law and the Constitution', *Irish Law Times* (January 1996), pp. 8–12

Whyte, Gerard, 'The Role of the Supreme Court in Our Democracy: A Response to Mr Justice Hardiman', *Dublin University Law Journal*, vol. 28, no. 1 (2006), pp. 1–26

Whyte, Gerry, *Social Inclusion and the Legal System* (Dublin, 2015)

Whyte, John, *Church and State in Modern Ireland 1923–1979* (Dublin, 1980)

Woolf, Harry (Lord Woolf), 'Should the Media and the Judiciary Be on Speaking Terms?', *The Irish Jurist*, vol. 38 (2003), pp. 25–33

Notes

Introduction

1 Thomas O'Malley, *Sexual Offences: Law, Policy and Punishment*, pp. 97–8.

2 *Irish Mirror*, 31 May 2006.

3 Charles Louis de Secondat, Baron de Montesquieu, *The Spirit of the Laws*, p. 163.

4 Rossa Fanning, 'Hard Case, Bad Law? The Supreme Court decision in A v The Governor of Arbour Hill Prison', p. 219.

5 *Kant's Critique of Teleological Judgement*, translated by James Creed Meredith (Oxford, 1928).

6 T. C. Kingsmill Moore, *A Man May Fish* (London, 1960).

7 Peter Charleton, *Lies in a Mirror: Essays on Evil and Deceit* (Dublin, 2006).

8 James Creed Meredith, *The Rainbow in the Valley*.

9 The former Chief Justice Tom O'Higgins published a memoir, *A Double Life*, in 1996, but his eleven-year period at the helm of the judiciary is dealt with in twelve pages out of 297.

1. Beginnings

1 Ernie O'Malley, *The Singing Flame*, p. 114.

2 Gerard Hogan, 'Hugh Kennedy, the Childers Habeas Corpus Application and the Return to the Four Courts', p. 179.

3 Ibid.

4 C. P. Curran, 'Figures in the Hall', p. 176.

5 Ronan Keane, 'Kennedy, Hugh', in James McGuire and James Quinn (eds.), *Dictionary of Irish Biography*.

6 Richard Ellmann, *James Joyce*, p. 70.

7 Ibid., p. 378.

8 Papers of Hugh Kennedy, IE UCDA P4/1388, letter from Kennedy to Cosgrave, 18 August 1923.

9 A. W. B. Simpson (ed.), *Biographical Dictionary of the Common Law*, p. 293.

10 Tom Garvin, *1922: The Birth of Irish Democracy*, p. 159.

11 Thomas Towey, 'Hugh Kennedy and the Constitutional Development of the Irish Free State, 1922–1923', p. 355.

12 Eunan O'Halpin, 'Politics and the State, 1922–1932', p. 109.

13 Margery Forester, *Michael Collins*, p. 282.

14 Hugh Kennedy, 'Character and Sources of the Constitution of the Irish Free State', American Bar Association Journal, vol. 14, no. 8 (August–September 1928), p. 445.

15 Papers of Hugh Kennedy, IE UCDA P4/1090.

16 Ibid., IE UCDA P4, letter from Kennedy to MacNeill, 22 August 1922.

17 Ibid., IE UCDA P4/30, letter from Kennedy to Cosgrave, 13 August 1923.

18 Ibid., IE UCDA P4/1689–91 July/December 1923, draft article by Kennedy under the heading 'Judicial Re-organisation in the Irish Free State'.

19 Letter from George Gavan Duffy to the *Freeman's Journal*, 19 August 1922.

20 Hugh Geoghegan, 'The Three Judges of the Supreme Court of the Irish Free State, 1925–36', p. 31.

21 Ronan Keane, 'The Voice of the Gael: Chief Justice Kennedy and the Emergence of the New Irish Court System 1921–1936', p. 215.

22 Papers of Hugh Kennedy, IE UCDA P4/1390, letter from Kennedy to Cosgrave, 13 August 1923. Glenavy was at this time chairman of the Free State senate.

23 Ibid., IE UCDA P4/1165, letter from Kennedy to Yeats, 13 August 1924.

24 Ibid., IE UCDA P4/6, letter from Kennedy to Louis J. Walsh, 31 May 1923.

25 Ibid., IE UCDA P4/1165, letter from Kennedy to Yeats, 13 August 1924.

26 Ibid., IE UCDA P4/1123, letter from Kennedy to Louis J. Walsh, October/November 1923.

27 Ibid., IE UCDA P4/1125–6, letter from Louis J. Walsh to Kennedy, February 1924.

28 Ibid., IE UCDA P4/1168, letter from Kennedy to Cosgrave, 12 July 1926.

29 Ibid., IE UCDA P4/1168, letter from Kennedy to Yeats, 22 September 1926.

30 Ibid., IE UCDA P4/1168, letter from Kennedy to Cosgrave, 12 July 1926.

31 Keane, 'The Voice of the Gael', p. 213.

32 Papers of Hugh Kennedy, IE UCDA P4/1104, letter from Kennedy to Louis J. Walsh, July/August 1923.

33 Ibid., IE UCDA P4/11, letter from M. K. Kennedy to Clare Kennedy, 12 July 1923.

34 Gerard Hogan, 'Chief Justice Kennedy and Sir James O'Connor's Application', p. 154.

35 Ibid., p. 155.

36 Blathna Ruane, 'Regime Change: The Fate of the Senior Crown Judiciary Following the Anglo-Irish Treaty 1921', p. 100.

37 Ibid., p. 103.

38 Ibid., p. 104.

39 Ibid., p. 103.

40 Ibid., p. 113.

41 *Irish Law Times and Solicitors' Journal*, 8 September 1928, p. 217.

42 Ciara Meehan, *The Cosgrave Party*, p. 32, and Ronan Fanning, *Independent Ireland*, p. 54.

43 Meehan, *The Cosgrave Party*, p. 33.

44 *Irish Times*, 12 June 1924.

45 Keane, 'The Voice of the Gael', p. 221.

46 *Freeman's Journal*, 12 June 1924.

47 Martin John McAndrew, 'Revisiting the Courts of Justice Act, 1924, from a Political Perspective', p. 1.

48 Keane, 'The Voice of the Gael', p. 37, and Fanning, *Independent Ireland*, p. 67.

49 Papers of Hugh Kennedy, IE UCDA P4/51(4), diary entry for 9 February 1929.

50 Ibid., IE UCDA P4/1058, letter from FitzGerald-Kenney to Kennedy, 16 September 1931.

51 Hogan, 'Hugh Kennedy, the Childers Habeas Corpus Application and the Return to the Four Courts', p. 207.

2. Stand-off

1 *Nenagh Guardian*, 28 April 1934; *Irish Times*, 28 April 1934.

2 See Fergal F. Davis, *The History and Development of the Special Criminal Court, 1922–2005*, p. 43; Eunan O'Halpin, *Defending Ireland: The Irish State and Its Enemies since 1922*, p. 79; F. S. L. Lyons, *Ireland since the Famine*, p. 497.

3 Davis, *The History and Development of the Special Criminal Court*, p. 43; Tim Pat Coogan, *De Valera: Long Fellow, Long Shadow*, p. 409.

4 Davis, *The History and Development of the Special Criminal Court*, p. 45.

5 Constitution (Amendment No. 16) Act 1929.

6 Constitution (Amendment No. 17) Act 1931.

7 *State (Ryan) v. Lennon* [1935] IR 170. Lennon referred to Captain Michael Lennon, the governor of the Military Detention Barracks at Arbour Hill in Dublin.

8 Ronan Keane, 'Murnaghan, James Augustine', in James McGuire and James Quinn (eds.), *Dictionary of Irish Biography*.

9 Gerard Hogan, 'Chief Justice Kennedy and Sir James O'Connor's Application', p. 156.

10 Ibid.

11 J. M. Kelly, *Fundamental Rights in the Irish Law and Constitution*, pp. 16–17.

12 In letters to his two colleagues in October 1933, Kennedy addressed Murnaghan as 'My dear James' and Fitzgibbon as 'My dear Judge'; NAI 2011/21/25.

13 Papers of Hugh Kennedy, IE UCDA P4/41.

14 Gerard Hogan, *The Origins of the Irish Constitution*, p. 33.

15 Ibid., p. 35.

16 Ibid.

17 Ibid., p. 43.

18 Ibid., p. 42.

19 *Irish Independent*, 14 December 1936.

20 Kennedy's view of judicial independence brought him into conflict with the Fianna Fáil government in 1932, when he resisted pressure from de Valera to carry out the functions of the Governor General. Kennedy argued that this would be incompatible with the separation of powers and the idea was quietly dropped. See Deirdre McMahon, 'The Chief Justice and the Governor General Controversy in 1932'.

21 Ronan Keane, 'Across the Cherokee Frontier of Irish Constitutional Jurisprudence. The Sinn Féin Funds Case: Buckley v. Attorney General (1950)', p. 188.

22 James Geoghegan's son Hugh would follow in his father's footsteps when he joined the Supreme Court in 2000.

23 Pauric J. Dempsey, 'Geoghegan, James', in McGuire and Quinn (eds.), *Dictionary of Irish Biography*.

24 Ibid.

25 Tadhg Foley, 'Meredith, James Creed', in McGuire and Quinn (eds.), *Dictionary of Irish Biography*.

26 Donal O'Donnell, 'A Partial or Uneven Administration of the Law: Lawyers, the Law and the Importation of Arms into Ireland, 1914', p. 103.

27 Ibid.

28 See Mary Kotsonouris, *Retreat from Revolution: The Dáil Courts, 1920–1924*.

29 O'Donnell, 'A Partial or Uneven Administration of the Law', p. 105.

30 The sculptor Rowan Gillespie is Meredith's grandson.

31 O'Halpin, *Defending Ireland*, p. 123.

32 Ibid., p. 124.

33 Ibid., p. 125.

34 Joseph J. Lee, *Ireland 1912–1985: Politics and Society*, p. 221.

35 Diarmaid Ferriter, *The Transformation of Ireland 1900–2000*, p. 419.

36 The power to detain was brought back up again to seventy-two hours only in 1998, but then the further twenty-four-hour detention after the first forty-eight hours had to be sanctioned by the District Court.

37 Gerard Hogan, 'The Supreme Court and the Reference of the Offences Against the State (Amendment) Bill 1940', p. 253.

38 Coogan, *De Valera*, p. 525.

39 Hogan, 'The Supreme Court and the Reference of the Offences Against the State (Amendment) Bill 1940', p. 255.

40 Maurice Manning, *The Blueshirts*, p. 116; Hogan, 'The Supreme Court and the Reference of the Offences Against the State (Amendment) Bill 1940', p. 259. Hogan also points out that, as a Supreme Court judge, O'Byrne would turn out to be something of an activist. If the Fianna Fáil government had had an inkling of that, it might not have chosen to appoint him.

41 Hogan, 'The Supreme Court and the Reference of the Offences Against the State (Amendment) Bill 1940', p. 259.

42 *Irish Press*, 24 January 1940.

43 Loren P. Beth, *The Development of Judicial Review in Ireland*, p. 50.

44 O'Donnell writes that the claim that Meredith withdrew from the case 'sounds like the overheated chatter in which lawyers excel, which

combines the maximum of scandalous speculation with a minimum of fact'. O'Donnell, 'A Partial or Uneven Administration of the Law', p. 107.

45 The 1937 Constitution allowed for technical amendments to be made by ordinary legislation by the Oireachtas for a three-year period (which could not be extended) from the date of the inauguration of the first President, which was June 1938.

46 Hogan, 'The Supreme Court and the Reference of the Offences Against the State (Amendment) Bill 1940', p. 279.

3. Separating powers

1 Rex Mackey and Ronan Keane, 'Conolly, Thomas James (Tommy)', in McGuire and Quinn (eds.), *Dictionary of Irish Biography*.

2 Anthony Cronin, *No Laughing Matter: The Life and Times of Flann O'Brien*, p. 202.

3 Ibid.

4 Ibid., p. 202.

5 Ibid., p. 166.

6 Gerard Hogan, 'The Sinn Féin Funds Judgment Fifty Years On', p. 375.

7 Ibid., p. 376.

8 Ronan Keane, 'Across the Cherokee Frontier', p. 189.

9 Memorandum of meeting written by Maguire, NAI 2011/21/27.

10 Ibid.

11 Hogan, 'The Sinn Féin Funds Judgment Fifty Years On', p. 376, and Keane, 'Across the Cherokee Frontier', p. 189.

12 *Irish Independent*, 13 March 1947.

13 *Irish Independent*, 30 April 1947.

14 Dáil Éireann transcript, 24 April 1947.

15 Ibid.

16 Ibid.

17 Hogan, 'The Sinn Féin Funds Judgment Fifty Years On', p. 379.

18 Ibid., p. 379. The story is described in G. M. Golding, *George Gavan Duffy* and, according to Hogan, was confirmed to him personally by the late Supreme Court judge Niall McCarthy, who was then devilling with Andreas O'Keeffe. Citing private correspondence with Gavan Duffy's son Colm, Golding writes that the judge told his son the

evening before the case that the government were in for a surprise and read the judgment to him. Golding, *George Gavan Duffy*, p. 116.

19 Ibid., p. 118.

20 A convention developed in the early years of the Free State that at least one judge of the Supreme Court should be a Protestant.

21 Hogan, 'The Sinn Féin Funds Judgment Fifty Years On', p. 379.

22 Keane, 'Across the Cherokee Frontier', p. 191.

23 Ibid., p. 192.

24 Ibid.

25 *National Union of Railwaymen v. Sullivan* [1947] IR 77.

26 *Irish Independent*, 2 August 2013. As the author Brian Murphy points out, Ó Dálaigh's view that the bill was 'clearly constitutional' is set out in his speaking note for the Council of State meeting.

27 Kingsmill Moore's judgment in *Buchanan v. McVey* [1954] IR 89 was reproduced in full in a subsequent House of Lords decision – a compliment no Irish judge has received since.

28 *In the Matter of Tilson, infants* [1951] IR 1.

29 Gerard Hogan, 'Duffy, George Gavan', in McGuire and Quinn (eds.), *Dictionary of Irish Biography*.

30 *Educational Company of Ireland v. Fitzpatrick* [1961] IR 323.

31 *The Pigs Marketing Board v. Donnelly* [1939] IR 413.

32 Donal Barrington, 'The Constitution in the Courts', p. 110.

33 Ibid., p. 111.

34 Ibid., p. 114.

4. *Changing of the guard*

1 Department of An Taoiseach, NAI S/5533 B/61.

2 *The Bar Review*, December 1998.

3 T. A. Finlay, 'Lavery, Cecil Patrick Linton', in McGuire and Quinn (eds.), *Dictionary of Irish Biography*.

4 Letter from John A. Costello to An Taoiseach, Seán Lemass, 15 November 1961, NAI S/14797 B/61.

5 Ibid.

6 Letter from Cardinal d'Alton to John A. Costello, 28 November 1961, NAI S/14797 B/61.

7 *Irish Times*, 18 December 1961.

8 Charles Lysaght, 'Walsh, Brian Cathal Patrick', in McGuire and Quinn (eds.), *Dictionary of Irish Biography*.

9 An Fórsa Cosanta Áitiúil: literally, 'the local defence force'.

10 Lysaght, 'Walsh, Brian Cathal Patrick'.

11 *Irish Times*, 18 December 1961.

12 *Buckley v. Attorney General* [1950] IR 67 (Sinn Féin funds case).

13 Gerard Hogan, 'The Early Judgments of Mr Justice Brian Walsh', p. 37.

14 *National Union of Railwaymen v. Sullivan* [1947] IR 77 established that workers in a particular industry could not be forced to join a prescribed trade union, while in *Educational Company of Ireland v. Fitzpatrick* [1961] IR 323 the court held that employers could not force their employees to join a trade union, as citizens were free to join or not to join an association or union as they pleased.

15 *Buckley v. Attorney General* [1950] IR 67 (the Sinn Féin funds case); *Foley v. Irish Land Commission* [1952] IR 118.

16 *Buckley v. Attorney General* [1950] IR 67; *In re Solicitors' Act* [1960] IR 239.

17 *In re Article 26 and the Offences Against the State (Amendment) Bill 1940* [1940] IR 470.

18 Garry Sturgess and Philip Chubb, *Judging the World: Law and Politics in the World's Leading Courts*, p. 419.

19 Correspondence with the author.

20 Ibid.

21 Ibid.

22 Ibid.

23 Garry Sturgess, audio interview with Brian Walsh no. 1 (March 1986).

24 Gerard Hogan, 'Mr Justice Brian Walsh: The Legacy of Experiment and the Triumph of Judicial Imagination', p. 2.

25 Garry Sturgess, audio interview with Brian Walsh no. 1.

26 Sturgess and Chubb, *Judging the World*, pp. 419–20.

27 Garry Sturgess, audio interview with Brian Walsh no. 3 (March 1986).

28 Diarmaid Ferriter, *The Transformation of Ireland 1900–2000*, p. 542.

29 Ibid., pp. 536–7.

30 Fergal Tobin, *The Best of Decades: Ireland in the Sixties*, p. 1.

31 Ferriter, *The Transformation of Ireland*, p. 537.

32 *Irish Times*, 19 June 2013.

33 Seth Stern and Stephen Wermiel, *Justice Brennan: Liberal Champion*, p. 165.

34 Letter from Brennan to Walsh, 8 August 1963, William J. Brennan Papers, Box II: 62.

35 Obituary of Gladys Ryan, *Irish Times*, 2 March 2013.

36 Appointed a Supreme Court judge in 1991.

37 Opening speech by Seán MacBride, *Ryan v. Attorney General*, 14 March 1963, Papers of Richie Ryan, IE UCDA P272/239.

38 *The State (Ryan) v. Lennon* [1935] IR 170.

39 Closing speech of Seán MacBride, *Ryan v. Attorney General*, 26 July 1963, Papers of Richie Ryan, IE UCDA P272/239.

40 *Ryan v. Attorney General* [1965] IR 294.

41 *Irish Press*, 2 June 1983.

42 Sturgess and Chubb, *Judging the World*, p. 420.

5. Vive la révolution!

1 In two previous cases, *The State (Dowling) v. Kingston (No. 2)* [1937] IR 699 and *The State (Duggan) v. Tapley* [1952] IR 62, the Supreme Court had decided that the backing of warrants under the 1851 act was constitutional.

2 *The State (Quinn) v. Ryan* [1965] IR 70. The highest court in the UK used to be the Judicial Committee of the House of Lords, which lawyers often shortened to 'House of Lords'. Since 2009, the UK's highest court has been called the UK Supreme Court.

3 Donal O'Donnell, 'James Joyce, Boss Croker, Oliver Wendell Holmes and the Influence of America on Irish Constitutional Law', p. 5. O'Donnell became a Supreme Court judge in 2010.

4 Ibid.

5 Gerard Hogan, 'The Early Judgments of Mr Justice Brian Walsh', p. 38.

6 'Appreciation by "B. W."', *Irish Times*, 31 January 1979.

7 *Mapp v. Ohio*, 367 US 643 (1961).

8 Colm Tóibín, 'Inside the Supreme Court'.

9 Rory O'Hanlon, 'A Court in Session', p. 32.

10 Ibid., p. 35.

11 Tóibín, 'Inside the Supreme Court'.

12 Letter from Stephen Roche to Michael McDunphy, 13 April 1937; Gerard Hogan, *The Origins of the Irish Constitution*, p. 473.

13 Hogan, *The Origins of the Irish Constitution*, p. 335.

14 Letter from Lemass to Maguire, 19 November 1959, NAI 2011/21/27.

15 Letter from Maguire to Lemass, 21 December 1959, NAI 2011/21/27.

16 Letter from Haughey to Ó Dálaigh, 16 October 1963, NAI 2011/21/28.

17 Letter from Ó Dálaigh to Haughey, 13 November 1963, NAI 2011/21/28.

18 Letter from Haughey to Ó Dálaigh, 6 December 1963, NAI 2011/21/28.

19 Tóibín, 'Inside the Supreme Court'.

20 O'Hanlon, 'A Court in Session', p. 32.

21 Letter from Walsh to Brennan, 28 February 1969, William J. Brennan Papers, Box II: 62.

22 Memorandum from the Office of the Minister for Justice to Government, 13 February 1963, NAI 6341/5F/62 (Dept of An Taoiseach).

23 Letter from Ó Dálaigh to Kingsmill Moore, 23 July 1963, NAI 2011/21/13.

24 Judicial Salaries: Memorandum from the Judiciary to the Government, 12 December 1967, NAI 6341/5F (Dept of An Taoiseach).

25 Letter from Brian Walsh to Brian Lenihan, 18 January 1967, NAI S 6341/5F (Dept of An Taoiseach).

26 *Irish Times*, 5 April 1968.

27 *Irish Times*, 1 July 1971.

6. *The limits of activism*

1 Colm Tóibín, 'Inside the Supreme Court'.

2 J. P. Casey, 'The Development of Constitutional Law under Chief Justice Ó Dálaigh', p. 3.

3 Garry Sturgess, audio interview with Brian Walsh no. 2 (1986).

4 *Attorney General v. Ryan's Car Hire* [1965] IR 642.

5 *McDonald v. Bord na gCon* [1964] IR 350.

6 *East Donegal Co-Op Ltd v. Attorney General* [1970] IR 317.

7 *Murphy v. Dublin Corporation and Minister for Local Government* [1976] IR 143.

8 Sturgess, audio interview with Brian Walsh no. 2.

9 Interview with Donal Barrington, *The Law Makers*, RTÉ Radio, Autumn 2012.

10 Ibid.

11 Ibid.

12 See Tomás Finn, *Tuairim, Intellectual Debate and Policy Formation, 1954–1975.*

13 Bryan Fanning, *The Quest for Modern Ireland: The Battle of Ideas 1912–1986*, p. 74.

14 Clíona de Bhaldraithe Marsh, 'Introductory Address'.

15 Finn, *Tuairim, Intellectual Debate and Policy Formation*, p. 171.

16 Lindsey Earner-Byrne, *Mother and Child: Maternity and Child Welfare in Dublin, 1922–60*, p. 193.

17 Mike Milotte, *Banished Babies: The Secret History of Ireland's Baby Export Business*, p. 23.

18 *The State (Nicolaou) v. An Bord Uchtála* [1966] IR 567.

19 J. M. Kelly, *Fundamental Rights in the Irish Law and Constitution*, p. 245.

7. *In the government's sights*

1 Paul C. Bartholomew, *The Irish Judiciary*, pp. 31–50.

2 Ibid., p. 33.

3 Ibid.

4 Ibid., p. 35.

5 Ronan Keane, 'FitzGerald, William O'Brien ('Billy'), in McGuire and Guinn (eds.), *Dictionary of Irish Biography.*

6 *Irish Press*, 6 March 1968.

7 Interview with Donal Barrington, in *The Law Makers*, RTÉ Radio, Autumn 2012.

8 Letter from Walsh to Brennan, 28 February 1969, William J. Brennan Papers, Box II: 62.

9 Ibid.

10 Letter from Brennan to Walsh, 10 March 1969, William J. Brennan Papers, Box II:62.

11 Garry Sturgess, audio interview with Brian Walsh no. 2 (1986).

12 Colm Tóibín, 'Inside the Supreme Court'.

13 Interview with Barrington, in *The Law Makers*.

14 Letter from Walsh to Brennan, 12 August 1968; Letter from Brennan to Walsh, 16 August 1968, William J. Brennan Papers, Box II: 62.

15 *State (Sheerin) v. Kennedy* [1966] IR 379.

16 *In re Gault*, 387 US 1 (1967).

17 Letter from Brennan to Walsh, 10 June 1969, William J. Brennan Papers, Box II: 62.

18 Charles Lysaght, 'Walsh, Brian Cathal Patrick', in McGuire and Quinn (eds.), *Dictionary of Irish Biography*.

19 *Magill*, May 1980.

20 Ibid.

21 Tóibín, 'Inside the Supreme Court'.

22 Letter from Walsh to Sturgess, 7 June 1989 (Private Collection).

23 Ibid.

24 Letter from Ó Dálaigh to Walsh, 16 August 1972, Papers of Cearbhall Ó Dálaigh, IE UCDA P51.

25 Ibid.

26 Letter from Walsh to Ó Dálaigh, 25 August 1972, Papers of Cearbhall Ó Dálaigh, IE UCDA P51.

27 Ibid.

28 Diarmaid Ferriter, *The Transformation of Ireland 1900–2000*, p. 617.

29 Michael Farrell, *Sheltering the Fugitive? The Extradition of Irish Political Offenders*, p. 56.

30 Ferriter, *The Transformation of Ireland*, p. 618.

31 Kevin Costello, 'Henchy, Séamus Anthony', in McGuire and Quinn (eds.), *Dictionary of Irish Biography*.

32 Keane, 'FitzGerald, William O'Brien ('Billy').

33 Ronan Keane, 'Ó Dálaigh, Cearbhall', in McGuire and Quinn (eds.), *Dictionary of Irish Biography*.

8. McGee v. Attorney General

1 *Irish Times*, 7 August 1989.

2 *Irish Times*, 9 June 1972.

3 *Irish Independent*, 10 June 1972.

4 *Irish Times*, 1 August 1972.

5 John Whyte, *Church and State in Modern Ireland 1923–1979*, p. 382.

6 *Irish Times*, 30 December 1972.

7 Diarmaid Ferriter, *Ambiguous Republic: Ireland in the 1970s*, p. 641.

8 Whyte, *Church and State*, p. 284.

9 *Irish Times*, 30 December 1972.

10 Ibid.

11 Kevin Costello, 'Henchy, Séamus Anthony', in McGuire and Quinn (eds.), *Dictionary of Irish Biography*.

12 Colm Tóibín, 'Inside the Supreme Court'.

13 *McGee v. Attorney General* [1974] IR 284.

14 *McGee v. Attorney General* [1974] IR 284.

15 *Irish Independent*, 20 December 1973.

16 *Cork Examiner*, 20 December 1973.

17 William Binchy, 'Marital Privacy and Family Law: A Reply to Mr O'Reilly', p. 330.

18 Letter from Walsh to Brennan, 8 November 1973, William J. Brennan Papers, Box II: 62.

19 *What If*, RTÉ Radio, 24 September 2006.

20 Gerard Hogan, '*Elegantia juris:* Mr. Justice Seamus Henchy: Some Thoughts on Two Leading Judgments', p. 5.

21 Whyte, *Church and State*, p. 409.

22 Ibid., p. 416.

9. Holding the line

1 Patrick Maume and Kevin Costello, 'O'Higgins, Thomas Francis', in McGuire and Quinn (eds.), *Dictionary of Irish Biography*.

2 Ibid.

3 The decision that de Valera, frail and almost blind, would not campaign because it was beneath the dignity of the office was taken by Charles Haughey, who was running the Fianna Fáil presidential election campaign, and was seen as a masterstroke.

4 The wife of Ronan Keane, Chief Justice from 2000 to 2004, was also named Terry Keane.

5 Maume and Costello, 'O'Higgins, Thomas Francis'.

6 Ibid.

7 *The Times*, Thomas O'Higgins obituary, 27 February 2003.

8 Dáil debate, 29 October 1974.

9 *Irish Press*, 24 October 1974.

10 Maume and Costello, 'O'Higgins, Thomas Francis'.

11 W. N. Osborough, 'Constitutional Law – A Waning of Judicial Activism?', p. 101.

12 J. P. Casey, 'The Development of Constitutional Law under Chief Justice O'Higgins', p. 13.

13 *People (DPP) v. Madden* (1977); *People (DPP) v. Shaw* (1982); *People (DPP) v. Lynch* (1982).

14 *In the Matter of Article 26 of the Constitution and in the Matter of the Emergency Powers Bill*, 1976 [1977] IR 159. See Maume and Costello, 'O'Higgins, Thomas Francis'.

15 *State (Lynch) v. Cooney* [1982] IR 337. See Casey, 'The Development of Constitutional Law under Chief Justice O'Higgins', pp. 24–5.

16 Ibid., p. 27.

17 *Irish Times*, 5 August 1971.

18 Garry Sturgess, audio interview with Máirín de Búrca (1986).

19 Law Reform Commission, *Report on Jury Service*, April 2013.

20 Ibid.

21 Sturgess, audio interview with de Búrca (1986).

22 Later an Attorney General (1977–81) and Supreme Court judge (1981–93).

23 Paul Carney would become a celebrated High Court judge (1991–2015).

24 Sturgess, audio interview with de Búrca (1986).

25 Ibid.

26 *De Búrca v. Attorney General* (1976).

27 *Irish Times*, 13 February 1976.

28 Sturgess, audio interview with de Búrca (1986).

29 Ibid.

30 *State (Byrne) v. Frawley* [1978] IR 326.

31 Casey, 'The Development of Constitutional Law under Chief Justice O'Higgins'.

32 Letter from Walsh to Brennan, 2 March 1977, William J. Brennan Papers, Box II: 62.

33 Letter from Walsh to Brennan, 2 October 1979, William J. Brennan Papers, Box II: 62.

34 Letter from Brennan to Walsh, 18 October 1979, William J. Brennan Papers, Box II: 62.

35 Gerard Hogan, 'Kenny, John Joseph', in McGuire and Quinn (eds.), *Dictionary of Irish Biography*.

36 Costello, 'Henchy, Séamus Anthony'.

37 Hogan, 'Kenny, John Joseph'.

38 Ibid.

39 A current judge of the Supreme Court. He was appointed in 2012.

40 A current judge of the Supreme Court. He was appointed in 2012.

41 *State (Healy) v. Donoghue* [1976] IR 325.

42 Yvonne Scannell, 'The Taxation of Married Women: Murphy v Attorney General (1982)', p. 329.

43 Ibid., p. 332.

44 Ibid., p. 344.

45 *Murphy v. Attorney General* [1982] IR 241.

46 Scannell, 'The Taxation of Married Women: Murphy v Attorney General (1982)', p. 351.

47 Ibid.

10. *The Norris challenge*

1 David Norris, *A Kick against the Pricks: The Autobiography*, p. 114.

2 A future judge of the High Court and Court of Appeal.

3 Norris, *A Kick against the Pricks*, p. 114.

4 Ibid., p. 115.

5 Ibid.

6 Garret Cooney was the brother of Paddy Cooney, Fine Gael Minister for Justice in the mid-1970s.

7 Mary Robinson, *Everybody Matters: My Life Giving Voice*, pp. 119–20.

8 Norris, *A Kick against the Pricks*, p. 116.

9 *Irish Independent*, 26 June 1980; *Irish Times*, 26 June 1980; *Irish Press*, 26 June 1980.

10 *Irish Times*, 27 June 1980.

11 Norris, *A Kick against the Pricks*, p. 119.

12 *Norris v. Attorney General* [1984] IR 36.

13 *Irish Family Planning Association v. Ryan* [1979] IR 295.

14 *Draper v. Attorney General* [1984] IR 277.

15 *O'B v. S* [1984] IR 316. See J. P. Casey, 'The Development of Constitutional Law under Chief Justice O'Higgins'.

16 Gerard Hogan, 'The Judicial Thought and Prose of Mr. Justice Seamus Henchy', p. 112.

17 Colm Tóibín, 'A Brush with the Law'.

18 Hogan, 'The Judicial Thought and Prose of Mr. Justice Seamus Henchy', p. 116.

19 Donal O'Donnell, 'Irish Legal History of the Twentieth Century', p. 114.

20 *Irish Times*, 23 April 1983.

21 V. Bradley Lewis, 'Natural Law in Irish Constitutional Jurisprudence', p. 174.

22 O'Donnell, 'Irish Legal History of the Twentieth Century', pp. 108–9.

23 Lewis, 'Natural Law in Irish Constitutional Jurisprudence', p. 175.

24 *McGee v. Attorney General* [1974] IR 284.

25 J. M. Kelly, *Fundamental Rights in the Irish Law and Constitution*, p. 43.

26 John Whyte, *Church and State in Modern Ireland 1923–1979*, p. 409.

27 Gerard Hogan, 'De Valera, the Constitution and the Historians', p. 3.

28 Ibid., p. 7.

29 F. S. L. Lyons, *Ireland since the Famine*, p. 544.

30 *In the Matter of Article 26 of the Constitution and in the Matter of the Reference to the Court of the Regulation of Information (Services Outside the State for Termination of Pregnancies) Bill, 1995* [1995] 1 IR 1.

31 Gerard Hogan, '*Elegantia juris*: Mr. Justice Seamus Henchy: Some Thoughts on Two Leading Judgments', p. 16.

32 *Bowers v. Hardwick*, 478 US 186 (1986). The *Bowers* decision was eventually overruled in 2003 by the US Supreme Court's decision in *Lawrence v. Texas*.

33 *Irish Times*, 23 April 1983.

34 *Irish Times*, 1 January 2016.

35 Norris, *A Kick against the Pricks*, p. 122.

11. The trouble with extradition

1 *The Springing of George Blake* (London, 1970).

2 *Irish Times*, 15 September 1990.

3 In 2007 Russian president Vladimir Putin presented Blake with the Order of Friendship, a major national honour, in a ceremony at the Kremlin. Now ninety-three, Blake still lives in a dacha outside Moscow.

4 Michael Farrell, *Sheltering the Fugitive? The Extradition of Irish Political Offenders*, p. 53.

5 *The State (Magee) v. O'Rourke* [1971] IR 205.

6 *Burns v. Attorney General* (High Court, 1974).

7 Farrell, *Sheltering the Fugitive?*, p. 61.

8 Gerard Hogan and Clive Walker, *Political Violence and the Law in Ireland*, p. 284.

9 Farrell, *Sheltering the Fugitive?*, p. 57.

10 Ibid.

11 Ibid.

12 Ibid.

13 *State (Furlong) v. Kelly* [1971] IR 132. In the English warrant for his arrest, Furlong was accused of having committed theft. When the case came before the Irish courts, the Attorney General argued that the English offence of theft corresponded with the Irish offence of larceny. In the Supreme Court, Ó Dálaigh compared the two offences and concluded that the ingredients specified as having to be present, in particular with regard to intent and the moment at which intent was formed in the alleged offender's mind, differed in each. That meant certain acts that in England would constitute 'stealing' would not amount to 'larcenies' in Ireland, so the two offences did not correspond.

14 Letter from Lord Hailsham to Billy FitzGerald, 21 September 1973, NAI 2011/21/29.

15 Letter from Billy FitzGerald to Lord Hailsham, 12 October 1973, NAI 2011/21/29.

16 Hogan and Walker, *Political Violence and the Law in Ireland*, p. 285.

17 The executive lasted barely five months, and collapsed in May 1974.

18 Hutton became Chief Justice of Northern Ireland in 1988.

19 Hilary Delany and Gerard Hogan, 'Anglo Irish Extradition Viewed from an Irish Perspective', p. 96.

20 *The State (Sumers Jennings) v. Furlong* [1966] IR 183. The British side also cited a judgment by former Chief Justice Conor Maguire, in the case of *The State (Duggan) v. Tapley* [1952] IR 62, in which he concluded that '[t]he attempt . . . to establish that the non-surrender of political refugees is a generally accepted principle of international law fails'.

21 Colm Tóibín, 'Inside the Supreme Court'; Kevin Costello, 'Henchy, Séamus Anthony', in McGuire and Quinn (eds.), *Dictionary of Irish Biography*.

22 Law Enforcement Commission Report, p. 27.

23 Ibid.

24 Seanad Éireann, 24 April 1975.

25 Dáil Éireann, 9 April 1975.

26 Farrell, *Sheltering the Fugitive?*, p. 72.

27 Ibid., p. 73.

28 Dáil Éireann, 31 August 1976.

29 Hogan and Walker, *Political Violence and the Law in Ireland*, p. 287.

30 As the case was not a constitutional matter, just three judges were required to make a ruling.

31 Farrell, *Sheltering the Fugitive?*, p. 96.

32 Ibid.

33 *McGlinchey v. Wren* [1982] IR 154.

34 See Alpha Connelly, 'Ireland and the Political Offence: Exception to Extradition', pp. 153–82.

35 For example, *Shannon v. Fleming* (1984) and *Quinn v. Wren* (1985).

36 *Quinn v. Wren* [1985] IR 322.

37 *Irish Times*, 19 March 1984.

38 Colm Tóibín, 'A Brush with the Law'.

39 Ibid.

40 *Irish Times*, 18 March 1998.

41 Ibid., 27 March 1998.

42 Ibid., 6 April 1998.

43 *Finucane v. McMahon* [1990] 1 IR 165.

44 Tóibín, 'Inside the Supreme Court'; *Irish Times*, 19 March 1984; Farrell, *Sheltering the Fugitive?*, pp. 99–100.

12. *Replacing O'Higgins*

1 *Irish Press*, 8 December 1984.
2 *Irish Independent*, 14 December 1984.
3 Ibid.
4 *Irish Times*, 12 January 1985.
5 *Irish Times*, 8 December 1984.
6 *Irish Independent*, 14 December 1984.
7 *Irish Press*, 8 December 1984.
8 McCartan was later a Workers' Party TD and was appointed a Circuit Court judge in 1997.
9 *Irish Independent*, 11 January 1985.
10 *G v. An Bord Uchtála* [1980] IR 32.
11 Adrian Hardiman, 'McCarthy, Niall St John', in McGuire and Quinn (eds.), *Dictionary of Irish Biography*.
12 *Sunday Tribune*, 9 December 1984.
13 Letter from Walsh to Brennan, 14 April 1981, William J. Brennan Papers, Box II: 62.
14 Letter from Walsh to Brennan, 17 December 1984, William J. Brennan Papers, Box II: 62.
15 Letter from Brennan to Walsh, 26 December 1984, William J. Brennan Papers, Box II: 62.
16 Garry Sturgess, audio interview with Brian Walsh no. 1 (1986).
17 *Irish Times*, 16 January 1985.

13. *Putting it to the people*

1 *Irish Times*, 21 May 2012.
2 Asmal, a South African, lectured at Trinity for nearly three decades. He became water minister in his country's first post-Apartheid government.
3 *Irish Times*, 10 November 1986. Another signatory who would go on to occupy senior office was the barrister Rory Brady, a future Attorney General.
4 Raymond Crotty, *A Radical's Response*, p. 118.

5 Ibid., p. 117.

6 Ibid., pp. 115–16.

7 *Irish Times*, 29 December 1986.

8 Crotty, *A Radical's Response*, p. 119.

9 Ibid., p. 121.

10 Ibid., p. 129.

11 *Crotty v. An Taoiseach* [1987] IR 713.

12 Dáil Éireann, 9 December 1986.

13 Dáil Éireann, 22 April 1987.

14 *Irish Times*, 11 April 1987.

15 *Irish Times*, 25 April 1987.

16 Hogan, 'The Supreme Court and the Single European Act', p. 55.

17 *Irish Press*, 1 June 1987.

18 *Pringle v. Ireland* [2013] 3 IR 1.

19 Gavin Barrett, *A Road Less Travelled*, p. 10.

20 *McKenna v. An Taoiseach No. 1* [1995] 2 IR 1.

21 The second vote on the matter in a decade. A previous referendum in 1986 had seen the proposal rejected.

22 *McKenna v. An Taoiseach No. 2* [1995] 2 IR 10; Barrett, *A Road Less Travelled*, p. 15.

23 Crotty, *A Radical's Response*, p. 97.

24 Peter Sutherland, 'The Constitution, the Courts and the Legislature'.

25 Barrett, *A Road Less Travelled*, p. 26.

26 Letter from Walsh to Brennan, 11 May 1987, William J. Brennan Papers, Box II: 103.

27 Letter from Brennan to Walsh, 21 May 1987, William J. Brennan Papers, Box II: 103.

28 *Irish Times*, 4 March 1987. Walsh's wide-ranging *Irish Times* interview, written by Fergus Pyle and headlined 'Final Bastion of the People's Rights', was part of a series of eight articles on powerful people in Irish public life.

29 *Irish Times*, 20 October 1988.

30 Ibid.

31 Gerard Hogan, 'The Judicial Thought and Prose of Mr. Justice Seamus Henchy', p. 112.

32 Letter from Walsh to Brennan, 20 March 1990, William J. Brennan Papers, Box II: 103.

33 Letter from Brennan to Walsh, 29 March 1990, William J. Brennan Papers, Box II: 103.

34 Letter from Walsh to Brennan, 19 February 1993, William J. Brennan Papers, Box II: 103.

35 Letter from Brennan to Walsh, 25 February 1993, William J. Brennan Papers, Box II: 103.

14. X

1 Tom Hesketh, *The Second Partitioning of Ireland?*, p. 12.

2 Ibid., pp. 2–3.

3 Ibid., p. 1.

4 James O'Reilly, 'Marital Privacy and Family Law', pp. 8–22; Donal O'Donnell, 'Irish Legal History of the Twentieth Century'.

5 William Binchy, 'Marital Privacy and Family Law: A Reply to Mr. O'Reilly', p. 330.

6 Ibid., p. 331.

7 Garry Sturgess, audio interview with Brian Walsh no. 2 (1986).

8 Gene Kerrigan, 'The Moral Civil War', p. 187.

9 *Irish Times*, 13 February 1981.

10 Kerrigan, 'The Moral Civil War', p. 186.

11 Linda Connolly, *The Irish Women's Movement: From Revolution to Devolution*, p. 163.

12 Diarmaid Ferriter, *The Transformation of Ireland 1900–2000*, p. 716.

13 *Irish Times*, 25 December 1981.

14 Hesketh, *The Second Partitioning of Ireland?*, p. 18. John Blayney would become a Supreme Court judge in 1992 and served for five years. In 2008 he was awarded a papal order and made a Knight of St Gregory. The award is presented for exceptional services to the church and society.

15 Hesketh, *The Second Partitioning of Ireland?*, pp. 18, 49.

16 Kerrigan, 'The Moral Civil War', p. 190.

17 *Irish Times*, 9 February 1983.

18 Hesketh, *The Second Partitioning of Ireland?*, p. 91.

19 *Irish Times*, 6 July 1982.

20 *Irish Independent*, 9 November 1982.

21 Hesketh, *The Second Partitioning of Ireland?*, p. 151.

22 *Irish Independent*, 20 December 1982.

23 Hesketh, *The Second Partitioning of Ireland?*, p. 216.

24 *Irish Times*, 6 September 1983.

25 Séan Duignan, *One Spin on the Merry-Go-Round*, p. 20.

26 *Attorney General v. X* [1992] 1 IR 1.

27 *Irish Times*, 15 February 1992.

28 *Irish Times Book of the Century*, p. 311.

29 *Irish Times*, 18 February 1992.

30 Ivana Bacik, *Kicking and Screaming: Dragging Ireland into the 21st Century*, p. 117.

31 *D (A Minor) v. District Judge Brennan, the Health Services Executive, Ireland and the Attorney General*, unreported judgment of the High Court.

32 Report of the Expert Group on the Judgment in *A, B and C v. Ireland* (November 2012), p. 117.

15. *The Whelehan affair*

1   Paul C. Bartholomew, *The Irish Judiciary*, p. 33.

2   Jennifer Carroll MacNeill, *The Politics of Judicial Selection in Ireland*, p. 138.

3   Shane Ross and Nick Webb, *The Untouchables*, p. 202.

4   Fergus Finlay, *Snakes and Ladders*, p. 246.

5   Ibid.

6   Albert Reynolds, *My Autobiography*, pp. 437–8.

7   Finlay, *Snakes and Ladders*, p. 246.

8   Ibid., p. 250.

9   Séan Duignan, *One Spin on the Merry-Go-Round*, p. 155.

10 Stephen Collins, *The Power Game*, p. 275.

11 *Irish Times*, 21 December 1994.

12 Noel Whelan, *Fianna Fáil: A Biography of the Party*, pp. 293–4.

13 Finlay, *Snakes and Ladders*, p. 260.

14 Dáil Éireann, 16 November 1994.

15 Reynolds, *My Autobiography*, p. 455.

16 Ibid.

17 Ibid.

18 Dáil Éireann, 29 November 1995.

19 Carroll MacNeill, *The Politics of Judicial Selection in Ireland*, pp. 64–5.

16. In the eye of a hurricane

1 'Report of the Chief Justice into the Circumstances Leading to the Early Release from Prison of Philip Sheedy' (14 April 1999).
2 *Sunday Independent*, 18 April 1999.
3 Pat Leahy, *Showtime: The Inner Story of Fianna Fáil in Power*, p. 154.
4 *Irish Times*, 17 April 1999.
5 Susan Denham, 'The Diamond in a Democracy'.

17. New judges, new ideas

1 *Irish Independent*, 22 January 2000.
2 Ibid.
3 In 1999 Terry Keane went public on her long-standing affair with Charles Haughey.
4 *Sunday Business Post*, 25 July 2004.
5 *Irish Examiner*, 26 January 2000.
6 John Kenny, 'The Advantages of a Written Constitution Incorporating a Bill of Rights', pp. 195–6.
7 Gerard Hogan, 'Unenumerated Personal Rights: The Legacy of *Ryan v. Attorney General*'.
8 *O'T v. B* [1998] 2 IR 321.
9 Ronan Keane, 'Judges as Lawmakers: The Irish Experience', p. 14.
10 See Oran Doyle, 'Conventional Constitutional Law', pp. 320–22.

18. Hitting the brakes

1 *Sinnott v. Minister for Education* [2001] 2 IR 545.
2 *Irish Times*, 5 October 2000.
3 *Dáil Éireann*, 5 October 2000.
4 *Sinnott v. Minister for Education* [2001] 2 IR 545.
5 *FN v. Minister for Education* [1995] 1 IR 409.
6 *DB v. Minister for Justice* [1999] 1 IR 29.
7 *TD v. Minister for Education* [2000] 3 IR 62.

8 Adrian Hardiman, 'The Role of the Supreme Court in our Democracy', p. 39.

9 Gerry Whyte, *Social Inclusion and the Legal System: Public Interest Law in Ireland*, p. 97.

10 *Irish Times*, 8 July 2013.

11 *Irish Times*, 15 April 2003.

12 *Irish Times*, 30 June 2004.

13 Gerard Hogan and Gerard Whyte (eds.), *J. M. Kelly: The Irish Constitution*.

14 Figure supplied by the Department of Health (2016).

15 *In the Matter of Article 26 of the Constitution and the Health (Amendment) (No. 2) Bill 2004* [2005] 1 IR 105.

16 *Maguire v. Ardagh* [2002] 1 IR 385.

17 Gerard Hogan, David Kenny and Rachael Walsh, 'An Anthology of Declarations of Unconstitutionality'.

18 Ibid.

19 Rozenberg is a British legal journalist and commentator who had worked with the BBC and the *Daily Telegraph*.

19. Supreme conflict

1 The economic collapse from 2007 reversed this trend.

2 Eamon Leahy was the husband of then government chief whip, Fianna Fáil TD Mary Hanafin. When the Distillery Building on Church Street, where many barristers have their offices, was extended in 2006, rooms were dedicated to Leahy and Peter Shanley, a High Court judge with Fine Gael connections who died in 1998.

3 Carroll MacNeill, *The Politics of Judicial Selection in Ireland*, p. 127.

4 Ibid., p. 129.

5 Robert Elgie, Adam McAuley and Eoin O'Malley, 'The (Surprising) Non-Partisanship of the Irish Supreme Court'.

6 Letter from Ernest Blythe to Hugh Kennedy, 23 January 1932, NAI 2011/21/13.

7 Letter from Hugh Kennedy to Ernest Blythe, 4 February 1932, NAI 2011/21/13.

8 Letter from Ernest Blythe to Hugh Kennedy, 5 February 1932, NAI 2011/21/13.

9 Letter from Conor Maguire to John A. Costello, October 1950, NAI 2011/21/13.

10 Letter from John A. Costello to Conor Maguire, 21 April 1951, NAI 2011/21/13.

11 Letter from Seán MacEntee to Conor Maguire, 5 September 1951, NAI 2011/21/13.

12 *O'Byrne v. Minister for Finance* [1959] IR 1. See Raymond Byrne and Paul McCutcheon, *The Irish Legal System*, p. 174.

13 Byrne and McCutcheon, *The Irish Legal System*, p. 175.

14 *Irish Times*, 16 May 2009.

15 *Irish Independent*, 27 June 2009.

16 New, continental-style gowns were introduced in the Supreme Court in 2012 and the Court of Appeal in 2015.

20. Détente

1 *Irish Times*, 5 October 2010.

2 *Irish Times*, 7 May 2011.

3 Birmingham is a former Fine Gael TD and junior minister.

4 *Attorney General and the Society for the Protection of Unborn Children v. Open Door Counselling and the Dublin Well Woman Centre (No. 2)* [1994] 2 IR 333.

5 *Irish Independent*, 2 March 2013.

6 *Pringle v. Ireland* [2012] 3 IR 1. In his 2012 case, the Independent Donegal TD Thomas Pringle argued that the treaty establishing the European Stability Mechanism, which was to act as a permanent source of financial assistance for EU member states in financial difficulty, was incompatible with the Constitution and therefore that a referendum was required to validate Irish ratification. The challenge was rejected by a 6-1 majority in the Supreme Court.

7 *MR and DR v. An t-Ard-Chláraitheoir* [2014] 11 JIC 0701.

8 Ibid.

9 *Damache v. DPP* [2012] 2 JIC 2306.

10 *DPP v. Gormley* [2014] 3 JIC 0601.

11 *DPP v. JC* [2015] 4 JIC 1502.

Acknowledgements

In the past two years I have racked up debts I cannot possibly repay. I am immensely grateful to Michael McLoughlin, managing director of Penguin Ireland, for suggesting I write the book and for his constant encouragement and support throughout the process. Patricia Deevy was the ideal editor; her clear-eyed vision of the project, her Stakhanovite work ethic and her adroit work on the text has enhanced the book in countless ways, big and small. Thanks to everyone at Penguin, including Cliona Lewis, Carrie Anderson and Brian Walker in Ireland and Keith Taylor in London, and to Kieran Kelly and Matthew Taylor for their vital contributions.

In attempting to slot the story of the Supreme Court into a broader narrative account, I have been able to draw on the writings of those who have led the way in chronicling Ireland's post-Independence legal history. They include Charles Lysaght, Ronan Keane, William Binchy, J. P. Casey, Gerry Whyte, Hugh Geoghegan and the late John Kelly. In particular, I have benefited greatly from the extensive writings of Gerard Hogan, who has done more than anyone to illuminate the history of the Constitution, the judiciary, the legal system and the ways in which all three have interacted in the past century. I took inspiration and encouragement from Colm Tóibín and Vincent Browne. Tóibín's seminal work on the Supreme Court for *Magill* in the 1980s lit the path for others to follow, while Browne has over the past three decades consistently subjected the court to the sort of informed and critical scrutiny it should receive but seldom has.

I am grateful to Catriona Crowe and the staff of the National Archives of Ireland for their help in tracking down new material. The staff at the National Library of Ireland, the library of Trinity College Dublin and the UCD Archives were unfailingly helpful. For access to the papers of Justice William Brennan, I am indebted to the Brennan estate and to Stephen Wermiel. At the Manuscript Division of the Library of Congress, Jeffrey Flannery and his colleagues made a trip to snowbound Washington DC last winter more fruitful than I had dared hope. Thanks also to Garry Sturgess in Melbourne, who went beyond the call of duty by digitizing a series of revealing interviews he carried out with judges in the 1980s.

The project has benefited from conversations I have had with many people about the court and its place in Irish life. For sharing their insights and expertise, I am grateful to Diarmaid Ferriter, John Bowman, Kevin Costello, Yvonne Scannell, Raymond Byrne, Eileen Barrington, Eunan O'Halpin, Bill Shipsey, Peter Ward, Frank Callanan, Gerry Whyte, Mary Kotsonouris, Michael Collins, Donncha O'Connell, Ivana Bacik, Conor O'Mahony, John O'Dowd, Carol Coulter, David Nolan, David Barniville, Tony McGillicuddy and Brice Dickson. I especially wish to thank David Kenny, Paul Anthony McDermott and Rossa Fanning for their guidance on points of law and their astute observations.

I am grateful to May and Séamus McGee and to Anthony Coughlan for sharing their recollections of their landmark cases. Mary Carmel was a brave and remarkable interviewee; I hope I have done her some justice.

Much of the research and writing was done early in the morning, late at night, on holiday and in transit. It could not have been completed without the support and forbearance of a great many people. I am especially grateful to friends and colleagues at the *Irish Times*, including Kevin O'Sullivan, Paul O'Neill, Roddy O'Sullivan, Chris Dooley, Mark Hennessy, Conor Goodman, Eithne Donnellan, Geraldine Kennedy, Denis Staunton, Enda O'Doherty, Evelyn Bracken, Dave McKechnie, Simon Carswell, Paddy Smyth, John Fleming, Fiona Gartland, Mary Carolan and Colm Keena. Thanks to stalwart colleagues on the legal beat – the great high-wire act of Irish journalism – including Orla O'Donnell, Dearbhail McDonald, Vivienne Traynor and Conor Gallagher – and to Maurice O'Mahony, Sally de Foubert, Gerry Curran, Averil Henchy and Mark Coughlan.

The great bulk of interviews on which I draw in the book – more than 140 in all – were given on condition that their subjects would remain anonymous. These interviewees invited me into their homes and offices, patiently fielded my questions, often late into the night, and took repeated calls stretching over many months with generosity and good humour. Some of them will not agree with my conclusions, but I hope they will recognize in these pages the value of their contributions.

Tá buíochas ar leith tuillte ag mo thuismitheoirí fadfhulangacha, Breandán agus Máire, agus mo dheirfiúracha, Aoife agus Fionnuala, as ucht a gcuid tacaíochta. Lastly, I'm grateful beyond words to Jean O'Mahony, to whom I already owe so much, for her unwavering support, her sharp critical eye and her unflagging enthusiasm for the book from start to finish.

Index

Cases and decisions of the Court can be found brought together under the heading 'Supreme Court cases/judgments'.